# Organizational Behaviour

**V. S. P. Rao**
*Associate Professor*
*Sri Venkateswara College,*
*University of Delhi,* New Delhi.

AF798807

Himalaya Publishing House
ISO 9001:2015 CERTIFIED

© **Author**

No part of this publication may be reproduced, stored in a retrieval system, or transmitted in any form or by any means, electronic, mechanical, photocopying, recording and/or otherwise without the prior written permission of the publisher.

**First Edition : 2011**
**Edition : 2017, 2018**
**Edition : 2020, 2021**
**Edition : 2025**
**Edition : 2026**

**Published by** : Mrs. Meena Pandey
for **HIMALAYA PUBLISHING HOUSE PVT. LTD.,**
Vishal Industrial Estate, 1st Floor, Office No. 63/64,
Bhandup Village Road, Subhash Nagar (Opp. CEAT Tyres),
Nahur (W), Mumbai - 400 078. **Phone:** 022-35131464/65/66/67
**E-mail:** himpub@bharatmail.co.in; **Website:** www.himpub.com

**Branch Offices** :

**New Delhi** : "Pooja Apartments", 4-B, Murari Lal Street, Ansari Road, Darya Ganj, New Delhi - 110 002. Phone: 011-23270392, 23278631; Fax: 011-23256286

**Nagpur** : Kundanlal Chandak Industrial Estate, Ghat Road, Nagpur - 440 018. Mobile: 09325409992, 09325908881

**Bengaluru** : Plot No. 91-33, 2nd Main Road, Seshadripuram, Behind Nataraja Theatre, Bengaluru - 560 020. Phone: 080-41138821; Mobile: 09379847017, 09379847005

**Hyderabad** : No. 3-4-184, Lingampally, Besides Raghavendra Swamy Matham, Kachiguda, Hyderabad - 500 027. Phone: 040-27560041, 27550139

**Chennai** : No. 34/44, Motilal Street, T. Nagar, Chennai - 600 017. Mobile: 09380460419

**Pune** : "Laksha" Apartment, First Floor, No. 527, Mehunpura, Shaniwarpeth (Near Prabhat Theatre), Pune - 411 030. Phone: 020-24496323, 24496333; Mobile: 09370579333

**Cuttack** : Plot No. 5F-755/4, Sector-9, CDA Markat Nagar, Cuttack - 753 014, Odisha. Mobile: 09338746007

**Kolkata** : 3, S.M. Bose Road, Near Gate No. 5, Agarpara Railway Station, North 24 Parganas, West Bengal - 700 109. Mobile: 09674536325

**DTP by** : Elite-Art, Delhi.

**Printed at** : Trinity Academy, Delhi. On behalf of HPH.

# PREFACE

Organizations employ the indispensable services of people to convert resources into useful products and services. In a way, organisations are people. People can make or break a firm. If they contribute to the best of their abilities, the firm will be able to withstand economic shocks, face competition, win over customers and produce outstanding results. The case of Southwest Airlines is a shining example of one man standing up against every possible hurdle that one can conceive of. With the help of a team of ordinary people—mind you ordinary people—he is able to produce extraordinary results for over three decades. To me excellence is nothing but making people work with zeal, commitment and dedication. You inspire them to give their best and expectedly they would rise to the occasion and fulfil your dream—howsoever impossible it might be. To this end, share every piece of information honestly. Explain your dream in simple terms.

Clarify what they are supposed to do. Set goals that are neither too easy nor too difficult to reach. Leave the ivory tower image and join the mainstream. Show them through exemplary character and conduct that you are there to help them, listen to them, and share the plus and minus points of work. Demolish the status walls between people. Remain accessible to your people. Use every opportunity to make them laugh and enjoy what they do. Connect them to their passions. Encourage them to do ordinary things in an extraordinary manner. Be there –always-to receive their suggestions.

Convert those creative ideas into concrete action plans. Recognise and reward those who suggested a different path, a creative route and a novel idea. Give them the feeling that they are the real heroes in the work spot. Empower them to take up anything and do everything in the interest of the organisation and the customer. Allow them to commit mistakes and learn. Appreciate their effort genuinely. Encourage them to think and act like owners. Not through lip service but through committed actions. Catch every opportunity to celebrate small successes. Let the celebrations continue, on and on, forever. Create that exciting feeling that they are part of a large family, out there on a picnic. Work becomes fun. Workers become partners. Customers become friends. Ordinary contributions bring in extraordinary profits. Competitors become copycats. You become a long distance runner. One man can bring about dramatic, stunning changes and can make a lot of difference—enriching our lives for ever. This is what Herb Kelleher of Southwest Airlines did for over three decades. On the way to stardom, he fought multifarious legal battles valiantly—Pushed rivals to the wall; Cut costs to bare bone level; brought smiles to millions of passengers, making air travel affordable and converted employees into stock owners. In short, he made everyone look big. He made us all realise that employees are the real heroes in the corporate world. The journey from zero (Kelleher was a lawyer and had no previous experience of running a business) to hero is truly fascinating and very inspiring.

Not that India is having a chronic shortage of talented leaders like Kelleher. We have Narayana Murthy—who made a graceful exit from Infosys only the other day—running the global IT Company, Infosys, and showing that great companies can be built around sound principles and high moral values—Followed by Ratan Tata who seems to have changed the rules of the game in auto industry forever through beautiful Indica and the sexy Nano—Producing outstanding innovations by assigning a seemingly impossible task of developing a new car from scratch through a small team of young engineers, when the global auto giants are in the midst of gloom and doom. Indian corporate history, too, is replete with successful stories of companies that have made it big, leveraging on the knowledge, skills and capabilities of their employees' Successful companies in the end are known by what they achieve rather than what they have. You may have everything but may remain at the bottom of the corporate ladder if you do not convert your strengths into opportunities and do not put your resources to best use. Companies that have been able to understand the dynamics of human behaviour and have used that power to build want-satisfying products and services have a great story to tell.

**Special Features of the Book**

The present work—primarily meant for BBA students of Guru Gobind Singh Indraprastha University—tries to highlight the time test principles of human behaviour in a simple, easy to understand style. Wherever necessary, practical aspects of organisational life have been highlighted. Live corporate examples have been inserted to enrich the contents. The ethical and moral issues surrounding human behaviour have also been critically examined. A balanced and integrated view of the subject is being presented—reflecting various themes, viewpoints that have gained currency in recent times—in a dispassionate way. One important objective of this book is to present theoretical concepts in a clear and concise form. Unlike other foreign texts, it is completely devoid of jargon. To the extent possible, terminological conflicts have been put to rest and the most popular view of a topic is being tossed around for further elaboration. Every attempt is made to develop arguments in a logical way. To clear the fog surrounding complex subjects, a number of examples have been pressed into service. The practical side of various themes that have gained popularity in recent times is also brought into focus wherever necessary. The most recent research evidence is being used to support an established theoretical viewpoint. Newspaper clippings, journalistic viewpoints, scholastic opinions and simple, down to earth facts of life have also been liberally used to make the presentation more lively and interesting. In the end, everything has been structured to meet the unique requirements of students through a number of study aids such as figures, charts, tables, diagrams, illustrations, contemporary examples, summary boxes etc.

**V. S. P. Rao**

# ACKNOWLEDGEMENTS

I am forever indebted to my dear wife, Vani, for her support, encouragement, love and affection and for single—handedly managing the household while I was busy revising this book. I am extremely thankful to my son, my daughter in law and daughter for their words of support and encouragement. Sincere thanks to my colleagues at S.V. College—Dr. R.K. Arora, Dr. Sarvesh, Prof V.P. Jain, Dr. Venkat, Dr. Mamta, Prof. Sunita, Prof. Shruti, Prof Pooja, Prof. Sindumani, Prof. Divya and Prof. Neha--- who generously shared their ideas with me, offered constructive feedback and refined my thinking and understanding of human resource management. I take this opportunity to thank Prof. Srinivas (XLRI), Prof. P. Satyanarayana (MIT, Dartmouth), Prof.P.C.K. Rao (Director), Prof. Surbhi, Inbuss School; Prof. Rashmi, Prof. Charu Chaudhry (ITS); Sri. K.V. Ramesh, General Manager, GMR group; Prof. Sanjay Sehgal (Head, Department of Financial Studies, South Campus) for their insightful comments and valuable suggestions.. I am deeply obliged to Prof. N.J. Yasaswy, Member, Board of Governors, ICFAI, Hyderabad who always encouraged me to give my best to the academic world in my own humble way. Special thanks go to Nimisha, the Production Manager for her unstinting support, monumental patience and editorial help that was indeed required to convert my manuscript into a fine product.

I take this opportunity to thank Shri Niraj Pandey—the young, dynamic and dashing publisher —for bringing out the text with passion, love and commitment at an amazing speed. I would also like to thank Shri Vijay Rawat—the marketing genius at Himalaya—for motivating me to join the ever expanding family of Himalaya through his personal charm and incomparable persuasive skills. Without the divine blessings of my mother—who gave me so much and loved me so much when she was alive—I would not have been what I am today and I respectfully remember her on this day and dedicate this book to her with folded hands.

**V. S. P. Rao**

# CONTENTS

## Unit 1: Introduction



## Unit 2 : Individual and Interpersonal Behaviour

## Unit 4: Organisation Culture And Conflict Management

# UNIT 1: INTRODUCTION

1. Concept and Nature of Organisational Behaviour
2. Organisational Behaviour: Challenges and Opportunities

# 1

# Concept and Nature of Organizational Behaviour

## INTRODUCTION

People work in organisations in order to build their careers, realize their dreams and achieve success. They join organisations with high expectations. When they get what they want, they get along with others quite happily. Unlike in the past most employees now a days are in search of jobs that are interesting and challenging. They want to contribute, get recognized and rewarded. They want to find meaning in their day to day work life. Striking a balance between what the employee wants and what the organisation can offer has become a knotty issue for many managers. Organisations are nothing but groups of people who work interdependently toward some purpose. When employees are presented with jobs that have stretch, pull and challenge—they are encouraged to put their best foot forward and produce wonderful results. They are motivated to work with passion, zeal and commitment. Unfortunately, the scene out there in the market place is not all that rosy. Most people work in organisations, since they do not have a choice. They do not get what they want. They are made to work in poor surroundings. They are made to fight for everything almost on a daily basis with their own colleagues—thanks to the scarcity of critical resources and lucrative opportunities. They are pushed to the wall and made to swallow their pride and work unhappily wearing a mask to cover up their inner feelings, thoughts and concerns. Yes, this is where Organisational Behaviour steps in to help managers understand what people think, feel and do in and around organisations. In fact the present text is all about people working in organisations. We try to look at the soft side of the coin—that is the feelings, emotions, concerns, expectations and reactions of people to any organisational initiative. We also look at how individuals and groups work toward common goals within the boundaries set by the organisation. We also look at how the organisation responds to the demands of people—both individually and collectively—and tries to put out fires from time to time. In a way, we are going to focus attention on what people do in an organisation and how their behaviour affects an organization's performance.

## UNDERSTANDING ORGANISATIONS

Before proceeding further, it is necessary to clear the fog surrounding the term 'organisation'. The term 'organisation' is used in many ways. It means different things to different people. Currently, the following uses of the term are popular: (i) A Group of people who are united by a common purpose (ii)An Entity, an ongoing business unit engaged in utilizing resources to create a result.(iii) A Structure of relationships between various positions in an enterprise. and finally, (iv) A Process by which employees, facilities and tasks are related to each other, with a view to achieve specific goals. The static (as a structure) and dynamic (as a process) interpretations of the term organisation are quite commonly used and these are explained below:

### Organisation As A Structure

According to classical theorists (Fayol, Taylor, Weber) structure is essential for achieving stated goals. The manager determines the work activities to get the job done, writes job descriptions, puts people into groups and assigns them to superiors. He then fixes goals and deadlines and establishes standards of performance. Operations are controlled through a reporting system. The whole structure takes the shape of a pyramid. Thus the team Organisation Structure describes the organisation's framework. It reveals the established pattern of relationships among the constituent parts of the organisation. According to Koontz and O'Donnell, 'organisation is a structural relationship by which an enterprise is bound together and the framework in which individual effort is coordinated'. It is nothing but a chart of relationships. However, organisation is much more than a network of formal, superior-subordinate relationship. Informal relationships also play an important role in processing work. Organisation, as a structure, has the following features:

- ***Two or More Persons:*** Organisation is a form of human association for achieving common goals. The human association consists of two or more persons.
- ***Common Goals:*** The organisation exists to achieve some common goals. Structure ensures the smooth achievement of goals.
- ***Cooperative Efforts:*** Structure permits members to work in a cooperative way, without any friction. The members combine their efforts with a view to achieve goals.
- ***Division of Work:*** The work is divided into small parts and assigned to people working at various levels. This ensures speedy execution of work.
- ***Communication:*** People communicate along specified routes. Mainly downward communication takes place in the form of superiors issuing commands, orders, directives, etc.
- ***Rules and Regulations:*** Rules and regulations define the territorial jurisdiction of members. Members have to observe and implement these rules consistently.
- ***Pyramidial Shape:*** Organisation structure takes a pyramidial shape generally. Each superior will have a limited number of people reporting to him at any point of time.

### Organisation as a Process (Organising)

Organising is the process by which employees, facilities and tasks are related to each other, with a view to achieve specific goals. It refers to the way work is arranged and allocated among members of the organisation, so as to achieve the goals. As a process, 'organisation' refers to one of the important functions of management, i.e., organising. According to Allen, organising is' the process of identifying and grouping the work to be performed, defining and delegating responsibility and authority and establishing relationships for the purpose of enabling people to work most effectively together in accomplishing objectives'. The process of organising, thus, involves the following steps:

- ***Identifying the Work:*** We organise to achieve objectives. So, it is essential to identify the total work necessary to achieve the goals. The work must be classified in a systematic way so that each person in the organisation gets a separate and distinct task. Work must be divided and distributed because no one can handle the total work in an organisation single handed. Identification and classification of work enables managers to concentrate on important activities, avoiding unnecessary duplications, overlapping and wastage of efforts.
- ***Grouping the Work:*** Division of work creates the need for coordination. In order to provide for a smooth flow of work all closely related and similar activities must be grouped together. Thus, departments and divisions are created under the direction of a manager.
- ***Establishing Relationships:*** In order to secure compliance to organisatonal directives, reporting relationships must be specified. Once formal relationships are established, it would help individuals know what must be done, how it must be done, to whom the matters must be referred and how particular jobs relate to one another, etc. Without formal relationships, it would be difficult to process the total work because there is no way to know how the work is progressing, who is supposed to handle the work, where the work has to be coordinated so as to achieve enterprise objectives. As soon as the formal relationships are established, they would provide a framework for assigning duties and responsibilities to individuals in a clear fashion.
- ***Delegating Authority:*** Authority is the right to act, to issue orders and exact obedience from others. Without authority a manager may not be able to perform the tasks with confidence and show results. While assigning duties the manager should clearly specify authority and responsibility limits, so that the subordinate knows well in advance as to what type of work is expected of him by the superior.
- ***Providing for Coordination and Control:*** The interrelationships between various positions must be specified clearly. The activities and efforts of various individuals must be coordinated. The performance must be measured, evaluated and controlled at frequent intervals. If deviations occur, they must be spotted early and appropriate remedial steps taken immediately.

In short, organisations basically conduct their operations through two things: differentiation and integration. **Differentiation** means that the organisation is composed of many different units that work on different kinds of tasks, using different skills and work methods. **Integration** means that these differentiated units are put back together so that work is coordinated into an overall product.

## Organization as a Group

Some writers have tried to strike a balance between the two aspects–dynamic as well as static–by placing greater emphasis on human interaction in an organization. In the words of C.I. Barnard, "Organization is a system of consciously coordinated activities or forces of two or more persons." Etzioni, in a similar vein expressed thus: 'Organizations are social units (or human groupings) deliberately constructed and reconstructed to seek specific goals.' A more refined version is provided by W.J. Duncan, "An organization is a collection of interacting and interdependent individuals who work toward common goals whose relationships are determined according to a certain structure." These definitions clearly bring out five essential features common to all organizations:

- An organization always refers to people.
- An organization is developed for people.
- People interact with one another in some way.
- These interactions are specified by some sort of structure.
- Interactions are ordered to achieve joint objectives.

## IMPORTANCE OF SOUND ORGANISATION

Sound organisation is an essential prerequisite of efficient management. It helps an organisation in the following ways:

***1. Enlarges abilities:*** It helps individuals to enlarge their capabilities. Division of work enables an individual to specialize in the job in which he is proficient leading to better utilization of resources and talents.

***2. Facilitates administration:*** It facilitates administration by avoiding waste motions, overlap in work and duplication of effort. Departmentation enables proper planning of work. Confusion and misunderstanding over who is to perform what work is avoided by specifying the role of managers clearly. Proportionate and balanced emphasis is put on various activities.

***3. Facilitates growth and diversification:*** Sound organisation helps in keeping activities under constant vigil and control. The organisation can undertake more activities without dislocation. Talents and resources are put to good use. Opportunities are seized quickly and exploited fully, ultimately, paving the way for growth and diversification.

***4. Permits optimum use of resources:*** Human, technical and material resources are put to good use. Right persons are given right jobs. There is proper allocation of work. People know that they are supposed to do, well in advance. Necessary functions are determined and assigned so that personnel and physical facilities are utilized effectively.

***5. Stimulates creativity:*** If offers stimulating opportunities to people at all levels to use their skills on jobs best suited to their nature. Delegation helps people at lower levels to do more challenging work. The higher-ups, in turn, can concentrate on strategic issues–putting their creative abilities to good use.

***6. Facilitates coordination:*** Organisation is an important way of achieving coordination among different departments of an enterprise. Clear authority relationships and proper assignment of work facilitate the task of achieving coordination at all levels. Poor organisation leads to improper arrangement of duties and responsibilities. As a result, unimportant and trivial issues are given top priority. Activities that should be integrated or centralized are spread out and put to improper supervision. Incompetent individuals are overused while talented people are under-utilized. Delays, duplications and waste motions occur with frustrating regularity. Expenses mount up. These would create utter confusion, chaos and conflict. Poor organisation may mean improper arrangement of facilities and failure to achieve goals.

## WHAT IS MANAGEMENT?

Management is the process of working with and through others to achieve organisational objectives in a changing environment. Central to this process is the efficient and effective use of limited organisational resources. By efficient, we mean utilizing resources wisely and in a cost effective manner. It is nothing but *doing things right*—that is not wasting resources. For example a firm like Toyota Motor Corporation which produces high quality products at low costs is efficient. However, it is not enough just to be efficient. Management is also concerned with being effective. By effective, we mean making the right decisions and successfully implementing them. Effectiveness is nothing but *doing the right things*. A firm could very efficiently produce big screen black and white televisions with few options and limited capabilities but still not succeed because black and white televisions are no longer popular. A firm that produces products that no one wants is therefore, not effective. Thus, efficiency is concerned with the means of getting things done; effectiveness is concerned with the ends or attainment of organisational goals. Successful organisations, in general, are both efficient and effective. The above definition of 'management' contains three important components that require a closer examination.

- **Working with and through others:** Managers get results by working with and through others. Managers who do not get along well with others hamper their careers as revealed by a study of derailed managers. (Table )

**Table 1.1. Ten features of Derailed managers**

(i) Insensitive to others.
(ii) Cold, aloof and arrogant.
(iii) Do not accomplish stated purposes.
(iv) Overly ambitious, play politics.
(v) Over manage, by not effectively delegating things to others.
(vi) Unable to staff effectively.
(vii) Unable to think strategically.
(viii) Unable to adapt to a boss with a different style.
(ix) Over dependent on a mentor.
(x) Having specific performance problems with the business.

- **Achieving goals effectively and efficiently:** Managers are at the top to formulate and achieve stated goals. Organisations are more successful when their activities are guided by challenging, yet, achievable goals. As managers use their resources, they must strive to be both effective and efficient. They need to put the resources at their command to best use, treat their employees well , offer outstanding customer service and put their company ahead of competition—-*at all times.*

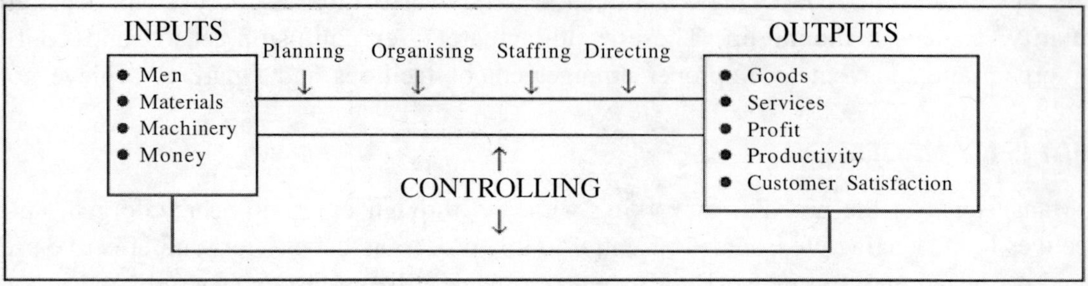


***Figure: 1.1***

The Process of Management: Converting disorganised resources into useful products/services

- **Coping with change:** The nature of management is to cope with diverse and far-reaching changes. An organisation that fails to monitor its environment and to change to keep pace with that environment is doomed to failure. Successful managers are the ones who anticipate and adjust to changing circumstances rather than being passively swept along or caught unprepared. Successful managers, according to Peter F. Drucker, do not wait for future; they make the future. Every day managers—in one way or the other— solve complex problems, turn organizations around and achieve stunning performances. To be successful, every organisation requires skilled managers.

**Box 1.1 Making a Difference**

***Lee Iacocca*** made a difference at Chrysler Corporation when he rescued it from bankruptcy through internal cost cutting, development of new products and obtaining concessions from the lenders, the union and government. ***Roberto Goizueta*** made a difference when he shook up the status quo at the Coca-Cola Company. When he took over Coke was into several unrelated ventures, the bottling system got badly dented and the entire marketing job was looked after by weak operators. Profits were miniscule, the stock price took a beating and the company's image suffered badly. Above all, the company seemed to suffer from lack of vision. ***Goizueta*** brought about dramatic changes and quickly turned the company into an enduring, everlasting brand. ***Herb Kelleher*** of Southwest Airlines has built a strong employee culture based on simple, fundamental principles of giving customers what they want and being happy in the work that one does. Herb's leadership has made Southwest's employees the most productive in the industry and leadership filters down through the company.

## Who are Managers?

Managers are the indispensable resources, the priceless assets of an organisation. They assemble resources, set goals, decide priorities, organise and coordinate effort and get things done through and with people. They are the 'coordinators' and 'directors' in the organisation. They are the individuals charged with examining the workflow, coordinating efforts, meeting goals and providing leadership. In terms of authority, managers possess the right to command others in their areas of responsibility. Each manager reports to someone higher in the organisation in what constitutes a theoretical chain of command from the top to the bottom of the structure. Managers usually do not directly perform any of the workflow activities. They are there to direct, coordinate and assist others in completing assigned work in a competent manner. They are also the activating elements that provide leadership and rewards to get results. They try to translate ideas into concrete action plans and produce results. When they succeed, they are able to keep everyone in good humour—including shareholders, employees and the general public. When they hit the bull's eye, they become the invincible corporate heroes and are sought after everywhere. When they fail, scarce corporate resources would have been squandered away and shareholder wealth would be burnt to ashes. Corporate failures are directly attributed to managerial incompetence and inept handling of situations. The outcomes of managerial actions, thus, are going to be deep, profound and decisive. To get past competition in this economic jungle, managers are expected to put their best foot forward, weighing the pros and cons of every decision carefully.

## What Managers do?

Managers generally work for long hours, their days are broken up into a large number of brief and varied activities, they interact with large number of different people, they do little reflective planning and spend most of their time engaged in oral communication (Reitz). They spend little time working alone. Time spent with others includes working with bosses, peers, subordinates, as well as outsiders, such as customers, suppliers and the like. They spend a lot of time getting, giving and processing information. Higher-level managers spend more time in scheduled meetings than do lower-level managers. According to Stoner, managerial work is characterised by the following things:

- *Managers' work with and through other people:* Managers work with internal (subordinates, supervisors, peers) as well as external groups (customers, clients, suppliers, union representatives etc.) in order to achieve corporate goals. They integrate individual efforts into teamwork. They plan things, create a structure, motivate people and achieve goals.
- *Managers are mediators:* People working in an organisation do not always agree on certain things, say, the establishment of goals and the means to achieve them. At the corporate headquarters of a large bank, managers may think about expanding into merchant banking, leasing, credit card business, whereas at the branch level, people may focus on expanding deposits by venturing deep into rural areas. Unless such differences are resolved quickly, employees find it difficult to think and act like a well-knit group. Their morale, too, may suffer. Managers often step in to put things in order, clear the paths to goals, clarify things to people, put out fires and meet goals.
- *Managers are politicians:* Managers must develop healthy relationships with various groups in order to achieve the goals smoothly. They may have to nurture groups and join certain coalitions within a company. They often draw upon such relationships to win support for their proposals and decisions.
- *Managers are diplomats:* Managers serve as official representatives of their work units at organisational meetings. They may represent the entire organisation as well

as a particular unit in dealing with external groups (clients, customers, government officials, etc.).

- *Managers are symbols:* Managers are symbols of corporate success or failure. They get applause when they succeed and get depreciated and attacked when they fail. In short, they represent corporate as well as employee aspirations. They are shown the door when these aspirations do not materialize.
- *Managers act as change agents and add value to organisational effort:* Managers set goals, put resources to best use, inspire people to give their best, coordinate effort and put everything on track. In an environment marked by complexity, uncertainty and rapid change, managers are virtually compelled to be on their toes and grapple with changes of various kinds on a daily basis. The ability to cope with change is the crux of the problem. For all practical purposes, managers are responsible for building an organisation's capabilities and then leveraging them through a strategy designed to give it an advantage over its competitors. They usually do this by creating more value for their customers than competitors.(Simon et all)

Managers, obviously, are there to utilise corporate resources in the best possible way. To achieve results, they change hats, shift gears and restructure and reorganize things continually. The diverse roles played by managers in discharging their duties have been beautifully summarised by Henry Mintzberg in the late 1960s, under three broad headings: interpersonal roles, informational roles and decisional roles.

## Research Evidence

A recent review of research on managerial behaviour, covering 40 books and articles on the subject, drew the following conclusions (Table): (McCall et al, Studies of Managerial Work, 1978, pp. 6-18).

**Table 1.2. Ten Facts of Managerial Life**

1. *Managers work long hours:* The number of hours worked tends to increase as one climbs the managerial ladder.
2. *Managers are busy:* A typical manager's day is made up of hundreds of brief incidents or episodes. Activity rates tend to decrease as rank increases.
3. *A manager's work is fragmented:* Episodes are brief. Given managers' high activity level, they have little time to devote to any single activity. Interruptions and discontinuity form the rule.
4. *The manager's job is varied:* Managers engage in a variety of activities (paperwork, phone calls, scheduled and unscheduled meetings and inspection tours/visits), interact with a variety of people and deal with a variety of content areas.
5. *Managers are 'homebodies':* Managers spend most of their time pursuing activities within their own organisations. As managerial rank increases, managers spend proportionately more time outside work areas and organisations.
6. *The manager's work is primarily oral:* Managers at all levels spend the majority of their time communicating verbally (by personal contact or telephone).

7. *Managers use a lot of contacts:* Consistent with their high level of verbal communication, managers continually exchange information with superiors, peers, subordinates and outsiders on an ongoing basis.
8. *Managers are not reflective planners:* The typical manager is too busy to find uninterrupted blocks of time for reflective planning.
9. *Information is the basic ingredient of the manager's work:* Managers spend most of their time obtaining, interpreting and giving information.
10. *Managers don't know how they spend their time:* Managers consistently overestimate the time they spend on production, reading and writing, phone calls, thinking and calculating and consistently underestimate the time spent on meetings and informal discussions.

## MANAGERIAL ROLES

Henry Mintzberg offered a view of the job of managing that throws considerable light on how managers perform their work. Managers, according to Mintzberg, must fill many roles as they carry out the management functions. These roles can be grouped into three categories: interpersonal, informational and decisional, as shown in Figure 1.2.

**1. Interpersonal roles:** Three interpersonal roles help the manager keep the organisation running smoothly. Managers play the figurehead role when they perform duties that are ceremonial and symbolic in nature. These include greeting the visitors, attending social functions involving their subordinates (like weddings, funerals), handing out merit certificates to workers showing promise etc. The leadership role includes hiring, training, motivating and disciplining employees. Managers play the liaison role when they serve as a connecting link between their organisation and others or between their units and other organisational units. Mintzberg described this activity as contacting outsiders who provide the manager with information. Such activities like acknowledgements of mail, external board work, etc., are included in this category.

**2. Informational roles:** Mintzberg mentioned that receiving and communicating information are perhaps the most important aspects of a manager's job. In order to make the right decisions, managers need information from various sources. Typically, this activity is done through reading magazines and talking with others to learn about changes in the customers' tastes, competitors' moves and the like. Mintzberg called this the monitor role. In the disseminator role, the manager distributes important information to subordinates that would otherwise be inaccessible to them. Managers also perform the spokesperson role when they represent the organisation to outsiders.

**3. Decisional roles:** There are four decision roles that the manager adopts. In the role of entrepreneur, the manager tries to improve the unit. He initiates planned changes to adapt to environmental challenges. As disturbance handlers, managers respond to situations that are beyond their control such as strikes, shortages of materials, complaints, grievances, etc. In the role of a resource allocator, managers are responsible for allocating human, physical and monetary resources. As negotiators, managers not only mediate in internal conflicts but also carry out negotiations with other units to gain advantages for their own unit.

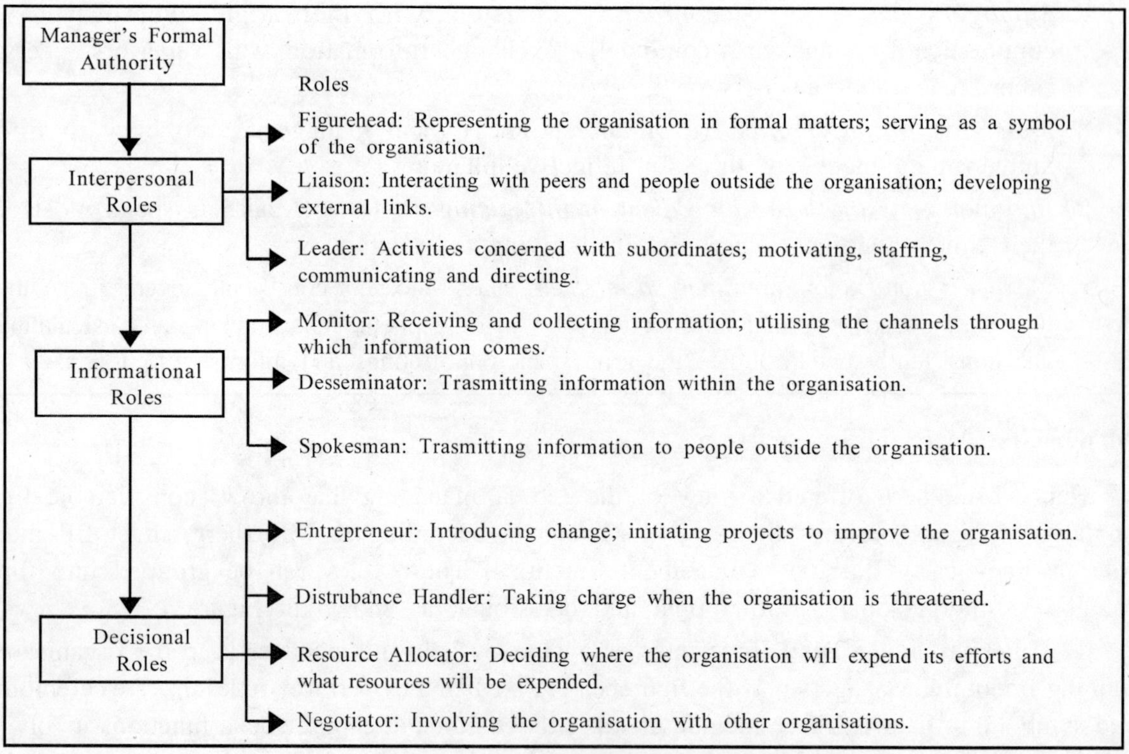


**Figure: 1.2. Managerial Roles**

Managers typically work 70 hour to 80 hour weeks and some work longer. They have to perform a great deal work at an unrelenting pace. Managerial work is a fast paced one and requires tremendous amount of energy. Apart from running through mountains of papers, they have to spend countless hours in conducting meetings of various kinds. Telephone conversations and handling e-mail messages might prove to be very taxing. Mintzberg's study found that in a typical day CEOs were likely to spend 59 per cent of their time in scheduled meetings, 22 percent doing 'desk work', More importantly, issues relating to people may confront them on a daily basis.

## FUNCTIONS OF MANAGEMENT

Managers are known by the work they do, the functions they perform. According to the functional approach, originated by Henry Fayol, in every organisation managers perform certain basic functions in order to achieve results. These functions may be broadly classified into five categories: planning, organising, staffing, leading and controlling. Managers perform these functions within the limits established by the external environment and must consider the interests of such diverse groups as government, employees, unions, customers, shareholders, competitors and the public. A brief discussion of the five basic functions is presented here.

- ***Planning:*** Planning is the process of making decisions about future. It is the process of determining enterprise objectives and selecting future courses of actions necessary for their accomplishment. It is the process of deciding in advance what is to be done, when and where it is to be done, how it is to be done and by whom. Planning provides direction to enterprise activities. It helps managers cope with change. It enables managers to measure progress toward the objectives so that corrective action can be taken if progress is not satisfactory. Planning is a fundamental function of management and all other functions of management are influenced by the planning process.

- ***Organising:*** Organising is concerned with the arrangement of an organisation's resources – people, materials, technology and finance in order to achieve enterprise objectives. It involves decisions about the division of work, allocation of authority and responsibility and the coordination of tasks. The function increases in importance as a firm grows. A structure is created to cope with problems created by growth. Through this formal structure, the various work activities are defined, classified, arranged and coordinated. Thus, organising refers to certain dynamic aspects: What tasks are to be done? Who is to do them? How the tasks are to be grouped? Who is to report to whom? Where the decisions have to be made?
- ***Staffing:*** A manager's greatest responsibility is to select, direct, develop and evaluate the people of the organisation. People are the source of all productive effort in organisations and hence, need to be nurtured carefully. Staffing is the function of employing suitable persons for the enterprise. It may be defined as an activity where people are recruited, selected, trained, developed, motivated and compensated for manning various positions. It includes not only the movement of individuals into an organisation, but also their movement through (promotion, job rotation, transfer) and out (termination, retirement) of the organisation. Staffing involves selection of the right man for the right job. It has four important elements:
- Recruitment may be defined as the process of attracting the maximum number of applications for a particular job.
- Selection is the process of screening the candidates and choosing the best ones out of them.
- Training involves imparting the necessary knowledge and skills required for the performance of a particular job.
- Compensation is the price paid to the workers for the services rendered to the organisation.
- ***Leading and Influencing:*** Leading is stimulating people to be high performers. It includes motivating and communicating with employees, individually and in groups. Influencing may be defined as guiding the activities of organisation members in appropriate directions. An appropriate direction is any direction that helps the organisation move toward goal attainment. The ultimate purpose of influencing is to enhance productivity. The leading and influencing function typically had a number of different labels and is being studied under various heads over the years. Let's look into these closely:
- ***Direction and Supervision:*** The function of guiding and supervising the activities of the subordinates is known as directing. According to Dale, direction is telling people what to do and seeing that they do it to the best of their ability. Acquiring physical

and human assets and suitably placing them on jobs will not suffice; what is more important is that people must be directed towards organisational goals. Supervision is seeing the subordinates do their work and do it as directed. It involves overseeing employees at work.

- ***Leadership:*** Leadership is the process of influencing the actions of a person or a group to attain desired objectives. A manager has to get the work done with and through people. The success of an organisation depends upon the quality of leadership shown by its managers.
- ***Motivation:*** Motivation is the work a manager performs to inspire, encourage and impel people to take required action. It is the process of stimulating people to take desired courses of action. In order to motivate employees, manager must provide a congenial working atmosphere coupled with attractive incentives.
- ***Communication:*** Communication is the transfer of information and understanding from one person to another. It is a way of reaching others with ideas, facts, and thoughts. Significantly, communication always involves two people: a sender and a receiver. Effective communication is important in organisations because managers can accomplish very little without it.
- ***Controlling;*** The objective of controlling is to ensure that actions contribute to goal accomplishment. It helps in keeping the organisational activities on the right path and aligned with plans and goals. In controlling, performances are observed, measured and compared with what had been planned. If the measured performance is found wanting, the manager must find reasons and take corrective actions. If the performance is not found wanting, some planning decisions must be made, altering the original plans. If the controlling function is to be effective, it must be preceded by proper planning. Thus, controlling includes four things: (i) setting standards of performance, (ii) measuring actual performance (iii) comparing actual performance against the standard and (iv) taking corrective actions to ensure goal accomplishment.

Successful management involves active participation by managers in the above basic managerial functions. These functions are interrelated and most managers use a combination of the four simultaneously to solve the problems facing their companies. All management functions are related and interrelated to each other. For theoretical purposes, it may be convenient to separate the management functions and study them independently but practically speaking, they defy such categorizations. They are highly inseparable. Each function blends into the other and each can be performed in any order or sequence, not necessarily in the order shown above, but tend to be performed (normally) in the planning, organising, leading and controlling sequence.

## MANAGERIAL SKILLS

In order to be effective, a manager must possess and continuously develop several essential skills. Robert L. Katz has identified three basic types of skills – technical, human and conceptual – which he says are needed by all managers.

**(a) Technical skill** is the ability to use the tools, procedures or techniques of a specialised field in a competent manner. Technical skill is considered to be very crucial to the effectiveness of lower level managers because they are in direct contact with employees performing work activities within the firm. For instance, the success of a drilling supervisor of an oil rig depends a great deal on his technical knowledge of drilling. However, as one moves to higher levels of management within the organisation, the importance of technical skill diminishes because the manager has less direct contact with day-to-day problems and activities. Thus, the president of an oil company does not need to know much of the technical details of drilling for oil or how to refine it. Horst Schulze, CEO of Ritz-Carlton, got his start washing dishes and waiting tables at hotels in Germany. Over the next several years he also worked as bellhop, a front desk clerk and a concierge. These experiences gave him keen insight into the inner workings of a quality hotel operation, insights he has used to take Ritz-Carlton to the top of the industry.

**(b) Human skill**—also known as interpersonal skill— is the ability to work with and through other people and to work effectively as a group member. This skill is demonstrated in the way a manager relates to other people, including the ability to motivate, facilitate, coordinate, lead, communicate and put out fires. A manager with human skills or people skills allows subordinates to express themselves without fear of criticism or ridicule and encourages participation. Interpersonal or people skills –including such things as sensitivity, persuasiveness and empathy— might often separate a successful manager from an unsuccessful one. Managers with good interpersonal skills are able to promote close working relationships between employees by making them feel part and parcel of a funny little world. Effective managers, after all, are cheer leaders, facilitators, coaches and nurturers. (J.McCune, Management's Brave New World, Academy of Management Review, 1997) At the end of the day, what does it take to grow good flowers, fruits and vegetables? It takes good soil, and that's what a manager tries to create by being sensitive, nurturing and trying to bring out the best in people..

**(c) Conceptual skill** is the mental ability to coordinate and integrate the organisation's interests and activities. It refers to the ability to see the 'big picture', to understand how a change in any given part can affect the whole organisation. Conceptual skills depend on the manager's ability to think in the abstract. They need the mental capacity to understand the overall workings of the organisation and its environment, to understand how the various parts of an organisation fit together and to look at the organisation in a holistic manner. Little wonder, these skills are often a major determinant of who reaches the highest management levels in the organisation. Management thinkers usually cite the example of Jack Welch, the former CEO at General Electric in support of this contention, who was primarily chosen for the job because of his conceptual skills in 1981. After taking over the reins, Welch immediately set out to put the company in shape and make it more competitive. He brought about radical changes at various levels, reduced a major part of GE's bureaucracy and presented a more flexible entity to the outside world. More importantly, he also changed GE's corporate culture to one based on the greater empowerment of employees. (Hitt et al 2009) The relationship between management levels and managerial skills is shown in Figure.

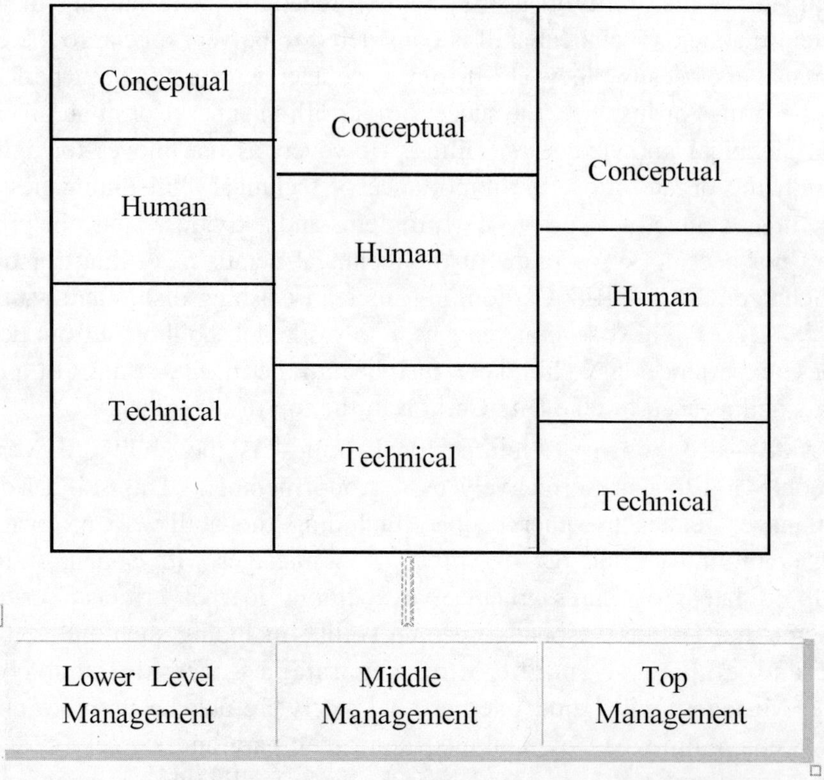


***Figure: 1.3. Relative Significance of Managerial Skills***

Technical skill is most important at the lower levels of management; it becomes less important as we move up the chain of a command. A production supervisor in a manufacturing plant, for example, is likely to need more technical skill than the company president, because he or she will have to deal with the day-to-day manufacturing problems that arise. On the other hand, the importance of conceptual skill increases as we rise in the ranks of management. The higher the manager is in the hierarchy, the more he or she will be involved in the broad, long-term decisions that affect large parts of the organisation. For top management which is charged with the responsibility for overall performance, conceptual skill is probably the most important skill of all. Human skill is very important at every level of the organisation. One reason this is so is because to get the work done through others; high technical or conceptual skills are not very valuable if they cannot be used to inspire and influence other organisation members. Supporting Katz's contention that specific skills are more important at some levels than at others is a study of managerial roles and behaviour by Jerdee and Caroll. More than four hundred managers from all levels of management and a variety of types and sizes of business are asked to estimate how much time they spent on eight management tasks: planning, investigating, coordinating, evaluating, supervising, staffing, negotiating and representing. Lower and middle-level managers replied that supervising was their dominant activity, while top managers claimed to spend proportionately more time on planning.

## CAONCEPT OF ORGANISATIONAL BEHAVIOUR

Organisations are not so much about plant and machinery as people. Everything else flows from that. People are what differentiate a Toyota from a General Motors, a Wal-Mart from a K-Mart (or for that matter a HDFC Bank from a Dena Bank), and an Apple from a Sony. People can make or break a company. In a competitive world, companies have to take care of the customer, innovate continually in order to deliver better goods or services, strive for continuous improvements in quality and render services better than competitors. Above all, they must recognise the importance of moving closer to the hearts of employees through novel compensation methods, participative schemes and retention plans. The relevant point to be noted here is that if people-related problems are not addressed properly, an organisation can go down the hill very rapidly. Hence, it makes sense to realize that '*the human side of work*' is a vital element in the functioning of any organisation. What people think, feel and do in and around organisations is the focal point of our attention in the ensuing paragraphs.

Precisely stated, OB is the study of human attitudes, behaviour and performance. *It is the study of what people do in an organisation and how that behaviour affects the performance of the organisation* (Robbins). There is a clear focus on the psychological, interpersonal and behavioural side of the organisation. As rightly indicated by ***J.W. Newstrom***, *OB is the systematic study and careful application of knowledge about how people-as individuals and as groups—act within organisations.* It is an action oriented and goal-directed discipline. Its **goals** are to make managers more effective at describing, understanding, predicting, and controlling human behaviour.

- *Describe behaviour:* how people behave under a variety of conditions
- *Understand behaviour:* understand why people behave as they do in organisations
- *Predict behaviour:* predict future employee behaviour, which employees might be dedicated and productive or which ones might be absent, tardy or disruptive on a certain day.
- *Control behaviour:* control and develop some human activity at work (skill development, team effort, productivity etc)

### Nature and Scope of OB

OB offers a set of tools—concepts and theories—that help people to understand, analyze and describe what goes on in organisations and why. Like why X wants to quit the job and Y is willing to hang on for over three decades in the same organisation. Why some people work with passion, love and commitment and why others waste resources and spend their time unproductively. The study of OB offers guidelines that help people at work to understand and appreciate the many forces that influence behaviour in organisations. It helps people working at all levels to make appropriate decisions about how to behave and get along with other people in order to achieve organisational goals.(George and Jones). The essential features of OB may be listed thus:

- **Three levels of analysis**: OB focuses attention on three distinct levels of analysis—individuals, groups and organisations. OB tries to look into the impact the individuals, groups and organisations have on the behaviour of members working in an organisation. It tries to utilise this knowledge with a view to improve organisational performance. (Greenberg and Baron)

- **Distinct field of study**: Over the years, OB has emerged as a distinct field of study—of what people think, feel and do in and around organisations. A large number of research studies and conceptual developments are constantly being added to its knowledge base.
- **Interdisciplinary in nature**: OB is an interdisciplinary field dedicated to better understanding and managing people at work. It draws on a wide variety of social science disciplines, including psychology, sociology, anthropology, economics, political science etc.
- **Use of scientific methods:** The field of OB seeks to develop a base of knowledge about behaviour in organisations by employing an empirical, research-based approach. As such, it is based on systematic observation and measurement of the behaviour or phenomenon of interest.
- **Focus on Application**: The field of OB lays emphasis on applications that can make a real difference in how organisations and people in them perform. For example, researchers have shed light on practical questions as: what steps could be taken to reduce work-related stress, what can be done to improve quality of organisational communication, under what conditions individuals make better decisions than groups etc. (Greenberg and Baron)

**Box 1.2 OB is both a science and an art?**

OB is both a science and an art. The knowledge about human behaviour in organisations lies toward the science end of the continuum; the skill in applying that knowledge clearly leans toward being an art, recognising the individual differences in managerial role can vary considerably. The fact of the matter is that OB is an inexact science. Since it deals with human behaviour, its predictive value is always questionable. As rightly pointed out by Luthans, it is possible to predict relationships between variables affecting behaviour on a broad scale but it is difficult to apply predictive models on an individual basis.

- **Contingency thinking:** OB relies on contingency thinking (meaning that *different situations require different behavioural practices for greatest effectiveness*) while trying to understand and solve work-related problems. The strength of the contingency approach is that it encourages a close examination of each situation prior to action while at the same time discouraging habitual practice based on universal truths about human beings. OB recognises that management practices must be tailored to fit the exact nature of each situation and rejects the classical thinking that there is one best or universal way to manage people and organisations(Schermerhorn, Hunt, Osborn)
- **Subset of management:** Management may be defined as the pursuit of organisational goals, effectively and efficiently. Efficiency means to use resources wisely and cost-effectively. Effectively means to achieve results to make the right decisions and successfully carry them out to achieve the organisation's goals. Since these goals are unattainable without human input, OB is a significant subset of management.
- **Positive and optimistic:** Modern OB is positive in nature and is very optimistic about human nature and behaviour. The traditional, negative thinking about employees (that they are basically lazy, irresponsible and require constant supervision and external

controls etc) is being rejected in favour of a more democratic approach where employees are trusted, treated with respect and every attempt is made to improve the quality of life at work.(*Greenberg and Baron*)

- **Integrative in nature:** OB seeks to balance human and technical values at work. It seeks to achieve productivity by building and maintaining employee's dignity, growth and satisfaction, rather than at the expense of these values. OB seeks to fulfil employees' needs and aspirations while trying to realize organisational goals.

**Box 1.3 Fundamental assumptions of the field of Organisational Behaviour**

The field of OB assumes that:

1. Organisations can be made more productive while also improving the quality of people's work life

2. OB is situational. There is no one best way to studying behaviour in organisations. OB scholars, therefore, embrace what is known as a contingency approach—an approach that recognises that behaviour in work situations is the result of many complex, unpredictable, interacting forces.

3. Organisations are not static, but are dynamic and ever changing entities. In other terms, organisations receive input from their environments and continuously transform it into output. This output gets transformed back into input and the cyclical operation continues. Thus, OB is based on the systems approach.

The focus of OB is on human behaviour at work. As we all know, human beings are complex. They are not alike and they are gifted with unique brains. Two people often act very differently in the same situation and the person's behaviour changes in different situations. Keeping this in the backdrop, we can safely conclude that OB does not offer any simple solutions or universal guidelines as far as human behaviour is concerned. It all depends on circumstance, situations and several other contingencies. OB certainly helps us to look at everything from a *refreshingly fresh angle* –paying attention to a wealth of research based theories about how people behave in organisations—before arriving at an informed decision.

## IMPORTANCE OF OB

OB tires to look into the impact that individuals, groups and organisation have on the behaviour of members, working in an organisation. It tries to utilize this knowledge with a view to improve organisational performance. As an applied behavioural science, it applies the knowledge gained about individuals, groups and the effect of structure on behaviour toward the objective of making organisations work more effectively. *(Robbins)* OB, more specifically, is important to managers because of the following reasons:

- *Uncover hidden aspects of organisation*: Often, managers in their anxiety to get results through others, tend to focus attention on strategies, objectives, policies, procedures, structure, technology, formal authority, chain of command etc—the formal side of the organisation—ignoring the human side of the coin completely. By forcing managers to focus attention on the actions of people at work, OB tries to uncover the hidden aspects of organisation such as attitudes, perceptions, group norms, informal relationships, interpersonal and intergroup conflict etc. it makes them realise the importance of taking the human element into account while translating mega corporate dreams into concrete reality.

- *Explain and predict behaviour*: OB helps managers to explain why individuals behave as they do in organisations, why individuals in groups behave differently than individuals acting alone, why monetary incentives have only a limited impact on individual motivation and satisfaction, why a certain amount of conflict is healthy for organisations, why people skills are most important to managers while running the show. By focusing attention on individual and group level characteristics, OB tries to explain and predict behaviour. Because they achieve results through others, managers will be more effective leaders if they have an understanding of human behaviour.
- *Acquire 'people skills' and win the race*: One popular reason for studying OB is to learn more about 'people skills' and apply them in work situations and come out of the race victoriously. People can distract the organisation from its professed path by engaging in conflict and misunderstandings, or they can pool their diverse talents and perspectives to achieve much more as a group than they could ever do as individuals.(*R.L.Daft*) By understanding what causes people to behave as they do, managers can exercise leadership to achieve positive, encouraging and even stunning results from time to time To succeed as a manager, one has to read OB and apply the knowledge in an intelligent manner.
- *Formulate informed judgements*: Generally speaking, OB does not offer magic solutions to behavioural puzzles in an organisation. (*Hamner and Organ*) There is no and there will never be any substitute for judgement of the practising manager in dealing with specific situations. OB can only help in formulating an informed judgement that can be derived from tenable assumptions; judgement that takes into account the important variables underlying the situation, judgement that assigns due recognition to the complexity of individual or group behaviour; judgement that explicitly takes into account the manager's own goals, motives, hang-ups, blind spots and frailties.

## LIMITATIONS

OB is not without its critics and problems. As Robbins rightly indicated, there are few absolutes in OB. Simple, universally acceptable solutions are not to be found anywhere. The reason is fairly obvious. It is a soft discipline and deals with complex and confounding behaviour exhibited by human beings at various points of time. As we all know, two people often act very differently in the same situation and the same person's behaviour changes in different situations. So instead of going for shortcuts or universal truths, one should look at solutions that are based years of fruitful research. And fortunately OB is a discipline that has got rich inputs from a variety of social sciences. If we are prepared to look at things keeping several contingent factors in mind, OB can offer a variety of guidelines that could be readily put into practice. Some of the limiting factors that impact OB may be listed thus:

1. **Theoretical soundness open to doubt:** OB is built around research that deals with complex human behaviour about which very little can be said with absoluteness. Based on research we cannot formulate and come out with certain generalizations that are applicable to all people and in all situations. The problem with OB is that it has no unified theory. Whatever little is known about human beings should be tempered with what the manager has gained through observation and practice.
2. **Behavioural flavor :** OB might stretch a point too far while trying to come to the aid of employees as human beings. No organisation can afford to miss other important elements of work in the name of meeting employee expectations, concerns and demands. You have many other stakeholders demanding their share of the cake. And you need to put all energies focused on getting results —results that are far superior to your rivals in your own self interest.
3. **Manipulative behaviour:** Often managers resort to manipulating people, putting OB concepts and guidelines to personal advantage. In the name of trying to get results you cannot obviously take people for a ride. There is an ethical and moral angle to everything you do. Results, of course matter. But you cannot ride over people—putting the knowledge, techniques and guidelines offered by OB to gain an upper hand over everything.

## DISCIPLINES CONTRIBUTING TO OB

OB is multidisciplinary in nature. It is, in fact, an applied behavioural science that is built on contributions from a wide variety of social science disciplines, such as psychology, sociology, social psychology, anthropology, political science, economics etc.

**Table 1.2. The Multidisciplinary Roots of OB**

| *Discipline* | *Relevant OB topics* |
|---|---|
| Psychology | Perception and learning, personality, emotion and stress, attitudes, motivation, decision making and creativity |
| Sociology | Group dynamics, socialization, communication, intergroup behaviour, power, conflict |
| Social psychology | Inter group collaboration, group decision making, integration of individual needs with group activities, effect of change on individuals |
| Anthropology | Organisational culture, leadership, organisational empowerment |
| Economics | Decision making, organisational power |
| Political science | Conflict, intraorganisational politics, manipulating power for individual self-interest. |

- **Psychology:** Psychology is a science that seeks to understand, explain and possibly change the behaviour of humans and other animals. The areas that have contributed and continue to add to the knowledge of OB include, understanding motivation at work, leadership effectiveness, perception and work stress, decision making, learning theories, personality and attitude analysis etc.

- **Sociology:** Sociology studies people in relation to their fellow human beings. The inputs from sociology flowing into OB include, group dynamics, work teams, organisational culture, interpersonal and intergroup communications, power, conflict, organisational structure, bureaucracy etc.
- Social Psychology: While psychology deals with individual behaviour and sociology deals with group behaviour, the social psychology examines interpersonal behaviour(influence of people on one another). The social psychologists focus attention on intergroup activities and decision making processes, integration of individual needs with group activities, effect of change on individuals and how people cope with 'change'.
- Anthropology: Anthropology is the study of societies, which helps us learn about human beings and their activities. It studies the cultural impact of individual behaviour. Our cultural roots, often, shape our value system and help us draw the curtain between what is right and wrong. the cultural upbringing and the values learnt over a period of time, would help us fit in with established norms of behaviour Anthropology, thus, contributes a lot in understanding the impact of culture on OB, values systems, norms, sentiments, group linkages etc.
- Political science: Political science examines the behaviour of individuals and groups within a political environment. Major areas of interest that are related to organisational behaviour include political manipulation, allocation of power, conflict and conflict resolution, using power for personal gains etc.

## MODELS OF OB

A model is a simplified presentation of some real-world phenomenon. The OB model, as mentioned earlier, focuses attention on three distinct levels of analysis—individuals, groups and organisations. It tries to look into the impact the individuals, groups and organisations have on the behaviour of members working in an organisation. It tries to utilise this knowledge with a view to improve organisational performance. The model of OB is generally built around two sets of variables, namely dependent variables (productivity, absenteeism, turnover, job satisfaction) and independent variables (individual level variables, group level variables and organisation system level variables). The basic objective of any model of OB is to make managers more effective at describing, understanding, predicting and controlling human behaviour.

### The Dependent Variables

The dependent variables, such as productivity, absenteeism, and turnover and job satisfaction are impacted by independent variables. Often, they are the important factors determining he effectiveness of an organisation.

- **Productivity:** Productivity is the ratio of an organisation's output to its inputs. It implies a concern for both effectiveness and efficiency. A service organisation, for example, is effective when it successfully meets the requirements of its customers. It is efficient when it can offer the service at a lesser cost.
- **Absenteeism:** Apart from productivity, absenteeism (failure to report to work) is also

an important factor having a direct influence on an organisation's effectiveness and efficiency. A high rate of absenteeism disrupts workflow, slows down decision making process and can even lead to a drastic reduction in quality of output.

- **Turnover:** Turnover is the voluntary and involuntary permanent withdrawal from an organisation. Turnover, for whatever reason, implies additional recruitment, selection and training costs.
- **Job satisfaction:** It is an indicator of one's attitude towards the job. Employees work better in a congenial work climate, well-supported by appropriate reward structure, benefit plans, and healthy human resource policies and practices. Every organisation, therefore, should always think of providing employees with jobs that are challenging and intrinsically rewarding.

## The Independent Variables

Employees have no control over the independent variables. Management, however, has full control over the individual, group level and organisation system variables. Our understanding of an organisation would improve considerably, as we move from the individual level to the organisation system level variables. These are, in fact, the building blocks of OB as each level is built upon the previous level.

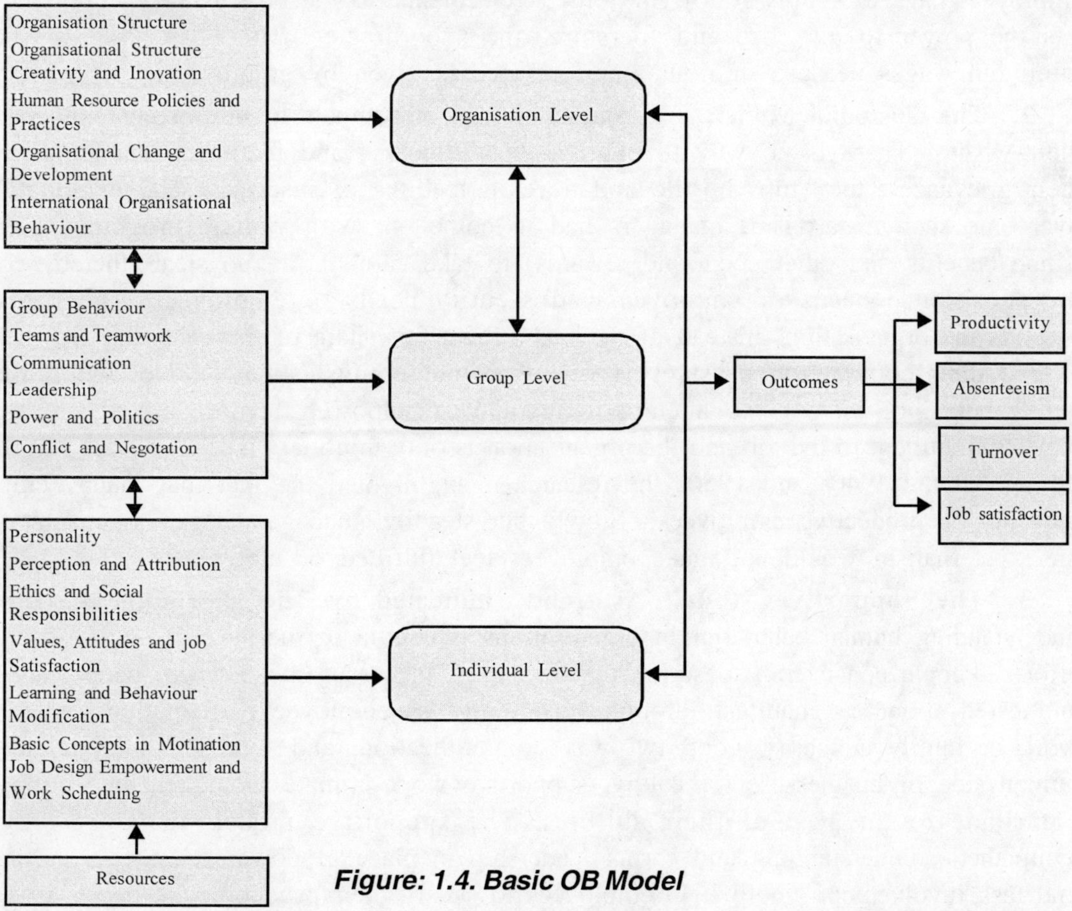


***Figure: 1.4. Basic OB Model***

The OB model—shown above— begins by examining the variables influencing individual behaviour. The knowledge obtained at the individual level will help us analyze the behaviour at the group level and in the organisation as a whole. These three levels of analysis in OB will enable us to unravel the complexities involved in OB in a systematic and organized manner.

## VARIOUS MODELS OF OB

Over the years, five different models of OB have emerged, typically representing beliefs that have significantly influenced management thought and actions, namely, autocratic, custodial, supportive, collegial and system.

**1. The Autocratic Model:** The autocratic model is based on a traditional set of assumptions about people. Managers believe that people have an inherent dislike of work and will avoid it whenever possible. Most people, being lazy, prefer to be directed, want to avoid responsibility and are relatively unambitious. They must, therefore, be controlled or even threatened with punishment to get them to work towards organisational goals. External control is appropriate for dealing with such unreliable, irresponsible and immature people. Managers have to be strict and authoritarian, if subordinates are to accomplish anything. Since the boss knows what is best for the employees and the organisation as a whole, employees have to simply follow the orders. Obedience to the boss is very important, as he has the power to hire fire and 'perspire' the subordinates. The boss pays, in the end, minimum wages because minimum performance is given by employees.

**2. The Custodial Model:** The autocratic model compels to be obedient, much against their wishes. There is no way to express their concerns and feelings. Unable to ventilate their grievances, they turn hostile and develop feelings of insecurity and exploitation. To overcome such negativism, managers had to come out with welfare programmes (mainly fringe benefits and other economic rewards) to take care of the physical (thereby covering the subsistence needs of employees)and security needs of employees. They now look towards the organisation (instead of the boss) for a fair share of the cake and are willing to extend their cooperation passively (remember, not enthusiastically). No doubt, they are happy but since there is no attempt to involve or empower them in organisational work, their commitment to the job and the organisation is only minimal. Therefore, not surprisingly, throughout the 1940s and 1950s the researchers highlighted the fact that 'happy employees may not be productive employees'. Slowly but steadily, managers began to understand that mere paternalism would not make employees feel fulfilled or motivated.

**3. The Supportive Model:** As rightly indicated by The Hawthorne Experiments, understanding human behaviour in organisations is central to the success of any cooperative effort. People consistently describe the best work places as those where people are valued and cared about, as manifest through such things as employee participation, sensitivity to work or family concerns, good two-way communication, and fun. These all relate to the human side of businesses. A healthy, supportive work climate would enable employees to contribute to the best of their abilities. The supportive model, therefore, advocates sympathetic, understanding and caring leadership in place of power or money. Participation and task involvement would help employees to satisfy their psychological needs, in addition to the physiological and safety needs. The manager's role is one of helping employees solve their problems and achieve results.

**4. Collegial Model:** The term 'collegial' relates to a body of people working together cooperatively. The model is found to be useful while carrying out unstructured work, somewhat intellectually challenging and requires a kind of 'meeting of minds'. In this case, the managerial orientation is toward teamwork. The manager would rather act like a coach and motivate team members to take charge of work independently. They are forced to exercise self-discipline, set a reasonable pace for themselves and meet the targets enthusiastically. They are encouraged to uphold quality standards so that they can bring laurels to their company in the end.

**5. The Systems Model:** This is reflective of the values underlying positive Organisational Behaviour. The model is in sync with modern management thought that essentially believes that organisations can take advantage of the imagination and intellect of all their employees. Employees with exercise self control and will contribute to organisational goals when given the opportunity. A sense of caring is said to be the foundation of managerial success. The need of the hour is to find leaders who are willing to" give people the freedom to do what they want" and facilitate employee accomplishments through a variety of actions(J.W.Newstrom)

**Table 1.3. Facilitator roles for managers in the systems model of OB**

- Support employee commitment to short and long term goals
- Coach individuals and groups in appropriate skills and behaviours
- Model and foster self esteem
- Show genuine concern and empathy for people
- Offer timely and acceptable feedback
- Influence people to learn continuously and share that learning with others
- Help individuals identify and confront issues in ethical ways
- Stimulate insight through interviews, questions and suggestions
- Encourage people to feel comfortable with change and uncertainty
- Build cohesive, productive work teams.

## REVIEW QUESTIONS

1. What is organisational behaviour and why is it important?
2. Examine the fundamental concepts that form the basis of OB. Which concepts do you think are more important than the others? Explain
3. Discuss the nature, scope and importance of OB
4. Why we have to study OB? Can you provide some justification?
5. Explain briefly the features of Modern OB
6. What is OB? Discuss its nature. What are the contributing disciplines to OB?

7. Examine the trends in the models of OB as they have developed over a period of time. Why have the trends moved in a positive direction?
8. What is a contingency approach to OB?
9. What are the three levels of analysis in the OB model suggested in the text. Are they related? If so, how?

## CRITICAL THINKING QUESTIONS

1. .Assume that a friend comments thus: "OB is selfish and manipulative, because it serves only the interests of management" How would you respond?
2. Do you think OB can contribute to both the effective functioning of organisations and to the well-being of individuals at the same time? Illustrate through some examples.
3. OB deals with human thoughts, feelings, emotions and actions in a work setting. Explain how an individual's behaviour at home and in society affects his behaviour in organisational environment.
4. "Why do managers often describe people problems as their most frequent and challenging difficulties?"
5. "Understanding human behaviour in organisations is central to the success of any cooperative effort" Critically examine the statement.

## CASE STUDY: Dealing with Unwanted Hands

Baleram was to celebrate his 60th birthday in a few days. As per the rules of the company the age of retirement of all employees was fixed at 60 years. Accordingly, a notice was served on Baleram terminating his services for after completing 60 years as per company records. Four days later, Baleram produced a birth certificate certifying that his age was 57 years. The company was obliged to withdraw the notice served on him and to continue his employment for three more years.

Baleram worked in the processing section of the company's mills. In his youth, he had a good physique and a dominating personality. He was a group leader in the Communist Party and was always a terror to his workers, and supervisory staff. His performance on the job was not bad. However, for the last five years, he had become sick and weak and he could not even walk straight. During the eight-hour shift period, he used to sleep quietly in one corner to the knowledge of everyone, including the Factory Manager, who did not take action against him because he was about to retire in a few years. Baleram also remained absent on many occasions on medical grounds. Fearing that he would be discharged on medical grounds, he produced a fitness certificate from one of the panel doctors of the Employees' State Insurance scheme so that the management would be legally bound to employ him. The management wondered how a fitness certificate was issued to a person who could not stand even for half an hour by a doctor approved by the Employees' State Insurance Scheme.

Baleram himself orally admitted before the management that he could not work at all. He had offered to resign if (1) the management gave him 25 months' salary as compensation in addition to what was entitled to under the retirement rules (he was then earnings Rs 4,500 per month); or (2) the management appoint his son. Baleram's son was equally active in party affairs and was believed to be the leader of a group of gangsters. Considering the other alternative of paying him 25 month's wages, management wondered whether such a course of action, apart from its financial implications, would set a good precedent. Management also knew that such a situation never arose before in the history of the company. They also considered why disciplinary action should not be taken against a person who could not stand even for a few minutes. While considering all these alternatives, management was well aware of the Union's strength and the desirability of avoiding any situation that might disturb union-management' relations. However, management was certain that some action should be taken in the matter.

Discuss the Pros and Cons of each of the following alternative courses of action:

(a) Take no action. Continue Baleram in employment till he retires.

(b) Appoint Baleram's son in his place.

(c) Pay him 25 months' salary as compensation and get rid of him.

(d) Take disciplinary action on Baleram for his inefficiency and irregularity and discharge

# 2

# ORGANISATIONAL BEHAVIOUR: CHALLENGES AND OPPORTUNITIES

## THE NEW WORK PLACE : CHALLENGES AND OPPORTUNITIES

The old work place is characterized by routine, specialised tasks and standardised control procedures. It is built around physical assets, machines, tools and equipment. Employees used to carry out work in a fixed location. The hours of work are predetermined and the quantum of effort is fairly well known. Appraisal mechanisms are put in place to guide human effort along desired lines. Juicy carrots are placed before humans in order to extract work. Punishment systems are put in place to check deviant behaviour. Order, discipline and control are emphasized at every level at all times. The organisational effort is coordinated by the vertical hierarchy with decision making power being held by top management.

The new work place is significantly different from the old work spot of yester years. The Internet coupled with rapid political and social changes has broken down old national barriers to competition. Markets, technologies and firms are fairly well integrated now and operate in a highly interconnected global arena. The new emerging scenario is dynamically different from the old economic order in many respects. Firstly, no managers in today's world can ignore the impact of technology and the way it impacts their jobs and firms. Secondly, it is the globalization trend that is compelling firms to go lean and fit in every respect in order to compete with the best in the world. Thirdly, the need to preserve intellectual capital—that could often turn out to be a crucial differentiator and the principal source of competitive advantage in this networked, globalized world.

**Table 2.1. The rewards and challenges of being a manager**

| *Rewards* | *Challenges* |
|---|---|
| Create a positive work climate enabling employees to work to the best of their ability<br>Provide opportunities to think creatively and use imagination<br>Help others find meaning and fulfillment in workSupport, coach and nurture others | Burn the candle of energies in the service of an organisation; at the end of the day managerial work is nothing but 'blood, sweat, toil and tears'<br>Confront issues head—on; handle difficult people, face tricky situations and encounter seemingly insurmountable problems almost on a daily basis |
| Work with people from diverse backgrounds and learn from each other<br>Receive recognition and status in organisation and community<br>Play a role in influencing organisational outcomes<br>Receive compensation in sync with effort, dedication and commitment | Motivate employees in chaotic and uncertain situations<br>Blend knowledge, skills, ambitions and experiences of a diverse work group<br>Be accountable for final outcomes, irrespective of success or failure<br>Remain brutally frank while placing facts before internal and external public and lead from the front showing exemplary character and conduct at all times |

(Adapted from S.P.Robbins *et al,* Management, 2010)

## 1. MANAGING INFORMATION TECHNOLOGY

The new work place is dominated by technology and knowledge workers (who spend more time using their brains rather than muscle power ) capable of handling non-standardized tasks, as dictated by changing markets and conditions. It is powered and propelled by information and ideas. By integrating computer, cable and telecommunication technologies, modern organisations are able to compete in a better way. In networked organisations, time, distance and space become irrelevant. A networked organisation can do business anytime and anywhere, which is essential in the global market place.(Daft, 2010) In this regard a bewildering variety of information technology choices confront modern businesses. Technology choices have to be made, of course, carefully keeping the end user and the work to be accomplished. Wrong choices could put managers in a tight spot. Any failure on the part of managers to incorporate new technologies into their organisations would put brakes to organisational growth. Modern organisations require IT—adept managers. Some may be able to work for several organisations simultaneously without ever leaving their homes. The aspiring manager today must be immersed in IT and be aware of the opportunities and threats. Managing a vast army of workers having a grip over emerging technologies is not going to be easy. Rapid innovations could bring in additional complexities (Nelson and Quick, 2009)

- Managers therefore need to be well equipped with appropriate technology related competencies and be able to guide effort along desired lines—if they want to command respect from others.
- Alternatives such as Telecommuting, Satellite offices, Hotelling should be explored carefully in order to enhance worker productivity. Telecommuting means workers either stay at home or travel short distances to telecentres to link to the workplace via IT. Satellite offices comprise another alternative work arrangement where large facilities are broken into a network of smaller work places close to employees' homes. Hotelling is a shared-office arrangement wherein employees have mobile file cabinets and lockers for personal storage and hotel work spaces are furnished for them. These alternative work arrangements cut down costs dramatically. AT&T for example has gained $550 million in cash flow from eliminating office space and reducing overhead costs through telecommuting. Alternative work arrangements help modern organisations hire and retain talented employees who find the flexibility of working at home very attractive. Finally, the new work place is slowly getting converted into a virtual office.—wherein people work any time, any where, and with anyone. The concept involves work being where people are, rather than people moving to where the work is.
- They must be able to understand the physical, psychological and emotional pressures on workers handling advanced technologies of various kinds. To relive stress and to enable workers lead a fuller and enriched lives they must try every trick in the book— aimed at converting the work spot into a funny little world. The fear of losing jobs because of rapid technological change must also be handled properly. Training opportunities would help workers overcome the anxieties created by technological obsolescence. Training helps employees feel that they control the technology rather than being controlled by it. Training in any case must be in sync with the requirements of workers.
- Instead of trying to control the work force they must put focus on motivating, coaching and counselling workers. They must try to encourage workers to invent news for technology already in use. Innovators must be singled out for praise and be rewarded in an appropriate way. Managers must find ways and means to adopt new technologies more humanely and effectively.
- Since most of the assets of modern organisations are knowledge based—mostly in the form of intangible assets such as patent, copyrights and trade marks—they must design well conceived strategies to protect these from competitive attacks from time to time. Managers must not leave any thing to chance as far as the intellectual capital of the company is concerned.(in the form of knowledge, information, intellectual property, plus the skills knowledge and competencies of its work force )

## 2. MANAGING GLOBAL FORCES

The world is shrinking in all major respects. People, goods, capital and information are moving around the globe like never before with faster communication, transportation and financial flow, the barriers between nations have disappeared and the world is becoming a borderless market. In the 21$^{st}$ century, global companies seem to virtually dance all over the place. They are not constrained by national borders. Most corporations cover lot of ground while trying to exploit an opportunity in any part of the globe now. BMW builds cars in South Carolina. McDonald's sells hamburgers in China. Coca Cola has over 80 percent of its sales outside of its home market. Nestle has 50 per cent, Proctor and Gamble 65 per cent and Avon 60 per cent. They source and coordinate resources and activities in the most suitable areas, to offer cost-effective products and services to customers all over the globe. Businesses can hire, source and sell wherever they want now. For many of these global corporations, with the entire world as a market, national boundaries have become virtually irrelevant. It is not without reason that IBM dropped its organisational structure based on country and reorganized into 14 industry groups. In a border-less world, success in business increasingly depends upon offering products and services that are competitive on a world basis, not just on a local basis. If the price and quality of a firm's products and services are not competitive with that available elsewhere in the world, the firm might be racing towards extinction. Global competition, whether you accept or not, has become a reality in all but the most remote corners of the world. The world, in short, has become a small but a very complex and dynamic neighborhood.

## Challenges in Managing a Global Corporation

Managing a global corporation in the 21st century, however, could be truly challenging. Global operations have

More functions: global corporations raise money in one market, buy raw materials in other markets, manufacture in a different location, obtain components from another country and the products are being sold in several other places. The corporation has to tackle multifarious design, production, distribution and servicing problems in addition to internal issues.

More heterogeneous functions: there are bound to be vast differences in the way each of the above functions is being carried out, depending on country-specific cultural differences.

More involvement in the employee's personal life

More complex external influences, such as from societies and governments

More cultural differences (with completely different languages, foods, values, beliefs and ways of doing things).

Different approaches to management, since the population of expatriates and locals varies

**Table 2.2. Types of organisation members found in global corporations**

- *Host country nationals (HCNs):* Also called local nationals, they are the employees from the local population. A worker from Bihar employed by an American firm operating in India would be considered a host country national.
- *Parent or home country nationals (PCNs):* Also called expatriates, they are the people sent from the country in which the organisation is headquartered. An American manager on assignment in India is an expatriate.
- *Third country nationals (TCNs):* TCNs are from a country other than where the parent organisations' headquarters or operations are located. If the American firm employs a manager from Great Britain at facilities in India, he would be considered a third country national

Organisations that operate in the global market place often employ all three types of employees. The use of host country nationals, however, is increasing because they are usually the least expensive to employ. They need not be relocated or undergo training in the culture, language or tax laws of the country where the company carries out its operations. Both expatriates and third country nationals, on the other hand, would have to be relocated and undergo training relating to local languages, customs, traditions, business norms and practices etc.

Global corporations require employees with transferable skills- employees who can adapt to different cultures, customs, values, social practices, political systems and management approaches—employees who are willing to work with colleagues with a different mental make-up altogether. They require people who understand the local customs, habits and societal norms very well and able to comply with a complex set of unique, country-specific rules and regulations. They need to build a deep reservoir of talent to compete with tiny local players, national champions and global competitors to succeed in the 21st century. Cascio summed it up appropriately: "attracting and retaining top talent will require more than just huge paychecks. Organizations will need to create the kinds of cultures and reward systems that keep the best minds engaged. The old command and control hierarchies are fast crumbling in favor of organizations that empower vast numbers of people and reward the best of them as if they were owners of the enterprise" To remain at the top, corporations need to invest time money and energies in building a strong work culture empowering people to think and act like real owners, carry out tasks creatively and experiment continuously to cut down costs—all in an atmosphere of great fun. You have to connect people to their passions and make them work for a higher purpose (the way the world works, lives and plays) rather than merely to collect a pay cheque. Corporations have to deal with diverse forces in this shrunken globe—suppliers, producers, distributors, service providers, customers who are connected to each other in some way or the other—and begin to exploit opportunities wherever they come. The lesson for managers is clear Get ready or get lost.. In the present day economic jungle, companies which are able to attract and retain talent will only emerge as star performers.

**Table 2.3. Attributes of the Global Manager**

A global manager has the international awareness and cultural sensitivity required to work well across national boundaries. Often multilingual, the global manager thinks with a world view, appreciates diverse beliefs, values, behaviours and practices and is able to map strategy accordingly.(Schermerhorn, Hunt, Osborn)

Adapts well to different business environments

Respects different beliefs, values and practices

Solves problems quickly in new circumstances

Communicates well with people from different cultures

Speaks more than one language

Understands different government and political systems

Conveys respect and enthusiasm when dealing with others

Possesses high technical expertise for a job.

## 3. MANAGING TALENT

One of the most visible changes that has impacted organisations in the past decade or so has been the growing realization that people are the most important assets of an organisation. Without their positive contributions, the organisation will never be able to realize its dreams. They are the backbone of an organisation and they are the primary sources of a firm's competitive advantage. It is now widely accepted that a firm's success is determined by decisions employees make and behaviours in which they engage. The strategic potential of people, therefore, must be utilized thoroughly in order to deliver extraordinary results. Simply delivering results is not enough; you need to be the best in meeting the expectations of your own employees and also the external public. It has never been more important for organizations to foster and tap the strategic potential of people. Managing people as an organization's primary asset has inspired modern managers to become increasingly more effective at developing programs and policies that leverage talent to align with organizational competencies and at executing organizational strategy. MacDonald (2003) states that "creating the next generation work environment— highly collaborative and capable of not just fostering, but also encouraging, the instant, seamless movement of ideas and expertise will present both intellectual and technical challenges for us as professionals"

### Put your Best Foot Forward to Attract and Retain Talent

Talent management implies recognising a person's inherent skills, traits, personality and offering him a matching job. Every person has a unique talent that suits a particular job profile and any other position will cause discomfort. It is the job of the Management, particularly the HR Department, to place candidates with prudence and caution. A wrong fit will result in further hiring, re-training and other wasteful activities. No matter how inspiring the Leaders are, they are only as effective as their team. A team's output is healthy only if the members are in sync. To achieve such harmony, the key ingredient is "putting the right people in the right jobs". While there is no magic formula to manage talent, the trick is to locate it and encourage it. Let us examine the issue more closely:

**Recognise talent:** Notice what do employees do in their free time and find out their interests. Try to discover their strengths and interests. Also, encourage them to discover their own latent talents. For instance, if an employee in the operations department convincingly explains why he thinks he's right even when he's wrong, consider moving him to sales!

**Box 2.1 Tapping into talent at Best Buy**

In the retail industry, the most influential ideas are often generated from the front-line managers and employees who interact with customers daily. With over 900 stores, Best Buy – a major U.S. retailer – has focused on tapping into and incorporating the ideas of every on-the-ground employee. Part of Best Buy's four-year-old customer centricity" strategy is to ask its employees to spot fresh customer groups – North Carolina retiree clubs and newly returned soldiers in Georgia, for example – that would otherwise fall far below the radar of headquarters-based strategists. Based on these insights, Best Buy stores are able to adjust offerings and product placements to best appeal to these uniquely local groups. Best Buy executives also want to give local managers leeway in setting sales strategies, inventory levels and product mixes. Local store managers are even influencing Best Buy's merchandising tactics. 7 Away from the stores, at corporate headquarters, another talent-focused endeavor is underway. With ROWE (Results Only Work Environment), all 4,000 corporate staffers are free to work wherever they want, whenever they want – as long as they get the job done. The company is planning to take ROWE to stores where employees involved in the "customer centric" campaign might benefit from increased flexibility, just like their headquarters cohorts. Since ROWE's implementation, staff retention has been much higher and productivity in departments participating in ROWE is up 35 percent.8 Best Buy offers a compelling example of how talent management initiatives can tie directly into the strategic plans of a company. While Best Buy did not invent the concepts behind ROWE, allowing customer-facing retail talent to embrace such a flexible approach is very much outside of the "big box".

**Attracting Talent:** Good companies create a strong brand identity with their customers and then deliver on that promise. Great employment brands do the same, with quantifiable and qualitative results. As a result, the right people choose to join the organisation.

**Box 2.2 Attracting and retaining talent at Capital One**

Capital One is a diversified financial services company with more than 21,000 associates in the U.S., Canada and the UK. Relatively early in its growth cycle, the company recognized the requirement to create a lean, engaged and productive workforce. Given the turbulent environment in which it operates, Capital One saw the need to align its organizational design and staffing to meet current and future business requirements while accommodating rapid and unexpected changes. To meet this challenge, Capital One developed an integrated workforce-planning framework using a cross functional team that honed in on both the staffing mix and staffing dynamics of the business. Using multi-dimensional scenario modeling, optimal mixes of internal and external human capital could be determined – laying out the number of positions available at each level for Marketing, Operations, IT and Staff groups. The modeling helped identify which groups should focus on attracting talent at any given time, and helped establish ceilings on attrition rates by allowing for greater control over promotion rates. The impact on the company has been positive and measurable. Not only has Capital One been able to better maintain stab le executive headcount levels, it has also broadened its control over staffing issues and set a floor for promotion rates. The latter has had a positive effect on retention.

**Selecting Talent:** Management should implement proven talent selection systems and tools to create profiles of the right people based on the competencies of high performers. It's not simply a matter of finding the "best and the brightest," it's about creating the right fit – both for today and tomorrow.

**Box 2.3 Motivating and developing talent at Google**

Much has been written about Google's unique approach to business, including the way that the company seeks to motivate and develop its talent. As founders Sergey Brin and Larry Page have written, talented people are attracted to Google because "we empower them to change the world" through the many "data democratizing" endeavours the company pursues. Google allows every developer to "change the world" as they see fit by devoting up to 20 percent of his or her time to non-core initiatives of their own choosing. Google also motivates its talent through its "learn fast, fail fast" approach to experimentation. Motivated employees can try something new with few sign-offs, but they must develop ideas that generate positive feedback from colleagues in order to garner significant resources for their initiatives. Since the notion of changing the world is built into Google's culture, the ideas that get the most positive feedback tend to be the type that might eventually attract millions and millions of users. Motivating employees to find the next big market winner is further enhanced through multi-million dollar stock grants called "Founders Awards" that are granted to individuals or teams that make outsized contributions to Google's success. So far the approach has worked, with non-core projects consistently resulting in new product launches for the company. (Human capital management, IBM Study, August, 2008)

**Retaining Talent:** In the current climate of change, it's critical to hold onto the key people. These are the people who will lead the organisation to future success, and you can't afford to lose them. The cost of replacing a valued employee is enormous. Organisations need to promote diversity and design strategies to retain people, reward high performance and provide opportunities for development. (see www.firehow.com)

What kind of intrinsic rewards would create a 'fire in the belly?'

Intrinsically motivated employees faithfully perform their task because it gives them a feeling of accomplishment. These individuals are not seekers of monetary rewards but instead find satisfaction in the job itself. So, as long as you can satisfy the esteem needs of these individuals you will keep them happy. Keep in mind that money is not the main motivator for everyone. Just follow these valuable steps for inspiring the intrinsically motivated employees and cut some company expenses.

- **Meaningful Work Assignments:** Intrinsically motivated employees want work that is challenging and meaningful. They tend to get bored and loose focus if they are not doing work they feel is valuable to them or to the company. Meaningful work makes them feel that they are a valuable asset to the company. To keep these individuals motivated, delegate meaningful task, then compliment them when they successfully complete them. A simple verbal thank you will work just fine.

- **Personal and Professional Growth:** They are happy when they can grow within the organization and will put forth great effort to apply what they have learned in the current position. They will go above and beyond the call of duty. Overall, opportunities for professional growth help to boost their esteem.

• **Remember employee's birthday/ and years of service:** Although intrinsically motivated employees do not seek after monetary rewards, it is a good idea to celebrate their birthday with them. This will make them feel that you really appreciate them. A birthday card, a cake, and maybe a small gift work just fine for them. You should also honor and celebrate them during an awards ceremony, after they have been with the company for a certain number of years (e.g. 5, 10, 15 years of service). This shows your appreciation for their loyalty to the company. And it also gives them more motivation to continue to work for your company.

• **Praise and recognition:** These individuals are motivated when they receive praise and recognition for their work. Make it a point to recognize them for their work and praise them in private or openly. You should also involve them in decision-makings for company projects and give them praise and recognition for those ideas and suggestions that are put into practice.

• **Job security:** Job security is very important to these individuals. They are not interested in leaving the company to get another job that pays more money; instead they seek longevity with your company. They are very dependable and rarely take time off from their job. They will strive to align their goals with the goals of the company with great enthusiasm.

• **Cost effective for the company:** Concluding, intrinsically motivated employees are lest expensive to employ than extrinsic workers because money is not the main motivator. As long as you satisfy their esteem needs, they are happy to work for you. Managers should keep in mind that a happy employee is a productive employee

The war for talent will continue. It is not easy to find people with requisite skills, knowledge and experience in the market place readily. To compound the problem further, you need to find people with the right kind of mental attitude. As long as there is a cultural mismatch, employee attrition rates will keep rising in the years ahead. Managing layoffs would be a matter of great concern as this will cause serious heart burn among employees leaving the firm. The survivors would look at every move of management with great suspicion. Modern managers, therefore, need to perform the balancing act, keeping the ever changing dynamics of the work place in mind. Cost pressures will compel managements to weed out inefficient people. in a labour surplus and capital hungry country like India, this is easier said than done. Workers will put up strong resistance to any such moves and the recent violent attacks on supervisors and HR managers should force every one to exercise caution and restraint while showing the door to employees. Companies will be ready to do anything possible to get the best results out of people. Because they have a compelling reason to remain at the top in this era of global competition. They have to deal with competitive attacks from any corner, from anywhere, from any player—small or big is not going to make much of a difference, as long as they leave a gap to be exploited by others to advantage. This is where managers could play a major role that of aligning business strategy with operational dynamics.

## 4. DEALING WITH WORKFORCE DIVERSITY

Competition in every conceivable area or sector is hotting up every where. So there is no use talking about local talent and local management. You have to think global and deliver results matching the performance of global majors in terms of cost, quality, design and service. You get bulldozed when you begin to take rest on past laurels. You have to be on your toes constantly and run like a race horse if you want to be in the reckoning. This is where companies have to hire people with relevant skills, experience and knowledge. Workforce is also turning young and, more importantly, mobile. They are willing to switch gears and change hats if the inducements are exciting enough. So, not surprisingly, most companies are bombarded with numbers from almost every corner of the globe. Workforce diversity, as a result, has become a real challenge staring at the face of most managers in recent times. You have to align your systems, practices with the multifarious expectations of a diverse work group—in terms of race, religion, caste, region, age, education and what not.

## India—missed her tryst with destiny?

India is a country of interesting contradictions. People from Nepal, Bangladesh, Pakistan, Tibet, Bhutan and other neighboring countries have been pouring into different parts of the country since times immemorial. In terms of population, it is a continent by itself. The vast majority of Hindus live in close proximity to Muslims, Christians, Jains, Budhists and people from other religious faiths. But for occasional flare ups between people belonging to different religious faiths, it is a fairly accommodative and tolerant state. The problem of gender inequity is assuming monstrous proportions in recent years. In 1981, India had 962 girls for every 1,000 boys. In the 2001 census, the ratio was 927 to 1,000. Current statistics might be very distressing. Indian Prime Minister Manmohan Singh recently called the problem a "national shame." The class divide between the rich and the poor, too, is tolerated admirably. The highest tax payer (incidentally actor, Akshay Kumar who paid Rs. 31 crore in 2009) pays crores of rupees in tax whereas the vast majority of those living below the poverty line cannot have the luxury of two square meals a day! India has the largest number, 200 million, of hungry people in the world. On the Global Hunger Index (GHI) India's rank is 66 out of 88 developing countries.(BT, November 16,2008) We have juggi clusters sprouting up along side Taj Mahals and Five Star Hotels, Super Malls of the world.. In states like Kerala the literacy levels are excellent whereas in other states like Bihar, UP, MP, Rajasthan the literacy levels are very poor. We have more number of doctors than nurses. Engineers outnumber skilled technical personnel. India has 300 million people (the number of poor remained 300-320 million for over 45 years now!) who will never read the newspaper they deliver, work in the factory they build, or drive the tractor they unload. Over a quarter of the world's new workers in the next five years will be in India, but our education and work schemes are unprepared for the demographic dividend. (See India Today, May 11, 2009) The educated do not get jobs, due to lack of relevant skills and knowledge; the uneducated do not have anything to live by. With the result the pains and pleasures of life stare at you in the face wherever you go. How to save the 160 million people from poverty during the next decade and complete the last leg of our journey from independence to freedom is the biggest challenge before administrators now. *Because everything said, an unemployed, unemployable and illiterate Indian is not a free India.* For managers it's really a challenge to understand the dynamics of society and initiate appropriate actions that are in sync with local, political, social, religious, legal and cultural interests of not only internal groups but also external groups such as customers, suppliers, and community at large. Those who fail to live up to the expectations of society, tend to pay a heavy price in the end.

**Box 2.4 Labour force in India**

Out of the estimated 24 million labour force over 1.6 million are unemployed in India. (2008 estimated) Currently over 300 million people live on less than one dollar a day. Poor agricultural returns over the years have contributed to the exodus of people to urban areas, converting urban areas into biggest slums. Over ten million people enter the labour force every year. The unemployment levels according to the NSS survey (61st round) are very high, because the number of those seeking jobs is also growing phenomenally. The 1400 employment exchanges in the country could only offer two lakh jobs to the four crore registered so far. Sad to report, over 90 per cent of the total employment in India is generated in the informal economy. (ILO report-Global Employment Trends) Only about 8 percent of the total workforce is in the organized sector; the remaining 92 percent are in the unorganized sector, self-employed, or employed as casual wage labourers.(See Team Lease's India Labour report) "*Over 50% of India is self-employed. This is not a badge of India's entrepreneurial instincts but our failure to create employability and non-farm jobs.*" Employment generation in private sector is primarily in hot sectors such as retail, telecommunications, IT, electronics, power etc. The contribution of public sector is very negligible. According to the National Sample Survey (62nd round), nearly fifty per cent of Scheduled Caste, Scheduled Tribe and Other Backward Caste members live below the poverty line (the corresponding figure for upper castes is less than 16 per cent) and the literacy levels are miserably poor. The percentage of Dalits and members bellowing to backward castes and economically poorer sections of society making it to factory floors is shrinking by the day. The caste divide in Indian society is very high. Scheduled castes and tribes constitute 24.4% of the population, but make up a fraction of the private sector workforce. The reservation policy adopted by the government during the last five decades or so has remained more or less on paper. Most units shy away from implementing the policy citing one reason or the other. Indian Institute of Dalit Studies conducted a series of studies in 2007 and found that dalits and other minorities are discriminated against in the Indian job market—irrespective of what the captains of industry might claim. There is no one to answer the question posed by Milind Kamble of Dalit India Chamber of Commerce and Industires, Pune: "why is it that a majority of vendors, distributors and dealers of Bajaj Auto belong to a particular community?". Private sector majors such as Infosys (offers a special programme imparting technical and soft skills to dalits and grooms them for corporate life); IBM (where a division head has to meet targets in terms of hiring and mentoring the differently-abled), Pepsico India, HSBC India are doing their best to reduce caste and gender based inequity in employment in recent times.(Outlook Business, May 2, 2009; National Sample Survey 62nd round; Pocket Book of Labour Statistics, 2008; ET 3rd Sep 2008; India Today, May 11, 2009 and en.wikipedia.org )

## Diversity' in the Indian Context

The moral of the story is very clear. One important element in the firm's continued success is its ability to attract, motivate and retain talented employees with divergent backgrounds and expectations and to meld them into a focused and dedicated workforce. Their multicultural backgrounds pose challenges for the firm but also offer an exciting opportunity—of harnessing human potential to firm's competitive advantage. Diversity may be defined as the situation that arises when employees differ from each other in terms of age, gender, ethnicity, education etc. The term 'diversity' as we use the term in 21$^{st}$ century is far more than skin, colour and gender. It refers to multifarious differences including religious affiliation, age, disability status, sexual orientation, economic class, educational background, and life style in addition to gender, race, ethnicity and nationality.

**1. *Composition of Workforce:*** Thanks to the opening up of the economy, especially after the 1990s, the composition of workforce in most organisations is changing. The 21$^{st}$ century is unique in that it accommodates three different generations—-Baby Boomers (born between 1946 and 1964), Generation X (also known as 'baby busters'—born between 1965 and 1979) Generation Y (born after 1980).(Cascio, 2006) —and is struggling to come terms with multifarious expectations of workers in various industries.

- The *Baby Boomers* who were battered by economic shocks and survived lay offs, restructuring exercises and reengineering efforts have either retired or will be retiring soon—leaving a vacuum in the labour markets all over the globe. They had to fight for everything ranging from privacy to freedom of speech.
- The *Baby Busters* have grown up in times of rapid change. Gen Xers are more practical, focused and future oriented. They demand interesting work assignments and thrive on open ended projects that demand sophisticated problem solving. They want control over their own work schedules and seek to refine their skills so as to be relevant and useful.
- *Gen Y* is the fastest growing segment in the workforce now. (India boasts of 550million below the age of 25) Members of Gen Y have grown up amid more sophisticated technologies. They want their work to be meaningful and interesting. They place a premium on their life style and seek to strike a fine balance between work and life. They look for work place perquisites as natural entitlements. Challenging work, company's culture and environment, relations with co-workers and leadership roles are some of the important things that are closer to their hearts than perquisites, benefits and bonuses.

**2. *Dealing with Ageing Workforce:*** Years of fruitful experience, knowledge and skills do not count in the modern world, as most companies compulsorily retire employees at the age of 60. Millions of 'baby boomers', as a result, are shown the door in recent times. There are three issues that merit immediate attention when a company is confronted with the issue of ageing workforce (see the AWF Leadership Pulse Study)

- *Culture change*: The AWF will have a strong effect on their company's culture, some view this as a strategic opportunity to reshape their organisational culture in a new and desirable direction
- *Knowledge gap*: As older employees, leave their talent knowledge, deep relationships and extensive on the job training exits with them
- *Leadership gap*: There will be loss of leadership knowledge, skills and abilities as well.

In a tight labour market situation, loss of experienced employees may have serious long term impacts. Finding a suitable replacement may be difficult or may take time. Even when a new hire is available, it may take time to get him appropriately trained and adequately prepared for a challenging job. Corporations, thus, all over the globe are caught in a— to be or not to be kind of —dilemma. Experts have offered useful suggestions to overcome this problem (M Welbourne, www.eePulse.com)

- *Retention planning*: A key employee may be asked to stay on the project and asked to guide new members
- *Succession planning*: A succession plan must be in place well in advance. The key issue here is the need to find out what types of organisational value older workers possess (e.g. , leadership skills, client relationships etc), then, figure out how to transfer these to the individuals who are expected to step into key roles
- *Targeted selection*: If experience and in-depth knowledge are important attributes in your industry, implement a selection system that will capture these skills
- *Culture change*: Whether desirable or not, a large influx of new employees can potentially change the cultural underpinnings of an organization. So it's important to understand your current culture and assess if a shift in basic values is necessary to help your business. If a planned change will benefit the organization, then selection procedures can help increase the likelihood of choosing the employee attributes that will foster the new cultural values ( Also See "The ageing workforce: challenge or opportunity", R.R.Feinsod and T.L.Davenport, WorldatWork Journal, Third Quarter, 2006)

Many older workers in India are compelled to work beyond retirement, due to the steep fall in pension amounts—in real terms. In a tight labour market situation, older people will make an increasingly vital contribution to the workforce. Keeping this in the background, employers must take informed decisions about retirement—based on peoples' abilities and not on their age. Where there is a chronic shortage of talent, retiring employees based on age would decrease the supply of talent on the one hand and also people who are loyal and committed to the company. The issue of older employees continuing to serve a company beyond retirement age—of course—depends on their health, relevance of knowledge and skills possessed by them; their willingness to undertake jobs across locations, the savings that may result in by keeping on rolls instead of hiring new recruits at higher wage levels; the motivational issues among older workers who may have to work longer hours now etc

**3. *Women at Work:*** Women employees today constitute a major share of the workforce. In India alone, nearly 35 per cent of workforce in software industry at present is women. In other sectors, however, the percentage of women employees is not very high. Over 500 million are employed in various streams due to a combination of factors like: women's emancipation, greater equality of sexes, increased literacy rate, The initial reluctance of employers to give jobs to women seems to be a thing of the past (due to increased financial burden in the form of maternity benefits, crèches, prohibition of women in night shifts and in hazardous jobs, etc.). They handle both 'hard' and 'soft' jobs now in areas such as accounting, hospitality, banking, insurance, airways, police, teaching, beauty care and even driving. The principle of equal pay for equal work has more or less become the rule now in most industries (barring plantation, construction industry, etc.). The Equal Remuneration Act of 1976 specified equal pay for equal work, regardless of gender and prohibits gender discrimination in hiring practices. The phenomenon of Indian women 'breaking the glass ceiling' is being increasingly highlighted in recent times—thanks to the entry of women into the boardrooms as well.

## Women at the top

According to latest finding of Grand Thormton International Business Report, 14% of the Indian women have made it to the top corporate rungs. Though the figures are low, there is no denying the fact that the numbers are steadily climbing up. And still counting. About 56% of the businesses in India have women at senior level as against the global average of 55%. ICICI, known to promote female talents, boast of 30% of the work force comprising of women alone. 3 out of 5 members of Board and 13 out of 40 of its Managers comprises of women. Once Slammed as a "petticoat brigade" by the Banking fraternity, ICICI today has transformed itself from a staid, "also ran" institution in to an aggressive, nimble- footed, financial power house The female brigade of the Bank, Ms Lalita Gupta, Ms Kalpana Moraparia, Ms Chandra Kochar played a tremendous role in scripting its success story. At Bharathi Airtel, 18% of the company workforce comprises women as against a national average of 4% as is revealed by the estimates of Confederation of India Industry. According to experts, companies, which have women employees out perform financially the performance of other companies that don't have women on their rolls.(" Re-assertion of Women Pride-India Inc. leads the way",N.R. Aravamudhan, March 21, 2007)

For women at work—especially in India— the problem of striking rapport between family demands and work place pressures still remains. The journey to the top is not going to be easy without a certain amount of support from the employer. Additionally, female employees have to tackle the problem of sexual harassment at work—which has become a very challenging issue for HR professionals all over the globe. Harassed women are not taking any chances by playing the role of a victim but dragging the culprits to the court rooms and beating them up mercilessly in the street. Educated women are not leaving anything to chance to overcome the glass-ceiling barrier. They are also trying to burn up their candle of energies and carrying a full briefcase of corporate problems back home—determined they are to prove to the world that they can do it better than their male counterparts.

**Box 2.5 Sexual harassment at the workplace: the Indian context**

The Visakha judgement in 1997 by the SupremeCcourt provides a useful framework now. Sexual harassment can involve physical, visual, verbal and non-verbal conduct of a sexual nature, which is uninvited and unwelcome. When the employer or a person in authority seeks sexual compliance from an employee with a promise of reward for compliance or threat of adverse job consequences –it's called quid pro quo harassment (The Industrial Disputes Act and the Industrial Employment(Standing Orders) Act, 1946 provided for this; Section 354 of the Indian Penal Code is the criminal provision that is applied in most cases of sexual harassment) It also includes subtle forms of sexual harassment in the form of physical contact or advances, sexually coloured remaks, display of pornography etc would create a hostile and intimidating work environment affecting a female's work performance.(http://www.lawyerscollective.org/wri/projects-activities/sexual-harassment) The employer has to put the anti-sexual harassment policy in place. It must come in black and white and made known to all through repeated communications. Displaying it at prominent places may be an effective way to remind rascal characters not to indulge in this kind of prohibitive behaviour. instances of inappropriate behaviour need to be brought to the notice of superiors immediately and to this end, awareness campaingns need to be undertaken—so that female employees come forward and voice their concerns in a bold and fearless manner. A complaints committee could be constituted to look into each case carefully and impartially—without invading the privacy of involved parties. Appropriate disciplinary proceedings must be carried out immediately once employee misconduct is established beyond doubt *(see The Sexual Harassment of Women at Work Place (prevention, prohibition and redressal) bill, 2006)*

**Box 2.6 Ways to Cheer up Female Employees**

- Provide *alternative career paths*
- Offer extended *leave facilities* so that they can meet their pressing commitments according to their convenience
- Allow female workers to create their *own schedules* and process work at home
- Permit *job sharing* especially in case of relatively independent tasks such as filing, faxing, word processing, photo copying etc.

Another gender-related problem, the so called glass ceiling needs to be looked into carefully, especially where a large number of women employees are working. The glass ceiling describes a barrier that comes in the way of women advancing to top management positions in many organisations. To overcome this, women running short of specific skills could be asked to undergo training from specialised institutions. They might be asked to acquire diplomas or degrees from reputed educational institutions—charging the expenses to the company. When implemented proactively, such steps will go a long way in overcoming the glass ceiling problem.

Other *facilitating initiatives* could be in the form of providing for child care, elder care, subsidized food plans, insurance plans, counselling services to strike balance between work and the home; realistic work loads etc. The percentage of female employees in various industries is going to increase substantially in the years ahead. Many companies (IBM, P&G, HLL, Sony, H-P, Infosys, TCS, MindTree, Agilent Technologies, Texas Instruments Marriott Hotels India, etc) have family-friendly policies to attract and retain talented women. Strict policies governing sexual harassment, glass ceiling, and gender discrimination have also been adopted to avoid legal hassles. In short, every attempt is made to see that women are truly empowered to think and act the way they like and assume highest positions of profit in industry.

4 ***THE DIVIDE BETWEEN PUBLIC AND PRIVATE SECTOR EMPLOYEES*:** The gap between pay levels and working conditions of public sector and private sector employees is also narrowing down—due to the highly sensitive nature of the issue. Political parties—both regional as well as national—trade unions, religious heads often use this platform—whipping up sentiments against the companies—to further their own selfish interests.

**5. *MINORITY GROUPS :*** The traditional Indian image of diversity has been one of assimilation. A kind of a melting pot wherein differences based on caste, race, religion, economic status were blended into an Indian puree. The socially deprived and economically poorer sections of society never really raised their head protesting against national leadership as to why they have to remain at the bottom of the ladder even after six decades of Independence. Despite fifty years of reservation, SCs/STs haven't even made to the senior management of most Public Sector Units, with the number of SC/ST directors on their boards not even averaging one per company. According to a FICCI study, a shocking 81 per cent of all reserved seats in technical institutes such as ITIs remain vacant, while 88 per cent of all reserved seats in IITs remain vacant. This is largely because of over 60 per cent school drop out rate. (Rajeev Dubey, 'Dump Reservation", BW, 5 May 2008)

**Box 2.7 Policy of Reservations**

The policy of statutory job reservation for SCs and STs has been extended for another ten years, starting from the year 2,000 through a government notification, in all public sector undertakings. The list of OBCs had also been expanded by the government, to extend employment benefits to other neglected sections of society. The 'sons of the soil' policy ensures reservation of certain category of lower level jobs to local people in preference to outsiders. Shiv Sena, for example, is a strong supporter of this policy ever since its inception as a political party in Maharashtra. Farmers who have lost their small parcels of land in favour of Special Economic Zones, Industrial belts have also joined hands with political parties demanding employment rights Displaced persons too get preferential treatment for lower level positions advertised by the company which has acquired their land/house sites, etc. (Essar Steel, Reliance,Tata Motors etc.), for building factories/production facilities.

The minorities, too, did not demand a fair share of the fruits of the so-called economic progress till recently. In fact, most sections of society have never realised the importance of using their 'voting right' as a powerful weapon to bring about radical social, economic and political change in the country. Not any more. Poorer sections of society, minorities, backward castes and the silent majority living in atrocious conditions have started demanding a fair share of the cake—*collectively.* This has brought about a sea change in the thinking of political parties and industry leadership. They cannot think of postponing issues relating to minorities, backward castes and the weaker sections of society—including marginal farmers, landless labour— even for a second. So we have violent demonstrations,

- *when industry leadership is trying to usurp land from the landless all over India;*
- *when political leadership is trying to distribute mining rights to corrupt industry leaders for a pittance;*
- *when companies have forgotten their promises to hire the locals who have lost their land parcels while trying to accommodate the setting up of industrial units ;*
- *when companies have shown scant respect for environmental and ecological concerns and started polluting the surroundings with reckless ease and callous irresponsibility.*

In a nutshell, there is a dramatic change in the thinking and actions of the large majority who, till yesterday, were mute witnesses to social, economic, cultural, religious, sexual exploitation.

**6. *TEMPORARY WORKERS (Temps)*** In a globalized business environment, employees are now compelled to work in three major time zones—namely, Europe, U.S and Asia. This development has compelled many Indian companies to hire workers on a temporary basis on short-term projects (also known as Temping). A temp is a temporary employee who works with a client company, but is on the pay roll of a third party staffing agency. The temping agency would hire a temp either on a commission basis (charging 10-20 per cent of fee paid by client to the temp) or hire the temp on a fixed salary basis plus some extra benefits when the temp takes up a project actually. Factors such as demanding customers, shrinking product life cycle, constantly churning markets, changing attitude of workers entering labour force, companies trying to avoid extra welfare costs payable to permanent labour etc— have paved the way for temping in Indian industries in a big way—especially after early 1990s. The Indian temping staff market is estimated to be nearly $150 million out of a global business pegged at nearly $140 billion. As Indian companies begin to operate in a global market, they are compelled to bring costs down and improve productivity and operating efficiencies. When bombarded with extra work—say to meet additional demand for refrigerators or air conditioners during summer— they go on a hiring spree. When there is subsequent contraction in demand, they are able to show the door to temps. When the company does not have people with specific domain expertise, they do not hesitate to tap the temping agencies to get the right man with requisite skills at a right time. Same is the case when you want to start a new venture, develop a new product, or enter a new market. You can take the help of the temping agency in getting people with relevant skills and expertise. The company is able to concentrate on its core areas of strength and outsource staff from outside in areas where the company does not want to specialize. When you hire people with unique skills and specialised domain expertise you are able to meet highest standards of quality—set by your clients—and also save costs significantly because you need not pay anything when the work ceases to exist. You need not train these people since they already possess relevant skills in the chosen area. Bharti Airtel for instance has hired thousands of temps in an attempt to bring down costs to bare bone levels. The company out sources everything from outside and has, in fact, built a telecom empire in less than a decade by remaining focused on customer service—its core area of strength. Since the company need not bear the extra welfare cost that comes with permanent staff, it can afford to increase its head count depending on the ebb and the flow of its business. if the company does not want to part with the services of good temporary employees, there is always the attractive option of hiring them on a permanent basis. You enjoy a decisive cost advantage as long as you wish and if qualified people are turning restless you can entice them with an irresistible job offer. Temping is a big hit with IT and IT enabled services space in India. Banking, Insurance, Financial services, FMCG, Retail, Pharmaceutical, R&D, Manufacturing companies have also shown pronounced preference for temps in recent times. Most of temping in India is taking place at the low end of the skill spectrum such as data operations, accounts, sales, back-end operations, administration and marketing. Unlike what many people say, temping is not going to be a new management fad. It's likely to witness exponential growth in the days ahead. Much depends on the temping agencies' ability to customize the temp model to the requirements of the clients. The ever-expanding size of the market should make the agencies realize the importance of creating a reservoir of talent through ethical conduct and excellent business practices. The trick is to turn the volume play into a value play. ( N.R. Aravamudhan, "Temping: Redefining the Indian Job Market", April 23, 2007)

## The New Employment Relationship and The Role of Managers

The relationship between the employer and the employees has undergone a radical change in the 21st century. The employer has a compelling reason to bring down costs, remain competitive, and offer the best products and services to get past competition. To attract talent, he is willing to offer a challenging job, come out with an attractive compensation package and bombard the prospective job seekers with benefits and concessions that were never heard of before. But not job security. When there is an economic downturn or when the employee is not contributing enough the employer wants the headcount to be cut down to size, without any hesitation. The employee, on the other hand, is looking for a rewarding job, full of challenge, excitement and fun. He is constantly on the look out to get past rivals and reach a top position—sometimes, by any means.. The moment he finds an irresistible opportunity outside, he is prepared to shift gears and change positions. In this competitive environment, traditional ideas such as commitment to the job, loyalty to a company and remaining faithful to a work group do not seem to excite anyone in the job market. It is more or less a contractual arrangement now between the employer and the employee—in place of a life long commitment of service to each other. Both parties exhibit a pronounced preference for flexibility in thinking as well as actions. The employer is willing to pay more for quality. The employee is willing to go that extra mile to improve his career prospects. The employer has to invent ways and means to attract talent. Training opportunities, profit sharing plans, extra bonuses, two way communications, flexible work arrangements are all part of that strategy. This is where HR managers are expected to play a strategic role, using their "soft skills" to good advantage. They have to go beyond the rule book, find out what the employees want, customize job offers that are in sync with expectations of job seekers, put talented employees on jobs that are challenging, motivate people to give their best, develop employee skills and knowledge constantly, and explore creative paths to enrich campus atmosphere. Managing knowledge workers is not going to be easy, especially when every company knows that talent is going to be the key differentiator between a successful company and an unsuccessful one. ('What it means to be a Strategic HR leader in the 21st Century", SHRM Foundation, 2003)

## MANAGING DIVERSITY

In the light of above discussion, managing diversity may look like a contradiction within itself. It means being precisely aware of characteristics *common to a group* of employees, while also managing these employees as *individuals.* It is not just tolerating or accommodating all sorts of differences arising out of diverse backgrounds and divergent expectations but supporting, encouraging and utilizing these differing points of view to a firm's advantage. (Bateman and Snell)

**Box 2.8 DIVERSITY AS A SOURCE OF COMPETITIVE ADVANTAGE**

- *Gaining and keeping market share*: As businesses expand their operations and gain entry into global markets, managers having exposure to multiple markets are in great demand. If a manager with a deep understanding of Indian retail business were to join Lifestyle, the Landmark Group's retail venture in India, for example, he will be in a position to assess customer preferences and choices better. (See "Differences can be strengths", People Management, April 20,1995). It becomes relatively easy to position a product matching customer expectations in terms of size, colour, fragrance etc. Morrison, who carried out a study of 16 private and public organisations in United States, cites a case in which one company lost an important opportunity for new business in a southwester city's predominantly Hispanic community. The lucrative business ultimately went to a competitor that had put a Hispanic manager in charge of the project who solicited input from the Hispanic community.
- Companies with a reputation for offering excellent opportunities for diverse employees such as Avon, Prudential, McDonald's, FedEx, Eastman Kodak, Toys "R" Us will definitely have an edge in the labour market and will be sought out by the most qualified applicants from premier institutions. When employees believe that their divergent views and perspectives are not merely tolerated but valued and even encouraged at every stage, they tend to become more loyal, productive and committed. A diverse workforce can offer a company with vast knowledge about the preferences and consuming habits of a diversified marketplace. Such knowledge would help companies design appropriate products and develop interesting marketing campaigns in tune with unique, local customer preferences and choices. A diverse workforce can also give a company competitive edge in a global economy by facilitating understanding of other customs, cultures and marketplace needs (for details see chapter 19, organisational culture and chapter 22 international organisational behaviour)
- *Significant cost savings*: According to Morrison, companies face huge penalties if any employee were to drag them to the court on charges of discrimination. (In one case a bypassed woman manager got $17.7 million from Texaco) They also incur high costs in recruiting, training, relocating and replacing employees and in offering competitive compensation packages. A little bit of compassion, nurturing attention and equitable rewards would help retain nontraditional managers on their jobs and this would, in turn, increase comfort levels of employees working at lower levels—especially those belonging to the same group—leading to significant cost savings.
- *Increased productivity and innovation* Many executives quoted in Morrison's study have found that employees who were treated with respect and were at ease in their work setting enjoyed coming to work and performed at a high level. Her study also concluded that a multicultural approach had a positive impact on employees' perception of equity. They were found to be more innovative, agile and productive.
- *Better quality management* Morrison also found that including nontraditional employees in fair competition for advancement usually improved the quality of management by offering

a wider pool of talent. The interactions with colleagues having diverse backgrounds helped managers develop breadth and openness.

- *Enhancement of organisational flexibility*: a diverse work organisation has to live with different styles and multiple approaches. It cannot afford to be restrictive on the operational front. Policies and procedures have to be kept very flexible to accommodate divergent points of view. This would certainly help organisations to become more flexible and thus better able to respond quickly to environmental changes.

As things stand today, many organisations are taking a more practical view of diversity, especially while trying to convert the challenge into an opportunity. The positive results of increasing amount of research highlighting the advantages of diversity have also improved sentiments further. A study by the Department of Labor's Glass Ceiling Institute (1995) showed that the stock performance of firms that were high performers on diversity related goals was over twice as high as that of other firms. Another recent study (Business Week, January 26, 2004) found that companies with the highest percentage of women among senior managers had a significantly higher return to shareholders than companies with the lowest percentage. (I am sure; ICICI Bank is having a close look at the data)

## CHALLENGES IN MANAGING A DIVERSE WORKFORCE

Diversity can turn out to be a big liability in the hands of a manager who is not sensitive to the needs, concerns and expectations of a diversified work group. It can pose lot of problems when a particular section of employees feel neglected or bypassed. The perceived inequity might reside only in the brains of some who might have been pushed to a corner on grounds of poor performance. Subsequent law suits could threaten the very existence of a company.. When the reputation of a company, for right or wrong reasons, takes a serious dent, it may be difficult to attract talent later on. Some of the challenges may seem insurmountable but with commitment and sincerity managers can cross over the hurdles

- Unexamined assumptions: seeing the world from someone else's perspective is a real challenge. Our own assumptions and viewpoints seem perfectly in tune with the requirements of a situation. We see no reason why we should pick up a female when a more qualified male is available for a front office job. Reasons like friendly face, beautiful smile, polished accent, seem totally irrelevant. Paper qualifications make all the difference. When you change sides, shift gears and change hats—perhaps, you might begin to appreciate that after all a male may not fit into a front office job. He tends to move away from desk for a variety of reasons: have tea, pick up newspaper, and chat with a friend, smoke in the lobby and so on. A fresh set of unintended assumptions begin to engulf the mind.
- Lower cohesiveness: Diverse groups, typically, are less cohesive than homogeneous groups. There is visible lack of similarity in language, culture, experiences etc. so how can they get along and produce results cooperatively? Mistrust, miscommunication and attitudinal differences reduce cohesiveness and affect productivity negatively. Unable to get along, many may even quit the field in frustration. Unless managers take the lead and set

common goals and explain the rewards that follow performance, it may be difficult to bring them to a common platform and achieve results.

- Communication problems: Diverse groups carry lot of emotional baggage in the form of misunderstandings, inaccuracies, inefficiencies. You have to explain things again and again to achieve clarity. Members may fail to keep pace with the manager and come back with lots of questions. In any case, the whole process is reduced to a feeble walk.
- Mistrust and tension: because of limited interaction and low familiarity with members belonging to a particular community, region, race of religion you do not like to share your feelings and opinions freely. People generally prefer to get along with others who are like themselves. The way you dress, eat, and get along may be subjects of animated discussion in office corridors—especially in places where there is a clear dividing line between people.
- Stereotyping: we tend to see the world in a particular manner (stereotyping) based on our background and experience. Such a jaundiced view could have negative or positive connotations. As a result, we may stereotype women as not loyal to their careers, older workers unwilling to learn new skills, minority group members as incapable of doing things differently etc. Sometimes, a positive view may not be in sync with reality. We may stereotype Indians as good for software positions because they are good in English and Mathematics! "Unless managers are aware of their stereotypes, either their own or those held by others, the stereotypes can directly affect how people in their organization are treated. Employees stereotyped as unmotivated or emotional will be given less-stress-provoking jobs than their coworkers. Those job assignments will create frustrated employees, perhaps resulting in lower commitment, higher turnover and underused skills" (Adler; Cox)

In an increasingly multicultural business environment, managers need to develop appropriate skills and strategies to overcome diversity related problems. Before proceeding further let's quickly run through various diversity related issues in a sequential manner

## DIVERSITY MANAGEMENT STRATEGIES

In an increasingly multicultural business environment, managers need to develop appropriate skills and strategies to overcome diversity related problems

- *Managing DiversityOpen communication:* One way to deal with the problem of diversity is to create a truly multicultural organisation where all members of diverse cultural and social groups are involved in the divisions that shape the mission, operations, interactions, products and services of the organisation. To this end, managers must encourage open communication with young and old employees, workers, minorities, disabled, etc. In this way managers can learn more about a group's personal values and understand how individuals like to be treated. When they interact with disabled, for example, they may find that the disabled may not like any special attention or treatment to be given to them. They may want to be treated like everyone else, asking only for equal employment opportunities.

- *Encouraging feedback* from various groups regarding how they would like to be treated helps managers in formulating appropriate strategies. In male dominated offices, sexual harassment has become a nuisance in recent times. Before initiating steps to curb such unhealthy tendencies, managers must interact with women employees and elicit their opinions on how to improve relations between males and females. They must develop and communicate a strongly worded policy stating that racial or sexual harassment violates company rules.
- *Awareness building:* Certain proactive companies nowadays are developing awareness campaigns to help employees understand the pain and indignity of harassment. Awareness building is designed to increase awareness of the meaning and importance of valuing diversity. Its aim is not to impart specific skills but to sensitize employees to the assumptions they make about others and the way those assumptions affect their behaviours, decisions and judgement. At middle and higher management levels, charges of harassment could invite harsh punishment and often lead to termination of employment, followed by law suits. To protect the image and reputation of the company, managers must highlight rules in this regard so that everyone understands the policies of the company clearly.

To avoid charges of discrimination, managers must: (Luthans,):

- *Ensure that all types of applicants are sought without any discrimination (recruiting).*
- *Use of valid and non-discriminators selection tools and devices (selecting).*
- *Emphasise that all employees without exception are eligible to use training and development-oriented facilities (training).*
- *Apply performance appraisal systems without any bias or prejudice (appraising).*
- *Reward employee performance emphasising the principle of equity (compensating).*
- *Fix work schedules in a flexible way so that female employees, dual-career couples, disabled workers can participate in all organisational activities without any problem (scheduling).*

- *Diversity training and skill building*: Diversity training and skill building programmes attempt to identify and reduce hidden biases and develop the skills required to manage a multicultural, diversified workforce effectively. The training could help people learn more about their similarities and differences from others. Men and women can be taught to move and work together so as to gain insights into how their own behaviours affect and are interpreted by others. Some companies—like Motorola— even to the extent of offering language training for their employees as a vehicle for managing diversity. Skill building, on the other hand, aims at imparting interpersonal skills –such as active listening, coaching and giving feedback—to participants.
- *Organisational practices*: Another way to accommodate diversity is to come out with flexible work schedules and arrangements. Differences in family arrangements, religious festivals, cultural events may be accommodated in a flexible manner, keeping individuals and groups in mind. Benefit packages could also be structured in a similar fashion—like full insurance cover for employees having a bigger family, allowing employee to schedule

vacations to coincide with those of his spouse, parental leaves of absence, time off to care for sick family members etc.

7. ***KEEPING THE ORGANISATION DYNAMIC AND FLEXIBLE:*** Organisations need to be more agile and flexible in the years to come. They have to turn leaner and leaner as years roll by. Every attempt must be made to cut the extra fat wherever it is found. Flatter organisations, cross functional teams, decentralized structures will bring in the requisite flexibility needed to survive the ups and downs in a business cycle. HR managers will have to give their best while trying to strike the rapport between technology, resources, people and ideas. Investment in human capital (refers to the knowledge, education, training, skills and expertise of a firm's employees) would prove to be very rewarding. Without significant investments in human capital, organisations will not survive and flourish in a competitive world.

Events in today's world are turbulent and unpredictable, with both small and large crises hitting the corporate world with frustrating regularity. Under the circumstances strategic management of change is the need of the hour. Managers should put their best foot forward and build organisational capabilities leveraging on their core strengths and develop a strategy that would put the company ahead of competition. They need to be flexible in their approach and actions, while trying to overcome the hurdles on the way. The scarce resources—physical, financial and human resources— at their command must be put to best use. Success in the new workplace, of course, depends on the ability of managers to strike collaborative relationships with internal as well as external forces. To get the best out of people, employees need to be empowered fully. More importantly, they must stay connected with customers and employees at all times—taking care of their needs, aspirations and expectations in every conceivable manner. Good managers are aware of the fact that they are in a competitive struggle to survive and win. To survive and win, you have to gain advantage over your competitors and earn a profit. The fundamental success drivers in this regard would be innovation, quality, service, speed and cost competitiveness (Bateman & Snell,2008)

- ***Innovation:*** As we all know, products do not sell forever. In fact, they do not sell for nearly as long as they used to because so many competitors are introducing so many new products all the time. Under the circumstances, every firm has to innovate or be prepared to die. You have to be ready with new ways to communicate with customers and deliver the products with innovative features to them. Innovation is today's Holy Grail and is the most important source of competitive advantage (an edge or strength a firm has over rivals). When resources are rare (such as competent workforce) and capabilities are exceptional (brand management strengths of Proctor & Gamble) and competitively relevant (design engineering strengths of Mercedes-Benz) a firm is able to sustain its edge over rivals for a long time.
- ***Quality:*** Remember, Apple has had phenomenal success with iPod but the batteries in the first three version died after 4 months, instead of lasting up to 12 hours, as expected by buyers. Apple's settlement with consumers cost the company a fortune—close to $100 million. So innovations mean nothing unless you deliver what your promise and promise what you can deliver! Many experts believe that organisations unable to produce high quality products won't be able to compete and survive in the present day global scenario.

Quality, after all, is nothing but living upto the expectations of consumers. It is the ability of a product or service to reliably do what it is supposed to do and meet customer expectations. To this end, manufacturers all over the globe must constantly find ways and means to improve quality and achieve zero defects in manufacturing. This means that the end product must stand the test of times in terms of performance, customer service, reliability, conformance to standards, durability, aesthetics and many more things specified and unspecified by consumers.

- ***Service:*** Service means giving customers what they want or need, and when they want it. It means meeting the needs of customers in every conceivable manner—always. Look at what Best Buy is doing to get people to the stores. The chain's loud music and high—tech features had been aimed at young men. But the store found that women today influence 9 out of 10 electronics purchases. So Best Buy lowered the volume and the lighting, trained its staff to discuss what customers want the technology to do for them, rather than merely pointing out each item's bells and whistles. The chain is also trying to hire more female salespeople.
- ***Speed:*** It means rapid execution, response and delivery of results—that often separates the winners from losers. How fast can you develop and get a new product to market? How quickly you respond to customer complaints? If you are able to do these things better than your competitors you are on a safe wicket. GM needed 40 hours to assemble a vehicle in 1980s. Ford is able to do this now in less than 15 hours. From the product concept stage to making the car available in the showroom, Toyota used to take 30 to 40 months in 1980s, but today it does the same in less than 20 months!. Speed is no longer another objective of modern organisations. It is actually the survival mantra.
- ***Cost competitiveness:*** It means keeping costs low enough so that the company can realize profits and price its products at levels that are attractive to consumers. A low cost position means that the company can undercut competitors' prices and still offer comparable quality and earn a reasonable profit. Comfort Inn and Motel 6 are low priced alternatives to Four-Seasons or Marriott. Enterprise Rent A Car is a low priced alternative to Hertz. Dell's phenomenal rise to fame is entirely attributable to its cost competitiveness. To this end, every company must put resources to best use. Often, little things can save big money. So the aim should be to eliminate wastages of all kinds and saving every rupee. Investments in R&D are the only way through which companies can offer incremental benefits to customers.

8. ***MANAGING QUALITY ISSUES:*** Until a few years ago, Indian industry was roundly criticized for paying insufficient attention to the quality of goods and services. Today, things have come full circle and the quality movement is at a feverish pitch. Companies such as BPL, Wipro, Carrier Aircon, Maruti, Thermax, Bata, Philips, Titan, etc., trumpet their steadfast devotion to quality in their advertisements. Quality has become the most important word in the corporate lexicon and companies have realised the importance of investing in processes that contribute to better quality and customer relationships. The term 'quality' refers to a sense of appreciation that something is better than something else. It means doing things right the first time, rather than making and correcting mistakes. According to Edward Deming, TQM is a way of creating an

organisational culture committed to the continuous improvement of skills, teamwork, processes, product and service quality and customer satisfaction. TQM is anchored to organisational culture because successful TQM is deeply embedded in virtually every aspect of organisational life.7

## Deming's Advice on Achieving Quality

W E Deming was originally trained as a statistician and started teaching process control (a method of measuring variation and continuously improving work processes before the final inspection stage to prevent the production of flawed products) in Japan shortly after World War II. He is recognised internationally as an important contributor to Japanese quality improvement programmes. Deming advocates that the way to achieve product quality is to continuously improve the design of a product and the process used to manufacture it. According to Deming, top management has the primary responsibility of achieving product quality. Deming advocates that management should follow fourteen principles to achieve a high level of success in improving product quality:

a. Create and publish to all employees a statement of objectives of the company. The management must demonstrate constantly their commitment to this statement.
b. Learn the new philosophy, top management and everybody.
c. Understand the purpose of inspection, for improvement of processes and reduction of cost.
d. End the practice of awarding business on the basis of price tag alone.
e. Improve constantly and forever the system of production and service.
f. Institute modern methods of training.
g. Teach and institute leadership. Focus supervision on helping people to do a better job.
h. Drive out fear. Create trust. Create a climate for innovation.
i. Optimise toward the aims of the company, the efforts of teams, groups and staff areas.
j. Eliminate slogans, exhortations and targets for the workforce.
k. Eliminate numerical quotas for production. Instead learn and institute methods for improvement. Eliminate management by objectives. Instead, learn the capabilities of processes and how to improve them.
l. Remove barriers that rob people of pride of workmanship.
m. Encourage education and self improvement for everyone.
n. Take action to accomplish the transformation.

## TQM: The Main Ideas

TQM is built around four main ideas: Do it right the first time, be customer centred, make continuous improvement a way of life and build teamwork and empowerment. Let's examine these in detail:

**a.** ***Do it right the first time:*** Managers have been interested in the quality of their products, at least as an afterthought, since the Industrial Revolution. Thanks to the sustained efforts of quality gurus like Deming and Kaoru Ishikawa, product/service quality has become both a forethought and a driving force in effective organisations of all kinds nowadays. Today's hospitals, universities and public sector organisations are as interested in improving product/service quality as are manufacturing organisations, mines, airlines and railways. In its most basic form, the emphasis on quality has come through four distinct phases since World War II – from 'fix it in' to 'inspect in' to 'build it in' to 'design it in'. Present day managers are moving away from the first two approaches and toward the 'build it in' and 'design it in' approaches. Let's look into the differences in these approaches:

- *The 'fix it in' approach to quality:* Rework any defective products identified by quality inspectors at the end of the production process.
- *The 'inspect it in' approach to quality:* Here, quality inspectors sample work in process and prescribe machine adjustments to avoid substandard output.
- *The 'build it in' approach to quality:* Make everyone who touches the product responsible for spotting and correcting defects. Emphasis is on identifying and eliminating causes of quality problems.
- *The 'design it in' approach to quality:* Intense customer and employee involvement drives the entire design production cycle. Emphasis is on continuous improvement of personnel, processes and product.

Each stage of this evolution has broadened the responsibility for quality, literally turning quality improvement into a true team effort. Also, the focus has shifted from reactively fixing product defects to proactively working to prevent them and to satisfy the customer completely. Just having 'zero things gone wrong' is not sufficient now. The focus has shifted towards offering something of value to the customer and buy his loyalty. Today's quality leaders strive to exceed, not just meet, the customer's expectations. Putting quality first is the new slogan.

**b. *Be customer-centered:*** Organisations have to meet the expectations of both the internal and external customers. Internal customers are other members of the organisation who depend on your work to get their job done. For example, a corporate lawyer employed by Maurya hotel does not directly serve the hotel chains' customers by changing beds, serving meals or carrying luggage. But that lawyer has an internal customer when a Maurya manager needs to be defended in court. As far as external customers are concerned, TQM demands all employees who deal directly with outsiders to be customer-centered. Being customer-centered means:

- Anticipating the customer's needs;
- Listening to the customer;
- Learning how to satisfy the customer; and
- Responding appropriately to the customer.

**c. *Make continuous improvement a way of life:*** The Japanese word for continuous improvement is Kaizen, which means improving the overall system by constantly improving the little details. Kaizen practitioners look at quality as an endless journey, not a final destination. In order to improve things, they experiment, measure, adjust continuously. Rather than naïvely assuming that zero defects means perfection, they try to put the finger on the problem causing trouble. There are four ways of achieving improvements:

- Improved and more consistent product and service quality.

- ❑ Faster cycle times (in cycles ranging from product development to order processing to payroll processing).
- ❑ Lower costs and less waste (for example, eliminating needless steps, scrap rework and non-value adding activities).

TQM advocates emphasise the importance of achieving greater quality, speed and flexibility at lower cost and waste. You need not sacrifice something in order to give another thing. All things are possible, provided you work with a clear-cut focus, i.e., improving things.

**d. *Build teamwork and empowerment:*** TQM is built around employees, their needs, aspirations and expectations. It is employee-driven. It allows employees to exploit their full potential. Empowerment takes place when employees are properly trained, provided with all relevant information and the best possible tools, fully involved in key decisions and fairly rewarded for results. In order to carry out work effectively and efficiently, teams have to be created, drawing talent from various departments in a cooperative way.

**9. *DEALING WITH MERGERS, ACQUISITIONS:*** Global corporations often use the mergers and acquisitions route for various purposes: (a)to incorporate new technologies, (b) to enter new markets and gain market share, (c) to improve their market standing and stay at the top. In recent times, such marriages between known and unknown entities are taking place quite routinely. As a result we have M&A activity picking up in sectors like pharmaceuticals, health care, telecom, software, steel, aluminum, power, energy etc. The year 2007 will go down as the year of big-ticket mergers and acquisitions for India. India Inc overtook the Chinese counterparts in the race for M&A deals. In 2008, 1,270 deals with Indian participation and a known value of 50 bil. USD have been announced. Indian companies were involved in a total of 54 M&A deals, including cross-border and domestic transactions till April 2009 according to a study by the Chennai-based Venture Intelligence, a research service that focuses on private equity and M&A activity in India.

## Neglect of the 'people' side

Often, the people side of M&A activity is being thoroughly discounted by firms trying to catch up with rivals in the market place. When a merger is announced, employee concerns in respect of job security, reward structure, growth avenues, territorial jurisdictions, cultural issues etc begin to mount up. If not resolved quickly, such factors may come in the way of integrating the businesses. Most of the global mergers have failed to click simply because the people centric issues have not been dealt with appropriately.

**Table 2.4. Reasons for Failure of Mergers and Acquisitions**

Mergers and acquisitions fail for a variety of reasons, such as:

- Expectations are unrealistic.
- Hastily constructed strategy, poor planning, unskilled execution.
- Failure/inability to unify behind a single macro message.
- Talent is lost or mismanaged.
- Power and politics are the driving forces, rather than productive objectives.
- Requires an impossible degree of synergy.

- Culture clashes between the two entities go unchecked.
- Transition management fails.
- The underestimation of transition costs.
- Financial drain.
- Defensive motivation.
- Focus of executives is distracted from the core business.

("HR issues, activities and responsibilitiesin mergers and acquisitions" Randall S. Schuler and Susan E. Jackson, ILO, Geneva, MCC working paper 3)

When you are buying a company, you are not simply buying land and buildings, equipment and other physical assets. You are also investing in talent acquisition and intellectual capital and unless HR is involved in allaying the fears of people in merged entities, successful integration cannot be achieved. It must be taken into confidence along side legal, finance, and marketing, technology departments during the pre-deal and post-deal stages—to look into the following issues closely: The uncertainties of mergers and acquisitions need to be examined closely and explained properly—especially issues relating to lay offs, career prospects, compensation practices, reporting relationships, job profiles in the new set up etc

## Why the 'people' factor is discounted in M&A activity?

The belief that they are too soft, and, therefore, hard to manage.

- Lack of concern by top management for the impact on employees, unions and communities.
- Lack of awareness or consensus that people issues are critical.
- No spokesperson to articulate these issues.
- No model or framework that can serve as a tool to systematically understand and manage the people issues; and therefore
- The focus of attention in M&A activity is on other activities such as finance ,accounting, and manufacturing

The three step process suggested by Schuler and Jackson deals with issues that are most often present in every M&A activity, but are discounted due to managerial preoccupation with other issues relating to finance, marketing, technology etc.

**A. Pre-Combination:** There is an urgent need to create a dedicated and skilled leader and team for M&A activity. Ignoring HR issues before the merger takes place, could prove to be a costly mistake in the end. There is also an urgent need to understand the cultures of both companies. A meaningful assessment of culture prevailing in each entity should take place before hand. Culture permeates everything, so you need to be aware of it and integrate it into the M & A process. People in both companies might be speaking the same language with completely different meanings. Each company may have its own unique set of values which may come conflict with those of the acquired company. Employees may find it difficult to adjust to the new cultural norms and codes of conduct—explicit as well as implicit—and suffer what is popularly known as –culture shock. Any failure to resolve culture related issues would increase stress levels of employees and result in low job performance. Readiness to face integration related problems, adequate preparation to minize problems at a later stage, adopting practices of learning and knowledge transfer between the two entities are the other issues that require top management attention.

**B. Combination:** integrating both companies: Lack of integration planning is an oft-cited problem in M&A activity. Once this issue is addressed, the next step is to attempt an integration through a series of well-calculated steps. Integration, here, refers to the process by which two companies combine after a merger or an acquisition is announced and pre-combination activities are completed. Systematic integration is at the heart of a successful acquisition.

- o Put systems and processes in place: The day-to-days systems and processes need to be put in place to achieve key synergies. It is also essential to strike a balance between what is integrated and how it is to be done to the specific strengths and weaknesses of the acquired company.
- o Competent integration manager: The whole exercise must pin-pointedly focus on the key drivers behind integration—essentially guided by a competent integration manager brought into the system to carry out the operation in an objective and systematic way.. the person selected must have a feel of the company, think and act like a true owner and should actually believe that integration would deliver outstanding results in course of time. In short, very passionate about making the acquistion work.
- o integration teams: Top management could oversee from a distance, a number of such M&A projects—with appropriate inputs from several integration teams . another important HR issue is the selection of a capable, strong leader who will actually manage the new business entity.
- o Strong leadership would ensure proper direction and appropriate actions taken at the right time. Successful leaders of the new business are generally described as being: (a)?sensitive to cultural differences; (b) open-minded; (c)flexible; (d) able to recognize the relative strengths and weaknesses of both companies; (e) committed to retaining key employees; (f) good listeners; (g)visionary; (h) able to filter out distractions and focus on integrating key business drivers such as R&D and customer interfaces. Such a leader should also have solid knowledge about the company being acquired.
- o Quick surgery: He should conduct a kind of surgical operation quickly and efficiently. this would minimize the uncertainty of 'waiting for the other shoe to drop" "Decisions about management structure, key roles, reporting relationships, layoffs, restructuring, and other career-affecting aspects of the integration should be made, announced, and implemented as soon as possible after the deal is signed - within days ,if possible. Creeping changes, uncertainty, and anxiety that last for months are debilitating and immediately start to drain value from an acquisition "
- o Selection, retention, motivation, issues: . Issues relating to staff selection, retention and motivation, communications and cultural integration also need to be looked into seriously at this stage. the selection process should be in sync with employee expectations so that top talent does not leave from the back door.

- o Open, honest and straight-forward communications: Acquiring companies could use several means—internet, e-mail, internal company intranets, informal discussions—to dispel doubts and arrest rumours regarding the impending changes that are being undertaken in the best interests of all. Senior managers could also straight away talk to the newly acquired hires they are determined to keep.
- o Policies and practices for learning and knowledge transfer: A final HR issue is the need to create policies and practices for learning and knowledge sharing and transfer. Helping to ensure that knowledge and learning are shared across units are HR policies and practices that appraise and reward employee sharing, flexibility, development and long-term orientation.

**C Solidification and Assessment of the new entity:** This is a process of readjustment, solidification and fine tuning. Depending upon the nature of integration, HR professionals should undertake soft due diligence (implying thorough examination of the people-related issues in the company to acquire or merge especially its human resource proactive and policies, talent and leadership attitudes and values; includes an analysis of the impact on all stakeholders: communities, employees, unions, partners, and families of employees):

- o gaining knowledge of the make-up and motivation of the two work forces
- o understanding the potential impact on the companies' multiple stakeholders, including the employees, the communities, and the unions;
- o accessing management team of the other company;
- o conducting analysis of its organizational structure;
- o Comparing benefits, compensation policies, and labour contracts of both firms; assessing the cultural match between the two firms.

HR should offer appropriate inputs to top management so that the transition from one stage to the other takes place smoothly. HR should align the right people with the appropriate knowledge and skills to meet the shared objectives of the enterprise. HR must also advise top management on the merged entity's new organisational structure, staffing policies and practices and help employees cope with changes that seem to be hitting them from all over. Timely inputs in the form of appropriate communications would help in moving closer to the hearts of newly acquired hires.

**10. MANAGING ETHICAL ISSUES:** The ethical behaviour of business has become a major issue in recent times. Not only in India but all countries around the world have received great media attention and aroused the public's concern about ethics in international business. Ethical behaviour is not just a nicety; it has become a very important part of doing business now. As executives from Enron, Tyco, WorldCom, Adelphia and other companies in recent times got paraded in handcuffs before television cameras, people have started questioning the absence of ethical standards in global corporations increasingly. In one recent poll, 71 per cent of the public felt that the typical CEO is less honest and ethical than the average person.(W.W.George) Over the past 20 years, over two-thirds of the Fortune 500 companies have been involved in some form of unethical behaviour. Surveys of employees working therein indicated workplace pressures to be the cause for unethical conduct. (H.Fountain) The list of unethical business activities is frustratingly long:

- o Cut corners on quality control
- o Covered up incidents
- o Abused or lied about sick days
- o Lied or deceived customers
- o Falsified numbers or reports
- o Lied to or deceived superiors on serious matters
- o Withheld important information
- o Misused or stole company property
- o Took credit for someone's work or idea
- o Engaged in copyright or software infringement

**Box 2.9 Unethical practices of global corporations**

Mitsubishi Motors has admitted that it systematically concealed customer complaints in Japan for more than 20 years and some top managers knew about the cover-up. The company failed to inform car owners about possible auto defects and did not file this information with the government. One of the ways Mitsubishi did this was by maintaining two sets of records of customer complaints; those to be reported to the authorities and those to be hidden.(New York Times report)

Nike: Nike, employing more than 450,000 workers mostly in Asian countries has become the subject of controversy on a number of occasions over its policy of hiring the services of these workers through subcontractors. According to critics, these factory workers are subjected to substandard working conditions in the premises of subcontractors, such as exposure to dangerous toxins and carcinogens, poor ventilation and/or air quality, forced overtime, sexual harassment and corporal punishment and abuse. (as reported in Financial Times and Wall Street Journal)

Arthur Anderson: on June 15, 2002 a Texas Jury found the accounting firm guilty of obstructing justice for its role in shredding financial documents relating to its former client: Enron

Adelphia Communications: On July 24, 2002, John Rigas, the 77 year old founder of the sixth largest cable television operator was arrested along with two of his sons, and accused of looting the non-bankrupt company.

WorldCom: WorldCom got decimated after it admitted it hid $3.85 billion in expenses, allowing it to post net income of $1.38 billion in 2001 instead of a loss. Former WorldCom CEO, Bernie Ebbers was sentenced in July 2005 to 25 years for fraud, conspiracy and false filings.

Satyam computer Services: The Rs.7000 crore fraud that the Founder and Chairman of the company, Ramalinga Raju perpetrated in order to prop up valuations of the IT giant for over a decade—falsifying accounts, siphoning out money to privately held companies headed by his sons, bribing the CFO and the auditors, showing accrued interest of nearly Rs.400 crore on non-existent bank deposits is indeed one of the largest and the biggest in corporate scandals in India.

Reputed Indian companies too, have been questioned on grounds of unethical practices in recent times e.g. issue of warrants to promoters, buying at inflated prices in foreign soils, under invoicing of sales, hiking equity raising sentimental issues regarding takeover, switching of shares to favour relatives and friends etc. The following sections define ethics, explain why ethical issues are an important aspect of management practices, discuss ways and means to put the house in order .and offer some suggestions for creating an ethical workplace

## Defining Ethics

The word 'ethics' refers to principles of behaviour that distinguish between good, bad; right and wrong. It is a person's own attitude and beliefs concerning good behaviour. Ethics reside within individuals and as such are defined separately by each individual in his own way. What may be ethical behaviour to 'X' may be unethical to 'Y'. Ethics, in short, may refer to the following (Davis & Blomstorm; Harvard Business Review,Sturdivant)

- o *Ethics are principles, values and beliefs that define what is right and wrong behaviour.*
- o *Ethics is broader than what is stated by law, customs and public opinion. For example, accepting gifts from father-in-law might be socially acceptable but not ethical; owners pocketing profits without sharing the gains with workers might be legally permissible but not ethical.*
- o *Ethical behaviour may differ from society to society. For example, birth control is mandatory in Communist societies but not in Catholic Christian societies.*
- o *Ethical standards are ideals of human conduct. Defining ethical standards is not an easy task.*

## Why Ethics is a vital part of management practices ?

Ethical issues are important for mangers for various reasons. If ethics are missing, business and society as a whole cannot flourish. Likewise, when job values are in conflict with individual expectations, productivity suffers. The job holder remains unhappy and discontented. If the organisation fails to project a healthy image of itself in society – its quality, service and customer satisfaction – its very existence may be in danger. A positive public image, on the other hand, can attract customers who might view such an image as desirable. Again, where companies are said to be behaving unethically, the public is more likely to seek increased governmental intervention and regulation. In short, ethical concerns are of vital importance to individuals, organisations and the society in general and cannot be discounted or slighted away as unimportant and unnecessary. As Akers (former chairman of the board of IBM) rightly pointed out, "*no society anywhere will compete very long or successfully with people stabbing each other in the back, with people trying to steal from one another, with everything requiring notarized confirmation because you can't trust the other person; with every little squabble ending in litigation, and with government writing reams of regulatory legislation, trying business hand and foot to keep it honest* '

## Managerial or Business Ethics

Business ethics deals with application of moral principles to business problems. Here, the word, 'morals' refers to accepted customs of conduct in a society. The purpose of business ethics is to guide the efforts of managers in discharging their duties to the satisfaction of various stakeholders like employees, owners, customers, suppliers, and the general public. Managerial ethics, thus, are those principles that guide the conduct and thinking of managers with respect to what is good or bad; right or wrong. (Barry) It is not always easy to divide managerial actions into clear-cut compartments of ethical and unethical behaviour because of certain complicating factors.

**Box 2.9 What Constitutes Ethical Behaviour?**

A manager of Corporate Planning from India, for example, may be acquiring a non-Indian company with two sets of books to evade income taxes being standard practice for the country. Do we: (i) declare income and pay taxes, (ii) take the black money out the country (illegally), or (iii) continue tax evasion? Another type of dilemma confronts the manager who must decide whether to lay off an older, less efficient employee for a younger employee with greater skills and vigour. Again, how to resolve the conflicting interest while deciding on a particular issue? Can a business man make decision in favour of his employee, the government, society at large, or some other persons when he would personally profit more by making a decision contrary to that interest? Thus, decisions with ethical overtones are often complex. Often, there are conflicts in values, and the manager perceives different obligations which seem to conflict in their implications.

## Determinants of Ethics

The key forces that shape the ethics of a person may be stated thus (see www.bsr.org and www.ethic.org

**Family, School and Religion:** The formation of ethics begins early in life. As a child one learns about what is good and bad from parents. Through their reinforcing actions, (rewarding good behaviours), parents inculcate high or low ethical standards among children. Schools and Religion also greatly influence the formation of ethical values (such as truthfulness, honesty, sincerity, tolerance etc.) at an early age.

**Peers, Colleagues and Superiors:** In the company of good friends, the child realises the importance of high ethical standards in life. If he were to single with peers who steal, smoke and use drugs, he will probably accept those behaviours as ethical. Colleagues in an organisation too, shape the value system of an individual. He adopts the attitudes, beliefs and values of the group to which he belongs. Likewise, most people yield to pressure from superiors in doing things that many consider unethical otherwise.

**Experiences in Life:** Experiences in life teach many lessons. These could be bitter or sweet, depending on the ability of a person to reach goals. If a person is not given a 'pit on the back' for good behaviour while others earn rewards for bad behaviour, the person will probably alter both ethical standards and behavioural responses in future.

**Values and morals:** People who value material possessions in life may not have strong ethical standards regarding behaviours that lead to accumulation of personal wealth. On the other hand, people who place a premium on quality of life will probably have strong ethics while competing with others for various things in life.

**Threatening Situations:** An employee threatened with losing a permanent job may resort to unethical acts to save his job. To meet pre-determined targets, many Bank managers sanction loans to individuals with practically no credit-worthiness. A housewife may practically beat a thief to death, when threatened with the prospect of losing her ornaments or child. Situations like these, force people to change their ethics and respond in an unexpected manner.

**Organisational Demands:** There is growing research evidence to show that managers at top, middle and first level have compromised their personal principles to meet an organisational demand. Corporate goals are paramount and exert considerable pressure on executives to change their ethical views.

**Legislation:** Laws are generally passed in response to social demands. Factors, such as low ethical standards, corruption in public life, absence of social responsibility, exploitation, sexual harassment etc, often force people to demand legislative protection. A practice can be made illegal, if society views it as being unethical. For example, if contributions to political parties by companies are being viewed as excessive and unethical, the practice can be banned.

**Government Ruler Regulations:** Government regulation regarding product safety, working condition, statutory warnings (on cigarettes and other harmful products) etc are all supported by laws. These offer guidelines to managers in determining what are the acceptable standards and practices.

**Industry and Company ethical codes of Behaviour:** Many times specific guidelines are provided to managers by the company's ethical codes of behaviour. One important question in such cases, in whether individuals within the organisations are really governed by the code of ethics or provide only lip service to the guidelines.

**Social pressures:** Social forces and pressures have considerable influence on ethics in business. Society, in the recent past has demonstrated how a special status can be conferred on backward castes; boycotted products, and severe action to prevent the construction of nuclear power plants. Such actions by different groups in society may, in fact, fore management to alter certain decisions by taking a broader view of the environment and the needs of society.

## Ethical and Unethical Behaviour: Managerial dilemmas

The manager's real world of deciding shades of difference is far more challenging and complex than the textbook ethical problem situations. In addition to the above factors, there are other complicating factors in making choice between right and wrong. (Jones) Often, it may be difficult for the manager to free himself from bias and prejudice and look at issues objectively. In spite of good intentions, he becomes passionately involved in the situation and becomes identified with certain positions or points of view. It becomes difficult to step back and to take a detached point of view in examining the issue from an ethical standpoint

**Box 2.10 What constitutes unethical behaviour?**

- Falsifies information on application blank.
- Trading stocks on the basis of inside information.
- Padding expense accounts.
- Divulging trade secrets to competitors

Taking company property or materials for personal use.

Giving or receiving gifts in return for orders.

Quitting a job or firing someone without giving adequate notice.

Stealing.

Soliciting offering kickbacks.

Severely critical of competitors

Cheating customers, overselling, unfair credit policies.

The dynamics of ethics in managerial decision making, in actual practice, is often complex. (Adler) Many ethical questions may remain unresolved in day-to-day life. What is 'fair' profit? What is a 'just' price for a product? How 'honest' should a company is with the union?

## 'Fairness' in Managerial decisions?

How to arrive at 'fair' decisions concerning resource allocation, interpretations of organisational rules and policies? The answer lies somewhere between egoism (decisions leading to maximum personal gain) and altruism (decision leading to maximum social benefits). (Mill) Managers, who are extremely selfish, always seek what is pleasurable and evaluate actions in term of personal benefit – power, prestige, salary etc. If the action process is beneficial to the organisation and society as well, it is purely accidental. Basically, they would always do what is personally beneficial. A managers who follows altruism, seeks course of action that may offer much social benefit – greatest happiness to the greatest number. Between the two extremes lies another alternative that is, obliging a formal principle. According to egoism, an act is good if one derives benefits from it. On the other hand, altruism says that an act is good if society is the ultimate beneficiary. The criteria for both are consequences. The ethic of following a formal principle is based on the idea that the rightness of wrongness of an act is based on principle, not impacts.

**Box 2.11 Factors that raise Ethical Standards (Better Man)**

- Provide clear guidelines for ethical behaviour.
- Teach ethical guidelines and their importance.
- In grey areas where there are questions about the ethics of an action, refrain from it.

Set up controls (e.g., establish an auditing agency reporting to outside directors) that check on illegal or unethical deeds.

Conduct frequent and unpredictable audits.

Punish trespassers in a meaningful way, and make it public so that it may deter others.

Emphasise regularly that loyalty to the company does not excuse improper behaviour or actions.

Creating an ethical workforce:Guidelines for managers

## PROMOTING ETHICAL BEHAVIOUR: GUIDELINES

Creating, distributing and continually improving a company's code of ethics is one common step managers can take to establish an ethical work spot Ethics officers could also be appointed to recommend, help implement and reinforce strategies aimed at integrating appropriate conduct throughout all phases of company operations. Appropriate training programmes could be initiated to promote ethical conduct throughout the company. Such programmes do not necessarily teach managers what is ethically appropriate or not but offer them useful guidelines to determine how ethical a certain action might be when viewed against commonly accepted standards of behaviour such as( Gellerman)

- ***The golden rule:*** act in a way you would expect others to act toward you
- ***The utilitarian principle***(utilitarian approach) act in a way that offers greatest benefit to the greatest number of people. Nobel Prize winning economist, Milton Friedman argues that using resources in ways that do not clearly maximize shareholder interests amounts to spending the owners' money without their consent—and is equivalent to stealing. The utilitarian approach, thus, puts focus on behaviours and their results, not on the motives for such actions.
- ***Kant's categorical imperative***(universal approach) act in way that the action taken under the circumstances could be a universal law or rule of behaviour. if you follow this approach, you should choose a course of action that you believe can apply to all people under all situations and that you would want applied to yourself.
- ***The professional ethic:*** take actions that might be viewed as proper by a disinterested group of professional colleagues
- ***The TV test:*** managers should indulge in soul-searching questions such as: "would I be comfortable explaining to a national TV audience why I preferred this action?"
- ***The legal test***(Justice approach) is the proposed action or decision legal? The justice approach involves evaluating decisions and behaviour with regard to how equitably they distribute benefits and costs among individuals and groups. Generally speaking, costs and benefits should be equitably distributed, rules should be impartially applied, and those damaged because of inequity or discrimination should be compensated.
- ***The four-way test:*** if the answer to the following questions is "yes", then managers are said to be on track: is the decision truthful? Is it fair to all concerned? Will it build goodwill and better friendships? Will it be beneficial to all concerned?
- ***Natural duty test:*** this principle requires that decisions and behaviour be based on universal principles associated with being a responsible member of society. Four universal duties are to help others who are in need, not to harm or injure another, not to cause unnecessary suffering; and to support and comply with just institutions
- ***Moral rights test:*** The moral rights approach holds that decisions should be consistent with fundamental rights and privileges, that is, life, freedom, health and privacy. Many laws now a days require businesses to comply with society's view of appropriate standards for quality of life and safety. Employees, customers, shareholders and the general public have the right not to be intentionally deceived on matters about which they should be informed. Likewise, citizens have a moral right to control access to personal information about themselves and is use by public and private agencies.

(S.W.Gellerman, "Managing ethics from the top down", Sloan Management Review, Winter 1989; Don Hellriegel et al, Management, South Western, Kundli, 2007)

While resolving questions involving ethics, of course, a manager needs to evaluate the consequences on society, on the company and self carefully and also analyse personal value system.

## Institutionalising Ethics

Keeping the above guidelines in the background, top managers must create an organisational environment that fosters ethical decision making by institutionalising ethics. This means applying and integrating ethical concepts into daily action. According to Purcell and Weber, this can be achieved by (1) teaching ethics in management development programmes (2) formally appointing ethics committee/officers and (3) establishing a code of ethics.

## Whistle blowing

Two other practices have gained popularity in institutionalising ethics:

- appointing an ombudsperson. An ombudsperson is an executive outside the normal chain of command who handles serious ethical problems in an impartial way
- appointing a whistle-blower. A whistle blower is an employee who reports perceived unethical organisational practices to outside authorities (press, government public interest groups).

Anyone thinking about whistle-blowing should ask themselves four important questions before doing so (R..Dwyer and D.Carney and Johnson)

- Is this the only way? Do not blow the whistle unless you have tried to rectify things by reporting up the normal chain of command and failed to get results. also make sure your allegations are not minor complaints
- Do I have the evidence? Collect documentary evidence and keep in a safe place. Make sure you are seeing fraud, not merely incompetence or sloppiness
- Why am I doing this? Do not act out of frustration because you feel underappreciated or mistreated. Do not embellish your case and do not violate any confidentiality agreements you may have
- Am I ready? Carefully evaluate the consequences that may engulf your family and your career. You may lose the job anyway, but try to protect your self-respect and dignity by remaining calm. Better seek legal help before management tries to project you as the villain of the piece!

Since whistle blowing comes in the way of organisational self interests, not many companies encourage this in actual practice. It may also put the career of a brilliant employee on the line. To make it more viable, whistle blowing must be encouraged along the following lines.

**Box 2.12 Steps to encourage valid whistle blowing**

- Clearly communicate whistle-blowing procedures to all employees
- Allow for reporting channels in addition to the chain of command or reporting incidents to one's boss
- Thoroughly investigate all claims based on a consistent procedure

- o Protect whistle blowers who make valid claims. Recognise that the harsh treatment of a whistle-blower will probably lead to adverse public opinion.
- o Provide moderate financial rewards for valid claims
- o Publicly celebrate employees who make valid claims
- o (M.P. Miceli and J.P.Near, Blowing the Whistle, Lexington, M.A. Lexington Books, 1992)

## REVIEW QUESTIONS

1. Why should managers monitor demographic trends (such as composition, race, age, sex, education, etc.)?
2. What is meant by diversity, and what are the major reasons that have made it a challenge for today's organisations?
3. Outline the major characteristics of diversity.
4. How can diversity be managed? Offer suggestions at both the individual and organisational levels.
5. Discuss the relationship between technology and managerial strategies and actions. What can managers do to grapple with economic challenges and technological advancements?
6. Write short notes on:
   - o Why the people factor is put aside in mergers and acquisitions?
   - o What do you know about total quality management?
   - o What problems have come to surface due to the entry of women in corporate sector?
   - o What are the challenges managers are forced to face due to increased globalization?
   - o How can managers come to terms with technology related issues in $21^{st}$ century?
7. Define 'ethics'. Draw the distinction between ethical and unethical behaviour, quoting relevant examples.
8. What are the forces that shape the ethics of a person?
9. State the importance of ethics for organisations and their employees?
10. Describe three approaches that people use when making ethical judgements.

## CRITICAL THINKING QUESTIONS

1. Predict workplace changes that you believe might take place within the next 10 years. What challenges will these changes present to organisations?
2. What can you do to avoid being pressured into acting in ways that go against your own ethical principles?
3. Can the ethical culture of an organization be improved? If so, how? If you do not think it can be improved, why not?
4. Since 2000 a number of corporate scandals have been brought to light. Many companies have responded by, for example, appointing a chief ethics officer, starting an ethics training programme for employees, writing a formal code of ethics, settiup up a hotline for whistleblowers. In your opinion, are these measures likely to increase organisational ethics in the long run? If so why? If not, what would be effective in improving organisational ethics?

## Case Study: Fish out of the Pond

Sandeep Mulye has finished the ITI diploma from a leading technical institute in Delhi in 1998. He has joined as a trainee in Shanker Foams (P) Ltd. on the strength of his brilliant interview performance. He was asked to report to Suresh Kumar, the warehouse supervisor, immediately after the interview. On the first day Suresh assigned Mulye to a small group of 8 workers who were responsible for loading trucks that supplied the materials and carried back the foam mattresses, furniture, pillows, bolsters, cushions, bus seats, sheets etc. to various marketing centres.

Being a technician, Mulye was basically surprised to find workers not doing things properly. They were carrying out instructions, no doubt, but at a slow pace, indulging in gossip and even playing 'hide and seek' wherever there was lot of work to do. Mulye often found himself alone unloading the trucks while other members of the group were off messing around elsewhere.

Mulye was quick to indicate this to his crew members. He said, "I do not like this kind of waste in the workplace. You must be sincere to your job. Instead of standing around and talking, why don't you assist me in the unloading operations. Don't you think, by wasting your time on useless activities you are also cutting off the profits and consequently your own bonus packages"? The workers on this part were quick to retort: "if you don't like our company, better hang out outside. If you plan to complain, you better hold your tongue and indecent haste. Otherwise you may have cause to feel sorry later on."

After the unhappy exchange of arguments and counter arguments, the crew virtually boycotted Mulye from their social network, such as taking tea and lunch together, celebrations on Friday afternoon, weekend movies, celebration of festivals in company quarters, street-side card games etc. Being a bachelor, Mulye found this a bit too hard and, one day, picked an argument with Shanker Dada, one of the older workers thus:

'What's wrong with you guys? I am just trying to do my job. I am paid for the work here. I don't want to be a parasite on the company and I don't like others to run around without a spot on their shirts. Anyway, I am not going to stick my neck out for long here. I am glad that you guys have not been able to change me a bit."

Shanker Dada replied Comrade Mulye, if you had been here as long as we have, you would be just like us."

### Questions

1. Employing some of the theories, explain the possible reasons for the group formation of this work crew. What types of groups exist in this case?
2. Examine the role the supervisor is playing in encouraging or discouraging the group to do well on the job?
3. Why has Mulye been accepted by the group? Do you agree with Shanker dada's statement? Why or Why not?

# UNIT II : INDIVIDUAL AND INTERPERSONAL BEHAVIOUR

# 3

# Individual Behaviour

## INTRODUCTION

One important result of liberalization, privatisation and globalization (you may call this the LPG era) is that modern organisations have grown in size and complexity. The jobs have become quite complex in nature, in that employees are now expected to be proficient in a variety of areas including basic business skills, core job skills and human relations skills. The work place is being increasingly flooded with people with varied social, cultural and religious backgrounds. To complicate matters further, the employees have turned more vocal, aggressive, demanding and restless. They have huge expectations from the employer and are ready to quit the jobs at the slightest provocation. Armed with transferable skills, they are constantly on the look out for greener pastures outside. Under the circumstances, it is not surprising to find modern managers describing '*People*' problems as their most frequent and challenging difficulties. Knowing how to do a job is no more the key to managerial success. To produce efficient and effective results, managers should know how to work with people. So, *understanding human behaviour* is central to the success of any cooperative effort.

### Foundations of Individual Behaviour

Individual behaviour, according to Kurt Levin, is a function of the (p) person and the environment (E)

$$B = f\ (P \text{ X } E)$$

These two factors are closely related. Any one of these two factors individually will not be able to throw light on why a person behaves in a particular manner. The behaviour may change due to a variety of reasons, attributable to individual differences as well as environmental factors.

**Individual differences:** Individual differences in terms of age, sex, education, learning capabilities tell us why people behave differently in different situations. Surprisingly, even in similar situations, all people do not act alike, like the behaviours exhibited by different workers when the organisation wants to fully computerize its operations. In fact, as research evidence shows, people's behaviour is a function of three main influences: the *genetic*(born with a predisposition to be a certain type of person like being intelligent, being happy, being depressed etc), *physiological* (like brain abnormalities, differences in hormones, a healthy diet etc) and *learning* factors that predispose them to behave in certain ways. Here, we are referring to the situational factors that encourage or discourage behaviour; and the reasoning process including the factors that affect our ability to think and decide how we will behave in a given situation.

**Environmental influences:** Human behaviour is impacted by environmental influences—both physical and social—greatly. The physical environment consists of factors such as noise, heating, lighting, ventilation, cleanliness, nature of job, office furnishings, space utilisation etc. For example, people might feel happy to work in an environment where the office space is being utilized without any visible differences between the manager and the subordinate. The social environment consists of societal norms and rules of behaviour established over a period of time. The societal norms act as unwritten laws of behaviour governing the conduct of employees in an organisational setting. Behaviours such jumping the queue, not wearing a formal tie, smoking in a public place, talking in an aggressive tone etc might become the butt of jokes and hence, anyone exhibiting such behaviours might fall in line with the majority.

In the final analysis, therefore, human behaviour is impacted by the personality related factors as well as environmental influences. Both these factors are highly interconnected so that behaviour cannot be explained in itself by either of the two influences, independent of the other influence.

## INDIVIDUAL GOALS VS ORGANISATIONAL DEMANDS

When a person joins an organisation, he brings with him a unique set of needs such as need for making a living, gaining social status, attaining a prestigious position, grabbing a certain amount of power, developing relevant skills and become what he wants to be and what he is capable of. He tries to fulfil his multifarious needs through his association with the organisation. The organisation, in turn, has its own set of goals such as gaining market share, improvement in sales revenues, product development etc. Organisations cannot attain these goals without positive contributions from people. According to Schein, both the individual and the organisation, therefore, enter into a kind of 'psychological contract'. This contract is executed by the organisation by assigning task to individuals, setting certain rules and placing some obligations on individuals while performing the duties. The individual concerned is expected to put in his ability, loyalty, hard work, commitment while at work and show superior performance and earn his rewards. Unimaginable rewards could accrue to both the individual (in the form of monetary rewards, growth opportunities, promotions etc) and the organisation (grabbing market share, becoming the leader in the industry etc), when individual goals are in sync with organisational demands. In actual practice, however, the goals of individuals and the organisations rarely mesh with each other in a neat manner. A variety of differences traceable to individual personalities as well as their upbringing and a number of environmental factors could often spoil the show. Given the wide variation among individuals and among jobs, an important responsibility of managers is to try to match employee and job demands so that work is carried out by people who are well suited to do it. This requires that managers be clear about what they expect employees to do. They should know what kind of people would be able to achieve results, within a given set of opportunities and constraints. The extent to which a person's ability and personality match the needs of a job is known as person-job fit. When selecting people, therefore, managers should try to achieve person-job fit so that employees are more likely to contribute to the best of their abilities and remain satisfied.

## MODELS OF MAN

A number of explanations have been advanced, over the years, to explain the behaviour of individuals in an organisation, whether a person would act rationally always, whether the behaviour is in sync with the expectations of his work group, whether he would be able to exploit his potential fully, whether the behaviour is actually a product of a variety of complex factors etc.

### Rational economic man

In this classical model, a manager is depicted as an economic being trying to make consistent, value-maximising choices within certain limits. The model is built around certain assumptions

- The decision maker operates to achieve goals that are known and agreed upon. He would define a problem carefully and would have a clear and specific goal.
- The decision maker tries to gather complete information about the problem. The model assumes that people have access to complete and perfect information. All alternatives and the potential results are calculated.
- Criteria for evaluating alternatives are known. The decision maker has the freedom to select that alternative which would maximise his satisfaction.
- The decision maker is rational and uses logic to assign values, order preferences, evaluate alternatives and make the decision that will maximise the economic return to the organisation.

The rational economic man model is characterised by 'hedonism' and is motivated by economic incentives. Man is being viewed as an automaton, a kind of a self-centred animal, devoid of human characteristics that all of us possess.

The rational economic man model, evidently, is an ideal that can rarely find expression in the real world, because of several reasons. Actually, it is not possible to give an accurate and precise description of real world problems. Frequently, the manager himself does not know that he has a problem. His knowledge of the problem, even if he is able to put the finger on the issue causing trouble, is not always perfect. Even when he is able to identify such problems, because of time and resource constraints, he may have to rush through such problems and settle for a choice that is based on imperfect data. His own capacity to run through bundles of data concerning various problems is also open to doubt. Sometimes, powerful political groups within an organisation may not allow him to pick up an alternative that would maximise return to the organisation. (like unions coming in the way of hiving off a division or striking an outsourcing deal with a foreign company etc).

### Social Man

This model is the outcome of behavioural science research and human relations movement.

Man is a social animal. He, therefore, tries to move closer to the expectations of the groups with which he has an active association. The model is based on certain assumptions

- Work is basically a social experience and therefore, most people find satisfaction in being members of a social group.
- Work group pressures, problems and sanctions often dictate the manner in which a person would behave, especially when faced with problems affecting the lives of the group as a whole.
- A person would be willing to obey and comply with management's orders so as long as these are not in conflict with the interests of the work group.
- It is, therefore, in the best interests of a manager to organise work in a democratic manner. He should be willing to encourage participation, take the whole group along with him and act more like a facilitator while resolving work-related issues and problems. Instead putting emphasis on achieving results at any cost, he should shift attention to the larger interests of the work group as a whole.

## Organisation Man

This model is an extension of the social man concept. Organisation man, according to William H. Whyte, is one who sacrifices his individuality for the sake of the group and the organisation. Competitive struggles are effectively replaced by cooperative efforts and the economic logic is discounted in favour of social ethic in this model. A person is willing to sacrifice his individuality for the sake of the group and the organisation. The model is built around three propositions:

- The group is the source of creativity. The individual by himself is isolated and meaningless; only when he collaborates with others does he operate. The individual helps to produce a whole that is greater than the sum of the part.
- Belongingness is the ultimate need of the individual. There should be no conflicts between man and society because what is normally considered conflict is merely misunderstanding and breakdown in communication.
- The application of science achieves the goal of belongingness. By applying the methods of science, the obstacles to consensus can be eliminated and equilibrium can be created where society's needs and the needs of the individual are one and the same.

According to the model, there is very little scope for conflicts to crop up between individuals and the organisation to which they belong. Eve when conflicts arise, it is easy to resolve them because people are used to sacrifice their self-interests in favour of the larger organisational interests. By implication, managers have to design work keeping the larger interests of the work group, so as to avoid friction between group goals and organisational demands.

## Self-actualizing man

Self actualization is self-fulfilment—the need to develop one's fullest potential, to become the best one is capable of being. According to A.H.Maslow, it is the desire to become what one is capable of becoming. A musician must make music, a poet must write, a general must win battles, an artist must paint, a teacher must teach if he is to be ultimately ahppy. What a man can be, he must be. However, this does not mean that one must always create poems, novels, paintings and experiments. In a broad sense, it means creativeness in realising to the fullest one's own capabilities, whatever they may be. As things stand now, a person's self actualization needs may not always find meaningful expression in a formal organisation where the requirements might be totally different. The assumptions about self actualization man that normally managers make in formal organisation are basically related to what McGregor proposed in Theory Y. They are:

- Human needs could be arranged in the form of a hierarchy, ranging from physiological, safety, love, esteem and self-actualizing. Self actualizing is the final goal of any individual.
- Man moves from a state of immaturity to a state of maturity to satisfy this particular need
- Man is essentially self motivated and does not require any external control or direction.
- Conflicts between self actualization man and the form of organisation structure are inevitable because the formal structure is based on the assumptions of immaturity of individuals.

## Complex Man

According to this model, man is complex and it is not possible to predict his behaviour with any amount of certainty. Attempts to establish a relationship between human needs and behavioural outcomes, hence, would be fruitless. Man is influenced by a bewildering variety of factors such as incentives, work group pressures, political influences, family concerns, social demands etc. To compound the problem further, he responds to managerial actions in unpredictable ways. To cut short a long argument, therefore, man is a complex mixture of needs, goals, aspirations, perceptions, attitudes and faculties. There is no one best way of dealing with such a complex being. A wide variety of contingency models of motivation, leadership and management have gained popularity, over the years, trying to solve this knotty issue. The basic theme of contingency theory is that there is no one way of managing people. It depends and varies with the situation.

According to the Contingency Approach, there are no plans, organisation structures, leadership styles, or controls that will fit all situations. There are few, if any, universal truths, concepts, and principles that can be applied under all conditions. Instead, every management situation must be approached with the 'it all depends' attitude. Managers must find different ways that fit different situations. They must continually address themselves with the question: which method will work best here? For example, in order to improve productivity, classical theorist may prescribe work simplification and additional incentives; the behavioural scientist may recommend job enrichment and democratic participation of the employees in the decision-making process. Instead, a manager trained in the contingency approach may offer a solution that is responsive to the characteristics of the total situation being faced. Organisations characterized by limited resources, unskilled labour force, limited training opportunities, limited products offered to local markets—work simplification would be the ideal solution. Job enrichment programme would work better if the organisation employs skilled labour force. Managerial action, thus, depends upon circumstances within a given situation. No one best approach will work in all situations. Applying a contingency/situational approach requires that managers diagnose a given situation and adapt to meet the conditions present.

According to Edgar Schein, the complex man model is built around the following assumptions

- Man is motivated by a variety of factors which are complex and unpredictable
- A person's needs, aspirations, attitudes etc will undergo significant changes as he begins to interact with his colleagues, organisation and the environment.
- There are wide variations among people in the same organisation. Such variations may be in terms of their need pattern, their behaviour and hence the need for direction and control

## Workforce to get multi-generational

Future workforce will be vastly different from what they are today—in age, aspirations as well as attitudes. The workers will be more youthful as they start taking up their first jobs much earlier in life. As a result they will be less skilled and companies will have to learn to groom and harness their potential. The workforce will also become more diverse with more women and many more nationals working together. It will also be multi-generational with a mix of almost four generations. They are matures(1909-1945), boomers(1946-1964), Gen X(1965-1979), and Gen Y (1980-2004). All of them with very different attitudes and needs. While the Matures work on their own terms, the Boomers tend to be more participative in nature. The Gen X demands to be told as compared to Gen Y which needs more guidance. For companies it will be a challenge to manage such a diverse set of people with different needs and mindset. (A.K.Mishra, Economic Times, 16.4.2007)

- A simple understanding of human need hierarchy is inadequate because empirical verification of the relationship between a particular need and the behaviour is difficult.
- A person could respond to managerial actions in multifarious ways, depending on his needs, aspirations, attitudes etc.

## REVIEW QUESTIONS

1. Give a detailed account of various models of man. Which of the models is superior, you feel, and why?
2. Behaviour is always not rational? What is the logic behind non-rationality in human behaviour?
3. Human behaviour is complex. Do you agree with this statement? Also explain the operational implications of complex nature of human being.
4. How do you explain the congruency between individual goals and organisational objectives
5. Human behaviour is more complex that what people generally believe. Do you agree with this? What are the factors that add complexity to human behaviour?

## CRITICAL THINKING QUESTIONS

1. "Human behaviour is a function of person and environment" Comment
2. Different approaches have made different assumptions about the needs that persons seek to satisfy through organisations. Discuss such assumptions
3. Examine the bondage between an individual employee and an organisation.
4. Is there any organisation where individual goals do not come in conflict with the organisational goals?

## CASE STUDY "Left or Right?"

Rajinder Kumar was a production worker at competent Motors Limited (CML) which made components and accessories for the automotive industry. He had worked at CML for almost seven years as a welder, along with fifteen other man in the plant. All had received training in welding both on the job and through company-sponsored external programmes. They had friendly relations and got along very well with one another. The played volleyball in the playground regularly before retiring to the quarters allotted by the company. They are together in the company canteen together, cutting Jokes on each other and making fun of everyone who dared to keep into their privacy during lunch hour. Most of the fellows had been there for some length of time, except for two men who had joined the ranks only two months back.

Rajinder was generally considered to be the leader of the group, so it was no surprise that when the foreman of the new was transferred and his job was posted, Rejinder applied for the job and got it.

There were only four other applicants for the job, two from mechanical section and two from the outside, when there was a formal announcement of the appointment on a Friday afternoon, everyone, in the group congratulated Rajender. They literally carried him on their shoulders, and bought him snacks and to celebrate.

On Monday morning Rajender joined duty as Foreman. It was company practice for all foreman to wear blue jacket and a white shirt. Each man's coat had his name badge sewn onto the left side pocket. The company had given two pairs to Rajender. He was proud to wear the coat to work on Monday.

People who saw him from a distance went upto him and admired the new blue coat. There was a lot of kidding around calling Rajender as 'Hero', 'Raja Babu' and 'Officer' etc. One of the guys went back to his locker and returned with a long brush and acted as though he were removing dust particles on the new coat. After about five minutes of horseplay, all of the men went back to work. Rajender went back to his office to get more familiar with his new job and environment there.

At noon, all the men broke for Lunch and went to the canteen to eat and enjoy fun as usual. Rajinder was busy when they left but followed after them a few minuter later. He bought the food coupon, took the snacks and tea and turned to face the open canteen. Back in the for left-side corn of the room was his old work group; on the right-hand side of the canteen sat all he other foreman in the plant - all observed in their blue coats.

At that point of time, Silence descended on the canteen Suddenly as both groups worked at Rajinder anxiously, waiting to see which group he would eat with.

**Questions**

1. Whom do you think Rajinder will eat with? Why?
2. If you were one of the other foremen, What could you do to make Rajinder's transition easier?
3. What would you have done if you were in Rajinder's shoes? Why?

# 4

# Personality

## INTRODUCTION

Human behaviour is influenced by personal and environmental factors. It is, therefore, essential to study the individual and his personality concepts before proceeding to see how he behaves in an organisation. Behaviour, as psychologists indicate, is the result of a complex interaction between a person and the situation. Often, how he behaves in a particular situation, largely depends on the surrounding events and situations. To a large extent, however, it depends on his own unique, physical and mental characteristics finding expression through consistent behavioural patterns.

*Personality*, thus, combines *a stable set of physical and mental characteristics that reflect how a person looks, thinks, acts and feels.. It is the sum total of unique ways in which an individual reacts and interacts with others*. We can also interpret personality as having a **core**—features common to most of us—and a **periphery**—those that have become part of us because of what we have observed and learnt from the environment.

## FEATURES

***Each person is unique and distinct:*** The term personality represents the overall, broad profile of certain stable characteristics of an individual—what X has in common with others and what separates X from others in terms of certain traits and behaviours.

***Each person has some stable patterns of behaviours and consistent internal states:*** This means that how X would behave in case of an accident to his colleague, how he would react when someone breaks the queue, what he would do to mend someone smoking in a public place etc. Although a person's personality undergoes certain changes over time, (as the saying goes, the journey of an individual through life can take infinite number of paths) most behaviour patterns are visible and understandable to his own family members and friends.

***Personality, thus, has both internal and external elements.*** One can easily form an opinion by observing the external traits of a person. The internal states such as feelings, thoughts, emotions and values make a person somewhat unique and even mystical. Every person is different from every other person in some respects, while being similar in other respects.

Although there is a biological bias to personality, the specific development is *a product of social and cultural environments.*

## DETERMINANTS OF PERSONALITY

The major determinants of personality are generally grouped by researchers under the following heads:

## BIOLOGICAL CHARACTERISTICS

Personal characteristics such as age, sex, marital status, dependants, ability etc. may often be obtained through personnel records. Such information would help find the relationship between an individual's background and his motivation level and the impact of these variables on employee productivity, absence, turnover and satisfaction.

***Age:*** The relationship between age and *job performance* has been a point of intense debate and discussion over the years. It is widely believed that job performance declines with increasing age. *Employee turnover* too tends to be low as employees grow in age. There are less chances of such employees quitting the job suddenly because of two reasons: one, the outside opportunities may not be very tempting or may not be available, second, you begin to get more by staying back in terms of higher wages, benefits, bonuses, stock options etc. On the other hand, older workers are perceived to be lacking in flexibility and offering resistance to new technology. Such negative feelings, often, come in the way of hiring older workers for any possible vacancies in an organisation. Keeping this in the background, let's now look into the research evidence. The *Age vs. absenteeism* relationship is somewhat inverse because older employees have lower rates of avoidable absence than do their younger counterparts. They have generally higher rates of unavoidable absence due to poor health and longer recovery period older workers require when injured. Coming to *age vs. productivity* relationship, it is generally believed that an individual's skills decay over time; he may lose interest in job and the intellectual stimulation may also depreciate over time. However, this may not always hold good as recent research studies proved. Intact, researchers now opine that age and job performance are unrelated and the decline in physical skills sometimes is more than offset by benefits due to the experience gained by the employee on the job. Finally, the *age vs. satisfaction* relationship is also somewhat hazy unless we classify employees into two categories: professional and non professional employees. Among professionals, satisfaction generally increased with age, whereas it fell among non professionals during middle age and then rose again as they advanced in age later on.

***Gender:*** It is generally believed that gender differences between males and females affect their job performance, especially in situations demanding physical effort. However, there are no consistent male-female differences in problem-solving ability, analytical skills, motivation, sociability, competitive drive etc. At lower levels, women are willing to conform to authority, whereas men are more aggressive. The differences in productivity and turnover were also negligible. The rate of absenteeism among females was found to be higher because of home and family responsibilities.

***Marital Status:*** Research evidence suggests that married employees tend to have fewer absences, undergo fewer turnovers, and more satisfied with their jobs than unmarried co-workers.

***Number of Dependents:*** The number of children an employee has is positively correlated with absence (especially among females) and job satisfaction. Employee turnover, however, was found to be not so closely related with number of dependents.

***Tenure:*** There is no valid reason to believe that experienced people are more productive than those with less seniority. Seniority has a negative correlation with absenteeism and turnover. The past behaviour of an employee in this regard could be used to predict future turnover and absence rates quite safely. The evidence also shows that tenure and job satisfaction are positively related.

***Ability:*** It refers to an individual's capacity to perform the various tasks in a job. An individual's abilities are of two kinds (a) *Intellectual abilities:* These are required to carry out mental activities. These include number aptitude, verbal comprehension, perceptual speed, spatial visualisation, reasoning and memory. Selection tests employed to measure the above are found to be strong predictors of job performance. They also help place a candidate on a right job, suitable to his mental make-up (b) *Physical abilities:* These include stamina, dexterity, strength and similar skills. These physical abilities are more important for performing less skilled and more standardised jobs at lower levels in an organisation.

## PERSONALITY FACTORS

Our behaviour at any given time is a complex combination of our unique personality traits and the demands of the environment. An early argument in behavioural science research was, whether the personality of an individual predetermined at birth or was it the result of an individual's interaction with his environment. To find the answer, let's examine the major determinants of personality.

***a. Heredity:*** Heredity (genes) plays an important role in determining one's personality, Physical stature, facial attractiveness, sex, muscle composition and reflexes, energy level, temperament are the characteristics that are substantially influenced by who your parents were. Research evidence suggests that traits such as fear, shyness, distress etc., are most likely caused by inherited genetic features. However, personality characteristics are *not completely dictated by heredity* (i.e., fixed at birth and not possible to change through experience). Further, the importance of heredity varies from one personality trait to another. For instance, heredity is generally more important in determining a person's temperament than values and ideals. Current research subscribes to the view that about fifty percent of the personality differences may be traceable to genetics and over thirty percent to occupational and leisure activities.

***b. Brain:*** There is a general feeling that brain plays a significant role in the development of one's personality. Results from the electrical stimulation of the brain (ESB) offer evidence that better understanding of human personality could come from a close study of the brain. The evidence in this regard, however, is not very clear.

***c. Physical features:*** An individual's external appearance— whether short or tall, fat or skinny, handsome or ugly etc, — is said to be having a major impact on his personality. For example, a short person, who generally becomes a butt of jokes, develops a defense mechanism which is reflected in his personality.

Personality characteristics, as most would readily agree, are not completely determined by heredity. In actual practice, there are other factors which could influence the personality of an individual in a major way. Let's run through these factors quickly.

## CULTURAL FACTORS

Among the factors that shape our personality in early stages are the *culture* in which we are raised, our early conditioning, the norms among our family, friends and social groups and other influences we experience, Culture is a complex set of these beliefs, values, and techniques for dealing with the environment which are shared among contemporaries and transmitted by one generation to the next." Culture requires both conformity and acceptance from its members. There are several ways of ensuring that members comply with the dictates of the culture. Such socialisation takes place through the early training given to the young persons of a culture, through establishing mores and through informal pressure to obey certain ways of behaving. The personality of an individual is thus determined by the culture in which he is brought up. Often the person and his culture are so interconnected with each other that it becomes to difficult to separate the person from his cultural surroundings. There is, however, one point that merits our attention here. Culture, no doubt, helps determine broad patterns of behavioural similarity among people, but differences in behaviour usually exist among individuals within a society due to age, education, skill levels, socio economic classes, geographic location etc. For example, work ethic (hard work is valued, an unwillingness to work is sinful) usually associated with Western cultures. But this value may not influence everyone with Western cultures to the same extent. (Hellreigel and Slocum)

## FAMILY AND SOCIAL FACTORS

Family and social factors are also important in shaping the personality of an individual. In order to understand the effect of family on individual's personality, we have to understand the socialisation process and identification process.

***Socialisation process:*** The contribution of family and social group in combination with the culture is known as socialisation. In the words of Mussen "socialisation is the process by which an individual infant acquires, from the enormously wide range of behavioural potentials that are open to him at birth, those behaviour patterns that are customary and acceptable according to the standards of his family and social group." It initially starts with the contact with mother and later on, the other members of the family (father, sister, close-relatives) and the social group plays an influential role in shaping an individual's personality.

***Identification process:*** Identification is fundamental in understanding personality. Identification starts when a person begins to identify himself with some other member of the family. Normally, a child tries to behave as his father or mother. He tries to emulate certain actions of his parents.

According to Mischel, identification process can be examined from three angles: (a) it can be viewed as the similarity of behaviour between child and the model, and (b) it can be looked as the child's motives or desires to be like the model, and (c) it can be viewed as the process through which the child actually takes on the attributes of the model.

Apart from the socialisation and identification processes, the personality of an individual is influenced by the *home* environment. There is a substantial empirical evidence to indicate that the overall environment created by parents at home is critical to personality development.

## SITUATIONAL FACTORS

Human personality is also strongly influenced by situational factors. Knowledge, skill and language are obviously acquired and represent important modifications of behaviour. Learned modifications in behaviour are not passed on the children, they must be acquired by them through their own personal experience, through interaction with the environment. In one research by Milgram it was found that situation plays a vital role in human personality. According to Milgram "situation exerts an important pressure on the individual. It exercises constraints and may provide push. In certain circumstances, it is not so much the kind of person a man is, as the kind of situation in which he is placed, that determines his actions."

In short, each person in some ways is like other people and in some other ways is unique and distinct. An individual's personality is shaped by inherited traits and on the job and off the job experiences. Experiences generally take place within the framework of a person's biological, physical and social environment—all of which are modified by the culture, family and other groups to which a person belongs.

## THE BIG FIVE PERSONALITY DIMENSIONS

A review of the personality literature and personality traits offers useful guidelines that can lead to effective job performance. As such, it can improve recruitment, training, transfer and promotion decisions. Because personality traits create the parameters for people's behaviour, they offer a framework for predicting behaviour. For example, outgoing, venturesome, experimenting people are clearly not suitable for desk jobs. Does this mean that we can predict the behaviour of individuals, based on their personality traits? The answer is no. But a clear view of personality traits help us avoid, to a great extent, selection, placement, promotion errors; reduce turnover and absenteeism.

The problem with personality traits is that the list of individual traits is fairly long. In one study 17,953 individual traits were identified. Another researcher isolated 171 traits from out of which 16 primary traits were found to be most helpful in predicting behaviour patterns:

Using more sophisticated techniques, recent investigations identified five personality dimensions (these dimensions of personality are assumed to underlie many specific traits) which are worth mentioning here

- **Conscientiousness**: the extent to which individuals are hardworking, organized, dependable, and persevering (high conscientiousness) versus lazy, disorganized and unreliable (low conscientiousness)

o I keep my room neat and clean

o People generally find me to be extremely reliable

- **Extraversion**: the degree to which individuals are gregarious, assertive, and sociable(high extraversion) versus being reserved, timid and quiet (low extroversion or introversion)

o I like lots of excitement in my life

o I usually am very cheerful

- **Agreeableness**: the extent to which individuals are cooperative and warm (highly agreeable) versus cold and belligerent (highly disagreeable)

o I generally am quite courteous to other people

o People never think I am cold and sly

- **Emotional stability**: the degree to which individuals are insecure, anxious, depressed and emotional (emotionally unstable) versus calm, self-confident, and secure (emotionally stable)

o I often worry about things that are out of my control

o I usually feel sad or 'down'

- **Openness to experience**: the extent to which individuals are creative, curious and cultured (open to experience0 versus practical and with narrow interests (closed to experience)

o I have a lot of curiosity

o I enjoy the challenge of change

These factors are measured on a five point scale, agree strongly (5 points), agree, neither agree nor disagree, disagree and disagree strongly (1 point). When measured on a continuum, therefore a person may exhibit a low, moderate or high degree of each quality. A person who has an extremely high degree of agreeableness would likely be described as warm, friendly, and good mannered, while one at the opposite extreme might be described as cold, rude and difficult to get along with. Several studies have found that these personality dimensions affect work-related behaviour and job performance. Two of the above – conscientiousness and emotional stability—have been found to be good predictors of success in many different jobs. Another dimension, agreeableness is found to be positively related to the interpersonal aspects of work.

## Myers—Briggs Type Indicator (MBTI)

The Myers—Briggs Type Indicator measures how people prefer to focus their attention, collect information, process and evaluate information and orient themselves to the outer world. The MBTI is an extension of what Carl Jung proposed in 1920s, that is, how people prefer to perceive their environment, collect and process information, judge and decide on action. The MBTI goes a step further by picking up a fourth dimension, that is, how people orient themselves to the external world. It is essentially a 100-question personality test that asks people how they normally feel or act in particular situations. Based on the answers given, individuals are classified as:

- Extroverted or introverted: extroverted persons are dependable, friendly, outgoing, sociable, and assertive. They are pragmatic, methodical and like jobs that involve active human interaction and public relations. Introverts are quiet, shy, introspective and unexpressive.

**Box 4.1 Introverts Vs Extroverts**

According to Carl Jung, individuals can be classified into two categories: Introverts and extroverts. Introverts are inward – directed people. They are guided by their own ideas and philosophy. They are rigid, subjective – oriented and rarely speak to others on their own. They have very few friends, avoid social contacts, withdrawn, quiet and enjoy solitude. Extroverts, on the other hand, are friendly, enjoy interaction with others, crave excitement and dislike solitude. Extroverts prefer job environments that offer opportunity, variety, unpredictability and sporadic bursts of intensity. If the job environment is not sufficiently stimulating, extroverts may play practical jokes and games or display other kinds of distracting behaviour to produce additional stimulation. On the other hand, introverts do not require as much excitement from external stimulation, and, consequently, they tend to perform better than extroverts on repetitive tasks or tasks occurring in environments that offer very little sensory stimulation.

- Sensing and intuitive: Sensing types are practical and base their decisions on facts and details. Intuitives rely on subjective evidence as well as their intuition. They are capable of synthesizing large quantities of data to arrive at conclusions quickly.
- Thinking and feeling: Thinking types use logic and scientific methods to arrive at decisions. They weigh the collected data objectively and unemotionally. Feeling types rely on their personal values and emotions.
- Judging and perceiving: judging types prefer order and structure in their interactions with the external world. They want control and quick resolution of problems. Perceiving types, on the other hand, are flexible in their approach. They adapt themselves to situations spontaneously.

Now the relevant question here is how managers could get the benefit out of MBTI assessment. Those who support the instrument believe that it is important to know these personality types because they ultimately impact the manner in which people interact and solve problems.

## OTHER PERSONALITY TRAITS INFLUENCING BEHAVIOUR

There are other personality attributes that influence the behaviour of individuals in an organisation. These are listed below:

## LOCUS OF CONTROL

People belong to two categories: Internals who believe that they are masters of their own fate and externals who believe that what happens to them in their lives is due to luck or chance. Individuals raised in families in which effort and achievement are properly rewarded tend to become internals. On the other hand, individuals raised in families in which rewards seem to occur in a random manner tend to develop as externals. Internals perceive a strong link between their effort and their performance. They are more satisfied with their work than externals. They generally, hold higher level jobs, advance more quickly in their careers, earn more money and play a key role in motivating others while at work. They handle stressful situations better than externals. Externals are more compliant and willing to follow commands. They tend to do well in jobs that are well-structured and routine. Internals, in contrast, do well on sophisticated tasks that demand complex information processing and learning; on jobs that require initiative, drive and independence of action. Managers with a high internal locus of control often adjust more readily to international assignments than do managers with a high external locus of control.

## AUTHORITARIANISM

Authoritarianism is the belief that power and status differences should exist within the orgaisation. Individuals high in authoritarianism tend to be fascinated with power and toughness, show respect to superiors having more authority, stick to traditional values, critically judge others and are against the use of subjective feelings. Due to their preference to hierarchical order, authoritarian people often turn out o be good followers, work reasonably better and deliver results under a directive supervisor

## MACHIAVELLIANISM

Another personality dimension that is helpful in understanding work behaviour is Machiavellianism, which is characterised by the acquisition of power and the manipulation of other people for purely personal gain. Niccolo Machiavelli proposed a ruthless strategy in early 1500 for seizing and holding political power. His approach was simple: other persons can be manipulated or used for our purposes if we follow certain rules: (a) never show humility – arrogance is far more effective when dealing with others (b) morality and ethics are for the weak – powerful persons should feel free to lie, cheat and deceive wherever required to achieve personal goals (c) it is better to be feared than loved. Those who want power should be willing to do whatever it takes to get his way. Persons with a Machiavellian orientation (called High Machs) are true pragmatists. Any means is justified as long as it helps High Machs to achieve their ends. This often gives them an edge over others who are guided by principles of morality – High Machs are confident, eloquent and competent. When they combine these traits with pure pragmatism, they achieve success easily. High Machs are often adept at picking up situations where their favourite tactics are most likely to work. Such situations are the ones in which they can interact with their intended victims in a face-to-face manner (and so make use of their persuasive skills), in which there are few firm rules (this leaves High Machs considerable room for manoeuvre), and in which others' emotions are running high. Since High Machs themselves never let their "hearts rule their heads," they can take full advantage of the fact that others' emotions make them especially vulnerable to manipulation. Finally, High-Machs are also skilled at forming alliances with others – alliances that usually work to their advantage

**Box 4.2 High Machs are con artists?**

High Machs are generally described as psychopaths or even con artists. Such persons are glib and charming, lie easily, have no qualms about manipulating or conning others, have little remorse or guilt over harming others, and are callous and show little empathy toward others. Additionally, they also tend to be impulsive, irresponsible and prone to feeling bored. High machs are definitely not team players, their only concern is themselves and their own well being. They are prepared to do anything to achieve success.

McHoskey et al, Machiavellianism and psychopathy, Journal of Personality and Social Psychology, 74, 1998

Low Machs, on the other hand, believe that there is no excuse for manipulating or lying to others. They are sensitive to the effects of their decisions on others and believe they should take action only when they are sure it is morally right. In loosely structured situations, high Machs actively take control, while low Machs accept the direction given by others. High Machs are particularly good in jobs that require bargaining skills or that involve substantial rewards for winning. (R.Christie and F.Geis, Studies in Machiavellianism, New York, Academic Press, 1970)

## ENDOMORPH AND MESOMORPH

Willam Sheldon has presented a unique temperamental model that represents a link between psychological traits and characteristics of an individual with his behaviour. Sheldon identified some relationship between the physique types of individuals and their personality temperaments. He identified three body types—endomorphic, mesomorphic and ectomporphic.

*Endomorph*: He is bulky and beloved. Sheldon contends that the endomorph would be rather fat and thick in proportion to his height. He seeks comfort, loves fine food, eats too much, jovial, affectionate and liked-by-all persons (viseertonic temperment).

*Mesomorph*: Mesomorph He is basically strong, athletic and tough. His physique is appreciated by all. In fact, it is this personality all other “morphs” wish for. According to Sheldon, he is found of muscular activity; tends to be highly aggressive, and self-assertive. He can run faster, smile brighter, and beat along the other two ‘morphs’ together (somatotonic temperment).

*Ectomorph*: Ectomorph is thin, long and poorly developed physically. Though physically weak, he leads the league in the intellectual department. His temperament is Cerebrotonic i.e. excessive inhibition, restraint, and advoidance of social contacts etc. He is labelled as absent-minded, shy, but brilliant university professor stereotype.

## TYPE A AND TYPE B BEHAVIOURS

Two cardiologist Meyer Friedman and Ray Rosenman have identified the typical characteristics of Type A personality and type B personality way back in early 70s, while conducting research on the impact of job stress on heart disease. Table gives a comprehensive list of the characteristics of the Type A personality:

**Table 4.1. Characteristics of Type A Personality**

- Move, walk and eat rapidly
- Have a habit of hurrying the ends of your sentences
- Hurry the speech of others, say very quickly, over and over again. “Uh huh, uh huh” or “yes, yes, yes: to get others to speed up their rate of talking
- Try to do two or more things simultaneously (e.g. Read the mail while you are on the phone)
- Try to bring conversations around to work-related topics that particularly intrigue you
- Feel guilty when you relax or do absolutely nothing for several hours to several days.

- Tend not to notice non-instrumental aspects of a situation (eg. Not noticing a new carpet, a new hair-do etc.)
- Feel acquisitive of money and personal possessions
- Over schedule yourself; do not make allowances for unforeseen contingencies
- Feel challenged and threatened by the success of others
- Have nervous tics like clenching your fists or banging your hand upon the table
- Keep on trying to do things faster and faster
- Evaluate your own performance and the activities of others in terms of 'numbers'.

Type A personalities are aggressive. They are willing to oppose others to get what they want. When placed in circumstances where there are a lot of obstacles, they will keep on plugging away rather than give up. Type A people are ambitious and hard-driving. They have very high standards for themselves. They try to schedule more and more in less and less time. They are also competitive; they have to win all the time, even in leisure activities and casual conversation. They do not find time to enjoy life. For them work is not a means to an end, but an end in itself. They live to work and do not work to live. For them, work is an addiction; and work outside the company is unproductive, disinteresting and meaningless. Type As, tend to lack skill in interpersonal relations and the ability to get along harmoniously with all types of people in various situations. Because of their impatience and irritability, Type As tend to rub their co-workers on the wrong side quite often. As a result, conflictful situations crop up almost suddenly, putting them in a spot. Lack of interpersonal skills would force them to lose their tempers and even lash out at others, leading to noisy, aggressive, counterproductive outbursts. Type As could become '*cyclones of activity*' but there is also the danger of being swept away by the winds, if they irritate their co-workers too often.

In contrast, Type B personalities feel less pressure. They keep a steadier pace, rather than working against the clock. Type Bs are more likely to extend the deadline or to accept a lower standard of work for themselves in the short run. They are likely to 'let things roll off their backs' rather than fight every issue. They are not as easily angered or disappointed by their own work or the work of others. They tend to be more relaxed and non-competitive. Because of their contemplative approach to problem-solving, Type Bs tend to be more creative than Type As.

Types Bs, typically, are highly skilled in interpersonal relations. They get along well socially. They have an innate understanding of people. They are quick to grasp the underlying motivations of other people. This insight serves them in excellent stead when they wish to gain the support of others who may have conflicting views. They not only understand people but also enjoy them. They rarely feel at a loss in public contact situations A Types B person can easily and happily manipulate an irate client.

**Table 4.2. Characteristics of Type B**

- Patient and composed
- Never suffer from a sense of time urgency; concerned with quality rather than quantity.
- Do not generally discuss their achievements unless demanded by the situation

- Play for fun and recreation
- Can relax without guilt
- They are wise, not hasty, they vary their responses to specific challenges in their milieu; their behaviour, hence can't be predicted easily.

The differences between type A and Type B persons have important implications for behaviour in the work spot. For example, hard driving, competitive individuals would be expected to act in very different ways from their more easy going counterparts. Type As tend to be more impatient with others and get angry quickly if things do not move as desired. They prefer to work by themselves, given a chance, rather than with others. They are definitely 'loners' rather than 'team players'.

## PERSONALITY AND SELF CONCEPT

**The self concept** describes the relatively stable perceptions; a person has about him self. It includes our conception of what is special about ourselves, what separates us from others and what makes us similar to others. It is like a mental mirror that reflects how we look at ourselves. Our self concepts are derived primarily from four sources:(a) our social interactions with others (b)own comparisons with others (c)what others say about us and (d) our view of how we see ourselves. Three important things about the self concept are worth mentioning here:

- Self concept is learned. No one is born with a self concept. It gradually emerges in the early months of life and is shaped and reshaped through repeated perceived experiences, as one interacts with others.
- Self concept is organized, that is it is characterized by orderliness and harmony. Each person maintains countless perceptions regarding one's personal existence, and each perception is orchestrated with all the others. It is this generally stable and organized quality of self-concept that gives consistency to the personality. At the heart of self-concept is the self-as-doer, the "I," which is distinct from the self-as-object, the various "me's." This allows the person to reflect on past events, analyze present perceptions, and shape future experiences.
- Self-concept development is a continuous, dynamic process. In the healthy personality there is constant assimilation of new ideas and expulsion of old ideas throughout life. Individuals strive to behave in ways that are in keeping with their self-concepts, no matter how helpful or hurtful to one self or others. Self-concept usually takes precedence over the physical body. Individuals will often sacrifice physical comfort and safety for emotional satisfaction. Self-concept continuously guards itself against loss of self-esteem, for it is this loss that produces feelings of anxiety.

According to Carl Rogers, Individuals have within themselves relatively boundless potential for developing a positive and realistic self-concept. This potential can be realized by people, places, policies, programs, and processes that are intentionally designed to invite the realization of this potential.

**Self efficacy** refers to one's personal ability to do a task. Unlike locus of control this characteristic is not about how much fate controls events. Rather, it is about one's personal belief about what it takes to get ahead and succeed in life.

**Box 4.3 How self-efficacy affects behavior?**

**Joy** of activities: individuals typically **choose** activities they feel they will be successful in doing.

**Effort** and **persistence**: individuals will tend to put more effort end activities and behaviors they consider to be successful in achieving.

Learning and **achievement**: students with high self-efficacy tend to be better students and achieve more

For example Erik Weihenmayer,35, is but also a self described unrealistic optimist who was the first blind climber to scale Mt. Everest. Low self efficacy is associated with learned helplessness, the debilitating lack of faith in one's ability to control one's environment. The implications for managers are fairly obvious. Complex, challenging and autonomous jobs tend to enhance people's perceptions of their self-efficacy. Boring, tedious jobs generally do the opposite. Self efficacy is a quality that can be nurtured through appropriate counselling and mentoring.

**Self esteem** refers to the extent to which people like or dislike themselves, their overall self evaluation. Some of the characteristics that may be associated with high and low levels of self esteem may be listed thus:

**Table 4.3. Characteristics that are associated with high and low levels of self esteem**

| High Self Esteem | Low Self Esteem |
|---|---|
| Inspires others to have confidence in him | Does not inspire confidence in him |
| Seeks responsibility | Lacks initiative |
| Outgoing | Introverted |
| Open minded | Closed-minded |
| Optimistic | Pessimistic |

Research evidence on self-esteem offers interesting insights into organisational behaviour. High-SEs believe that they have the ability to succeed at work. They take more risks in job selection and are more likely to choose unconventional jobs. Low-SEs are more vulnerable to external influences than high-SEs. They are more likely to seek approval from others and are willing to conform to the beliefs and behaviours of those they respect, than high-SEs.

Some ways in which managers can build employee self esteem may be listed thus.

**Box 4.4 Ways to boost employee self esteem**

Reinforce employees' positive attitudes and skills

Provide positive feedback whenever possible

Break larger projects into smaller tasks and projects

Express confidence in employees' abilities to complete their tasks

Provide coaching whenever employees are seen to be struggling to complete tasks.

**Self monitoring** refers to the ability of an individual to adjust his behaviour to external, situational factors. High self monitors show great flexibility in adjusting their behaviours to external situational influences. They pay more attention to what others say and how others behave. They can put on different faces for different individuals. They will be more successful on jobs that require position holders to play multiple and even contradictory roles. High self-monitors are criticized for being chameleons, always able to adapt their self-presentation to their surroundings, low self-monitors are often criticized for being on their own planet and insensitive to others.

## THEORIES OF PERSONALITY

Over the years, researchers have developed a number of personality theories while trying to find answers to questions such as what is personality. How is behaviour influenced by personality etc. These are listed below

### Psychoanalytical Theory

The theory, developed by Sigmund Freud, emphasizes the unconscious determinants of behaviour. According to Freud, personality is the outcome of three inter-related and interacting forces, namely, the id, ego and superego.

- **Id** consists of everything that is inherited psychologically and is present at the time of birth. It is the foundation of the unconscious mind and is the source of libido (psychic energy that seeks pleasure, tries to avoid pain and wants immediate satisfaction of all desires) drives. It strives for sexual gratification and other biological pleasures. It is instinctive, often unconscious and unrecognized and is unaffected by socially or culturally determined restrictions. Id basically represents an individual's natural urges and feelings. However, it cannot act on its own; it can only fantasize and force the person to satisfy the desires immediately. Id is largely childish, irrational, never-satisfied and always demanding.
- **Ego** is the logical, rational and realistic side of the personality. it keeps the Id in check and take decisions rationally after evaluating the facts in a realistic and objective manner. The demands made by Id, of course, would be met but only at an appropriate time and in an acceptable manner.
- **Superego** is the moral side of the personality. It represents the noblest thoughts, ideals, feelings that are acquired by a person from his parents, teachers, friends, religion, organisation, and colleagues etc. Labelled as the 'ego-ideal' it tells a person whether the action proposed by 'ego' is right or wrong so that the person acts in accordance with the values and standards set by the society. Acting as a kind of moral police, superego thus restricts the freedom enjoyed by the 'ego' and in some respects it is antithesis of Id. In actual world, the Id is striving for satisfaction, the ego is trying to delay it and the superego demands morality above all. If people violate the prohibitions set by superego, they may feel guilty and even indulge in self-punishment.

By nature, therefore, the id, ego and superego will always be in a state of constant friction and tension. Conflicts between the id (the pleasure seeking element), the superego (the noble and idealistic element) and the ego(the compromising element) will often force people to develop certain defence mechanisms(such as aggression, regression, rationalization, denial etc. Such defence mechanisms, according to Freud, are necessary to reduce the tension and anxiety caused by conflict between the three elements of personality.

## Evaluation

The psychoanalytical theory proposed by Freud has undoubtedly revealed the importance of unconscious processes in human behaviour. Researchers have assigned a place of importance to the theory on account of four specific reasons:

- It is deterministic: Behaviour is assumed to have been caused. Surprisingly, even unconscious slips are considered to exhibit or reveal a certain meaning
- It is dynamic: It assumes that human action results from psychic energy called libido (i.e., life maintaining and pleasure-seeking energy that becomes attached to or withdrawn from various goals and objects
- It is developmental; Human development begins at birth and progresses through life.
- It is structural: The three basic structures of personality are id, ego and superego. These three elements are iinter-related and each cannot exist in isolation from others.

The idea of a person being motivated more by unseen influences than by conscious and rational processes is universally welcomed and is being used by behavioural scientists all over the globe. However, researchers have attacked the theory on methodological grounds. Scientific verification of what Freud has proposed through repeated experimentation is not possible because his constructs are difficult to define and are largely ambiguous.

## Type Theories

The type theories try to bring some amount of order into the theories of personality, by classifying individuals into convenient categories. Sheldon's physiognomy theory and Carl Jung's extrovert and introvert theories are the two important type theories that merit attention here:

***Physiognomy Theory*:** According to Sheldon there is some relationship between the physique types (like the features of the face or body type) of individuals and their personality temperaments. He identified three body types—endomorphic, mesomorphic and ectomorphic. One pitfall of this theory is the inherent generalization. There is almost unfailing tendency on the part of many people to pigeonhole every person into one category or another.

***Extrovert-Introvert Theory*:** According to Carl Jung an extrovert is sociable, lively, impulsive, seeking novelty and change, carefree and emotionally expressive. Introverts, on the other hand, are basically shy, prefer to remain aloof, and are unexpressive. They are quiet, introspective, intellectual, well-ordered, and value-oriented. Few persons are complete extroverts or introverts but a combination of the two types help capture a snapshot of an individual.

## Trait Theories

A trait is an enduring attribute of a person that appears constantly in a variety of situations. According to the trait theory:

- Traits distinguish one person from another

- Traits can be measured, and used to summarize behaviour
- Traits and the resultant behaviour patterns are said to be fairly stable over time. So, on the basis of trait theory, people can be described as aggressive, impulsive, sentimental or romantic.
- Although there are many traits that are common to most people, there are many other traits that are unique to an individual and are not shared by other people.

The problem with personality traits is that the list of individual traits is fairly long. In one study 17,953 individual traits were identified. Another researcher isolated 171 traits from out of which 16 primary traits were found to be most helpful in predicting behaviour patterns:

**Table 4.4. Sixteen Primary Traits (Cattell)**

| | | |
|---|---|---|
| Reserved | vs. | Outgoing |
| Less Intelligent | vs. | More Intelligent |
| Affected by feelings | vs. | Emotionally stable |
| Submissive | vs. | Dominant |
| Serious | vs. | Happy go-lucky |
| Expedient | vs. | Conscientious |
| Timid | vs. | Venturesome |
| Tough-minded | vs. | Sensitive |
| Trusting | vs. | Suspicious |
| Practical | vs. | Imaginative |
| Forthright | vs. | Shrewd |
| Self-assured | vs. | Apprehensive |
| Conservative | vs. | Experimenting |
| Group-dependent | vs. | Self-sufficient |
| Uncontrolled | vs. | Controlled |
| Relaxed | vs. | Tense |

Source: "Personality penned Down," Psychology Today, July 1973.

## EVALUATION

Trait theories, on the negative side, suffer from the following limitations:

- Traits may be too abstract. For example, the scale of measuring, anxiety may be abstract
- Trait theory focuses attention on isolated traits without specifying how these traits are organised within a person. Without knowing which traits are more important and how they are related to other traits of an individual, it is not possible to come out with an appropriate description of an individual's personality.
- Another drawback of trait theories is that they are essentially descriptive rather than analytical.

## Self Theory

According to the Self Theory, the individual himself is the centre of experience. His self image is a reflection of how he looks at himself (Rogers terms this as "I") and his perception of how others view him (termed as "Me" by Rogers). Rogers has defined "Me" as social self and "I" as personal self. Personal self is nothing but one's own mirror image guiding our beliefs, thoughts and actions. Social self is the way a person appears to others or others appear to him. Behaviour is the outcome of the realisation of "Me" or is a reflection of inner self. "Me" is what "I" believe others expect from me. The relationship between "I" and "Me" shapes one's personality. As the individual interacts with his environment, his own concept of self develops, grows and matures over a period of time. Positive responses from the environment would reinforce our self image and likewise, any negative responses from the environment would lower our self image creating tension and anxiety. As Rogers commented "the basic nature of the human being when functioning fully, is constructive and trustworthy. The self generally takes the initiative in improving the conditions in its environment so that the values of the self can be achieved."

## Evaluation

The self theory is appreciated on the ground that it is organised around the concept of self. It is the one in which personality and behaviour are largely determined by the individual, whereas, in other theories, the individual is the only medium through which behaviour is elicited after having been acted on by elements over which one has no control. In analysing organisational behaviour, it would be beneficial for the manager to understand the self concept because this concept influences the manner of applying various reinforcement, motivation and leadership techniques for achieving desired results. For instance, monetary rewards for performance, authoritarian leadership style and motivational strategies when applied to intelligent, independent, confident workers may prove to be ineffective. These techniques may yield fruitful results when applied to the unintelligent, insecure, indecisive workers.

## Social Learning Theory

The main idea in Julian Rotter's Social Learning Theory is that personality represents an interaction of the individual with his or her environment. One cannot speak of a personality, internal to the individual, which is independent of the environment. Neither can one focus on behavior as being an automatic response to an objective set of environmental stimuli. Rather, to understand behavior, one must take both the individual (i.e., his or her life history of learning and experiences) and the environment (i.e., those stimuli that the person is aware of and responding to) into account. Rotter describes personality as a relatively stable set of potentials for responding to situations in a particular way. In fact, much of human learning is vicarious or observational.

The social learning theory uses 'reinforcement and punishment' approach in understanding personality. For example, repeated failures caused by external circumstances may compel an individual to act tough and be aggressive. On the other hand, many acts of kindness that are rewarded by society in various forms may reinforce good behaviour. Thus, behaviour is caused by environment and is affected by environment in many ways.

**Box 4.5. General principles of social learning theory**

1. People can **learn by observing** the behavior is of others and the outcomes of those behaviors.
2. Learning can occur **without a change** in behavior. Behaviorists say that learning has to be represented by a permanent change in behavior, in contrast social learning theorists say that because people can learn through **observation alone**, their learning may not necessarily be shown in their performance. Learning may or may not result in a behavior change.
3. Cognition plays a **role** in learning. Over the last 30 years social learning theory has become **increasingly cognitive** in its interpretation of human learning. Awareness and expectations of future reinforcements or punishments can have a major effect on the behaviors that people exhibit.

Rotter sees personality, and therefore behavior, as always changeable. Change the way the person thinks, or change the environment the person is responding to, and behavior will change. He does not believe there is a critical period after which personality is set. But, the more life experience you have building up certain sets of beliefs, the more effort and intervention required for change to occur. Rotter conceives of people in an optimistic way. He sees them as being drawn forward by their goals, seeking to maximize their reinforcement, rather than just avoiding punishment.

## HOW DO WE MATCH PERSONALITIES AND JOBS?

Given the enormous amount of differences among individuals and among jobs, an important job of managers is to try to match a person and job characteristics so that work is carried out by people who are best suited for it. This requires that

- Managers be clear about what they expect employees to do.
- They should have a sense of the kinds of people who would succeed at work that needs to be executed.

The attempt to strike a rapport between the person and the requirements of the job is called ***person-job fit.*** When hiring and leading employees, managers should attempt to achieve person-job fit so that employees are more likely to contribute and remain satisfied. Whenever the nature of work changes, due to various reasons, managers should look into questions such as: how prepared are the employees? Are they going to voice their concerns? Will the employees be able to shoulder the additional burden? Personality, in the final analysis, does not lend itself to change. When person-job fit is poor, the manager must think of replacing employees or restructuring work. Research in this area indicates that job satisfaction is highest and turnover lowest when person-job fit is achieved. So for fairly obvious reasons, social individuals be in social jobs and conventional people be in conventional jobs. Now-a-days, researchers also point out the need to achieve the person-organisation fit as well, in order to show excellence. In a way, this means selecting people who fit better with organisational culture and get along with people easily.

## REVIEW QUESTIONS

1. How do you define personality? What are its major determinants?
2. What is the role of personality in the study of organisational behaviour?
3. What is the Myers—Briggs Type Indicator?
4. Briefly explain the various theories of personality How will you integrate various theories to get a satisfying view of personality?
5. Describe the Type A and Type B behaviour patterns and describe the nature of Machiavellianism
6. What are the major personality traits that managers need to be aware of in order to understand workplace behaviour?
7. Write short notes on
   - the self concept
   - locus of control
   - introvert vs. extrovert

## CRITICAL THINKING QUESTIONS

1. Personality is an organised whole, without which an individual would have no meaning. Comment on the statement
2. Critically analyse the statement that "the various psychological processes can be thought of as pieces of jigsaw puzzle, and personality as the completed puzzle picture".
3. Why might two individuals whose personalities are very similar behave differently in a given situation?
4. Why is it important for managers to achieve person-job fit when they are hiring employees?
5. Think of an important event in your life. Do you believe that the success or failure of the event was your responsibility (internal locus of control) or the responsibility of outside forces or people (external locus of control)? Has your belief changed since the event took place? How does your locus of control affect the way you now view the event?
6. Do you think that a Type A person or a Type B person would be better suited to managing a health care facility? Why?
7. Have you ever known someone you considered to be high in extraversion? If so, what kind of jobs do you think they would perform best? Worst?

## CASE STUDY : UMA NAIR-RATHAN SINGH

Uma Nair grew up in a small town near Trivandrum in Kerala State. She was the third generation of the Nair family in this town. Her grand-parents had come from Delhi after retirement to take care of herself and her younger brother. Her parents had always kept themselves busy in social functions and social service activities. However, neither of Uma's parents had undergone formal college education. Surprisingly, her father's I.Q. level was relatively very high. She used to get adequate encouragement from her parents at every stage, to do well in education. They used to save their hard earned money to let her pursue university education. Brought up under this affectionate parental care, Uma had tried to improve her mental faculties in every conceivable way. To support herself, she had also started taking up odd jobs during summer season. She always came out with flying colours both in her school and college days. She had very little difficulty in securing admission in Calicut University where she did her M.B.A. Her creative abilities had been immediately recognised by an Advertising Agency in Bombay, where she had gone to attend a seminar on International Marketing during her University life. Uma, now 38 years old, had been working in the same company for 15 years and had earned a creditable work record over the years.

One of Uma's co-workers is Rathan Singh. He grew up in small town near Bhopal. His parents hold post-graduate degree in Commerce. His grand-father had retired from military service very recently. Despite this rich family background, Rathan could not do well during his school and college days. He could however, prove his mettle in organising debates, functions and extra-curricular activities. After finishing his degree, he obtained a Diploma in Journalism from a prestigious institute in Bombay. He has been working in the present company for 5 years and has a wonderful work record to his credit. He maintains good relations with all the employees in his section.

He is young, dynamic and aggressive. He decides things quickly and his success rate is quite high in the company. Of course, his competitive spirit had always earned him, no doubt, praise from the 'top' but, at the same time, has bought him many enemies both within and outside the company. Though liked by his workers for his social behaviour, he is disliked by his colleagues and competitors in the organisation. Now, the job of Chief Copy Editor has fallen vacant for which Uma Nair, Rathan Singh are the two potential candidates. The General Manager of the company declared: "The job demands a good personality. The prospective candidate should be able to maintain good relations with all the people in the organisation. We need someone who can get along with customers, coordinate organisational work and meet the deadlines",

**Questions**

1. Based on the above brief sketches, explain the personalities of Uma Nair and Rathan Singh.
2. In your opinion who deserves the job?

## Suggested Answers

### Ans. 1 Personality of UMA NAIR

Uma hails from a small town in Kerala. Her parents loved and actively participated in social service activities. They have encouraged Uma to do her best always. Uma grew up under the love and care of affectionate parents, who saved every penny for her university education. Uma, naturally knew her responsibilities well and tried to fulfil the parental expectations using her mental faculties to good effect. She did odd jobs to support herself. She, thus, grew up as a confident, responsible, and self-made person struggling with surrounding forces and events successfully. Academically, she came out with flying colours–signifying her determination to succeed in life. Participation in seminars during her university life reveals her interest to equip herself fully and learn the basics of the subject by mixing up with others actively. Her creative potential during her MBA course attracted the attention of an advertising agency. She has served the same agency for a period of 15 years, revealing her zest for creative work and continued loyalty to the job as well as company.

## Personality of Rathan Singh

The following table reveals the personality features of Rathan Singh clearly.

2. In your opinion who deserves the job? Why?

| ***Major plus points*** | ***Major minus points*** |
|---|---|
| 1. Good extracurricular activities. | Could not do well during school and college days. |
| 2. Has a good family back-ground, whose parents are well-educated. | Aggressiveness and competitive spirit—working against him and producing many enemies within and outside the company. |
| 3. Wonderful work record liked by the management as well as workers. | Controversial, as he is disliked by colleagues and competitors. |
| 4. Young, dynamic. | |
| 5. Decides things quickly | |
| 6. High success rate in the company. | |
| 7. Keeps good social relations with workers. | |

Before deciding the issue, let's look into the requirement of the job closely:

1. A good personality

**Ans. 2. Good relations with all persons in the organisation.**

3. Ability to get along with customers.
4. Ability to coordinate organisational work
5. Ability to meet deadlines.

Let's now see how far the candidates would meet the above requirements.

| ***Job demands*** | ***Uma Nair*** | ***Rathan Singh*** |
|---|---|---|
| (a) Personality | Confident, responsible and self-made; wants to learn things by mixing up with people, creative and loyal to the company, middle aged, non-controversial, creditable work record; the urge to do well in studies reflecting in the workspot also. | Young and dynamic wants to do well and run ahead of others. Good social behaviours, aggressive and competitive, proving to be a 'winning' horse, for the company. |

| | | |
|---|---|---|
| (b) Relations with all people | Creditable work record and continued loyalty to the company for 15 years; no negative mark on this score as she seems to be getting along with all people reasonably well. | Ability to get along with workers in general and employees in his section in particular.Not liked by colleagues and competitors. |
| (c) Relations with customers | Creditable work record speaks about her ability to get along with customers as well. | High success rate in the company speaks about his ability to get along with customers. However, 'enemies outside the company' may mean customers as well? |
| (d) Coordinating capacity | Seems to be doing well. | May not do well, as he is disliked by colleagues; they may put hurdles whenever and wherever possible. |
| (e) Ability to meet deadlines | Seems to be a person doing her work at a leisurely pace; creativity does not mean meeting deadlines and running around in a competitive and aggressive manner. | Young, dynamic aggressive and competitive. Wants to do well and run ahead of others.'Winning' seems to be his motto as he seems to have earned many enemies within and outside the company in the process. Can meet the deadlines and secure results to the satisfaction of superiors. |

**Option I:** Where the intention of management is to find an aggressive and dynamic person, who has the ability to coordinate the work and meet the deadlines, Rathan Singh fits in the slot very well. Also, if the management does not like to hand over the reins to a female person, the choice would be in favour of Rathan Singh.

**Option II:** Uma Nair can get along with all people, unlike Rathan Singh who is not liked by colleagues and competitors; has a creditable work record: creative and seems to be doing well and is loyal to the company. She, obviously, lacks aggressiveness and the ability to push things ahead of others. Where the intention of management is to find a creative person who can organise things well, who can get along with people and who can deliver the goods creatively; the choice should be in favour of Uma Nair. Except the last dimension, that is the ability to meet the deadlines. Uma has major plus points on other personality requirements. If I were to decide the issue my choice would be in favour of Uma Nair. The reasons are fairly obvious I do not like to hand over the reins of an important section in the company to a controversial person, who is not liked by colleagues and competitors. Even if Rathan Singh is able to deliver the goods much to he satisfaction of management, the long-run costs of getting results seem to be high. Colleagues may not allow him to function well; or alternatively they may even see that he fails in his attempts.

# 5

# Perception

## PERCEPTION VS. REALITY

The world, psychologically, is not the same for different people. Individuals may look at the same thing differently. A manager may evaluate an assistant who takes time to decide things, as thorough and thoughtful. Another may interpret such behaviour as slow, disorganized and afraid of taking prompt decisions. Thus, most often, we do not see reality. *We interpret what we see and call it reality.*

### Box Your point of view affects your reaction!

Read the following incidents first, fairly quickly and note down your initial reactions. Now, how would you react after having a look at what happened in reality?

> 1. While riding on the subway, you see a man with three small boys ranging in ages from about five to nine. The boys run up and down the aisles, yelling and screaming. The father sits totally oblivious of the behaviour of his kids
>
> 2. At lunch time you decide to walk a few blocks for a quick sandwich. As you are crossing the street at a busy intersection, a car races through it, apparently trying to beat the red light. The car comes so close that you literally jump out of the way to avoid being hit.
>
> *1. They are on the way home from the hospital where his wife died after weeks of suffering from cancer. 2 The driver is your 70 year old father who recently had an eye operation!)*

The point to be noted is that as a manager you should not take ***initial*** perceptions at face value. You should get as much information as possible before you firm up perceptions into opinions that influence your actions. A good way to avoid such misperceptions is to understand how the perception process actually works. Let's look into this more closely now.

## WHAT IS PERCEPTION?

Perception is the process by which people select, organise, interpret and respond to information from the world around them. It may be described as *a person's view of reality.*

## Features

**Sensory experience:** Perception is our sensory experience of the world around us and involves both the recognition of environmental stimuli and actions in response to these stimuli.

**Subjective** Perception is a subjective process, because different people may look at the same event from different angles and interpret the same in multifarious ways. The world is not the same for different people. Often, people tend to behave on the basis of what they perceive reality to be and not necessarily as what reality is.((a quick look at the following figure reveals that the first line is shorter than the second line. If you actually measure them they are equal in length!)

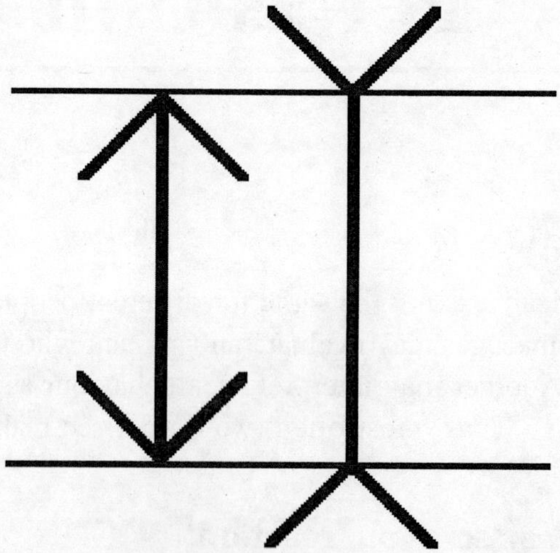

***Chart 5.1. An example of optical illusion: Are these two lines the same size?***

**Filter:** Perception is a way of forming impressions about oneself, other people and daily life experiences. It serves like a filter through which information passes before it has an effect on people. The quality or accuracy of a person's perceptions, therefore, has a major impact on his or her responses to a given situation (*Schermerhorn* et al)

**Unique interpretation:** Perception is a unique interpretation of the situation, not an exact recording of it. It is, in fact, a very complex cognitive process that yields a unique picture of the world, a picture that may be quite different from reality. (*Luthans*)

The President was working alone, very late at night, in a hotel room while on a trip. He opened the door, beckoned to a waiting aide and ordered, "Get me Coffee". The aide immediately responded to the directive. Most of the activities at the hotel including the kitchen were not operating at such a late hour. Hotel personnel had to be called in and a fresh pot of coffee brewed. All of these activities took some time and the President kept asking about "Coffee" while waiting. Finally, a tray was made up with a carafe of coffee, cream, sugar and some sweet rolls and was rushed to the President's suite. It was only at this point that the aide learned that the President did not want coffee to drink, but rather wanted to talk to an assistant whose name was Coffee"

*From Rather Dan and G.Paul Gates, "Palace Guard,' Harper & Row, 1970*

**Seeing things differently;** Seeing things differently is an inevitable outcome of perception. Because of individual differences in what people perceive and how they organise and interpret it, perceptions vary among people and differ from objective reality. Our experiences, expectations and interests influence what we see, and what we see may actually differ from the truth. As rightly pointed out by Plato, we see reality only as shadows reflected on the rough wall of a cave (that is reality being filtered through an imperfect perceptual process).

**Basis of human behaviour:** There can be no behaviour without perception and perception lies at the base of every individual behaviour.

## THE PERCEPTUAL PROCESS

Perception is the process of interpreting and understanding one's environment. It is a complex psychological process, but it can be boiled down to four steps: observation, selection, organisation and interpretation. First we observe information (sensory data) from the environment through our senses: sight, hearing, touch, taste and smell. Next, our mind screens the data and will select only the items we will process further. Finally, we organise the selected data into meaningful patterns for interpretation and response. The key elements in the perceptual process are selection and organisation.

### A. Observation & Selection

Every second of every day individuals are bombarded by countless stimuli through the human senses of sight, hearing, touch, smell and taste. We attend to only a small portion of these stimuli (Certo and Certo). Since we are not in a position to digest all that we observe, we engage in selectivity. We collect bits and pieces of information from environment – depending on our interests, background, experiences etc. Also, we tend to see only what we want to see. Out of a hundred children playing in a park, 'X' often would look at what his own kids are doing. Thus, people perceive what is most important for them in a particular situation. While in a bus, for example, an employee who is already late for his office is quite likely to look at his watch time again and again rather than two lovers sitting in front of him

**Box 5.1. Importance of relevancy in perceptual selection**

Relevancy is one important criterion for selective perception. People perceive things that are pleasing to them, ignore what is mildly disturbing, and pay close attention to what are considered as threat to them. An event or object looks meaningful only when it is closely related to the perceiver. We may read the news that war is broken between Iran and Iraq but hardly pay any attention to it. We, however pay attention when our friend is at the war site on a peace mission. The more clearly an event is related to us, the greater will be its effect on perception.

*Perceptual Selection, thus, is the tendency to filter out information that is discomforting, that seems irrelevant, or that contradicts one's beliefs*. Perceptual selection depends on several factors, some of which are in the environment and some of which are internal to the perceiver

## External Factors Influencing Perception

Perception is influenced by the characteristics of the perceived object, event or person. These include:

**Size:** The larger the object, the more likely it will be noticed. Big televisions, refrigerators in a shopping mall stand out very clearly and attract our immediate attention(because of their size elative to other things in that area) In advertising a full page spread is more attention getting than a few lines in some corner of the newspaper. People often pay more attention to an exceptionally tall or unusually short person than to a person of average size.

**Intensity:** The intensity principle of attention states that the more intense the external stimulus, the more likely it is to be perceived. A loud noise, strong odour, or bright light will be noticed more than a soft sound, weak odour or dim light. For example, at a cocktail party, the more boisterous and outgoing people have a greater probability of being heard. You may think a loud person is prohibitive or you may enjoy his or her antics, depending on your feelings toward the person. In either case, the probability is high that owing to the intensity of the person's action, you will pay more attention to him or her. Bright packaging, loud price off announcements and celebrity endorsements are often used by advertisers to gain consumer's attention.

**Contrast:** Stimuli which contrast with the surrounding environment are more likely to be selected for attention than stimuli which blend with the environment. Figure 6.2 illustrates this perceptual principle. The while circle on the left appears much larger than the one on the right because of the contrast with the background circles. Both white circles are exactly the same size.

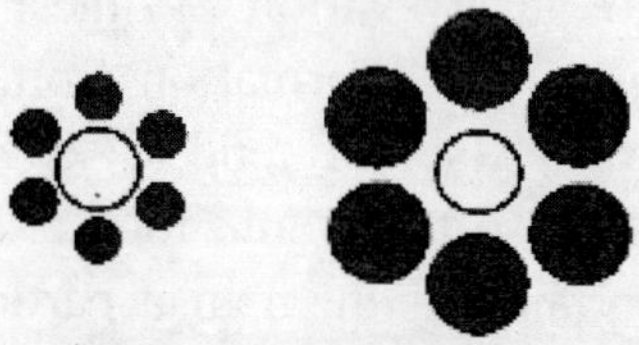

***Figure: 5.1. The contrast principle. Which white circle is larger?***

Again, the "no smoking" sign written in black against a yellow background is likely to be noticed more quickly because of the contrast factor. Women brokers in a stock exchange making presentations to their clients are likely to be remembered (not merely the face but also the name) for a while, than their male counterparts.

**Repetition:** A repeated external stimulus is more attention getting than a single one. People are attracted to a stimulus that is repetitious, that is repetitious, that is repetitious. If we listen to a CD that skips, continuing to play the same message over and over again, we are very quickly attracted to the sound; we want to correct it before it drives us nuts! The principle of repetition is used extensively in advertising to attract the attention of buyers. For example Nike uses 'swoosh' symbol consistently throughout the globe on all its products so that the prospective buyers are bombarded with the same message wherever they go.

**Motion:** A moving stimulus is more likely to be noticed than a stationary object. An animated sign, for example, attracts more attention than a fixed billboard.

**Novelty and Familiarity:** A stimulus that is new and unique will often be perceived more readily than stimuli that have been observed on a regular basis. Thus, new objects in a familiar setting or familiar objects in a new setting will draw the attention of the perceiver. An elephant walking along a city street is noticed almost instantaneously. A mother is likely to notice the face of her child first among a group of approaching school children.

## Internal Factors Influencing Perception

Several characteristics of the perceiver also can influence the selection of sensory data. Some of the more important internal factors include:

- **Personality:** People pay the most attention to stimuli that reinforce their personality. Persons who accept themselves and have faith in their individuality perceive things favourably. Likewise a person with a positive self concept is likely to notice positive attributes in another person.
- **Personal moods:** Our emotions often filter out large blocks of information that threaten our mental state. When you feel depressed or insecure, the world is a very different place than it is when you are confident. We generally remember information that is in line with our mood than information that Is not in sync with our state of mind.
- **Experience:** Successful experiences enhance and boost the perceptive abilities and lead to accuracy in perception of a person whereas failure comes in the way of self-confidence.
- **Values and beliefs:** We tend to remember information that is consistent with our values and attitudes and ignore information that is inconsistent with them. 'Employees only do enough work to get by' "In spite of all their mistakes, our employees are doing the best they can". Beliefs such as these can shape the way a manager interprets an employee's action.
- **Expectations:** Expectations can influence your perceptions in that you will see what you expect to see. If you imagine your boss is unhappy with your performance, you will likely feel threatened by the termination notice. However, if you imagine that your work is exceptionally good, you will probably spend your weekend in a happy manner.
- **Learning**: *Learning refers to any relatively permanent change in behaviour that occurs as a result of experience*. Learning usually plays big role in developing perceptual set. *A perceptual set is an expectation of a particular interpretation based on past experience with the same or similar object.* For example read the phrase in the triangle below in a routine way.

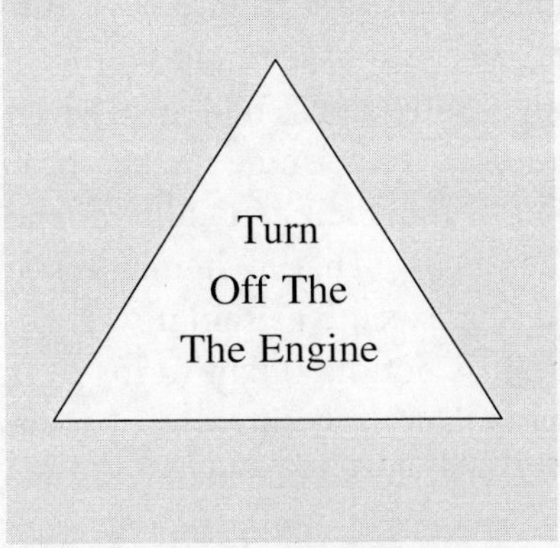


***Figure: 5.2. Read the sentence quickly***

Because of familiarity with the phrase, we tend to read, 'turn off the engine'. After a few seconds, you tend to notice the fact that the word 'the' appears in the triangle twice. Many illustrations could be used to demonstrate the impact of learning in the development of perceptual set. What do you see in the following picture? (fig 5.3)

***Figure: 5.3. Ambiguous picture of a woman***

A young woman or an old woman? (Psychologists reported that when shown first, 60 percent saw a young woman and 40 percent saw an old woman) Which woman is seen depends on how the person is set to perceive. Now take a look at the following two clear pictures.

***Figure: 5.4. Clear pictures of the old and the young woman***

When first shown a clear, unambiguous picture of a young woman (figure 5.4) and then shown figure 5.3, the person will almost always report seeing the young woman in figure 5.4. If the clear picture of the old woman is seen first (figure 5.4), the viewer will subsequently report seeing the old woman in figure 5.3 because of learning that has taken place because of previous exposure. Perceptual set has many implications for organisational behaviour. One classic study found that when executives were asked to determine the key problem in a complex business case, they identified the problem as falling within their particular functional area of work—they evidently filtered out information about other areas. That is, human resource managers said the particular problem was a people issue, marketing executives said it was a sales issue, and production people said it was a manufacturing issue. It is not important for us to find out who is right or wrong in this case, rather, the relevant point is that all the involved personnel perceived the same situation in completely different ways. Likewise, in labour management disputes also, management may often confront the wage related disputes by saying that workers are already overpaid, whereas workers feel that they get considerably less than their counterparts in competing organisations.

1. **Motivation:** Motivation also plays a significant role in influencing the process of perception. A hungry person would react quickly to the sight or scent of food than a non-hungry person. Any mention of sex, especially in a traditional society like ours, is likely to grab headlines An outgoing employee with strong affiliation motives would always seek situations where he can join a group and enjoy the fun. Likewise, power-hungry people would look for opportunities where they can show their dominance and exercise their will over others. For example, if you had just been in a serious automobile accident, you would likely perceive the white-jacketed paramedic rushing to your help as a fine person. Yet if you were not motivated by a need for medical help and you saw this same individual in a restaurant or shop, your perception might be entirely different. "That person looks like a vagabond to me". Same person—different perceptions. In short, our perceptions are guided by our needs, interests and motives. Generally speaking, people perceive things that promise to help satisfy their needs and that they have found rewarding in the past.(Hellriegel & Slocum).

Perceptual selectivity has important implications for managers. It compels managers to understand and appreciate why one person sees things differently from others, and why one should not speed read situations and come to conclusions quickly based on oversimplified assumptions. In the end, both managers and employees have to realise that perceptual differences are bound to come in the way of effective group efforts and learn to deal with such diversity through open communication.

## B. Perceptual Organisation

Once people have selected the sensory data to be perceived, they begin grouping the data into recognizable patterns. Perceptual organisation is the process by which people categorize stimuli according to their frame of reference, based on their past learning and experiences. While organising the incoming information into a meaningful whole, people generally depend on the following principles:

### Figure Ground Principle

In the perceptual field, certain factors are considered significant and give a meaning to the person, and certain others which are rather unimportant for a person or cannot be studied are left as insignificant. The meaningful and significant portion is called the 'figure and the insignificant or meaningless portion is labelled as 'ground'. For instance, the printed words on this page are the 'figure' and the white space is the 'ground'. The information we classify as figure is assigned more importance than that which we view simply as background. The employee's psychological storage and subsequent interpretation of information will be affected by whether he classified the information as figure or ground. Figure 5.5 (a) and (b) presents a classic example of figure-ground differentiation.

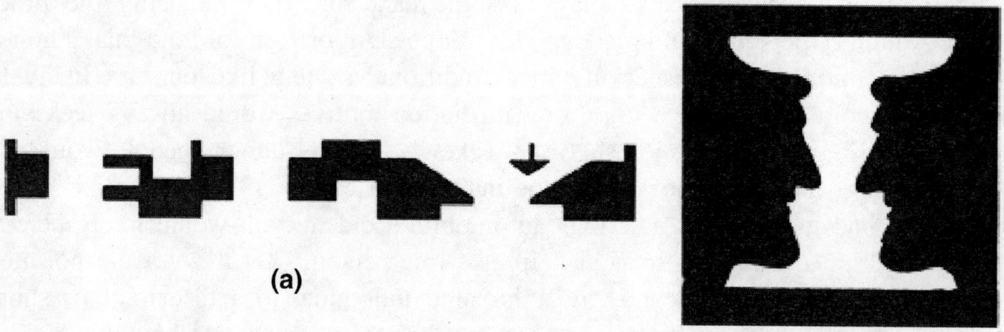

(a) (b)

***Figure: 5.5. illustration of Figure Ground Principle***

Figure 5.5 (a) At the first glance of this figure, you may perceive a jumble of black, irregular shapes against a white background. But when white letters are seen against a black background you get the words "FLY", that jumps out with clarity, (b) This is the famous cup-faces illustration. If you concentrate on black portion you notice white cup. On the other hand if you concentrate on white portion you get two faces facing each other. What becomes ground or what becomes figure is largely influenced by our needs and expectations. For instance, when we enter a dark movie theatre, we do not immediately consider what is going on the screen; rather we focus on the seat. Once we find a seat, the seat becomes ground and movie switches from ground to figure.

When there is no figure-ground pattern to organise information, we have to live with lot of ambiguity. For example in figure 5.6 do we see a white wine glass or a white table leg against a non-white background or do we visualise two persons facing each other against a white background?

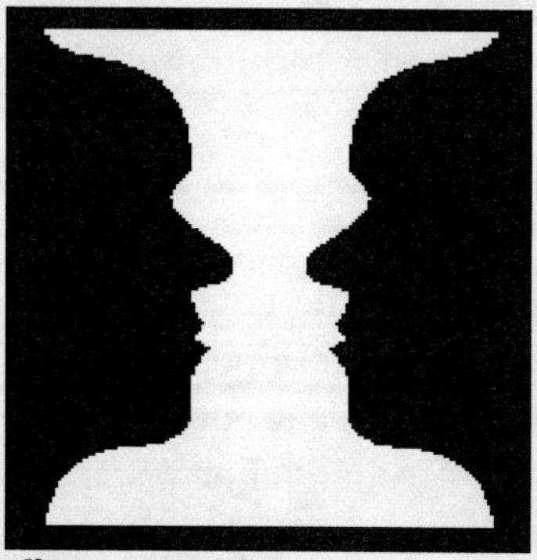

***Figure: 5.6. Is the figure a white vase (or goblet, or bird-bath?***

## Perceptual Grouping

People or things can be grouped on the basis of similarity or proximity. The greater the similarity in the events, the greater is the probability that we tend to perceive them as a group. Further, objects that have close proximity are also grouped under one head, howsoever, they are unrelated. For instance, if in a department two people suddenly resign, then people tend to perceive that their departures were closely related; whereas in reality it might not be so. One might have got a foreign assignment; other might be starting his own business.

***a. Closure:*** People when faced with incomplete information have a tendency to fill in the gaps themselves. When presented with a set of stimuli that are incomplete, people fill in the missing parts and make it more meaningful. The tendency to organise perceptual stimuli so that they form a complete message is known as 'closure'. in the drawing below, we mentally close the gaps( and perceive a picture of a duck. This tendency allows us to perceive whole objects from incomplete and imperfect forms.

***Figure: 5.7. The Principle of Closure: Illustration***

In organisations, managers usually do not have complete information on the basis of which to judge the employees. Managers in such cases fill the missing lines and make decisions.

***b. Simplification:*** Whenever people are overloaded with information, they try to simplify it to make it more meaningful and understandable. Simplification occurs when the perceiver subtracts less salient information and concentrates on the important one.

***c. Continuity:*** This is the tendency to perceive sensory data in continuous patterns if if hey are not actually continuous. The principle of closure supplies missing stimuli, whereas the principle of continuity says that a person will tend to perceive continuous lines or patterns. In the following example, for instance, we are more likely to identify lines a-b and c-d crossing than to identify a-d and c-b or a-c and d-b as lines.

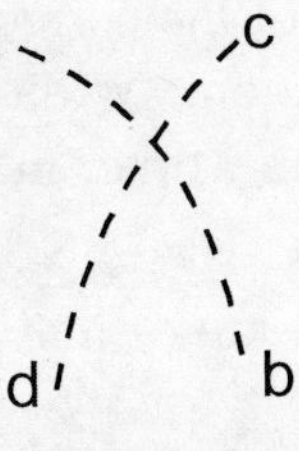


***Figure: 5.8. Principle of Continuity***

This principle is that contours based on smooth continuity are preferred to abrupt changes of direction. Because people tend to organize messages in a way that makes sense to them, managers must be extremely careful in how they communicate messages that may be unexpected or difficult to understand

***d. Proximity:*** This is the tendency to perceive sensory data as related because of close physical location. We are more likely to associate the lines in the following figure 6. which are close together than those which are further apart. In this example we tend to see three pairs of lines which are fairly close together (and a lonely line on the far right) rather than three pairs of lines which are further apart (and a lonely line on the far left).

***Figure: 5.9. An illustration of the principle of proximity***

As a result of the principle of proximity, managers usually blame the entire group in case of production failure in a particular plant, instead of actually picking up those inefficient workers who are regularly irregular.

***e. Similarity:*** The principle of similarity states that the greater the similarity of the stimuli, the greater the tendency to perceive them as a common group. In a large shopping mall, for example, all employees who wear a blue dress may be perceived as a group of sales persons, when in reality, each worker is a unique individual. Another example could be our general preference to put minorities and women employees as a single group

## Perceptual Constancy

Perceptual constancy denotes the tendency of animals and humans to see familiar objects as having standard shape, size, colour, or location regardless of changes in the angle of perspective, distance, or lighting. The impression tends to conform to the object as it is or is assumed to be, rather than to the actual stimulus. Perceptual constancy is responsible for the ability to identify objects under various conditions, which seem to be "taken into account" during a process of mental reconstitution of the known image. For example, an orange will be perceived with its characteristic colour under different kinds of light. Without perceptual constancy the world would be perceived as a booming blur of chaotic confusion in which the sizes, shapes, and colors of objects would be constantly shifting.. An example in this regard would be the worker who must choose a piece of material or a tool of the correct size from a wide variety of materials and tools at varying distances from a workstation. Without perceptual constancy, the sizes, shapes, and colours of objects would change as the worker moved about and would make the job almost impossible (Luthans)

## Perceptual Context

Another important form of perceptual organisation relates to perceptual context. The perception of an object or event depends in part on the context (surrounding conditions). Context gives meaning and value to stimuli, objects, events and situations. In an organisation, a pat on the back, an appreciative gesture, a raised eyebrow etc will be meaningless unless they are viewed against a contextual background. A pat on the back, for example, would assume special significance when the worker is complimented for showing superior performance.

## C. Perceptual Interpretation

This is the third step in perception. Once we select and organize perceptions, we draw further conclusions about their meaning through interpretation. The perceived world would look meaningless without interpretation. For example as a manager you might be complimented by a friendly subordinate profusely almost on a daily basis. You may try to dismiss this as a genuine appreciative move from an admiring subordinate, whereas others might interpret the behaviour as insincere flattery. Interpretation is a subjective, judgemental process and is, usually, influenced by several factors in an organisation

## REASONS FOR PERCEPTUAL DISTORTIONS

Errors in perceptual judgement are called perceptual distortions. As pointed out earlier, we cannot assimilate all that we observe and hence, we try to speed-read others, based on our interests, background, experience and attitudes. Such pieces of selective perception often put us in a spot because we only see what we want to see. Apart from selective perception, there are other reasons which force us to draw unwarranted conclusions from foggy situations (you can also name these as ***barriers to perceptual accuracy***!)

- ❑ Stereotyping
- ❑ Halo effect
- ❑ Projection
- ❑ Expectancy Effects
- ❑ Primacy Effect: First impressions
- ❑ Recency Effect
- ❑ Perceptual Defense
- ❑ Attributions

## STEREOTYPING

Judging people on the basis of the characteristics of the group of which they belong, is called stereotyping. Stereotyping greatly influences perception in organisations. Stereotypes are a kind of schema that often have problematic consequences in terms of justice. In the past women were seen as too flighty and flaky to be entrusted with voting, so they were not allowed to vote. Blacks are often seen as dumb, violent and lazy. Men are often seen as aggressive, competitive and sexual predators. The consequences of these stereotypes, besides the obvious, is that stories about individuals are often judged as true simply because they fit preconceptions about the class. For example, it is easy for people to believe that a crime was caused by a black man. Similarly, accusations of sexual harassment tend to stick even without evidence because people believe that "men are like that". In organisations, we often hear comments that reflect stereotypes based on gender, age, nationality and even weight. Females can't be good salesmen; older workers can't learn new skills, Japanese are industrious (Americans are materialistic), over-weight people lack discipline etc. As Robbins commented, "from a perceptual stand point, if people expect to see these stereotypes, that is what they will perceive, whether it is accurate or not."

**Box 5.1 Two commonly cited stereotypes**

From an organisational point of view, two commonly-cited stereotypes merit our attention here:

***Sex role stereotypes:*** a sex role stereotype is the belief that differing traits and abilities make males and females particularly well suited to different roles. A classic study found that women were viewed as relatively less competent, less independent, less objective and less logical than men. Although research shows that men and women do not differ in such stereotypical way, the stereotypes still persist.

***Age stereotypes:*** Age stereotypes tend to present older workers as less involved in their work, less satisfied, less motivated and less committed than younger workers. However, research evidence shows that as employees' age increases, so does their job involvement and satisfaction, work motivation and organisational commitment. Stereotypes depicting older workers as less productive or having more absenteeism in comparison to younger workers have also not been supported by research

## HALO EFFECT

It is the process of using a single personality attribute while evaluating a person. in other words, a halo blinds the perceiver to other attributes that also should be taken into account in order to have a complete, accurate picture of the other person. A stunningly beautiful girl, who has applied for a typist's job, for example, may be viewed by a male interviewer as intelligent and highly skilled. In reality, she might be quite dull and poorly skilled in typing. As if to prove a point that life is unfair, it has been generally found that attractive people generally are treated better than unattractive people. Teachers have higher expectations of them in terms of academic achievement. Potential employers are more apt to view them favourably. Attractive employees are generally paid higher salaries than unattractive ones are. In general, however, if a manager fails to look at all an individual's traits, he or she has no right to complain if that employee does not meet expectations.

## PROJECTION

Projection is the tendency for people to see their own traits in other people. That is, they project their own needs, feelings, values and attitudes into their judgement of others. For instance, if you like jobs with stretch, pull and challenge, you tend to assume that others want the same. If you are sincere, honest and dedicated, you take it for granted that other people are equally honest and committed to their jobs. Dishonest people, again, tend to see dishonesty in others. Attributing one's own attributes to others could often distort perceptions made about others and put people on the wrong side of the fence. People who suffer from this tendency tend to perceive others according to what they themselves are like rather than according to what the person being observed is really like. The best guards against errors based on projection are self awareness and empathy. Empathy means being able to put yourself in someone else's shoes, to recognise what others are feeling without them needing to tell you.

## EXPECTANCY EFFECTS

We constantly make mental guesses about how people, events, or things will be. Sometimes we are right; other times we are wrong. Occasionally we are deliberately misled. Such expectations, often, create a mindset in us that causes us to anticipate future behaviours or events. A new manager, for example, is being introduced to employees as very energetic, very demanding and strict. As one can understand, the people who are going to be managed by this person would immediately feel the heat. The perceptual expectancy in this case is that they are going to have a tough time with the new boss! Expectancy effects, thus, are the extent to which prior expectations bias perceptions of events, objects and people. An important aspect of expectancy effects is the self-fulfilling prophecy.

Self fulfilling prophecy (also called **the Pygmalion effect**) occurs when our expectations about another person causes that person to act in a way that is consistent with those expectations. As a manager, for example, if you expect your employees to perform badly, they probably will and when you expect them to perform well, they probably will.

**Box 5.2 Leadership lessons from the Pygmalion effect?**

When leaders display enthusiasm toward people and express optimism about each person's potential, such positive expectations become contagious and spread throughout the organisation. As a case in point, consider the great enthusiasm and support that Gordon Bethune showed toward employees of Continental airlines in 1995 when he took over as that bankrupt company's CEO. It would have been easy for him to be unsupportive and to show his disappointment with the workforce but he did just the opposite. Only a few years after Bethune was at the helm, the airline turned around to become one of the most successful carriers in the sky today. Although the changes he made to the airline's systems and equipment helped, these things alone would not have been enough if the employees had felt like failures. Indeed, Bethune's acceptance and enthusiasm toward members of Continental's workforce contributed greatly to giving the encouragement needed to bring the airline "from worst to first"

*Greenberg and Baron, 2007, p 50*

## PRIMACY EFFECT: FIRST IMPRESSIONS

According to Anderson ((1981) our judgments of other people are weighted averages of the information we have about them. In other words, while assessing other people, we tend to take everything we know about them, giving some information a greater weight, and then produce an average of the information we have. Negative information will generally be given more weight than positive information.

The common adage that first impressions count is known technically as the *primacy effect*. Weighted averaging would explain this effect by saying that the information we get first is weighted more heavily because it is assumed to be more important. Also because it is not easy to remember every detail about a person initially, we tend to categorize people fairly quickly. For example, an ugly looking employee may be perceived to be unproductive by the manager, where in reality he may be a very sincere and hard-working person. If someone fails to maintain eye contact and speaks rather softly, we speed-read the person and conclude that the person lacks self-confidence. Unfortunately, such unfavourable impressions are difficult to change, because we tend to attribute the negative features to the person, whereas positive features are often attributed to the situation. Generally, the first impression lasts longer unless it is greatly contradicted by information received later.

## RECENCY EFFECT

It is generally accepted (and perhaps paradoxically) that, if there is a time lag between the first piece of information and the next, then the last piece of information will carry more weight. This is known as the *recency effect*. The recency effect is found to be stronger than the primacy effect when there is a long gap between the time when the first impression is formed and the person is evaluated. Not surprisingly, therefore, many employees bring their best work to the manager's desk just before the starting of the performance appraisal process.

## PERCEPTUAL DEFENSE

Perceptual defense is the tendency of people to protect themselves against ideas, objects, situations or people that are threatening. Generally people perceive things that are satisfying and pleasant but tend to discount things that are disturbing and unpleasant. They conveniently develop blind spots in the perceptual process itself so that negative sensory data do not hurt them. Sometimes, such perceptual errors can result in manager's inability to creatively solve problems before they turn into emergencies. As a result, the individual simply proceeds as in the past even in the face of evidence that business as usual is not accomplishing anything worthwhile.

## ATTRIBUTION THEORY: WHY PEOPLE BEHAVE AS THEY DO?

This is a theory about how people explain things. Attribution refers to the way people try to understand the behaviour of others (depending on what meaning we attribute to a given behaviour). When we begin to explain why things have happened in a certain way, we may submit, "the devil made me do it" (external attribution. Attributing the outcome to an outside agent or force) or we may admit "I am guilty, grant me forgiveness" (internal attribution, claiming responsibility for the event). A manager for example, might believe Raja's performance is poor because he is lazy. Alternatively he may also believe that Raja's performance is poor because his machine is old.

According to Attribution Theory, (**Kelly**), *three* factors influence this internal or external determination.

- **Distinctiveness** considers how consistent a person's behaviour is across different situations. If Raja's performance is low, regardless of the machine on which he is working, we tend to view poor performance being caused by internal factors (lazy, inefficient, disinterested etc).
- **Consensus** examines how likely all those facing a similar situation are to respond in the same way. If all employees using machinery like Raja's have poor performance, we tend to give his performance an external attribution. If others do well, we attribute internal causation to Raja's performance.

- **Consistency** considers whether an individual responds the same way across time. If Raja has a batch of low-performance figures, we tend to view the performance as internally caused. On the other hand, if Raja's low performance is an isolated incident, we attribute the same to an external cause.

It has been suggested that people attribute behaviour to personal factors when they perceive low consensus, high consistency and low distinctiveness. They attribute behaviour to external factors when they perceive high consensus, low consistency and high distinctiveness.

## Attribution Errors

However, in actual practice, certain factors tend to distort attributions based on the above criteria. Research evidence suggests that when we made judgements about the behaviour of other people, we tend to underestimate the influence of external factors and overestimate the influence of internal or personal factors. This is called the ***fundamental attribution error*** (the tendency to attribute the behaviour of other people more to internal than to external factors) this partly explains why a sales manager is prone to attribute the poor performance of his salesman to laziness rather than the new product line introduced by a competitor.

Again, individuals tend to attribute their own success to internal factors like ability or effort but put the blame for failure on external factors like luck (called '***self-serving bias,*** means people give themselves too much credit for what they do well and give external forces too much blame when they fail). For example, a student blaming the teacher or the college for his poor grades and taking credit for showing excellence in examinations. In the organisational context, if your manager says you don't communicate well enough, and you think your manager does not listen well enough, the truth may actually lie somewhere in between

The interesting question here is, whether it is possible to make common men do uncommon things by simply encouraging them to realize their untapped, unrecognised potential—that is, by looking at what they have more closely than what they lack or do not find normally in the environment

Attributions can be managed by recognising a typical overemphasis on internal causes of behaviour and an under emphasis on external causes. An overemphasis on internal factors tends to lead to assignment of failure to employees with accompanying disciplinary measures, negative performance appraisals and the like. An under emphasis on external factors tends to lead to lack of workplace support. For example a manager who feels that subordinates are not meeting the targets and attributes the reason to an internal lack of effort is likely to respond with attempts to motivate the subordinates to work harder. In the process, the possibility of changing environmental factors eliminating job constraints and ensuring better organisational support might be discounted thoroughly. Such an oversight might come in the way of achieving major productivity gains.

## HOW TO DEVELOP PERCEPTUAL SKILLS?

Though there are no set formulas to develop the perceptual abilities some guidelines can definitely help promote the skills of the perceiver.

Avoid perceptual distortion: Some managers have a tendency to form opinions about employees without reading them properly. If the opinions are biased they lead to perceptual distortion. Further, managers can be misled by people who deliberately mistrack other employees. When such a possibility of perceptual distortion exists, managers should be careful in evaluating their perceptual judgements.

Make accurate self-perception: People are not without some limitations. Therefore, one very important thing a person should do is that he should understand himself. The more accurately he understands himself, the more accurate his perceptual skills would be. But some people are unaware of the skills they possess. These skills remain unexploited, hidden and unproductive as long as the people are unaware of these skills. This happens due to inaccurate self-perception. Maslow contends that self-actualising individuals have more accurate perceptions about themselves than those who are not self-actualising. Positive attitude towards ourselves and 'self-fulfilling prophecy' are likely to further self-improvement and understanding of the self and proper introspection.

Put yourself in another person's place: To understand other people properly we must live in their shoes. But people seldom follow this because it is very difficult to be empathetic. By changing the frame of reference and assuming others' position, managers can improve their interpersonal skills.

Create a good impression about yourself: In social settings how one appears is very important. We must show ourselves in a positive light creating and presenting an honest image of ourselves in order to improve social status and earn respect. It is an essential requirement for socialisation.

## REVIEW QUESTIONS

1. What do you mean by perception? Briefly explain the perceptual process in organisations?
2. Elaborately analyse the perceptual mechanism.
3. How two people can see the same thing and interpret differently? Can you list some reasons why they do so?
4. Briefly explain how managers develop their own perceptual skills.
5. 'People's responses are always based on their perceptions'. Critically examine this statement.
6. What are the factors on which perception is based?
7. Give some examples of the external factors that affect perceptual selectivity
8. Explain how perceptual constancy works
9. Whay does stereotyping mean< Why is it considered to be a perceptual problem?
10. What do you mean by halo effect? Summarize the current thinking on halo error.
11. What do you mean by impression management? What are the major strategies employees can use in impression management/
12. Provide examples of impression management based on your personal experiences. In your opinion, why do people try to manage impressions?.

13. Describe how a manager or coach could use the process of self-fulfilling prophecy to enhance an individual's performance.
14. Think of someone you know personally who is an effective decision maker. What key characteristics would you use to describe this person?

## CASE STUDY : BOMBAY PRINTERS

Bombay Printers is a large printing firm located in Bombay. It has specialised in printing calenders and greeting cards. Right from inception, this concentration brought rich dividends and over the years sales have increased considerably, much to the envy of competitors. Slowly but steadily, it has captured a major share of the market. Since Bombay Printers is a family held company, exact figures are not readily available. Despite this statistical deficiency, competitors knew very well that Ramakant Patil and his children who own the company are extremely wealthy. The fact that the Patil Foundation grants several lakhs of rupees every year to Charitable Institutions speaks volumes. Over the years the company has been investing its surplus funds in real estate and equity capital in a calculated manner. Supported by a vast reservoir of funds, it is small wonder, the company has achieved a stupendous growth rate leaving everyone behind in the race.

Currently, Bombay Printers is the dominant employer in the printing industry. Though there is no union, employees are well-paid. The demand for calenders and greetings has increased considerably, in the recent past, and most of the employees receive a fat overtime allowance. In an interview, given to a local magazine, Ramakant Patil proudly declared, "Workers in Bombay Printers are highly motivated. They're currently the highest-paid employees in the country. The future is rosy. Within a few days we are going to introduce a new productivity incentive plan under which employees are likely to get annual bonus based on a novel productivity formula devised by our Accounting staff. We always want our employees to grow along with us."

To his surprise and dismay, Ramakant Patil received a nasty letter, containing a long list of demands, from a group of anonymous employees—after the publication of the interview in the magazine. Among their complaints were the following:

"We're sick of all this overtime. You and other officers in the company may like working day and night. We prefer the company of our families and friends to machines and tools during holidays."

"The new bonus plan is a hoax. None of us can understand how it operates. As usual, it will be those people who lick the boots of management that'll benefit. Stop playing these dirty tricks. We hate working harder for something we don't have any chance of getting."

"You are-talking as if we're one big happy family, and yet trying to throw us all on the roads at the same time. Stop manipulating us. We know pretty well that the company has bought land in Delhi and you're going to settle there only throwing us all out of work. Why should we care for a company that is abandoning us on streets?"

**Questions**

1. From the standpoint of employee perceptions, what is going on here'
2. How can the company avoid these negative reactions?

# 6

# Values, Attitudes and Emotions

## INTRODUCTION

Values define what is good or bad, right or wrong. They guide our behaviour wherever we go and are the primary sources of our actions. That is why stories of what happened in an organisation, often, offer valuable insights into the organisation's culture. At Southwest Airlines, '***having fun***' is a value shared by the airline's employees and the customers alike. After the terrorist attacks on September 11, 2001 the custom of flight attendants sharing jokes with customers was suspended for more than a year. But gradually letters from customers began to pour in complaining about the missing jovial spirit. Soon the humour that is so much a part of Southwest's culture returned. Right from childhood, we are guided by our parents to be honest and true to ourselves and to be accountable for our actions. When we grow up and enter organisations we continue to judge events, people and situations with preconceived notions of" what ought "and" what ought not" to be. (Robbins) Values, for all practical purposes, reveal more than what a naked eye could possibly see. Not surprisingly, in organisations artefacts such as stories offer valuable insights into an organisation's spirit and its culture

**A well known story about UPS culture**

Just before Christmas a railroad official called a regional United Parcel Service's manager to inform him that a flatcar carrying two UPS trailers had unfortunately been left on a siding in the middle of Illinois. Most of the packages in these two cars were Christmas presents. Without permission or authorization, the regional manager paid for a high-speed diesel locomotive to fetch the stranded flatcar and haul it to Chicago. The manager then diverted two of UPS's Boeing 727 jets to Chicago to pick up the packages and fly them to their destinations in Florida and Louisiana in time for Christmas. Headquarters wasn't even informed of these extraordinary expenses until weeks after the incident. Once informed, top management applauded the regional manager's decision.

*(C.Hawkins and P.Oster, "After a U-turn UPS Really Delivers", Business Week, May 31, 1993)*

Attitudes, on the other hand, have a significant role to play in shaping our lives as well as the organisations that we serve People with positive attitudes are the greatest assets of an organisation. The saying, "they can conquer who believe they can" says it all in one sentence. People with positive attitudes are a treat to watch because they are pretty sure about their competencies and are very confident about outcomes. They are not rattled by defeats and instead look at failures as stepping stones to success. They have the ability to laugh at themselves and easily forgive and forget when others commit mistakes

- When asked to comment on film censorship Helen, India's celebrated film vamp, said: " I have spent my whole career dancing between a pair of scissors1" (reported in India Today)
- Thomas Edison failed nearly 10,000 times while he was working on the light bulb. Henry Ford was broke at the age of 40. Young Beetoven was told that he had no talent for music. Lata Mangeshkar was told that she had a feeble voice.
- An actress at a Society party, seeing an authoress whom she disliked, went over to congratulate her on her latest book

  "I enjoyed, it my dear", she said. "who wrote it for you?"

  "Darling", replied the authoress, " I'm glad you liked it. Who read it to you?"(A.P.Pereira)

Finally, we take a look at job satisfaction— which is nothing but a general collection of attitudes that an employee holds toward the job. This is a topic of great interest to managers because the overall level of satisfaction among employees does have an important bearing on organisational effectiveness.

## NATURE OF VALUES

Values (such as freedom, honesty, self-respect, equality etc) are perceptions about what is good or bad, right or wrong. They tend to be broad views of life and are influenced by parents, teachers, peer groups and associates. Infact, peoples' values develop as a product of the learning and experience they face in the cultural setting in which they live. Value differences basically arise because learning and experiences differ from one person to another. As a result, one person may give more importance to money whereas another person may look at honesty and truthfulness as more important than money. Such differences are likely to be deep seated and somewhat difficult to change, many have their origins in early childhood and the way a person has been raised.(Rokeach)

**Box 6.1 Features of Values**

- Values don't just reflect what we want; they specify what we 'ought' to do—socially blessed ways to achieve our needs. They, thus, influence our preference for goals and the means to achieve those goals. They dictate our priorities, our preferences and our desires. In fact, without values to guide us, it would be difficult to make any decisions.
- Values contain a judgemental element in that they showcase a person's ideas as to what is right, good or desirable. They, thus, contain both content and intensity attributes. The

content attribute says that a specific way of behaviour is important. The intensity attribute shows how important it is.

- Values are emotionally charged priorities and are passionately defended. They tend to be fairly broad views of life and are influenced by parents, peer groups and associates
- They are moralistic in nature.
- They are relatively permanent and resistant to change. They are , in a way, stable, evaluative beliefs that guide our actions and judgements across a variety of situations
- In most cases, values cloud objectivity and rationality since individuals enter organisations with preconceived notions of what "ought" and what "ought not" to be.

(W.H.Schmidt and B.Z.Posner Managerial Values in Perspective, New York, AMA, 1983; M.Rokeach, Beliefs, Attitudes and Values, San Francisco: Jossey-Bass, 1968)

From a managerial standpoint, it is important to know that values are those concepts, principles, things, people or activities for which a person is prepared to work hard and even make sacrifices for. Compensation, recognition and status are common values in the workplace (A.Sagie and D.Elizur) Values, quite often, help managers to tie the knot between employee decisions and actions with overall corporate goals. ( B.M.Meglino and E.C.Ravlin)

## TYPES OF VALUES

Depending upon its nature, a value according to Rokeach may be of two different types:

**Terminal value**s: They reflect a person's preferences regarding the 'ends" to be achieved. (e.g. prosperity, achievement, world peace, freedom, equality, happiness, inner peace, friendship, wisdom, personal and family security, stimulating life etc) They are the goals individuals would like to achieve during their lifetime.

**Instrumental value**: They represent the "means" for achieving desired ends (e.g. ambition and hard work, open-mindedness, competence, cheerfulness, courage, honesty, courtesy, responsibility, cleanliness). They indicate how you might go about achieving your important end states, depending on the relative importance you attached to the instrumental values.

Another values schema, developed by Maglino and associates, is aimed at people in the workplace ( B.M.Maglino et al)

- achievement: getting things done and working hard to achieve difficult things in life
- helping and concern for others: being concerned with other people and helping others
- honesty: telling the truth and doing what you feel is right
- fairness: being impartial and doing what is fair for all concerned

A more recent values schema, developed by Schwartz, draws the distinction between espoused values and enacted values. Espoused values represent the explicitly stated values and norms that are preferred by an organisation. They are generally established by the founder of a new or small company and by the top management team in a larger organisation. In actual practice, however, aspirations do not always produce desired behaviours because people do not always "walk the talk". Enacted values, on other hand, reflect the values and norms that are actually exhibited or converted into employee behaviour.

### Value Congruence

Value congruence occurs when individuals express positive feelings upon encountering others who exhibit values similar to their own. The relevant question here is: What would happen when employee values do not align with organisational values? When values differ, or are incongruent, conflicts over such things as goals and the means to realize them may arise. Value incongruence (a situation where two or more entities do not have similar value systems) may lead to lower job satisfaction and organisational commitment as well as higher job stress and turnover among employees. Maglino and associates found greater follower satisfaction with the leader when there was such congruence in terms of achievement, helping, honesty and fairness values. Despite the best efforts of management, in actual practice, some level of value incongruence is inevitable and may even be desirable. Too much congruence may undermine original thinking and organisational flexibility

## VALUES AND BEHAVIOUR

People are not born with values; rather they acquire and develop them early in life. Parents, teachers, relatives, friends and others influence an individual's values. Values such as stealing is bad'. 'Honestly is the best policy'. 'Respect your elders & teachers. 'Be kind to people' are taught and reinforced in schools, religious institutions and social groups. Over the years these values become relatively stable and enduring. As we grow in years, we often seek environments that are compatible with the values we learned as children. For example, values help find out what companies we are attracted to and how long we stay therein. They also influence how motivated we are at work; people who share same values as the organisation are committed to the organisation that those who do not.

### Impact

Whenever people make decisions or talk about what constitutes appropriate behaviour at work, we can easily see the impact of values or even conflicts between different values. For example, consider the question of laying-off employees. Managers with dominant economic values would be less hesitant to lay them off quickly than would managers with high social values.

### Criterion for behaviour

Once a particular value is internalised, it becomes a standard for guiding action. It becomes instrumental in developing and maintaining attitudes towards relevant objects and situations for justifying one's own and others actions and attitudes, for morally defining self and others and for comparing self with others.

### Cloud objectivity & rationality

When individuals enter an organisation with certain pre-set values, of what is right or wrong, they tend to look at the world through coloured glasses. For example, you believe that an organisation should promote people on the basis of merit and not on seniority. However, the organisation does the opposite thing, you tend to feel disappointed and totally out of place. Your attitude and behaviour towards the organisation perhaps would be very optimistic if your values match with organisation's promotion policies. Values, thus, overpower objectivity and rationality.

## VALUE SYSTEMS OF MANAGERS

The concept of the value system suggests a rank-ordering of values along a continuum of importance. Within a person's total belief system, there are varying numbers of attitudes and values. Thousands of beliefs may result in a large number of attitudes and a number of these attitudes are conditioned by social and cultural factors and may further get condensed to a few dozen values. According to Pestonjee, "this value attitude system is more internally consistent and determines behaviour. Any change in any part of this system will affect other connected parts and will lead to behavioural change."

George England and others have conducted extensive research on personal value systems of managers and reported the following (England)

1. There are large individual differences in personal values of managers–some have a pragmatic orientation, some have an ethical moral orientation and some have a feeling orientation. Some managers have very small set of values: others have a large set.
2. Personal value systems of managers are relatively stable and do not change rapidly.
3. Personal value systems of managers are related to and/or influence the way managers make decisions. For example, those who have profit maximisation as an important goal are less willing to spend money on cafeteria and rest room improvements than those who do not have profit maximisation as an important value. Values influence the choices of managers and, choices, in turn are important in determining managerial effectiveness as they influence outcomes. For example, the value a manager holds may influence the choice of his subordinates as well.
4. Personal value systems of managers are related to their career success as managers. Successful American managers favour achievement oriented values; less successful managers prefer passive values.
5. Viewed broadly, the value systems of managers in different countries studied (US, Korean, Japanese, Australian, Indian) were similar: yet, there were some distinct differences. Interestingly, social factors as against technological factors were found to be more influential in explaining value differences and similarities.

### Values Across Cultures: Hofstede's Study

Hofstede's study of thousands of IBM employees in 50 countries about their work related values revealed interesting differences among countries in terms of five value dimensions:

**Power distance**: The degree to which less powerful members of society accept that influence is unequally divided is the measure of its power distance. Managers operating in countries ranked low in power distance are expected to be generally supportive of equal rights and equal opportunity for example, managers in Canada and United States typically support equal opportunity. In countries like Mexico, France and India where power is somewhat centralized, decisions are made at the top.

**Uncertainty Avoidance**; The extent to which members of a culture feel threatened by risky or unknown situations is the measure of its uncertainty avoidance. In the United States and Canada employees and managers ranked low on uncertainty avoidance, sharing a relatively high tolerance for uncertainty, compared with their counterparts in Japan and France. In France and other cultures with high uncertainty avoidance, individuals often try to make the future more predictable by following established rules and procedures that foster tradition.

**Individualism**: Individualism is the tendency of people to look after themselves and their immediate family only. Collectivism is the tendency of people belonging to groups or collectives and to look after each other in exchange for loyalty. In countries like Japan group incentives and strong seniority systems prevail in organisations whereas in United States and Canada individual merit and incentive pay systems are valued greatly. High individualism culture often provokes managers and employees to move from company to company more frequently. They do not believe that their organisations are primarily responsible for their welfare; nor do they expect decisions made by groups to be better than decisions made by individuals.

**Masculinity**: It is a situation in which the dominant values in society are success, money and things. Femininity, on the other hand, is a situation in which the dominant values in society are caring for others and the quality of life. Countries with a high masculinity index, such as Mexico Japan, Austria, and Italy place great importance on earnings, recognition, advancement and challenge. Countries with a low masculinity index such as Norway tend to give great importance to cooperation, a friendly atmosphere and employment security.

**Long-term/Short-term Orientation**: People in cultures with long term orientation such as China, Hong Kong, Japan, stress the importance of thrift, ordering relationships by status and persistence. In the United States, Canada, France practices such as thrift, gift giving, seniority etc are not highly valued and practiced.

**Table 6.1. Differences among core values in three cultures**

| *American* | *Japanese* | *Arabic* |
|---|---|---|
| ▪ Competition | ▪ Group harmony | ▪ Reputation |
| ▪ Risk taking | ▪ Belonging | ▪ Family security |
| ▪ Material possessions | | ▪ Religious belief |
| ▪ Freedom | | ▪ Social recognition |

(F.Elashmawi and P.R.Harris, Multicultural Management, Gulf Publishing Co,Houston, Texas, 1998)

Values of managers, thus, may differ from culture to culture. These differences influence managerial decisions significantly. To arrive at sound decisions, today's managers must not only be aware of their own values, but also of others inside and outside the organisation.

## Values in Indian Society

The Indian society exhibits the following cultural components and dominant values(Udai Pareek, 2008)

**Table 6.2. Values in Indian Society**

**Karta:** The had of the family, known as karta, is nurturing, caring, dependable, sacrificing yet demanding, authoritative and a strict disciplinarian.

**Relationships**: the family ties are strong. Each one is exposed to strong personal relationships with parents, grandparents, siblings and others. Therefore, according to Ramachandran," individuals come to the workplace with a strong need to relate with others. Values like empathy,intimacy, togetherness, concern for one another, mutual understanding, and respect are shown in the workplace"

**Proximity to power:** the powerlessness and dependency experienced in childhood and adolescence in India results in people placing a high value on the power source as well as a need to be close to the power source

**Security**: a profound desire to go after safety, security and comfortable living is exhibited by large majority.

**Simple living and high thinking**: The Gandhian ideals exhibit themselves in more than one way, whether you go to South India, Gujarat or Mumbai. Living by ideals is something that is greatly valued in India, even in 21st century—though this may not be the case in the political system.

**Karma:** Indians have immense faith in luck and fate and also in past. They strongly believe that these factors govern their destinies.

## Managing Individual Differences in Values

Achieving the desired 'fit' between the person and the job is not always easy. It requires special attention and consistent effort on the part of managers. While administering sound human resource practices, managers must pay attention to individual differences in employees. To develop strong and desired values among employees, the following things need to be looked into carefully:

- **Clarify and communicate:** Managers must explicitly state and clarify values respected by the organisations. This can be achieved through formal orientation programmes. Every attempt should be made to expose new employees to the correct values & expectations and to teach them 'the way we do things here'.
- **Train and develop:** To improve skills of employees, managers must focus on training and development continually. Values can and should be emphasised along with other important individual attitudes.
- **Reward and reinforce:** Rewards can reinforce individual values and maintain enthusiasm in support of key organisational values. "Creative managers can find many ways to reward people for displaying the values that are considered essential to organisational success."

## Work Ethic

Work Ethic refers to the value to work in one's life. Most people consider dedicated work as a form of worshipping God and a service to humanity. Work viewed this way, is broader than job involvement and organisational commitment. There are three motives behind a belief in the work ethic.

- **Instrumental value:** Work is instrumental in achieving other virtues such as self discipline, personal happiness, organisational growth, rational productivity, etc. Work is good because of its contribution to society.
- **Terminal value:** Dedicated work is a mark of good character. It is a desirable activity in and of itself. We ought to be diligent and industrious.
- **Self worth:** Sincere and honest work builds up self-esteem. A worker develops feelings of self confidence and mastery by successfully accomplishing a task.

Work ethic is influenced by childhood experiences and the expectations of others in life. Children who are brought up in homes by parents who emphasized discipline and obedience tend to have stronger work values and display great social responsibility. Organisational experiences also play an important role in shaping work values. Sound human resource practices, proper reward systems, employee development plans-all help in achieving this to a great extent. Individuals who have strong work values tend to report greater job satisfaction. Older workers, for example, report such stronger work oriented values than younger workers. The reasons are fairly obvious. As workers become older, their values and perspectives change. Older workers have experienced unique events that taught the value of work. Older workers were taught different work values during their youth than were younger workers. Workers who entered workforce in 1940s believing in the protestant work ethic tended to be loyal and dedicated. The 1960s and 70s are marked by existential philosophy–the Hippi culture and employees in this period are more concerned with quality of life than material benefits. Individuals who entered the workforce since 1980 are more pragmatic in their approach and outlook, putting emphasis on achievement and material success. They look at organisations as means to achieve career success. They think that ends can justify means.

## ATTITUDES

An individual's behaviour is also a function of attitudes. An attitude is a learned predisposition, an evaluative statement—either favourable or unfavourable— toward a given object, a person or an event. The statement *'I like my Job'* reflects my attitude towards work. Attitudes are different from values. Values are the ideals that represent our beliefs about ideal conduct. They contain a judgemental element in that they carry an individual's idea about what is right, good or desirable. Attitudes are narrower in that they represent our feelings, thoughts and behavioural tendencies towards a specific object or situation. Over a period of time, our attitudes, unless we strongly believe in them, also undergo a change. For example young Japanese graduates entering the workforce desire to stay with their firm for a lifetime and may even say that they are willing to work hard to get ahead. After only a few years on the job, however, these attitudes change and many infact were observed to be leaving their firm. Attitudes are important since in virtually all aspects of our social lives we continually seek to discover other people's attitudes, tell others of our views, and try to change another person's opinions. Attitudes have a past, present and future; they evolve from past experience, they guide our current behaviour, and can direct our development inn the future( G.Hofstede; A.P.Brief,; M. Fishbein and I. Ajyen)

## Components of an Attitude

A person's attitude comprises of three vital components: cognitive, affective and behavioural.

**(1) Cognitive component:** "I believe" information and beliefs about a particular person or object. Beliefs are accepted facts or truths about a person or an object. The beliefs are generally based on a variety of learning experiences, rumours, misunderstanding, or any other information. You may believe that the boss is intelligent or stupid; ethical or unethical; good or bad; autocrat or democrat. The cognitive component is sometimes referred to as 'opinion'.

**(2) Affective component:** "I feel" It basically consists of the feelings, sentiments, moods and emotions a person has toward an individual, event, object or situation. This component is concerned with the evaluation and emotion and often expressed as like or dislike, good or bad, pleasing or displeasing, favourable or unfavourable. The expression of warmth, love, hate, and other emotional expressions also belong to the affective component. It is this affective feature that is most commonly associated with the idea of attitude. For example: "I hate putting on a suit for work" " I really like working from home"

**(3) The behavioural component:** "I intend" This is concerned with the way one intends to behave toward someone or something. Both the affective and cognitive components (feelings and beliefs) influence the way a person intends to behave toward an object. For instance, if a person has a negative feeling or belief toward an object (say junk food) he will be likely to behave negatively toward the object. "I'm going to turn a new leaf at New Year's and stop eating junk food" " In other words, the behavioural component of attitude consists of the tendency to act or reach toward an object in certain specified ways. Unable to lodge my complaint with a customer service executive of an electronics company, I may shout: "I'll never call them again. I'm not going to buy anything from this company in future. I'll not recommend this company's products to anyone"

## Functions Served by Attitudes

Attitudes serve a number of functions. According to Katz, attitudes serve four important functions ( D. Katz)

**Adjustment function**: People strive to maximise the rewards and minimise the penalties in their external environment. Attitudes are the means for reaching desired goals or for avoiding undesirable results. Attitudes are the expressions of sentiments based on experiences in attaining the motive satisfaction.

**The ego-defensive function**: People normally expend a great deal of their energies in the process of learning to live with themselves. Many of our attitudes serve the function of defending our self-image. For instance, when people cannot admit their inferiority feelings, they project their feelings over some convenient minority group and bolster their egos by attitudes of superiority toward this minority group.

**The value-expression function**: Many attitudes serve another,function in terms of positive expressions of an individual in the minds of other people. Value-expressive attitudes, according to Katz, not only give clarity to the self-image but also mould that self-image closer to the heart's desire. Attitudes make people bond or clash. They allow us to tell others our opinions and views. As social beings we need to communicate with others

**The knowledge function**: (mainly the belief components) - the world can be a confusing and strange place; attitudes help us to organise our social world, thus making the world more familiar and predictable.

## Sources of Attitudes

Attitudes are basically learned. People are not born with specific attitudes; rather they acquire them through a process of learning – especially from the following:

1. ***Experience:*** People gain experience in forming (developing) attitudes by coming in direct contact with an attitude object. Through job experiences, individuals learn attitudes. They develop attitudes about such factors as salary, performance reviews, job design, work group affiliation and managerial capabilities. But by the time a person goes for work in a specified organisation, he holds many attitudes toward the type of job which is acceptable to him, the expected pay, working conditions and supervision etc. Previous work experience can account for the individual differences in attitudes such as loyalty, commitment, and performance.

2. ***Association:*** People are highly influenced by the major groups or associations to which they belong. Our geographic region, religion, educational background, race, sex, age and income-class-all strongly influence our attitudes. The influence of groups on the attitudes of the individual is inversely proportional to the distance of the group from the individual.

3. ***Family:*** Family exerts influence on the initial core of attitudes held by an individual. Individuals develop certain attitudes from their family members—parents, brothers, sisters etc. The family characteristics influence the individual's early attitude patterns and control to which he is initially exposed. Family is primary to the group which an individual belongs to.

4. ***Peer groups:*** As people approach their adulthood, they increasingly rely on their peer groups for approval/attitude. How others judge an individual largely determines his self-image, and approval-seeking behaviour. "We often seek out others who share attitudes similar to our own, or else we change our attitudes to conform to the attitudes of those in the group whose approval is important to us."

5. ***Society:*** Social class and religious affiliation also play a vital role in forming attitudes of an individual. The culture, language and the structure of society, all provide an individual with the boundaries of his initial attitudes. At the very early age, an individual is taught that certain attitudes are acceptable and certain others are non-acceptable in the society. For instance, the attitudes of Hindus toward Lord Ram's birthplace, called Ayodhya, are radically different from those held by other communities such as Muslims or Christians in India. That is to say, what seem to be appropriate in one individual's culture and society may be totally unacceptable in another culture.

*6. **Personality factors:*** Personality differences between individuals play a major role in the formation of attitudes. This particular area has been the subject matter of great interest and it carries a great deal of weight in organisational behaviour.

## Attitudes and Behaviour: Cognitive Dissonance Theory

Attitudes, as stated above, predispose people to behave or act the way they do. For example, if you feel that attending college is good (attitude), then you will likely attend college (behaviour). To deal with employees in an organisation, managers can either focus attention on changing employee attitudes or employee behaviour. There are many theories about attitude change. One of the more famous theories, proposed in the late 50's by Leon Festinger, deals with cognitive dissonance.( Leon Festinger)

Dissonance means simply inconsistency. Cognitive dissonance refers to any incompatibility that a person might perceive between two or more of is or her attitudes, or between his or her behaviour and attitudes. According to Festinger any form of inconsistency is uncomfortable and that individuals will attempt to reduce the dissonance and thereby the discomfort. People seek consistency among their attitudes and between their attitudes and behaviour. That is to say individuals seek to reconcile divergent attitudes and align their attitudes and behaviour so that they appear to be consistent and highly rational. Since people are uncomfortable with inconsistency, Festinger theorized, they will seek to reduce the 'dissonance' or tension of the inconsistency. How people seek to deal with dissonance, of course, on three important factors:

**Importance**: How important are the elements leading to dissonance? Most people can put up with some ambiguities in life. You tend to drive fast every now and then, knowing fully well that "speed thrills but kills". You prefer greasy foods in place of home made items, even though you know that they may force you to the hear surgeon's table.

**Control:** How much control does one have over the matters that create dissonance? If your boss were to ask you to reduce the tax burden by manipulating balance sheet figures, dissonance exists but that can be rationalized and justified.

**Rewards:** What rewards are at stake in the dissonance? High rewards accompanying high dissonance tend to reduce the tension inherent in the dissonance. Once you believe that Rs. 1 lakh car is a possibility and you have invested time and money in the project, nothing can come in the way of such a belief.

Among the main ways to reduce cognitive dissonance are the following:

**1. Change your attitude and/or behaviour:** your fierce loyalty to the company might come the in way of your giving quality time to your kids on weekends. You may restructure your responsibilities so that you have time for both work and family, if you are able take charge of your working hours. Or you may change your attitude toward the company and reduce your workload steadily over time.

**2. Belittle the importance of the inconsistent behaviour**: Smokers find all kinds of reasons to explain away their unhealthy habit. Many smokers ignore the warning "smoking is injurious to health" and belittle the habit as not being as risky as the messages suggest. "My grandfather smokes, and he's over 80!"

**3. Find consonant elements that outweigh the dissonant ones**: students may justify cheating in an exam by saying" I don't usually do this but here I really have to do it". My future is at stake." This kind of rationalizing goes on quite often as when employees are confronted with moral and ethical dilemmas but fear losing their jobs. . R.Plotnik,2006 I.Ajzen 1996; Goliwitzer and J.A. Bargh I.Ajzen 1980)

In organisational life, too, many of us encounter situations where our attitudes conflict with each other or with our behaviours. Many a time we might be wondering why we are not able to leave the company that does not seem to take enough care of its employees. As a consequence of this dissonance, we tend to rationalise saying that the company is not all that bad, that there are no immediate options available and that the option of quitting at a right moment still exists.

## Theory of Reasoned Action (I.Ajzen and M. Fishbein, 1980)

To what extent do attitudes predict behaviour? Not very much really, as indicated by research evidence in early 70s. People's avowed feelings and beliefs about someone or something seemed only loosely related to how they behaved towards it. One reason was social pressures of various kinds: laws, societal norms and views of specific people can all prevent a person behaving consistently with their attitudes. So, while attitudes influence employee behaviours in the workplace, they are not perfect predictors of behaviours. To explain this phenomenon, Martin Fishbein and others have developed a model, called the theory of reasoned action, explaining the intricacies of attitude-behaviour relationship. According to this model, when a behaviour is a matter of choice, the best predictor of the behaviour is the person's intention to perform it. Intention is best

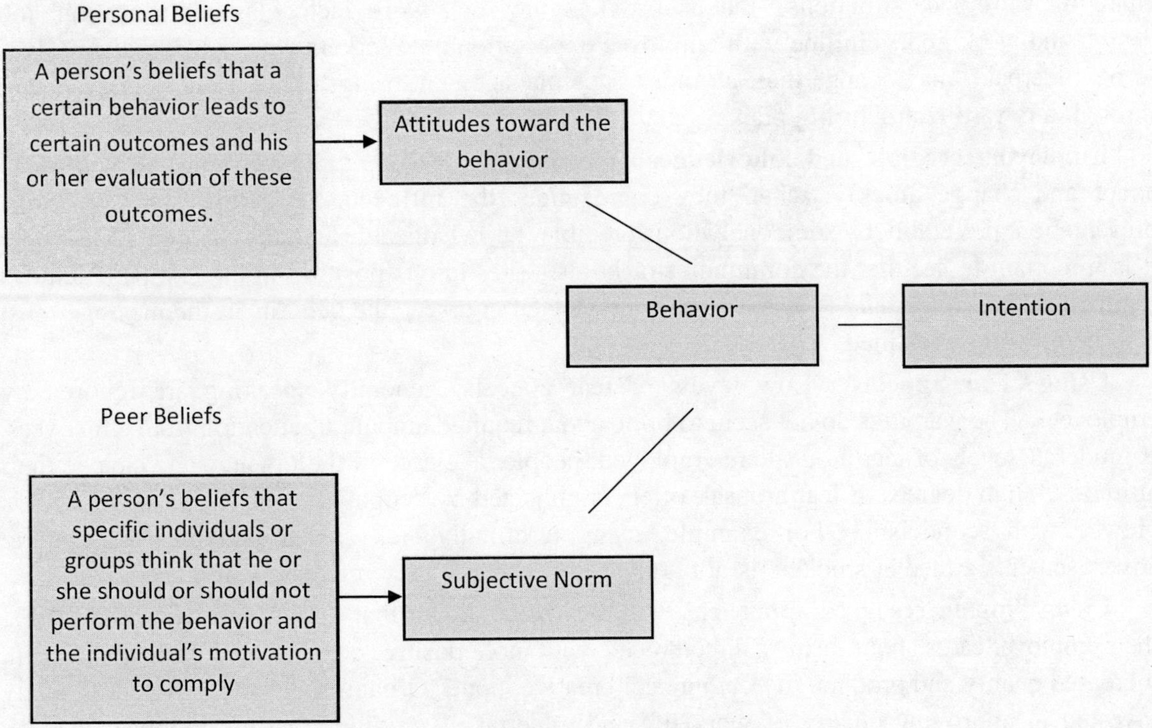


***Diagram The Theory of Reasoned Action***

predicted from two factors: (i) person's attitude toward performing the behaviour and (ii) person's subjective norm—the perception that he is expected by peers or others to perform a certain behaviour. The model thus, assumes that actions are best predicted by intentions and that intentions are in turn, determined by a person's attitude and their perception of social pressure.

The model clearly shows that a person's attitude can be predicted by his belief that a specific behaviour will lead to certain outcomes. More importantly, the value that he places on those outcomes. Likewise, a person's subjective norm can sometimes be predicted from his belief regarding how others (supervisors, coworkers, and friends) think about whether he should or should not perform a behaviour. Consequently, when people have strong beliefs and attitudes about a certain behaviour and perceive that it is expected of them, they are more likely to perform it. The reverse, of course, is also true.

## Changing Attitudes

Is it possible to change unfavourable attitude of employee toward a more favourable direction? The answer, to a large extent, is yes. Let's see how this happens . .R.Eiser; A.H.Eagly et al; J.R.Eiser and van der Pligt.J; T.M.Dembroski, et al)

**Provide new information**: In one classic study it was found that union workers had an antimanagement attitude. However, when some of the workers were promoted into the management ranks, their attitudes changed. They came to know how the company was doing to help the workers and this new information made them look at managerial efforts more favourably.

**Changing workplace situation**: managers may bring about change in employee attitudes by changing workplace situations—that is by changing such work factors as compensation, job design and work hours (in line with employee expectations). Workers who consider themselves to be underpaid, may change their attitudes once management brings about a big salary increase through a reward restructuring plan.

**Employing credible and knowledgeable communicators**: Employees may be willing to adapt and change quickly, when they come under the influence of a powerful persuasive presentation, preferably by someone who is credible, knowledgeable and convincing. To this end, it is important to see that the communicator holds a prestigious position in the company, enjoys the trust of employees and is liked by one and all. Of course, the benefits in the message must also be properly explained.

**Using "fear appeals":** Low levels of fear appeals, generally speaking are ignored by employees. The warnings do not seem to bring about required amount of attention from employees. If moderate levels of fear arousal are employed, people take note of the urgency and change their attitudes. High degrees of fear arousal, often, are rejected by people because the message itself is viewed with scepticism. For example, using terminally sick cancer patients for cigarette advertisements aimed at smokers is not a good idea because they refuse to listen.

**Using 'human resource approach'**: Studies have shown that employees who believe that their employer cares about them will reciprocate with more positive attitudes, reduced absenteeism, increased quality and productivity and greater creative input. Organisations that have consistently invested in improving quality of work life and undertaken activities that are highly valued by employees have certainly been able to improve employee attitudes and behaviours in recent times.

Employees who are strongly committed to their attitudes, of course, are not the ones who are easy to manage through above means. You may try any trick in the book but once they strongly believe—for example— that whatever management does is not going to benefit the large majority, nobody can reverse that position easily. Further, as revealed by several research studies, attitudes that are publicly accepted by people are more difficult to change. Again the more central the attitude to other attitudes and values, the less and less change is possible. Furthermore, people who appear to be self-confident, strong, and have high self-esteem are difficult to change because they feel their attitudes are absolutely right.( A.J.Kinicki et al) To sum up, unfortunately, managerial experience and research both indicate tat changing attitudes is not an easy task. In most cases 'bad attitude' is not the problem. The problem usually is *unacceptable behaviour*. So understanding why an employee is not performing satisfactorily is important because unless we are able to put the finger on the problem causing trouble, we may not be able to correct it. The real issues might be related to skill deficiency, emotional illness, financial crisis, alcohol, drug dependency, family unrest etc.

**Box 6.2 Dealing with negative attitudes**

***Confront negativity***: When negative attitudes begin to spread in an organisation, do not ignore them. Better to investigate and establish the truth behind the curtain, by identifying factors that are responsible for such negativity.

***Recognise good performance***: Give positive recognition to those who deliver results. show that you are behind them and is willing to share the fruits of progress.

***Promote loyalty:*** Encourage loyalty towards the organisation . treat your people with respect and admire their valuable contributions from time to time.

***Communicate well***: Communicate with your employees in a straightforward, unambiguous manner.. make every effort to gain their trust. Leave nothing to chance and make them feel responsibility by establishing clear goals. encourage others to be open with you

***Glass is half full***: Always carry a positive attitude. Focus on what has been achieved through collective efforts. Allow people to commit mistakes and learn. Mistakes in implementation and gaps in performance need to be analysed objectively without pushing people to a corner.

## KEY WORK RELATED ATTITUDES: JOB SATISFACTION

Work related attitudes are those lasting feelings, beliefs and behavioural tendencies toward various aspects of the job and the environment in which people carry out their work. Managers are particularly interested in exploring three such work related activities, namely, job satisfaction, job involvement and organisational commitment.

A positive attitude toward one's job is known as job satisfaction. According to Locke, it is "a pleasurable or positive emotional state resulting from the appraisal of one's job and job experience". It is basically an emotional response to a job situation. Therefore, it cannot be seen but only inferred. It is dispositional in nature. It is relatively stable and is learned through experience and information provided by others while at work. It is a result of employees' perception of how well their job offers those things which are viewed as important. Generally speaking, people experience job satisfaction when their work matches their needs and interests, when working conditions and rewards are satisfactory when the employees like their co-workers. (C.A.Kiesler)

**Table 6.3. Sources of job satisfaction**

- **The work itself:** the extent to which the job offers the individual with interesting tasks, opportunities for learning, and the chance to accept responsibility (job content factors such as recognition, responsibility, achievement etc)
- **Pay:** the amount of financial remuneration that is received and the degree to which this is viewed as equitable vis-à-vis that of others in the organisation
- **Promotion opportunities:** the chances for career growth and advancement in the hierarchy
- **Supervision:** the abilities of the supervisor to offer technical help and behavioural support; generally speaking, employee centred supervisory style enhances a great deal of job satisfaction as the leader looks after the subordinates carefully, displays friendship, warmth, respect etc towards employees.
- **Coworkers:** the degree to which fellow workers are technically proficient and socially supportive. Isolated workers generally dislike their jobs. The amount of satisfaction an individual derives from his association with the work group depends, to a large extent, on the relationship with the group members and also his own need for affiliation.
- **Working conditions:** clean, attractive (as against, hot, noisy and not-so-clean) surroundings in which work is actually carried out.
- **Occupation level:** Top levels positions carry lot of premium value and are generally sought after because they offer exciting opportunities for people to express themselves meaningfully improve financial standing of the person and are held high in public image as well. Studies have shown that blue collar workers are often the victims of severe dissatisfaction.

Other determinants of job satisfaction reveal interesting things. The relationship between age of the employees and their satisfaction from the job is complex. "People tend to begin their work with unrealistic assumptions about what they are going to derive from it, and notice that reality falls far short of their perceived expectations. But with their experience over a period of time, they realize their disillusionment and have accurate expectations because of which job will be seen in a positive perspective resulting in higher job satisfaction." Research evidence also indicates, though not emphatically, a negative correlation between the level of education of employees and their satisfaction. One reason could be that people with higher educational qualifications have a tendency to set higher expectations from their jobs. When posted on jobs not meeting their expectations or intrinsic capabilities, they tend to get dissatisfied.

## Why job satisfaction is important?

Job satisfaction has attracted the critical attention of researches for a variety of reasons:

**Impacts mental health:** It has some relation with the mental health of the people. Job satisfaction and life satisfaction are inextricably bound. The spill over effects of many unresolved personality problems, family-related issues and other maladjustments in social life could often be felt on the job. Job satisfaction, as research evidence, indicates is important for the psychological adjustment and happy living of a person.

**Influences physical well being:** It has some degree of positive correlation with physical health of individuals. People, who like their wok, are likely to live longer. Chronic dissatisfaction with work creates stress, which in turn, takes its toll on the physical as well as mental health of an individual.

**Spreads goodwill about the company:** People who feel positively about their work life are likely to voice favourable opinions about the company to the general public. In the long run, this helps the company gain a favourable image and attract talent without any difficulty.

**Allows a person to live with the organisation:** A happy and satisfied individual can find it easy to live with the company for a long time.

**Reduces absenteeism and turnover:** A number of research studies indicate negative relationship between satisfaction and absenteeism. Of course, the correlation is moderate. A satisfied employee has a positive attitude towards his work and will try to avoid being absent from work. On the other hand, there is strong negative correlation between job satisfaction and turnover. (Hom and Griffeth) Of course other important factors such as general labour market situation, availability of alternative job opportunities, length of tenure with the organisation also come in the way of deciding to quit a job.

## THEORIES OF JOB SATISFACTION

Researchers, over the years, have come out with various explanations about what makes some people more satisfied with their jobs than others. The important ones may be listed thus:

**Two factor Theory:** According to Herzberg, who proposed this theory, job satisfaction is caused by a set of factors referred to as motivators. Whereas job dissatisfaction is caused by a different set of factors, known as hygiene factors (see the chapter on motivation for details)

**Value Theory:** According to Locke, who proposed this theory, job satisfaction depends primarily on the match between the outcomes individuals' value in their jobs and their perceptions about the availability of such outcomes. The more people receive outcomes they value, the more satisfied they will be. This theory focuses attention on any outcomes that people value, regardless of what they are.

**Equity Theory:** According to Adam's, who proposed this theory, people strive to maintain ratios of their own outcomes(rewards)to their own inputs(contributions)that are equal to the outcome/input ratios of others with whom they compare themselves. If their ratio is greater than or lesser than that of the others, they feel dissatisfied because inequity has occurred. (see the chapter on motivation for details)

## MEASURING JOB SATISFACTION

Questionnaires, consisting of highly specialized rating scales, are generally used to measure job satisfaction. People record their reactions to their jobs by simply answering questions developed by researchers. Three popular methods of measuring job satisfaction are listed below:

**Job Description Index (JDI):** It is a rating scale for measuring job satisfaction. Individuals respond to this structured questionnaire by indicating whether or not various adjectives describe aspects of their work. For example, on the question of how employees look at their work, the alternatives offered could be: *routine, satisfactory, good* and employees may be asked to enter "yes" "no" or "?". In most cases JDI has proved to be a reliable and valid way of measuring job satisfaction.

**Minnesota Satisfaction Questionnaires (MSQ):** This is a rating scale for assessing job satisfaction wherein people indicate the extent to which they are satisfied with various elements of their jobs. People completing this scale rate the extent to which they are satisfied with say, their pay, by putting one number to each aspect : 1= extremely satisfied, 2=not satisfied, 3=neither satisfied nor dissatisfied, 4= satisfied, and 5= extremely satisfied. As a result, higher scores reflect higher degrees of job satisfaction. One important merit of both these scales is that they can be completed quickly and efficiently by large numbers of people. When administered over thousands of employees in various companies, the scores provide reasonably valid measures of relative satisfaction.

**Critical Incident Technique:** This is a procedure for measuring job satisfaction in which employees describe incidents relating to their work that they find especially satisfying or dissatisfying. Their responses are then examined to uncover underlying themes. For example, when workers praise their supervisors for standing by them in trying circumstances, that suggests the role of supervisory style in boosting employee confidence and thereby satisfaction.

## CONSEQUENCES OF JOB SATISFACTION

Looking at the devastating impacts of job dissatisfaction on employee well being, most organisations, now a days, take all possible steps to keep their employees in good humour.

How employees express their dissatisfaction?

**Voice**: Try to discuss the problems with superior; raise the issue in union meetings; attempt to improve conditions by suggesting viable alternatives in a constructive way

**Loyalty**: Try to keep the spirits high by optimistically thinking that management does everything right, reflecting loyalty towards the organisation and management

**Neglect**: Keep the mouth shut; not discuss anything with anyone; resigning himself to fate and allowing things to worsen day by day

**Exit**: Look for greener pastures outside, submit resignation at an appropriate moment.

(D. Farell, "Exit, Voice, Loyalty and Neglect as Responses to Job Dissatisfaction" Academy of Management Journal, December, 1983

They undertake frequent surveys to find out how happy their employees are while at work, in relation to those employed in other units. For example, FedEx has been so enamoured with tracking the attitudes of its employees that it has started a fully automated online survey. The company depends on insights obtained from survey of its US based employees as the key to identifying causes of dissatisfaction among them. The impact of job satisfaction on some important organisational and individual factors may be presented thus:

### How to improve job satisfaction?

Levels of job satisfaction can be raised by paying people fairly, improving the quality of supervision, decentralizing control of organizational power, assigning people to jobs that match their interests

**Funny jobs:** People are more satisfied with jobs they enjoy doing than those that are dull and boring

**Fair rewards:** people who believe that their organisation's pay systems –when compared with competing units—are fair tend to be satisfied with their jobs.

**Jobs that match with interests :** the more people find that they are able to fulfil their interests while on the job, the more satisfied they will be with those jobs

**Jobs with stretch pull and challenge:** most people like jobs that are interesting to handle and challenging to confront.

## EMOTIONS

Emotions are intense feelings that are directed at someone or something. They are reactions to a person (seeing your class mate after a long time may make you happy) or event (like dealing with a rude client may make you angry for a while). You show your emotions when you are happy about something, angry at someone, or afraid of something. Emotions are related to, but different from, mood. Emotions are specific reactions to a particular event that are usually of fairly short duration. Mood is a more general feeling such as happiness, sadness, frustration, contentment, or anxiety that lasts for a longer time. Individuals differ in their capacity to experience both positive emotions such as happiness, pride and negative emotions such as anger, fear, guilt etc. Employees need to cope with both positive as well as negative emotions while at work on a daily basis. Although there are dozens of emotions, psychologists have universally agreed on six emotions that affect us, namely anger, fear, sadness, happiness, disgust and surprise.

## COMPONENTS OF EMOTIONS

Emotions, specifically, have three parts:

- Subjective feelings: How one is experiencing for example, love, anger, hatred etc? This is most difficult to describe or measure. The person experiencing the same must describe it to others. Of course each person has his own story to tell , like two persons falling in love may not experience or describe their feeling in exactly the same way.
- Psychological responses : These responses are easy to measure—such as a pounding heart, sweating, blood rushing to the face or the release of adrenaline (a harmone or chemical messenger that is released in response to fear, anger, panic and other emotions—which increases heart rate, breathing etc) in response to a situation that creates intense emotion. People generally have very similar internal responses to the same emotion.
- Expressive behaviour: Expressive behavior is the outward sign that an emotion is being experienced. Outward signs of emotions can include fainting, a flushed face, muscle tensing, facial expressions, tone of voice, rapid breathing, restlessness, or other body

language. The outward expression of an emotion gives other people clues to what someone is experiencing and helps to regulate social interactions.

**Box 6.3 Why bother about emotions?**

Emotions control your thinking, behavior and actions. Emotions affect your physical bodies as much as your body affects your feelings and thinking. People who ignore, dismiss, repress or just ventilate their emotions, are setting themselves up for physical illness. Emotions that are not felt and released but buried within the body or in the aura can cause serious illness, including cancer, arthritis, and many types of chronic illnesses. Negative emotions such as fear, anxiety, negativity, frustration and depression cause chemical reactions in your body that are very different from the chemicals released when you feel positive emotions such as happy, content, loved, accepted.

## Why Do We Have Emotions?

Emotions appear to serve several physical and psychological purposes. Some scientists believe that emotions are one of the fundamental traits associated with being human. Emotions color people's lives and give them depth and differentiation. For many people, strong emotions are linked to creativity and expression. Great art, music, and literature deal on a fundamental level with arousing emotions and creating an emotional connection between the artist and the public. Some scientists also believe that emotions serve as motivation to behave in specific ways. Physiologically, emotions aid in survival. For example, sudden fear often causes a person to freeze like a deer caught by a car's headlights. Because animals usually attack in response to motion, at its simplest level, fear reduces the chances of attack.

***What functions do emotions serve?*** Emotions help us cope up with various events in life. As Darwin indicated, emotions motivate people to engage in actions that are important for survival. For example, disgust might force us to avoid dangerous or harmful things. Likewise, excitement might motivate us to take on situations in which we require energy and initiative. As an example here you can look at what Richard Branson—the owner of Virgin Group— is known for. Living and learning for Richard Branson means indulging in endless curiosity, being adventuresome, having fun and filling each day with a seamless integration of work and family life. Not without reason he has created 200 companies—ranging for records, airlines, retail goods, cell phones, space travel, consumer electronics etc— and is sitting on a massive wealth of over $2.5 billion. Branson thrives on adventure, taking risks and enjoying life to its fullest. He seems to thrive on a relentless stream of activity including hot air ballooning and tennis.

Emotions also help people monitor their social behavior and regulate their interactions with others. Every person unconsciously learns to "read" the outward expressions of other people and apply past experience to determine what these outward signs indicate about what the other person is feeling. If a person sees a man approaching who is walking very aggressively, holding his body stiffly and frowning, the person might correctly assume that the man is angry. Using this information, the person can decide whether to leave or to stay or what tone of voice and body language to use when approaching the man.

## SOURCES OF EMOTIONS

Some of the primary influences on emotions and moods may be listed thus: (Robbins 2010)

**1. Personality:** Some people experience mood swings more frequently and are easily taken for a ride by their inner emotions than others. This has got something to do with their mental make up and personality type.

**2. Day of the week and time of the day:** People rush to offices during early part of week and get impacted by negative emotions. Late in the week, people seem to be living with a positive frame of mind. Some people find it easy to get along with traffic, work pressures, colleagues etc during morning hours—the typical 'morning' people. Others might get this feeling in the 'evening'—the typical 'evening' people.

**3. Weather:** we generally think that mood swings are a matter of weather. Research evidence, however, does not support this. People do not dance when the sun shines and go into deep depression when the sun sets—especially those dark and rainy days.

**4. Stress:** People experience negative emotions when stress levels are high. Like just before the examination, a student might be flying off the handle easily. When stress builds up over time, negative emotions also erupt quite spontaneously. Some people might thrive on stress, but for most others stress impacts our moods and emotions quite negatively

**5. Social activities:** Social activities such as spending time with friends and like minded people, attending a party, eating with family and friends in a restaurant —are found to put people on a positive frame of mind than doing formal (attending a meeting) or sedentary activities (such as watching television)

**6. Sleep:** Poor sleep often puts people in a bad mood. Lack of sleep makes people grumpier. Poor sleep quality impairs our decision making capabilities and compels us to go off the track quite often.

**7. Exercise:** research has consistently shown that exercise helps people to be in a positive frame of mind—having full control over their emotions and moods.

**8. Age:** As people get older and older they do not seem to slip into a negative frame of mind more easily. One longitudinal research study reported by Carstensen stated that "periods of highly positive moods lasted longer for older individuals and bad moods faded for them more quickly than for younger people".

**9. Gender:** Research studies have confirmed a popular belief that— women are more emotionally expressive than are men; they experience emotions more intensely; they tend to hold on to emotions longer than men and they display more frequent expressions of both positive and negative emotions, except anger.

## EMOTIONAL LABOUR

Employees need to express themselves properly while at work, especially if they are working in a hotel, hospital, or a retail store. They need to keep the smile on their faces throughout. Because customers will not come if you show off your moods and expose your emotions openly. Since it is a bread and butter issue, you are compelled to hide your emotions and give a picture of having been in control of everything. Emotional Labour is an employee's expression of organizationally desired emotions during interpersonal transactions at work. However, this is easier said than done. Because we cannot put a lid on our emotions and keep looking at people with a smiling face always. The real challenge is when the employee is supposed to project one emotion (positive, displayed emotions you do not like to see the face of a friend who ditched you, but when you face the friend suddenly in a market place, you greet the person with a smile) while simultaneously feeling another (real, innermost, felt emotions you want to slap your boss on the face but you hide it). If you are not giving expression to your real feelings and are trying to hide them from public for long periods of time, it will have serious impact on your personal life. The emotional dissonance (the disparity between the two moods, one expressed and the other hidden one) and the pent up feelings of anger, frustration and resentment would burn up your candle of energies too soon. You become a mental wreck and get become a victim of emotional exhaustion and burnout.

Obviously, you cannot be acting always especially in day to day interactions. You tend to burst up on occasions and expose your emotions in an unashamed manner. Surface acting ( hiding one's inner feelings and forgoing emotions expressions in response to organisational rules—like greeting a customer with a smile while standing on your legs all the while in a huge departmental store) may prove to be extremely stressful in the long run because you are trying to deal with your felt emotions. Deep acting, the other alternative, ( trying to modify one's inner behaviour based on harsh realities of the game—like a hospital nurse trying to show empathy with patients whether she likes it or not, she tries to imbibe this and make it part of her work life). As years roll by, everyone exposed to such situations where their very survival is dependent on display of a happy and pleasant mood, will certainly try to get along with events more easily than someone who steps into the arena for the first time. For people working in such industries, it is well worth remembering what Mahatma Gandhi said: " the customer is the most important visitor and is not dependent on us. Rather we are dependent on him. He is doing us a favour by giving us an opportunity to serve him."

## WHAT IS EMOTIONAL INTELLIGENCE?

The term emotional intelligence refers to the ability to diagnose and recognize your own emotions, the ability to control your own emotions, the ability to recognize and diagnose the motions displayed by others and the ability to respond appropriately to those emotional cues. Thus, there are, essentially, four competencies that form part and parcel of emotional intelligence: n other words, it implies an awareness of other's emotions, and a sensitivity to one's own emotions and the ability to control them. Actually, according to Goleman emotional intelligence is a combination of five competencies, namely:

1. **Self-awareness** is the ability to recognize a feeling as it happens, to accurately perform self-assessments and have self-confidence. It is the keystone of emotional intelligence .

2. **Self-management** or self-regulation is the ability to keep disruptive emotions and impulses in check (self-control), maintain standards of honesty and integrity (trustworthiness), take responsibility for one's performance (conscientiousness), handle change (adaptability), and be comfortable with novel ideas and approaches (innovation).

**3. Motivation** is the emotional tendency guiding or facilitating the attainment of goals. It consists of achievement drive (meeting a standard of excellence), commitment (alignment of goals with the group or organization), initiative (acting on opportunities), and optimism (persistence reaching goals despite set backs).

**4. Empathy** is the understanding of others by being aware of their needs, perspectives, feelings, concerns, sensing the developmental needs of others.

**5. Social skills** are fundamental to emotional intelligence. They include the ability to induce desirable responses in others by using effective diplomacy to persuade (influence); listen openly and send convincing messages (communicate); inspire and guide groups and individuals (leadership); nurture instrumental relationships (building bonds); work with others toward a shared goal (collaboration, cooperation); and create group synergy in pursuing collective goals.

People who know their own emotions and are good at reading emotion cues—for instance, knowing why they are angry and how to express themselves without violating rules and regulations—are most likely to be effective. People with emotional intelligence are generally branded as street smarts, showing superior performance while at work. Such people are also able to respond appropriately to the emotions of others. In an organisation, the emotional intelligence of managers plays an important role in shaping the behaviours of subordinates. As Goleman explained it, "a cranky and ruthless boss crease a toxic organisation filled with negative underachievers who ignore opportunities,; an inspirational inclusive leader spawns acolytes for whom any challenge is surmountable". Of course, emotional intelligence is a vague concept and is difficult to measure. Most researchers also feel that being self aware or self motiated or having empathy is a matter of intellect. Some critics also argue that because emotional intelligence is so closely related to intelligence and personality, once you control for these factors, EI has nothing unique to offer.

## REVIEW QUESTIONS

1. Define 'attitudes'. How attitudes affect the behaviour of individuals?
2. Explain the various components of attitudes.
3. Can attitudes be changed? What are the factors that are to be taken into account while changing attitudes?
4. Elaborately explain "cognitive dissonance theory of attitudes".
5. "Attitudes are evaluative statements – either favourable or unfavourable–concerning objectives, people, or events". Do you agree with the statement?
6. Explain the major consequences of job dissatisfaction and ways of overcoming them.
7. Describe the concept of organisational commitment, the major consequences of low levels of organisational commitment and how to overcome them.
8. Write short notes on:

   Emotions

   Emotional labour

   Emotional intelligence
9. What are the primary sources of emotions and moods

## CRITICAL THINKING QUESTIONS

1. 'A happy employee is a productive employee'. Discuss.
2. Occasionally we say that another person 'has had a bad attitude'. What exactly does that mean in the contexts of the three attitude components—cognitive, affective and behavioural tendency? Give an example of each.
3. Think of a particular job you have enjoyed most. What did you like about it so much? Now think of a particular job that you enjoyed least. What made you dislike it so much? Do the factors you liked fall into the motivation category of two factor theory? Did the factors you disliked fall into the hygiene category of the two factor theory? Explain clearly.
4. Why is it so difficult to change people's attitudes? Think of a co-worker who has a negative attitude toward his or her supervisor. What can the supervisor do to change the attitude to a positive one?
5. "Twenty five years ago, young employees we hired were ambitious, conscientious, hardworking and honest. Today's young workers don't have the same values". Do you agree or disagree with this manager's comments? Support your answer.
6. When people have conflicting thoughts, we say they are experiencing 'cognitive dissonance'. How can a manager use cognitive dissonance to change a subordinate's attitude?
7. Think about the particular organisation at which you have worked the longest. What were the main reasons you stayed there/. How do these compared to the three forms of organisational commitment described in this chapter?
8. Most companies now days agree on one thing: It pays to keep employees in good humour and glued to their jobs. Of the various things that can be done to promote commitment to a firm, which tactics do you believe may be most effective? Explain through concrete examples.

## INDIVIDUAL EXERCISES

1. This weekend eat at a restaurant that serves ethnic food (e.g. Indian, Chinese, Mexican) and where the servers of that cultural background. Write down your opinion of the service. What do you base your opinion on? Do you think your opinion is based on your attitude about the culture? Would you be comfortable returning to that restaurant? Why or why not?

2. John felt that there was nothing wrong with drinking a glass or two of beer during lunch break while working for Crew Boss Products, a global supplier of leather items located in Gurgaon, Haryana. He could afford it easily enough. He claimed that his lunchtime drink never came in the way of his work performance during the afternoon. He felt more relaxed and invigorated afterwards. However, he could do without a drink without much difficulty if he had to. John liked the company and approval of other acquaintances and friends present in a nearby name-sake tea shop where all sorts of interesting rumours floated around. John, of course, liked his work and was keen to gain promotion. Sad to relate, though, his boss did not approve of alcoholic drink at lunchtime—or indeed at any other time. Nor did most of his colleagues, mostly women, with whom he had to work closely. They took a serious view of his problem and even lodged a formal complaint with his boss. Use the theory of reasoned action to decide whether John is likely to drink a glass of beer during his break on most working days in future.

## GROUP EXERCISE

## IDENTIFYING IMPORTANT VALUES IN A CLASSROOM SETTING

The purpose of this exercise is to help you think about what values are important to you in the classroom. Because values differ from person to person, it's beneficial to know which values people are willing to work hard to maintain and which values others feel are less important.

Below are 10 different values from the ***Rokeach Value Survey.*** Read the list and then rank each value according to which ones you feel are important in the classroom. Rank the values from 1 to 10 , with 1 being equal to "most important" and 10 being equal to "least important". Mark your results in the first column.

Once you rank the values, break into teams of five to six people. As a group, compare each of your individual results and discuss them. What do you notice about the differences in rankings? Were the group members' rankings similar to yours, or was there argument as to which values were important? As a team, take the average ranking for each value or devise some other method to reach a consensus on which values are important or not important. Mark those results in the second column, again using the scale from 1 to 10. Compare your team's results to the results from the rest of the class

| | | |
|---|---|---|
| Broad minded (open-minded) | | |
| Capable (competent, effective) | | |
| Honest(sincere, thoughtful) | | |
| Responsible (dependable, reliable | | |
| Polite (courteous, well mannered) | | |
| Sense of accomplishment (lasting contribution) | | |
| Equality (brotherhood, equal opportunity) | | |
| Self-respect (self-esteem) | | |
| Self recognition(respect, admiration) | | |
| True friendship (close companionship) | | |

### Questions for discussion

1. Were you surprised at how your results differed from the group's? Or were you surprised at how closely your results matched? Why or why not?
2. to what extent do you feel knowing your classmates' values will help you work more effectively with them in teams? Explain.

## True/False Questions

1. Attitudes are largely shaped by personal beliefs and values
2. Employee workplace attitudes are fairly stable over time and slow to change
3. People strive to minimise the rewards and maximize the penalties in their external environment
4. people are born with specific attitudes toward objects, people or events
5. Most people can put up with some ambiguities in life
6. Attitudes are perfect predictors of behaviour
7. attitudes are internal and largely kept to oneself
8. high degrees of 'fear arousal' are generally accepted by people
9. A positive attitude toward one's job is known as job satisfaction
10. In organisational life, our attitudes are rarely in conflict with each other or with our behaviours

(**Ans.** 1 True 2 True 3 False 4 False 5 True 6. False 7. False 8. False 9.True10 false )

## CASE STUDY THE LOYAL EMPLOYEE

Raman is the Sales Manager of a reputed Corporation. He has 25 employees in his Department, and all are paid commission for their sales in their territories. For the past three years, the market for the company's goods has been steadily growing and the majority of Raman's staff have met this growth with increased sales. However, one employee in particular, Krishnan has not kept up with the pace.

Krishnan has been with this Corporation for over 20 years and is now 56 years old. Krishnan is a friendly man and is liked by his peers and those to whom he sells the company's products on a regular basis. The company has always considered Krishnan dependable and loyal. Through the years Krishnan has been counted as an asset to the company, but at the age of 56 he has gone into a state of semi-retirement. Krishnan's sales have not increased as the others have and he does not have the determination to acquire a significant increase in sales.

Raman wishes to change this situation. He wants to motivate Krishnan into increasing his sales to match that of his younger peers. To accomplish this, Krishnan must begin to do more than put in his time, but Raman is not sure how to go about trying to motivate him. Unlike the majority of the new employees Krishnan is an old man, who within a few years will reach the age of retirement. If you were Raman what would you do?

### Questions

1. Would you threaten to fire him?
2. Would you increase his commission?
3. Would you increase the retirement benefits for Krishnan rather than offer him the increased commission rate?
4. Would you offer him more status by way of a new title or a new company car or place his table in a better position in the office?
5. Is there some way in terms of appraisal and rewards with which you can motivate Krishnan?

## Suggested Answers

(Please Note: Only suggested answers are given here. There can be any number of alternatives depending on the nature of the organisation, the leadership style, the environment in which the work is taken up, the mental make-up of the subordinates etc. These answers should help the students in developing their own alternatives working in the capacity of a decision-maker independently.

### 1. Would you threaten to fire him?

Firing on old player in the corporation will have serious negative consequences on the morale of other employees. Traditionally also, threats of punishment and dismissal have not yielded concrete results in the form of higher output, better discipline etc. Such treats would alienate the employee further. Moreover, the case in question speaks about the rapport Mr. Krishnan has with other employees and customers, his loyal and dedicated service to the company for more than two decades. Any attempt to fire such an employee will definitely tarnish the image of the company the eyes of the employees as well as the customers to whom Mr. Krishnan has been selling the company's products on a regular basis.

### 2. Would you increase his commission?

The power of money to motivate an established, senior employee in the company is open to doubt. Nevertheless, the commission payments could be structured in such a way that senior players get a fair share of the cake when compared to junior colleagues. Institution of group incentives would be a good idea i.e., rewarding Mr. Krishnan's efforts along with others in his team on an agreed basis.

### 3. Would you increase the retirement benefits for Krishnan rather than offer him the increased commission rate?

Increasing the post-retirement benefits would be a good idea, if Mr. Krisnan's present pay and allowances have come in the tax bracket in a major way. Substantial tax savings on post-retirement benefits may put Mr. Krishnan on the right track as laid down by management. But the whole exercise depends on how Mr. Krishnan values the monetary incentives offered by management from time to time.

### 4. Would you offer him more status by way of a new title or a new company car or place his table in a better position in the office?

High status titles have great motivational value, especially in the case of senior employees who have put in more than two decades of service. However, such a high-status position must be backed up by stimulators like luxurious office space, car and car parking space, interesting and challenging responsibilities etc. The position must be viewed as an important one by others in the organisation as well.

**5. Is there some way in terms of appraisal and reward with which you can motivate Mr. Krishnan? Argue out your action.**

Mr. Krishnan can be motivated through a package of incentives aimed at stimulating him to superior performance. The package may consist of the following elements:

1. Mr. Krishnan may be invited to present his case before the management as to why the sales are not picking up in his area. Any action plan should take into account the problems cited by Mr. Krishnan in this regard. A sincere attempt must be made by management to find a solution to all the vexing issues highlighted by Mr. Krishnan.
2. Group incentives may be offered to all the members in Mr. Krishnan's team with a view to link the rewards to their performance.
3. The compensation package of Mr. Krishnan may be made more attractive by:

Linking sales efforts to incentives based on sales, offering additional perquisites in the form of a company car; assigning an important location for Mr. Krishnan recognising his worth and importance to the company; giving as independent charge of promoting company's products in a particular area for a specified period of time and assess his performance against the targets set by management, Mr. Krishnan and his staff *jointly*

# 7

# Learning and Reinforcement

## INTRODUCTION

Learning can be defined as a relatively permanent change in behaviour or performance resulting from experience or practice. This definition contains many interesting points

- **Bring about change**: Learning involves a change, though not necessarily improvement in behaviour. Learning may be good or bad from an organisational point of view. For example, bad habits such as reporting late for work, fighting with coworkers when the supervisor is away, careless and reckless use of facilities etc can be learned, especially when management is viewed as weak or not very effective in enforcing discipline.
- **Result in relatively permanent change**: The change brought about by learning should be long lasting. Therefore, short-lived performance changes that typically occur prior to the visit of a top management team should not be confused with learning.
- **Arise out of experience or practice**: The change in behaviour should occur as a result of experience, practice, education or training. Any change in an individual's thought processes or attitudes, if not accompanied by change in behaviour should not be interpreted as learning.
- **Learning through reinforcement:** Reinforcement is the process by which an external reinforcer or reward produces and maintains a behaviour. Rewards for workers who are regular and sincere to their work, would induce others to learn such behaviours. Reinforcement increases the strength of response and tends to induce repetitions of the behaviour that precedes the reinforcement. The practice of learning, thus, must be reinforced in order that learning occurs. If reinforcement does not accompany the practice or experience, the behaviour will eventually disappear.
- **Differences in the learning process**: There are individual differences in the learning process. Two individuals who undergo similar experiences—for example transfer of two

professors working in Mumbai to two different locations, one to Lucknow and another to New Delhi probably will differ in terms of acquisition of skills, knowledge and ability to adapt appropriately to new challenges posed by such transfer (finding a school for kids, adjusting to local customs and traditions, etc )

## THEORIES OF LEARNING

People learn new behaviours through one or more of the four learning processes—classical conditioning, operant conditioning, observational learning and cognitive learning.

**1. Classical Conditioning:** It is a simple form of learning in which a conditioned response is linked with an unconditioned stimulus (a stimulus is something that incites actions and draws forth a response). Ivan Pavlov, a Russian psychologist developed classical conditioning theory based on his experiments to teach a dog to salivate in response to the ringing of a bell.

### Before conditioning

- When Pavlov offered meat (unconditioned stimulus) to the dog, he noticed a great deal of salivation (unconditioned response). Pavlov termed the food an unconditioned stimulus because food automatically led to salivation (that is, an unconditioned response) When the dog saw the meat, it salivated.
- On the other hand, when Pavlov merely rang the bell (neutral stimulus), the dog did not salivate.

### After conditioning

- Pavlov subsequently introduced the sound of a bell (artificial stimulus or conditioned stimulus) each time the meat (unconditioned stimulus) was given to the dog. Thus when the bell was paired with the meat, it produced a response. The dog eventually learned to salivate in response to the ringing of the bell *even when there was no meat*. (conditioned stimulus leading to conditioned response) Pavlov, thus, had conditioned the dog to respond to a *learned* stimulus. This is known as the "***law of exercise***' which states that behaviour can be learned by repetitive association between a stimulus and a response.

In organisations, however, only simple behaviours and responses can be learned in this way. For example, if the boss were to reprimand an employee for poor performance every Monday during a month, the next time the employee receives a call from the boss, he becomes extremely nervous, because of this association. Also, classical conditioning does not explain situations where people choose a course of action in a rational and objective manner. In actual practice, managers are more interested in how employees behave voluntarily and freely (as opposed to involuntary and reflex responses) in an organisational setting.

**2. Operant Conditioning:** Operant is defined as voluntary or learned behaviour (as against reflexive or unlearned behaviour suggested by classical conditioning) that produces effects. Operant conditioning, according to Skinner, is based on the premise that people learn to behave to obtain something they want or avoid something they do not want. Behaviour, thus, is a function of its consequences, and not a function of inner thoughts, feelings, emotions or perceptions—as suggested by classical conditioning. People, in short, learn to behave to get something they want or to avoid something they don't want. Operant behaviour, therefore, is something that is learned as against something that is reflexive or unlearned. The consequences of a given behaviour would ultimately decide whether the same behaviour is likely to occur in future or not. As a result, behaviours that are rewarded (or reinforced) get repeated and behaviours that are punished (or not reinforced) are avoided (known as the ***Law of Effect***). An employee who receives a written disciplinary warning after submitting a report 24 hours late is more likely to submit the report on time next month. The consequences, according to Skinner, determine the likelihood that a given operant will be performed in future. If, as a manager, you want more of behaviour, you must make the consequences for the individual positive. Skinner's emphasis here is on consequences that can be manipulated rather than consequences inherent in the behaviour itself.[4]

**Box 7.1 Classical and operant conditioning: Compared**

| Features | Classical conditioning | Operant conditioning |
|---|---|---|
| Type of association | Between the stimuli | Between a response and its consequences |
| State of the subject | Passive | Active |
| Focus of attention | On what produces response | On what follows response |
| Type of response typically involved | Involuntary response | Voluntary response |
| Range of responses | Relatively simple | Simple to highly complex |
| Responses learned | Emotional responses: fear, likes and dislikes | Goal-oriented responses |

(S.E.Wood, E.G.Wood, The World of Psychology, Allyn and Bacon, Boston, 1996)

**3. Cognitive Learning:** Cognition refers to an individual's ideas, thoughts, knowledge, interpretations, understandings etc about himself and his environment. According to Cognitive Theory—proposed by Tolman and Kohler—learning is considered to be the outcome of deliberate thinking about a problem or situation both intuitively and based on known facts and responding in an objective and goal oriented way. Edward Tolman, using rats in his laboratory, explained how the rats learned to through a complicated maze toward their goal of food. It was found that rats developed expectations at every choice point in the maze. They, thus, learned to expect that certain cognitive cues related to the choice point could ultimately lead to food. If the rat actually got the food, the association between the cue and the expectancy was strengthened, and learning took place. As against the S-R and R-S learning in the classical and operant approaches, Tolman's approach could be described as S-S (stimulus-stimulus_ or learning the association between the cue and the expectancy. The theory became highly popular in 1940s and 1950s and in fact several training programmes were designed along similar lines. The training programmes, basically, aimed at strengthening the relationship between cognitive cues (supervisory, organisational and job procedures) and worker expectations (incentive payments for good performance). The assumption was that the worker would learn to be more productive by building an association between taking orders or following directions and expectancies of monetary reward for this effort. Along similar lines, Kohler and his team6 were interested in finding how animals solved problems confronted by them. Chimpanzees were put in a cage with some fruit placed tantalisingly out of reach. A stick was kept in view, so that the chimpanzees employ the stick as a tool to bring the fruit into the cage. Expectedly, chimpanzees retrieved the fruit and Kohler proposed that the chimpanzees solved the problem through the use of insight.

**4. Social Learning:** People can learn through observation and direct experience (also known as vicarious learning which means capturing the lessons of others' experiences) Social learning takes place when people observe the behaviour of others, note their consequences and alter their own behaviour as a result. Thus, social learning is nothing but acquisition of knowledge through processing of information .Watching the boss reprimand someone for being late, would simply make you learn the importance of being punctual. People supposedly learn behaviours and attitudes at least partly in response to what others expect of them. Like operant conditioning, social learning theory also states that behaviour is a function of consequences.

## Modelling

As noted above, people learn a lot by simply observing others and *modelling* those behaviours that seem to lead to favourable outcomes and avoiding behaviours that invite negative consequences. The person whose behaviour is imitated (usually, parents, teachers, peers, motion picture and television performers, bosses etc) is referred to as the model. In a social setting, when those at the head of the table at a formal dinner begin to eat, their actions let the other diners know that starting to eat is now appropriate. According to Bandura[7] for people to learn by observing models, several processes must occur:

Attention: The learner must pay careful attention to the model; the greater the attention, the more effective the learning will be.

**Retention:** The learner must have good retention of the model's behaviour. For fairly obvious reasons, the learner will not be able to remember complex behaviour patterns or complicated sequence of operations enacted or carried out by the model. The behaviour being observed and imitated must be relatively simple. We cannot learn from observing behaviour we do not even remember.

**Reproduction:** The learner must have the physical ability to imitate the behaviour observed. Even after watching the cricket ball being hit with tremendous speed and mesmerising skill on television again and again, we may not be able to send the ball to the fence like Sachein Tendulkar. Also, the behaviour observed must be concrete, not intellectual. We probably cannot learn through simple observation how to write computer software.

**Reinforcement:** Finally, the learner must have some motivation to learn from the model. Obviously, we don't emulate every behaviour we observe. Instead, we concentrate on those we have some reason or incentive to match—such as actions where others were praised and rewarded profusely.

## Self Efficacy

According to Bendura, behavioural modelling enhances employees' self-efficacy. They gain more self confidence when they observe others doing the job rather than merely told to execute the same using discretion. Research evidence also suggests that people who think they can perform well on a task (high self-efficacy) do better than those who think they will fail (low self-efficacy). People with high self-efficacy believe that they have the necessary ability for a given job, that they are capable of the effort required, and that no outside events will hinder them from attaining their desired performance level. In contrast, people with low self-efficacy believe that no matter how hard they try, they cannot manage their environment well enough to be successful. Through constructive pointers (a pat on the back, a' thumbs up' sign, appreciative looks) positive feedback, rewarding small successes etc managers can help improve the self-efficacy of employees.

## Self-Control and Self-Reinforcement

This is the final element of social learning theory. Self-reinforcement occurs whenever an employee has control over a reinforcer but does not embrace the reinforcer without completing a self-determined goal.[8] Like, for example, the employee does not want to take any break before completing the assigned work, out of a strong, self-induced desire to complete the assignment to the best of his abilities. When employees begin to learn behaviours both on and off the job (like running a software package, carrying out performance appraisal, resolving pending customer complaints etc on their own, exercising what is called *self-control*, managers can spare themselves from the gruelling tasks of supervising and controlling from close quarters. In modern organisations, employees in supervisory roles have to inspire themselves through self-reinforcers because there is very little that they could get from "up-stairs" in the form of either positive reinforcement or punishment.

**Box 7.2. Guidelines for using Social Learning Theory to Improve Behaviour in Organisations**

- Identify the behaviours that will lead to improved performance
- Select the appropriate model for employees to observe
- Be sure that employees are capable of meeting the technical skills needed by the new behaviours
- Structure a positive learning situation to increase the likelihood that employees will learn the new behaviours and act accordingly
- Provide positive consequences (praise, raises or bonuses )to employees who perform as desired
- Develop organisational practices that maintain the newly learned behaviours

D.Hellriegel and J.W.Slocum, Organizational Behaviour, Thomson, Bangalore, 2004.

## LEARNING THROUGH REINFORCEMENT (BEHAVIOUR MODIFICATION)

*Reinforcement* is anything that causes a given behaviour to be repeated or inhibited, whether praising an employee for reporting to work punctually or reprimanding an employee for being regularly irregular! Basically, *reinforcement theory* tries to explain behaviour change by suggesting that behaviour with positive consequences tends to be repeated, whereas behaviour with negative consequences tends not to be repeated. The use of reinforcement theory and its concepts to change human behaviour is called behaviour modification.

*Behaviour modification(which is based on the law of effect)* focuses on encouraging appropriate behaviour by controlling the consequences of that behaviour. It takes the extreme view, that behaviour is totally dependent on the environment. Our experience with the environment enables us to change our behaviours so that we maximize positive consequences and minimize adverse outcomes. The *law of effect*, as mentioned above, also proposes that behaviour which is rewarded tends to be repeated, while that which is punished tends to be eliminated. 9

| *Antecedents* | *Behaviour* | *Consequences* |
|---|---|---|
| What happens before the behaviour? | What does the person say or do? | What happens after the behaviour? |
| Rewards for punctuality announced | Employee reports to work on time | Employee gets reward for punctuality |

***Figure: 7.1. A-B-C's of Behaviour Modification***

Although behaviour modification programmes typically involve the administration of both rewards and punishment, it is rewards that are generally emphasized because they are more effective than punishments in influencing behaviour. The term organisational behaviour modification (popularly called OB Mod) represents the application of reinforcement concepts to individuals in the work setting. More specifically, OB Mod, thus, is ***the systematic reinforcement of desirable work behaviour and non-reinforcement or punishment of unwanted work behaviour***

### Basic Steps in OB Mod

OB Mod, developed and used by Luthans and Kreitner, characteristically uses positive reinforcement to encourage desirable behaviours in employees. The basic steps in OB Mod may be listed thus:

**Identification of critical behaviour:** in order to apply OB Mod the manager should try to identify critical behaviours (which have a significant influence on the performance outcome of the employee)that is ,5 to 10 percent of the behaviours that may account for up to 70 or 80 percent of the performance in the area in question—that are observable, measurable and task related. To this end, only direct performance behaviours such as absenteeism or attendance, tardiness or promptness or complaints or constructive comments need to be picked up for close examination. The important point to be seen here is whether behaviour is measurable and if yes, then its impact on performance outcome. When someone is goofing off all the time, it is appropriate to break this down into measurable aspects such as not being at the workstation, being tardy when returning from the breaks, spending time at the water cooler, cutting jokes with co-workers all the time. It is always better to entrust this job of identifying critical behaviours relating to say, offering service to clients or customers to the person who knows the job best—either the job holder himself or his immediate supervisor. This can also be carried out through a systematic behavioural audit, utilising the services of internal staff specialists and/or outside consultants. Job analysis techniques would greatly help in analysing each job in question.

**Measurement of behaviours: O**nce critical behaviours that need to be changed get identified, it is necessary to measure such behaviours in an objective manner through baseline data. The data before the beginning of the change process are called baseline data (usually obtained by observing and counting or by extracting from existing records). The baseline measure would throw light on how the identified behaviour is occurring under present conditions—for example, whether the employee is reporting late less frequently or more frequently, whether such a problem is much smaller or much bigger than originally anticipated. The basic purpose of the baseline measure is to offer objective frequency data on the critical behaviour .Supervisors may complain that employees never seem to be doing assigned tasks. The baseline measure, however, may reveal over 95 percent attendance on an average. Attendance in such a case seems to be less of a problem than anticipated. To gain credibility, it is always better for managers to record behavioural frequencies objectively, rather than rely on general comments and observations.

**Functional analysis of the behaviour:** This step involves a detailed examination of present behaviours being shown by employees to find what consequences each produce, what conditions lead to their occurrence etc. If workers were to indulge in unscheduled breaks, a functional analysis could be carried out to find the antecedents and consequences of such behaviour, recording workers' entry and exit timings ( from the place of work to rest rooms and meeting friends in other departments routinely) as the basis. They might be indulging in such behaviour (unscheduled break) to avoid a boring job say between 11am to 11.15am (behaviour negatively reinforced) or to socialize with friends in other departments or simply light a cigarette between 3.30 to 4 pm immediately before or after tea (behaviour positively reinforced) once the manager is able to identify the antecedents and consequences of such a behaviour, it becomes easy to come out with an intervention strategy.

**Development of an intervention strategy:** This involves development of specific steps for modifying the critical behaviours. Intervention strategies (positive reinforcement, negative reinforcement, extinction, punishment—discussed in the next section) are designed to strengthen desirable critical behaviours and weaken undesirable critical behaviours. The strategy selected must be appropriate to the situation and should produce the desired result.

**Systematic evaluation to ensure performance improvement:** This is the final step that reveals whether the desired behavioural change has occurred or not, whether the intervention programmes have caused improvement in performance or not. In case no significant improvement in performance is noticed, the intervention strategy will be changed by the manager.

## CONTINGENCIES OF REINFORCEMENT[10]

OB Mod includes four basic reinforcement strategies (collectively known as contingencies of reinforcement) namely, *positive reinforcement, negative reinforcement, extinction and punishment*. The term 'Contingencies of reinforcement' explains the various relationships between a person's behaviour and the consequences resulting from it. They represent the conditions under which rewards and punishments would be either given or taken away. .

### 1. Positive Reinforcement

A positive reinforcement is a reward for desired behaviour. In fact, any reward that encourages an individual to repeat a behaviour may be classified as a positive reinforcer. There are two types of positive reinforcers:

- ***Primary reinforcers*** such as food, water and sex are of biological importance in that they are innately satisfying and have effects which are independent of past experiences. For instance, a primary reinforcer like food satisfies hunger need and reinforces the food producing behaviour. However, primary reinforcers don't always reinforce. For someone who has just completed a five-course meal, food may not be a reinforcer
- **A**. ***Secondary reinforcer*** (like money, job advancement, promotion, praise and esteem) is something that once had neutral value bust has taken on some value—positive or negative—for an individual because of past experience. Money is an obvious example of a secondary reinforcer. Although it can't directly satisfy a basic human need, money has value because an individual can use it to buy both necessities and discretionary items. Secondary reinforcers are basically learned ones. They are dependent on the individual and his past reinforcement history. In organisations, secondary reinforcers influence most behaviours. Regardless of whether the reinforcer is primary or secondary in nature, once it is established that the consequence has reward value for an employee, it can be deployed to increase performance.

### Principles of Positive Reinforcement

To ensure that work rewards have desirable positive reinforcement effects, managers should:

**1. Reward only desirable behaviour:** you should give rewards to your employees only when they exhibit desired behaviour. That is, the reward must be contingent on the desired behaviour.(the law of contingent reinforcement) for example, you should praise your employees not for showing up for work on time (an expected part of any job) but for showing up early

**2. Give rewards as soon as possible:** The reward must be given as soon as possible after the desired behaviour (the law of immediate reinforcement). Thus, you should praise an early-arriving employee as soon as he or she arrives, not later in the week. the more time that elapses after the behaviour occurs, the less effective will be the reinforcer.

**3. Clarify what kind of behaviour is desired:** You should tell employees exactly what kind of work behaviours are desirable and what the employees should do to earn rewards.

**4. Find whether the reward has any value for the employee**: The reinforcer will be effective only when it has some value from the employee's point of view. Thus, money would be less of an enforcer to an employee who expects praise and recognition for his effort more.

**5. See that the size of the reinforcer is large enough to entice employees**: The principle of reinforcement size says that the larger the amount of reinforcer delivered after the desired behaviour, the more effect the reinforcer will have on the frequency of the desired behaviour. To be effective in having more than a very limited impact on the motivation of a number of people, rewards should be visible not only to recipients but also to others who possibly could obtain them in future. The principle of reinforcement deprivation states that the more a person is deprived of the reinforcer, the greater effect it will have on the future occurrence of the desired behaviour.

**6. Have different rewards and recognize individual differences**: Recognizing that different people respond to different kinds of rewards, you should have different rewards available. It is always better to have positive reinforcers individually tailored so as to facilitate repetition of desired behaviours. You can offer a word of praise verbally to X, send a congratulatory e-mail to Y, and even send flowers to Z to indicate how delighted you are with their performances.

## Shaping

When the desired behaviour is specific in nature and is difficult to achieve, a pattern of positive reinforcement known as 'Shaping' can be used. Shaping is the creation of a new behaviour through positive reinforcement of successive steps leading to the desired behaviour. Suppose, you have to train new recruits in the customer relations department as to how to interact with customers in a smooth way. The gradual steps leading to the desired behaviour could be outlined thus:

- Greet customer with a smile Make the customer feel comfortable
- Enquire why the customer has come Give a patient hearing
- Get a complete picture of the complaints/suggestions/ideas advanced by customer
- Assure the customer of all possible help; show sincerity, zeal and commitment Lead the customer to the door and have a pleasant parting of ways

Offer praise only when the trainee comes closer to your expectations at each stage. Reinforcement should be given only when the entire first step and an aspect of the second step are completed successfully. Over time, trainees learn all four steps and are given contingent positive rewards immediately for doing the job in an appropriate manner as outlined by you. In this way behaviour is shaped by gradually reinforcing each successive step that moves the employee closer to the desired response (as against changing behaviour all at once)

**Box 7.3. Using reinforcement theory to shape employee behaviour!**

The key to a successful behaviour shaping programme lies in reducing a complex target behaviour to easily learned steps and then faithfully and patiently reinforcing any improvement using praise, recognition, constructive and credible feedback to good effect.

- *Some executives have, in the past, used reinforcement theory to shape employee behaviour quite effectively. Jack Welch of General Electric fame always made it a point to reinforce behaviour. As an up-and-coming group executive, Welch reinforced purchasing agents by having someone telephone him whenever an agent got a price concession from a vendor. Welch would stop whatever he was doing and call the agent to say "That's wonderful news, you just knocked a nickel a ton off the price of steel". He would also sit down and scribble out a congratulatory message to the agent!*

*(Tom Peters and Nancy Austin, A passion for Excellence, New York, Random House, 1985, p.267)*

- Emery Air Freight, a few years ago, encountered great trouble getting packers to use freight containers for shipments whenever possible. To encourage packers to use containers, management established a program of feedback and positive reinforcements. Each packer was asked to keep a checklist of his daily packings, both containerized and noncontainerized. At the end of each day, the packer computed his container utilization rate. Almost unbelievably, container utiliation increased to more than 90% on the first day of the program and stayed at that level. This simple program saved $2 million over a three year period..
- *Continental Airlines used a cash bonus programme to improve its on time arrival record from one of the worst in the industry to one of the best. Employees originally were promised a $65 bonus each month. Continental earned a top five ranking. Now it takes a second or third place ranking to earn the $65 bonus and a $100 bonus awaits employees when they achieve a No. 1 ranking.*

*Kinicki and R. Kreitner, Organizational Behaviour, New Delhi, Tata McGrawhill, 2006*

## 2. Negative Reinforcement

In positive reinforcement, people work hard to gain rewards. In negative reinforcement, people perform acts that help them avoid undesirable consequences For example you may stay late at the office one evening to finalise the project report because you believe that the boss will 'chew you out' if it's not ready in the morning. Most employees follow tea break and lunch hour guidelines to avoid the disapproval of managers or coworkers. The process by which people learn to perform acts leading to the avoidance of such undesirable consequences is called negative reinforcement. This strategy is also known as avoidance learning or escape learning because it forces people to behave in a certain way to avoid undesired or unpleasant consequences. We stop at a red light to avoid a traffic ticket. Negative reinforcement, as the word reinforcement indicates, strengthens a behaviour because It offers relief from an unpleasant situation It is therefore, *used to increase the frequency of a desired behaviour* (whereas punishment is used, it is worth remembering here, to decrease the frequency of an undesired behaviour) In avoidance learning an unpleasant event occurs, until an employee performs a behaviour or escape response to terminate it. Not surprisingly, most students come to class on time to avoid a reprimand from the teacher!

## 3. Extinction

It is the withholding or withdrawal of positive rewards that were previously provided for a desirable behaviour. When rewards are withdrawn for behaviours that were previously reinforced, the behaviour will probably become less frequent and eventually die out. To reduce tardiness, you may offer small incentives to employees reporting to work punctually. Absenteeism comes down as planned. When forced to reduce costs after a while, you may decide to withdraw the incentives. Soon absenteeism may begin to rise as usual. The incentives available for regularity made employees overcome barriers that they encountered in getting to work on time previously. Removal of incentives caused the extinction of valuable behaviour, that is, punctuality. Like a plant without water, a behaviour without occasional reinforcement eventually dies.

## 4. Punishment

Punishment involves presenting an undesirable or aversive consequence in response to an unwanted behaviour. It is the application of negative consequences to stop or change undesirable behaviour. Managers, often, try to check inappropriate behaviour at work by withholding rewards or by initiating company disciplinary procedure. When an employee is loafing, reporting to work late, doing poor work or interfering with the work of others, the manager might resort to reprimands, pay cuts, loss of privileges and discipline involving lay offs and termination

## Consequences

According to psychologists, punishment as a strategy to control behaviour is a lose-lose approach due to a variety of reasons:

- Because neither children nor adults like to be punished. The punished behaviour tends to be only temporarily suppressed rather than permanently changed. Punishment, evidently, reinforces behaviour rather than reducing it. By punishing people for exhibiting unwanted behaviours, managers are giving attention to rule-breakers and attention tends to be very reinforcing. "I call Vijay in, give him heck for goofing up, and he goes right back out and goofs-up again!"
- The punished individual tends to look at the punisher with lot of venom, hatred and resentment. Punishment frustrates the punished and leads to antagonism toward the punishing agent. At the first available opportunity, he (the punished) is ready to settle scores with the punisher in a hostile manner.
- Another problem is that control of the undesirable behaviour becomes contingent on the manager's presence. When the manager is not around, the unproductive employee behaviour is likely to recur.
- Some employees may display physical or psychological withdrawal symptoms when punished repeatedly, leading to high absenteeism and turnover.
- Punishment may suppress employee initiative and flexibility. Instead of exploring creative ways of solving problems on a daily basis, employees simply follow the rule book. Repeated punishments would reduce their self-esteem and self-confidence.
- Those punished would now begin to *hide* their feelings and are *less enthusiastic* to meet the managers who punished them on previous occasions. The reluctance to communicate freely and fearlessly would come in the way of discharging their duties to the best of their abilities.

The use of aversive control, as historical evidence indicates, is the most controversial method of modifying behaviour because it produces counterproductive side effects

## Administering Punishment

Punishment, as the above discussion clearly shows, has several unintended consequences impacting employee behaviour in a negative manner. This, however, does not mean that it should not be used at all. Prohibitive and unacceptable behaviours need to be punished strongly. For example an employee who steals stationery from office, or destroys office furniture in a fit of anger, sexually assaults a co-worker need to be disciplined appropriately. If such behaviours go unpunished, that will set a nasty example. Accordingly, in situations where punishment is desirable as a means of behaviour modification, certain checks and balances need to be incorporated so as to minimize the unproductive consequences.

- *Be clear about what behaviour is unacceptable:* Inform employees about what kinds of work behaviours are undesirable. In a way this is nothing but defining the limits, that is, being late means reporting to work beyond the permissible 30 minutes from the scheduled time.
- *Punish only undesirable behaviour:* you should give punishment only when employees show frequent undesirable behaviour. thus, for example, you should reprimand employees who show up, say, a half hour late for work but not 2 or 5 minutes late. If you begin the bombardment every time they are late by say 2 or 5 minutes, they begin to look at you negatively as a tyrannical boss.
- *Punish the specific undesired behaviour, not the person:* if it is directed at the person, punishment produces strong negative reactions leading to frustration, anger, resentment and hostility. The purpose of punishment should not be to undermine a person's confidence or sense of adequacy as a person.
- *The punishment should be enough to extinguish the undesired behaviour :* Under punishment will not deter the behaviour. over punishment may produce undesirable by-products.
- Punishment should quickly follow the undesirable behaviour. it is more effective when applied at the time the undesirable behaviour is actually performed than at a later time. Calling subordinates into the office to give them a warning for breaking a rule the week before is not effective. Moreover, punishment should follow every occurrence of the undesirable behaviour.
- *Punishment should be administered privately:* A private reprimand can be constructive. There is no use depreciating the worth of an employee in front of others. Those who get punished in public turn resentful and constantly look for opportunities to retaliate violently at the slightest possible provocation. Also, to avoid feelings of resentment toward the punishing agent, punishment should be administered by an agent other than the rewarder.
- *Combine punishment and positive reinforcement:* To avoid undesirable side effects of punishment, persons administering it must always provide an acceptable alternative to the behaviour that is being punished. That is, if you are reprimanding an employee be sure to say what he is doing right and state what rewards the employee might be

eligible for. For example, while reprimanding someone for being late, say that a perfect attendance record over the next few months will put that employee in line for a raise or promotion. If managers fail to provide such a desirable alternative path, the undesirable behaviour will tend to reappear and will unnecessarily cause fear and anxiety in the person being chosen for punishment.

## Schedules of Reinforcement

Now the next question deals with a tricky issue. Should the manager try to reward every instance of acceptable behaviour and punish every instance of unacceptable behaviour? Or is it better to apply reinforcements according to some plan or schedule. Of course, as you might expect, it depends on the situation. A great deal of research into reinforcement theory suggests that the timing of reinforcement has an impact on the speed of employee learning. ***Schedules of reinforcement refer to the frequency with which and intervals over which reinforcement occurs.*** They may be either continuously administered or may be sporadic.

**Continuous Reinforcement Schedule:** A continuous reinforcement schedule reinforces the desired behaviour each and every time it is exhibited. This schedule can be very effective in the early stages of learning new types of behaviour because every attempt has a pleasant consequence. However, performance would decline equally rapidly when the reinforcer is removed. Further, it is administratively impractical (because you have to observe employee behaviour continuously and from close quarters which is not desirable) because employees cannot be rewarded each time they produce something. It is more expensive to administer, especially if the rewards are monetary.

**Intermittent Reinforcement Schedule:** In the real world of organisations, often, it is not possible to reinforce every correct behaviour. Therefore, under intermittent or partial reinforcement, the rewards such as pay, praise, recognition, promotion etc are administered on a random basis. That is, rewards are administered partially with some desired responses reinforced and others not. Four varieties of partial reinforcement schedules have direct application to organisations"

1. **Fixed interval schedule:** The fixed interval schedule offers reinforcement at fixed intervals of time regardless of behaviour. A good example of this schedule is the weekly or monthly pay cheque. This method provides the least incentive for good work because employees know they will be paid regularly regardless of their effort.

2. **Variable interval schedule:** A variable interval schedule rewards desired behaviour at random intervals of time. For example, a bank auditor may make surprise visits to branch offices, say once every six weeks. Since the branch manager cannot tell exactly when the branch is going to be audited, the employees cannot afford to slack off. Another inspection may be closer than they think. Not surprisingly, variable interval schedules are more effective than fixed interval schedules.

3. **Fixed ratio schedule:** A fixed ratio schedule offers reinforcement after a fixed number of behaviours, regardless of the time that elapses between behaviours. For example, suppose members of a sales team know that they will receive bonus for each Rs.10,000 worth of goods they sell. Immediately after receiving the first reward, performance may slack off. But as their sales begin to approach Rs. 20,000, the next level at which reward is

expected, performance will pick up once again! Thus administering rewards under this method tends to produce a high response rate when the time for reinforcement is close, followed by periods of steady behaviour.

**4. Variable ratio schedule:** The variable ratio schedule is based on a random number of desired behaviours rather than on variable time periods. Reinforcement may occur sometimes after 5,10,15 or 20 displays of behaviour. One example is the attraction of slot machines for gamblers. Most of the time when people put a coin into the slot they lose. But, after some unknown number of plays, the machine will pay off. Because gamblers can never tell which pull of the handle will offer the jackpot, they are likely to keep on playing for a long time. An employee performing under a variable ratio schedule is motivated to work hard because each successful behaviour increases the probability that the next one will result in reinforcement. Of course, this schedule is difficult to use for formal rewards such as pay because it would be too complicated to keep track of who was rewarded when.

## CONTRIBUTIONS OF BEHAVIOUR MODIFICATION

OB Mod is a very useful tool for managers to understand human behaviour and improve organisational effectiveness. It helps management to modify or eliminate undesirable behaviour and replace it with behaviour that is more in sync with organisational goals. 'it encourages managers to analyze employee behaviour, explore why it occurs and how often, and identify specific consequences that will help change it when those consequences are applied systematically". As indicated previously, most behaviours in an organisation are shaped by the consequences. OB Mod helps managers to control and regulate the behaviour of subordinates by manipulating the reward system. To influence behaviour, managers have to simply manipulate the consequences. According to Chung and Megginson, the core strengths of OB Mod programmes may be listed thus:

- OB Mod deals with observed behaviours. Therefore, it can be put to testing
- It presents a set of tools by which people can learn new behaviours and skills
- It presents managers tools with which they effectively control and influence the behaviours
- Principles of behaviour modification and simple and easy to understand. Hence, they can become effective users of a Behaviour Modification programme.

## CRITICISMS OF OB MOD

Many people are uncomfortable with the notion of behavioural modification; we don't like to think of our behaviour as similar to pigeons or dogs. Some view the whole approach as manipulative, misleading, and unethical. The behavioural approach has met with lot of resistance and considerable criticism—both from an ethical and theoretical point of view. Let's examine these in detail

## ETHICAL OBJECTIONS

- Behaviour modification tends to equate rats with human beings. Skinner's operant conditioning principles were developed after a series of experiments on white rates. It is said 'organisations are more complex than Skinner's boxies"
- Operant conditioning techniques ignore the individuality of man and constitute a threat to the concept of personal autonomy. These techniques are employed to manipulate and control participants into another person's concept of ideal person.
- According to Waird, the whole idea of changing behaviour through reinforcement tantamounts to bribery as some reward is always offered when the person exhibits the desired behaviour according to the wishes of the change agent.
- Behaviour modification restricts freedom of choice, behavioural freedom and utilization of human capabilities. It tries to exaggerate the powers of behavioural control through psychological methods.
- Behaviour modification insults the intelligence of the average worker. A worker reporting later continuously will understand the relationship between being late for work and docked pay if he walks to the pay section – where he observes the clerk calculate and subtract the pay adjustment. In fact, this is an absurd and fallacious argument because most workers are well aware of the relationship between lateness and docked pay. Walking the individual to the pay section will do little if anything to increase the awareness of the relationship. Again, this may give a chance for workers to take additional time to meet the payroll clerk and manipulate.
- Behaviour modification emphasizes external rewards (money, praise, administered by someone other than the employee himself) and contingent profit plan and ignores the importance of task environment and internal rewards. Relating tasks either to punishment or reward actually reduces the intrinsic pleasure of the task. For example, a professor who derives satisfaction from the intrinsic challenge of doing research in addition to teaching may actually get less—not more—satisfaction when performance is tied to extrinsic rewards.

## THEORETICAL OBJECTIONS

- Behaviour modification disregards employee's perceptions, beliefs and expectations. It is, therefore, an exercise in over-simplification.
- Behaviour modification is not an innovative management technique. It is, in actuality, a revival of Tayloristic management and has some of the same problems as scientific management. Both are inherently autocratic methods of management. In both the cases, responses are made without cognitive attention given to the workers.

## PRACTICAL DIFFICULTIES

- Behaviour modification is labelled as a grossly overrated management technique and is said to be applicable to animals and other humans who cannot make full use of their intelligence. Behaviour modification has been applied primarily with such groups as younger students in schools, delinquents in institutions, patients with varying behavioural problems and mentally challenged persons. All these applications, interestingly, have several things in common like, subjects are dependent on the therapists, they are submissive to the therapists, they have a short term perspective, they carry out only those tasks that are assigned to them. To apply Behaviour Mod, these conditions must be present in an organisation. Organisational settings, in reality, are different from the laboratory environment and hence, the practical difficulty in applying Behaviour Mod programmes in organisations.

- It is an impractical tool because managers are compelled to psychoanalyze workers, tie rewards to performance continuously.
- It is basically a univariate method applied to a multivariate organisation. Quite often it is too difficult to measure the complex human behaviours most employees engage in
- It may be difficult to teach reinforcement principles to lower level managers, design reward systems that help creatively and are not manipulative.

OB Mod should not be treated as a panacea for all organisational ills. It requires considerable administrative skill and effort in managing reward contingencies. The above criticisms will certainly help managers in applying OB Mod carefully and in designing effective reinforcement strategies that will encourage creative, productive and satisfied work force. OB Mod, it must be realised now, is not a bag of tricks to be applied indiscriminately for the purpose of coercing unwilling people. Instead, it must be viewed as a practical tool for shaping, improving and motivating behaviour of organisational members. To this end, these days, it is being used quite extensively in mental asylums, clinics, group therapy, school rooms and even in the homes.

## REVIEW QUESTIONS

1. Describe the basic differences between classical conditioning and operant conditioning. Which type is most important for managers? Why?
2. Explain the concept of learning, supported by examples.
3. Outline the important elements of learning. Can learned behaviour be forgotten?
4. What is meant by reinforcement? What types of reinforcers could be employed by managers to make employees learn new behaviours?
5. Critically evaluate behaviour modification theory and its applications in work organisations
6. What are the controversies surrounding behaviour modification approach in actual practice?
7. Can you identify, discuss, and offer examples of reinforcement schedules?
8. What should be done to ensure that efforts to punish employees are as effective as possible?
9. Distinguish between positive and negative reinforcement
10. What schedules of reinforcement can a manager use to stop employees from fighting with each other?

**11.** How can a manager or a team raise an employee's level of self-efficacy?

**12.** What are the five steps of OB Mod? Briefly summarize the critical dimensions of each step that will help improve employee performance.

**13.** Explain the following briefly

a. Shaping

b. Punishment

c. Self efficacy

d. Law of effect

## CRITICAL THINKING QUESTIONS

**1.** 'Learning Theory can be used to explain behaviour and to control behaviour" Examine the validity of the statement.

**2.** "Any observable change in behaviour is prima facie evidence that learning has taken place" Comment on the statement

**3.** Discuss a situation wherein you have employed behaviour modification to influence someone's behaviour. What did you do actually and what was the outcome?

**4.** How can managers use social learning theory to achieve desired employee behaviours?

**5.** "Learning is involved in almost everything that everyone does" Explain.

**6.** "Behaviour is a function of its consequences". Do you agree? Why?

**7.** Discuss how behaviour modification operates to motivate people? Why is it still important to understand people's needs when using this approach?

**8.** Overall do you think that managers will be able to more effectively change their subordinates' performance by using reward or by using punishment? However you answer what specific steps would you take to make these efforts most effective? Explain your recommendations.

## Case Study: Difficult to Change People Indeed

Raghu Ram's new job as safety and welfare manager with Maruti Construction Ltd (MCL) a large construction outfit from South India, was extremely challenging. Construction industry in India had one of the worst accident records of all industries in recent times, thanks to the pressure on construction companies to complete projects at an unbelievable pace to meet deadlines set by highly demanding customers. MCL's safety record was, of course, better than its counterparts but it was still a matter of great concern. Raghu's understanding of the situation made him believe that when it comes to safety, workers generally resort to short cuts. For example, when it was mandatory to use protective goggles, gloves and face masks while employing power cutter, workers ignored the same completely and felt it was an inconvenient and time wasting tactic. Since site managers and supervisors were under great pressure to meet pre-determined targets, they also turned a blind eye to such unsafe practices. They were more interested in getting the work done on time.

Raghu examined the situation carefully and felt that changing workers' attitude toward safety practices through an education campaign might not work. He knew that to have any impact their behaviour need to change. He also knew that various previous attempts to improve safety, initiated by his predecessor, had failed. These included poster campaigns and lectures from safety experts and sometimes even from medical staff.

Raghu, without wasting much time, came to the conclusion that he should come down very heavily on those who indulge in unsafe acts. Site managers were also strictly instructed to this effect and were asked to reprimand people severely and cut the salaries of those not observing safety rules. Most of their reprimands were given to accident victims or (when it was not the victim's fault) others involved in causing the accident.

The policy seemed to work initially. The first few weeks of the campaign went off peacefully, with a perceptible decrease in accidents. When he discussed the issue with site managers in an excited mood, they did not share his pleasure. Immediately after the meeting, one of the site managers took Raghu to a nearby coffee shop and explained why the policy seemed to work the other way round. The operatives simply were not reporting normal accidents (unless they were really serious) to avoid punishment. As a result of this, the relationships between site managers and operatives had also deteriorated. Site workers did not like site managers reprimanding their unfortunate colleagues who were still shaken and in pain after an accident.

## Questions for discussion

1. Using the concepts and terminology of behaviour modification, explain what went wrong and why
2. offer suggestions about how Raghu might have gone about changing his goal by a more successful route, using OB Mod scheme.

(Adapted from J.Arnold et al., Work Psychology, Longman, London 1991)

# 8

# Interpersonal Behaviour and Transaction Analysis

## UNDERSTAND AND APPRECIATE INDIVIDUAL DIFFERENCES

A manager should be able to understand and appreciate individual differences while managing people, especially in 21$^{st}$ century where the workforce is becoming increasingly diverse—in terms of gender, age, culture and ethnicity. Self awareness helps a manager to find how unique he is in terms of skills, knowledge and experience and adapt himself to the multifarious expectations of people reporting to him. The differences that he is able to find out in others would help him find out that there is no one best way philosophy that he could readily adopt. He should remain flexible, adapt his style in sync with situational requirements and move closer to the hearts of employees through a process of honest communication, rapport building and by adopting appropriate reward management techniques.

### What is self awareness?

Self awareness is the ability to gain control over oneself. It involves setting up clear priorities in life, pursuing them with zeal and commitment. It means steering one's own life with the knowledge about where we are going, why we are going and what lies ahead if we choose a specific path. Self awareness involves being conscious of who you are and how you will react in certain situations. It means taking charge of your emotions and channelizing them to get what you want. Awareness of our selves often enables us to proactively take charge of future events and situations which could put us in a spot. Self awareness stems from reflection, on trying to understand what we do and how we might do it differently to achieve greater success. Self awareness involves self knowledge when we know ourselves we learn to trust ourselves and rely on our own judgment rather than the judgment of others. (my-personal-growth.com,) In short, self awareness is knowledge of one's own personality and individuality. As Coleman expressed it "self awareness means being aware of both our mood and our thoughts about that mood" It is a kind of nonreactive, nonjudgemental attention to inner states.

One way of achieving self awareness is to take time to think things through. Looking at events and situations that impact our lives more closely, more critically and more thoroughly so that we are ready to accept life as it comes. According to Carl Rogers, individuals with a positive self concept are able to take charge of situations in a better way. We generally develop a positive understanding of who we are by undertaking jobs that offer stretch, pull and challenge; by doing things that we like and by caring for something that we deeply love. Of course, experience is the best guide here. It tells us clearly that when we do things that give immense pleasure not just to ourselves but to others as well, we are less stressed and happier. ." It makes us feel not only that what we are doing is worthwhile but that we ourselves are worthwhile. Part of self awareness is recognition of the intrinsic value not just of ourselves but of others."( Kevin Sinclair) When you become self aware you grow as a person. You develop self-acceptance and this in turn makes you more accepting of others. You become more self reliant and self motivated. These are the qualities that help you to continue growing as a person and to be successful in your chosen field.

## The Sensitive Line

When we go deep into our inner-most chambers and find what we are, we get an uncomfortable feeling of not doing things to the best of our abilities and living up to our true potential. Complete honesty with ourselves compels us to get more information for putting us on the right path. The information that we get, sometimes, would be inconsistent with what we are actually. When we return from office, our neighbor would peep in and comment: "You look tired today. Are you feeling okay? Honestly speaking, you may not have done much at the office today, but looked exhausted due to the tiring bus journey that you have undertaken to reach home. The dichotomy between what you are and what others offer information in the form of comments like these—is somewhat minor and so you do not put up a strong defensive reaction. Such information does not compel you to reexamine your self concept from a new angle altogether. However if the information is highly prohibitive, offending and intolerable, you probably would react strongly. For example, if your coworker were to put an accusing finger at your not being able to meet targets and call you an incompetent fellow, you would defend your position to protect the image that you have of yourself. This is known as *sensitive line* which is nothing but *an invisible boundary around one's self image, which, if threatened, will evoke a strong defensive reaction.*

## Threat-Rigidity Response

Often, the uncomfortable information that poses a threat to your self concept would make you rigid, inflexible and uncompromising even (known as **threat-rigidity response** indicating the tendency of almost all individuals, groups and organisations to become rigid, meaning conservative and self protective when faced with a threat) Where the self concept is under threat due to any discrepant information, the individual tires to safeguard his familiar position. The individual, however, would be willing to relent a bit and listen and accept discrepant information(information that is not in sync with his own image of self) that (i) meets some objective criteria set by him over the years, (ii) that is not somewhat unexpected but hits him at regular intervals (iii) and that is within his control .In other words, the individual would be prepared to accept the feedback from others when the discrepant information offered by others is verifiable, predictable and controllable.

## Self Disclosure

The defensive posture of an individual in the face of discrepant information could also be overcome, if the individual is willing to open up before others and discuss aspects of the self that seem somewhat ambiguous or unknown to others. Such a move, known as self disclosure (*revealing to others ambiguous or inconsistent aspects of oneself*), is necessary for self growth. A lack of self disclosure affects self awareness and also negatively impacts other aspects of managerial skill development.

## How Self-Awareness helps managers to develop interpersonal relationships

Self-awareness helps managers identify gaps in their management skills, which promotes skill development. But self-awareness also helps managers find situations in which they will be most effective, assists with intuitive decision making, and aids stress management and motivation of oneself and others.

**Skill development**. Improvement projects should normally begin with an assessment of the gap between the current situation and the desired future situation. Having an accurate sense of who you are helps you decide what you should do to improve. Often, self-awareness will reveal a skills gap that you want to work on.

**Knowing your strengths and weaknesses**. Self-awareness helps you exploit your strengths and cope with your weaknesses. For instance, if you are someone who is good at "seeing the big picture" that surrounds decisions, but not as good at focusing on the details, you might want to consult colleagues and subordinates that are more detail-oriented when making major decisions. Cooperation between big-picture-oriented decision makers and detail-oriented decision makers can produce high quality decisions.

**Developing intuitive decision-making skills**. Leaders with well-developed emotional self-awareness are more effective intuitive decision makers. In complex situations, intuitive decision makers process large amounts of sometimes unstructured and ambiguous data, and they choose a course of action based on a "gut feeling" or a "sense" of what's best. This type of decision making is becoming more important for managers as the rate of change and the levels of uncertainty and complexity in their competitive environments increase. Managers who are highly emotionally self-aware are better able to read their "gut feelings" and use them to guide decisions.

**Stress**. Jobs that don't suit your personality tend to give you more stress than jobs that are more compatible. This is not to say that you should never take a job that conflicts with your personality. However, be aware that you will need to work extra hard to develop the skills for that job, and there are jobs that would be less stressful for you.

**Motivation**. It's very difficult to cope with poor results when you don't understand what causes them. When you don't know what behaviors to change to improve your performance, you just feel helpless. Self-awareness is empowering because it can reveal where the performance problems are and indicate what can be done to improve performance. In addition, awareness of your psychological needs can increase your motivation by helping you understand and seek out the rewards that you really desire such as a sense of accomplishment, additional responsibility, an opportunity to help others, or a flexible work schedule.

**Leadership**. When we understand "what make us tick"—what gets us excited, why we behave the way we do, etc.—we also have insight into what makes others tick. To the extent that other people are like you (and, of course, there are limits to the similarity), knowing how to motivate yourself is tantamount to knowing how to motivate others.

To perfect your management skills, the best place to start is self-awareness. Self-awareness means knowing your values, personality, needs, habits, emotions, strengths, weaknesses, etc. With a sense of who you are and a vision of the person you want to become, a plan for professional or personal development can be created. Moreover, self-awareness allows you to motivate yourself and manage your stress better, helps you with your intuitive decision making, and helps you to lead and motivate others more effectively. Self-awareness is very useful.

## INTERPERSONAL STYLE: THE JOHARI WINDOW

The term 'interpersonal style' refers to the manner in which an individual prefers to relate to others. Two people saying the same thing might do so very differently and communicate their

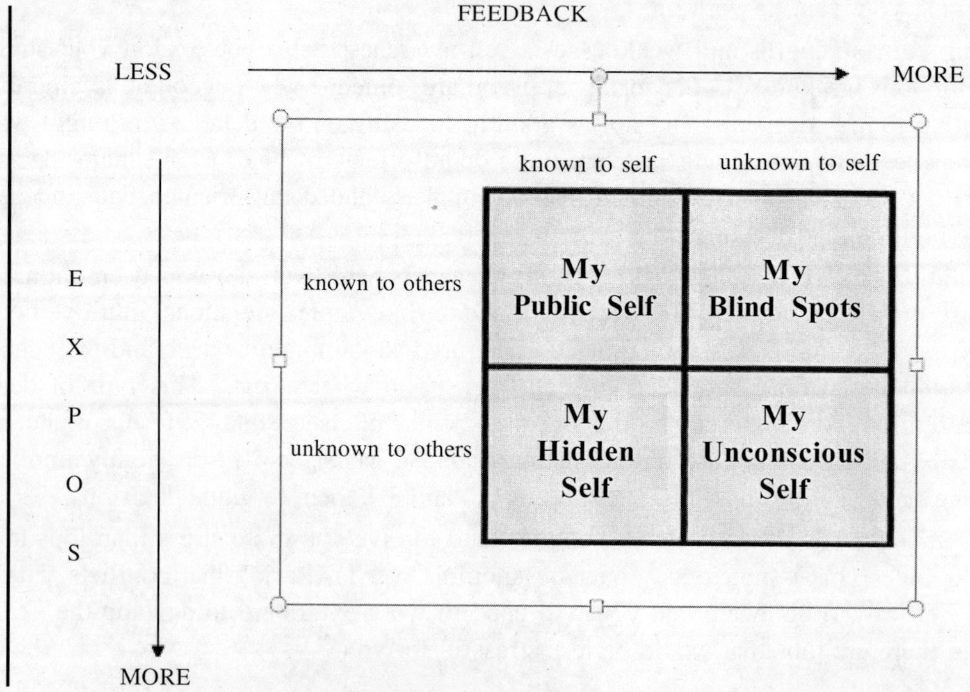


***Figure: 8.1 The Johari Window: Interpersonal Style and Communication***

messages in ways that may have different effects on you. Obviously, there are individual differences in the way people communicate their feelings, opinions and thoughts to others. Joe Luft and Harry Ingham, both researchers at the University of California in the 1950's coined the term Johari Window (a way of looking at how one's personality is expressed) to explain why we do not like to place our cards on the table while trying to relate to others. Luft and Ingham observed that there are aspects of our personality that we're open about, and other elements that we keep to ourselves. At the same time, there are things that others see in us that we're not aware of. As a result, you can draw up a four-box grid, which includes a fourth group of traits that are unknown to anyone:

- **My Public Self or ARENA:** The public area contains things that are openly known and talked about – and which may be seen as strengths or weaknesses. This is the self that we choose to share with others. Here all the information necessary to carry on effective communication is known to both the communicator (self) and the receivers (others). Arena, thus, is the area of common understanding. Parties can exchange information freely and gain understanding quickly when the arena is fairly large.
- **My Blindspots :** Here the relevant information is known to others but not to the self. Others have the advantage of knowing their own reactions, feelings, perceptions and so on while the self is unaware of these.
- **My Hidden self or Façade :** Here the information is known to the self but unknown to others. Information that we perceive as prejudicial to a relationship or that we keep to ourselves out of fear, desire for power or for any other reason, makes up the Façade (or the false front). This is a dangerous sign, because the subordinate knows something that the superior is not aware of. The façade like the blindspot diminishes the arena and reduces the possibility of effective communication.
- **My unconscious self or the unknown:** This is a tricky position. " I do not understand them and they do not understand me." Here the relevant information is not known to anybody. The unknown self is potentially disruptive because it contains hidden characteristics, drives and needs that can be handled effectively if they are understood. Through self disclosure I place my cards on the table and it encourages you to throw light on my blindspots. Such an interactive self disclosure helps me peep into the unknown area and improve my communication skills and you also begin to reap the benefits of improved communication.

## Feedback

As you can see from the above figure, if Arena is very small then there is very little open interaction between the parties. If the Arena is very large, parties get a chance to make correct perceptual judgements about each other and develop healthy working relationships later on.

Expanding the size of arena depends on whether one is willing to 'listen' and others are willing to give information that is essential for effective communication to take place. Active cooperation of others is necessary to get honest feedback.

### Exposure and the inherent risks

The application of the Johari Window comes in opening up the public area, so that the other three areas begin to shrink. This is done by regular and honest exchange of feedback, and a willingness to disclose personal feelings. The process that the self uses to increase the information known to others is called exposure. Of course exposure would put the self in a vulnerable position. Exposing one's true feelings by telling it like it is often involves risks. "If you give people information about yourself, you give them power over you," she says. Monica Lewinsky's disclosure to Linda Tripp and the ensuing scandal that enveloped President Clinton is a case in point. People also misjudge how others respond to secrets. Sometimes you get negative feedback. For example, a women who reveals that she was raped may be seen in the future as a victim, or by men as damaged goods. Now, if you must tell your secret to someone, chose that person very carefully. So you need to pick up some one whose response would help you see the picture correctly. Unfortunately, such a person is often hard to find. So if you are unable to find a trustworthy person, keep the secrets to yourself and remain in control of your own self. Exposure of course helps people to get to know each other closely. People around you will understand what "makes you tick", and what you find easy or difficult to do, and can provide appropriate support. And of course you can then do the same for them .Self-assessment questionnaires can be used to indicate the size of your public window, but any measure is purely subjective.

In order to improve interpersonal communication, both the communicator and the listener must be willing to share information honestly and openly. They must be willing to share feedback as well with an open mind. In terms of Johari Window, large hidden or blind areas hinder effective interpersonal communication.

## TRANSACTIONAL ANALYSIS

Dr. Eric Berne developed a technique (called Transactional Analysis) designed to help individuals communicate with others and understand both their behaviour and that of other people. At its simplest level, transaction analysis is the method for studying transactions between individuals. A transaction is nothing but a unit of social interaction—or simply the interaction between two or more people in a social setting. The basic purpose of TA is to provide better understanding of how people relate to one another, so that they may develop improved communication and human relationship. The central theme of TA is that each person has three ego states (defined as a consistent pattern of feeling and experience directly related to a corresponding consistent pattern of behaviour) that serve as important sources for behaviour—namely the parent, the child and the adult.

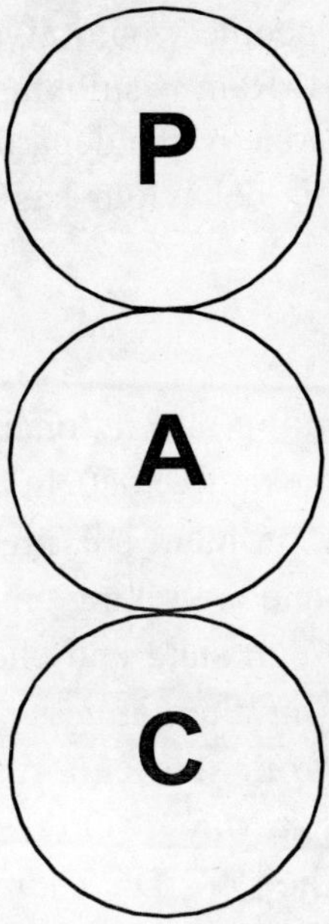


PARENT EGO STATE
Behaviours, thoughts and feelings copied from parents or parent figures

ADULT EGO STATE
Behaviours, thoughts and feelings which are direct responses to the here and now

CHILD EGO STATE
Behaviours, thoughts and feelings replayed from childhood

***Figure: 8.2. Three Ego States***

## The Parent

The Parent ego state is the sum total of feelings, thinking and behaviour that we have copied from our parents and significant others right from childhood. The overall imprint of either a nurturing parent ( be careful, do not hurt yourself; drive carefully, the roads are wet) or a critical parent ( you always get up late in the morning, try harder to improve your grades) is evident when individuals try to communicate with others. Nurturing parent is that part of a person which is understanding and caring about other people. Behaviour coming from the nurturing parent may set limits on and provide direction for people behaviour. It will not put the people down and make then feel not OK as individual. Critical parent behaviour attacks people's personalities as well as their behaviour. Critical parent makes people feel that they are not OK. When people are in their critical parent ego state they are very evaluative and judgmental.

## The Child

The Child ego state is a set of behaviours, thoughts and feelings which are replayed from our own childhood. Examples of recordings in the Child include: "When I saw the monster's face, I felt really scared" "The clown at the birthday party was really funny! These are characterized by highly emotional and/or uncensored behaviour. The child ego state is associated with behaviours that appear when a person is responding emotionally. A person's child contains the 'natural' impulses and attitudes learned from child experiences. There are several forms of the child ego state. However, two kinds of ego states viz. happy child and destructive child are commonly cited. People behaving from their happy child take up things they want to pursue without rubbing people on the wrong side. However, people in their destructive child undertake things that are either destructive to others or to themselves, or to their environment. In understanding the difference between these two types of child ego state, it helps to remember that behaviour by itself is not happy or destructive. Feedback from other people would give an indication whether one is behaving or responding from the child ego state. If Ram is smoking secretly while at work he might be doing so to rejuvenate himself. When someone in the department objects to this but Ram continues to smoke unmindful of consequences, his behaviour has moved from the happy child state to that of a destructive child.

## The Adult

The Adult ego state is characterized by logical thinking and rational behaviour. Instead of getting scared or making assumptions, the adult begins to examine data in an unemotional manner. Behaviour from the adult ego state is characterized by problem solving analysis and rationale decision-making. People operating from the adult ego state are taking emotional content of their child ego state, the value-laden content of their parent ego state and checking them out in the reality of the external world. These people are examining alternatives, probabilities and values prior to engaging in behaviour. Typical statements from this ego state include: consumer research shows we should introduce our new product next May" "On the basis of his education and experience, I think Ram has the best credentials for the job" Dr. Thomas Harris described the Adult as "a data-processing computer, which grinds out decisions after computing the information from three sources: the Parent, the Child, and the data which the adult has gathered and is gathering"[7]

## Analyzing Transactions

When two people communicate with each other, one will initiate a dialogue (transactional stimulus) and the other will respond (transactional response According to TA, a transaction is a stimulus plus a response. For example, if you say to one of your staff, "You really did a fine job on that project" that is stimulus: and he says, "Thanks", that is a response. In terms of Transactional Analysis, now we need to identify which ego state directed the stimulus and which ego state in the other person executed the response. According to Dr. Berne, the **simplest transactions are between Adults ego states.** For example, a surgeon will survey the patient, and based upon the data before him/her, his/her Adult decides that the scalpel is the next instrument required. The surgeon's Adult holds out his/her hand, providing the transactional stimulus to the nurse. The nurse's Adult looks at the hand, and based upon previous experiences, concludes that the scalpel is needed. The nurse then places the scalpel in the surgeon's hand.

**Complementary transactions:** They occur when the speaker is received by the appropriate ego state of the listener and in turn gets back the expected response.

A sick child might ask for a glass of water and the nurturing mother might give the water to the child. The transaction below shows a Parent - Child transaction, with the Child ego state providing the *transactional stimulus*, and the adult responding with the *transactional response.*

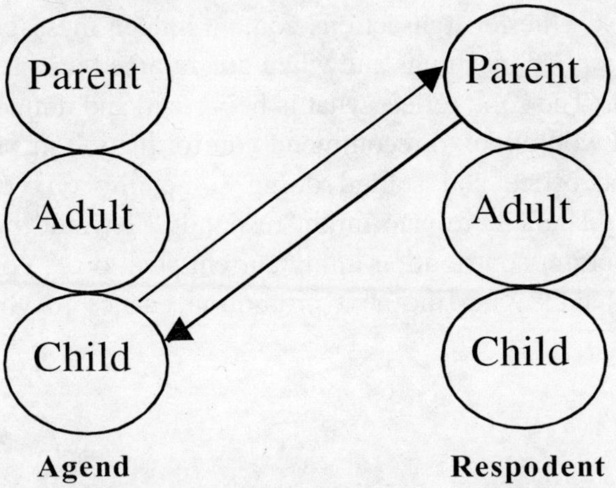


***Figure: 8.3 Complementary Transaction***

When the stimulus (sick child asking for water and responses (mother offering water) on the Parent-Adult-Child (PAC) transaction are parallel, the transaction is complementary. In a complementary transaction, the response must go back from the receiving ego state to the sending ego state. The manager might call a subordinate and say: Ram I would like you to analyse these data and tell me which investment offers the best return (stimulus—adult ego state). The subordinate might respond: "I will get on it right away. We will place the findings on your desk by tomorrow morning" (adult—response)

**Crossed Transaction:** A cross transaction would occur when the communicator receives a response from an ego state other than the intended one. The manager might ask a subordinate: Mr. Gupta it is your turn to prepare the control report. The subordinate might reply: Why me always? It's always my turn. How come you never ask Madhuri?" On a daily basis, the husband might ask: "where is my Parker Pen?" (obviously directed at the respondent's adult) look at the reply from the wife: "You always blame me for everything" Instead of the Respondent's Adult responding with "I think it is on the desk in your study room— it is the Respondent's Child that responds back.

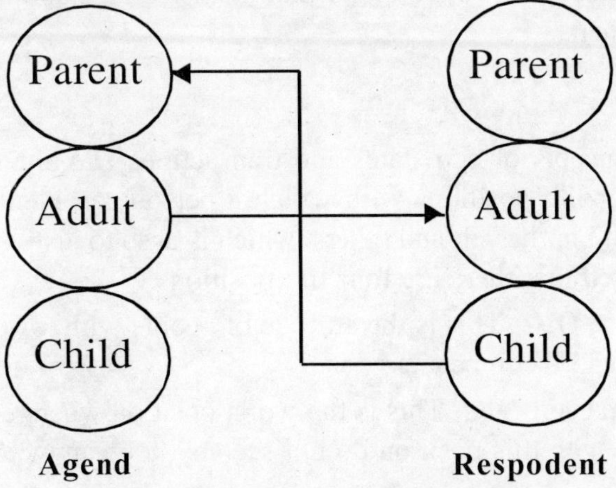


***Figure: 8.4 Crossed transaction***

**Ulterior Transactions:** Ulterior transactions contain hidden messages in addition to what is openly stated. There are implied meanings and when diagrammed it is necessary to use two types of arrows solid and dotted. The solid reflect what is being said and dotted indicate what is meant. The Manager might say: I would like to recommend you for the job in Mumbai. (It is about time you got out of the home office and started doing something on your own, assuming full responsibility for results) The subordinate might respond: " I would rather stay here. I really think I am making an important contribution in my current position. (You must be crazy to think that I would go to Mumbai, leaving the next promotion chance to your favourite guy in the department!)

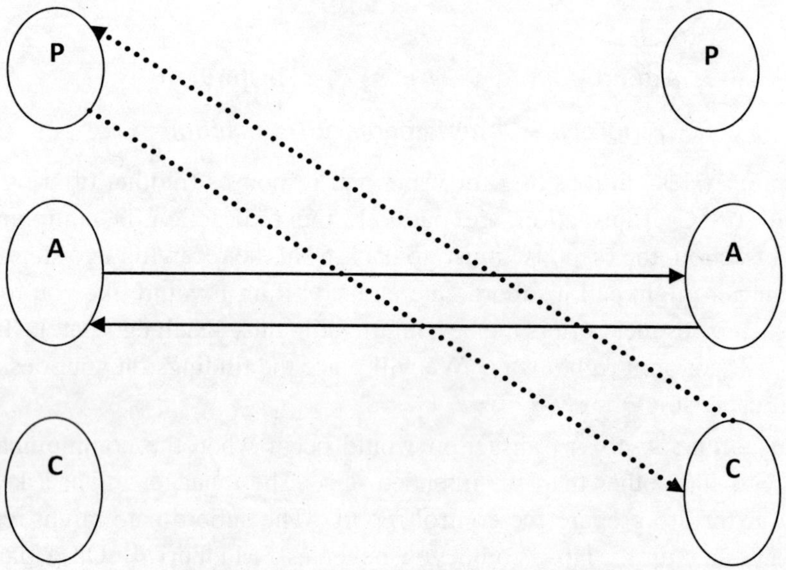


***Figure: 8.5 Ulterior Transaction***

This transaction shows that when there is more than one stimulus and response, communication breakdowns occur—because both parties try to hide their feelings and thoughts more than what they reveal in front of others.

## LIFE POSITIONS

In addition to the concepts of ego states and transactions, TA theory teaches that there are four basic philosophies or life positions with which a person can identify. A life position is a person's basic belief about him/herself and others, which is used to justify decisions and behaviour. Berne (1972; 84) suggested that there are four life positions.

**I am not OK you are OK**: This is the attitude of people with low self esteem. They suffer from feelings of despair and incompetence

**I am not OK—you are not OK**: This is the worst position where everyone is bring branded as a loser. People struck with this position do not see any hope anywhere

**Box 8.1 Four I ife Positions**

| | |
|---|---|
| **I am not ok, you are ok**<br>(Therefore the best I can do is to get away from others or hide myself)<br>DEPRESSIVE POSITION | **I am ok, you are ok**<br>(Therefore you and me can get on with being open with each other)<br>GOOD LIFE POSITION |
| **I am not ok, you are not ok**<br>(Therefore there is no hope. I can never be ok nor could you give me what I need) | **I am ok, you are not ok**<br>(Therefore I best get rid of you to be ok) |

**I am OK—you are not OK**: These people suffer from a bloated ego. They feel superior to others. They remain arrogant and try to put down others and in the process invite lot of problems on a daily basis.

**I am OK ——You are OK**: This is a healthy position. Differences are accepted. You begin to look at people as they are instead of judging them before hand using your own critical lenses—thereby paving ground for developing and sustaining healthy interpersonal relations.

Although people do occasionally embrace different life philosophies or positions, everyone has a dominant style that is reflective of their life perceptions. Most people in an organisation may begin their journey in an emotional manner. They are fond of telling Stories about how others have come in their way, how other people have betrayed them, how others have taken them for a ride. As they begin to understand the dynamics of life in a better way and show maturity in their interactions with others, the life positions seem to change. The journey from child ego state to adult ego state is not an easy one but one can certainly have a healthy outlook toward life—if one is willing to learn from past mistakes. People with an I am OK, you are OK position are able to get along with people—taking life as it comes instead of indulging in a constant game of mutual recrimination and shifting of blame.

## GAMES

It is the interaction of these parts of our personality with the equivalent child, adult and parent in others that make up our relationships. Often, when we are interacting with others, there can be two conversations going on at the same time - our adult can give the impression of talking to their adult, when in fact it's our parent who's talking to their child. Often, these interactions, or transactions as Berne calls them, are normal everyday parts of life. We all need to relate to one another to get along in the world, after all. What he's most interested in, and has spent a long time documenting, aren't these normal interactions - but what he calls "games". He defines such games as "an ongoing series of complementary ulterior transactions progressing to a well-defined, predictable outcome"

They are a series of interactions between people that are superficially plausible, but contain some kind of hidden motive. The ultimate aim of the primary player in such games is to achieve some sort of payoff - usually some kind of emotional reward. The early moves are set up so as to maximize the likelihood of this payoff being achieved. The use of the word "games" should not give the impression that such activities are necessarily fun or played light-heartedly. Often the outcomes, though predictable, can be very damaging and distressing.

**Box 8.2 Games and Outcomes**

| *Game* | *Description* | *Real benefit* |
|---|---|---|
| Stop me if you can | Damaging activity, for example using drugs. | Gets attention, avoids responsibility |
| Blemish | Finding fault with others. Being as picky as necessary | Distracts attention from self |
| Clever me | Boasting about what you have done | Get attention, sympathy, admiration |
| Courtroom | Describe 'logically' how I am right and others are wrong | Get support, sympathy and absolution |
| If it weren't for you | Blaming others for your non-achievements | Absolution of guilt |
| I'm only trying to help | Offering help then complaining when it is not accepted | Controlling others |
| Let's you and him fight | Get others to fight for you | Control of others, share of blame, friendship |
| Look how hard I've tried | Put in lots of effort that intentionally does not succeed. | Absolves oneself from responsibility. |
| Now I've got you (you son of a bitch) | Vents rage on someone and blames them for it | Displaces anger. Absolves responsibility |
| Poor me | Display self as unlucky and helpless | Sympathy and support |
| See what you made me do | Blaming others for one's own problems | Absolution of responsibility, instilling guilt |
| Honestly | Making empty promises | Getting one's way in the short-term |
| Uproar | Violent argument with deliberate pressing of hot buttons | Sustain attention, venting and displacing anger |
| Yes but... | Providing objections to refuse help | Maintenance of attention and control |
| Wooden leg | Acquire a handicap, real or imagined and ham it up | Sympathy, avoidance of responsibility |

## STROKING

Strokes—in the form of praise, recognition and rewards— are essential to inspire people to give their best to an organisation. Without them the spinal cord will shrivel up—according to Berne. Positive strokes sometimes called "warm fuzzies" are positive reinforcers such as a physical pat on the back or a verbal 'well done'. Positive stroking comes from a healthy state of mind where one begins to see the brighter side of life almost always and is willing to help others through inspiring words of encouragement. Negative strokes put people down and tell others that their words, actions and behaviour are not appropriate. Yelling, name calling, criticisms of various kinds are all part of this unhappy blame game. When played again and again, negative strokes can leave people completely shattered and demoralized.

## BUILDING POSITIVE INTERPERSONAL RELTIONSHIPS: COMMUNICATION

Communication is the bridge of meaning between two people. It certainly helps them move closer to each other and build positive interpersonal relations. Communication is important to all managers, and it is needed by all employees. It pervades everything managers do. In fact, a large part of the manager's time is spent in some form of communication—writing, reading, speaking or listening. Communication is the means by which he persuades, informs, motivates and leads employees towards organisational goals. Not surprisingly, most people judge managers on the basis of their communication skills. Everything a manager does, he does through communication only. An idea, no matter how great, is useless unless it is transmitted and understood by others. Managers might be blessed with extraordinary talent, but if they cannot sell their vision and dreams to others, their future is sealed. Years of formal education, the amount of coaching that young recruits receive in the majestic corporate world, the enormous amount of literature that is readily available on communication would compel us for a second to believe that communication is an easy job. In actual practice, however, it is not easy to communicate with people, that is, make them understand what you are trying to convey—howsoever big or experienced the company might be Take a look at the following examples and you will understand that it is not as easy as it looks like (A.M.Francesco and B.A.Gold; Helen Deresky; R.M.Hodgetts and Fred Luthans,)

**Box 8.3 Miscommunication can have deadly consequences!**

Americans call the storage compartment of the car the "trunk", the English call it the" boot". To get to the 50th floor, Americans take an "elevator", but the English use a "lift". When the English "table an item" in a meeting, they act on it immediately. When Americans table something they expect to deal with it later!

An early translation of Coca-Cola into Chinese meant 'bite the wax tadpole' Coca Cola has since found and trademarked a new Chinese name that means refreshing and delicious.

When Pepsi cola's slogan 'Come alive with Pepsi' was introduced in Germany, the company learned that the literal German translation of 'come alive' is 'Come out of the Grave'

Ford introduced a low cost truck, the 'Fiera' into some Spanish speaking countries.

Unfortunately the name meant 'ugly old woman' in Spanish. Needless to say, this name did not encourage sales.

Finally, one laundry detergent company certainly wishes now that it had contacted a few locals before it initiated its promotional campaign in Middle East. All of the company's advertisements pictured soiled clothes on the left, its box of soap in the middle and clean clothes on the right. But, because in that area of the world people tend to read from the right to the left, many potential customers interpreted the message to indicate the soap actually soiled the clothes.

We are all familiar with situations where we like the company of someone who greets us with a smile, talks pleasantly, shares our concerns, shows lot of empathy and boosts our morale through comforting words and gestures. Positive emotions such as joy, excitement, and interest are products of positive relationships. These emotions, in turn, expand our mental capacities. We are able to learn and perform better. Positive relationships create positive energy and help us realize goals easily.. Positive relationships help us cope better with stress, recover from illness quickly and help us get along with ups and downs in life in a cool and composed manner. When we build positive relations with people, we are less likely to be distracted by feelings of anxiety and frustration. Positive interpersonal relations are energy boosters for others as well. They feel like working to the best of their abilities, participate enthusiastically and remain committed to the assigned tasks. Cooperation among organisational members improves. The things that normally come in the way of organisational performance such as conflict, disagreements, confusion and ambiguity, unproductive competition, anger also get cleared. Every one, therefore, would seem interested in having positive relationships with people all around. But this is easier said than done—because not everyone would behave according to our expectations and dance to our tunes. Communication breakdowns occur for a variety of reasons. The messages, therefore, get coloured and misinterpreted.

**Box 8.4 Nature of communication**

Communication refers to the process of passing information and understanding from one person to another. It involves an exchange of facts, ideas, attitudes, opinions or emotions by two or more individuals. In fact, it is the" sum of all the things one person does when he wants to create understanding in the mind of another." Communication's purpose is to supply the information necessary for job performance and active cooperation—the skill to work and the will to work. Communication is a bridge of meaning between people. By using this bridge of meaning a person can safely cross the river of misunderstanding that separates all people. The essential features of communication are given below:

**Two People:** Communication requires both a sender, who begins the process, and a receiver who completes the communication link. When the receiver provides the feedback that the message was received as intended, the communication cycle is complete.

**Sequential Process:** Communication is a process, involving several steps. First, the sender has an idea to communicate. Second, the idea is translated into a recognisable form such as spoken or written language. This is called encoding information. Third, the encoded message has to usually travel a distance through various communication channels like telephone routes, mail routes etc. Fourth, once the receiver gets the message, he begins encoding — that is, transforming the message back into ideas. Finally, if the idea received by the receiver is the one which was intended, communication has taken place.

**Continuous activity:** Everything a manager does involves communicating not some thing, but everything. A manager must always be in touch with his subordinates, peers and superiors in order to get things done. It is an activity to which every manager devotes an overwhelming portion of his time.

**Pervasive function:** Communication takes place at all levels in an organisation. It is, infact, the artery of an organisation through which instructions, orders and decisions of the management flow down to the lower levels. It also conducts upward the pulse of the workforce — i.e., their ideas, feelings, suggestions etc. It is essential at all levels of management and in all areas of business.

**Transference of Meaning and Understanding**: Communication involves both information and understanding. It takes place when the receiver understands what the sender means to convey. If the idea received by the receiver is the one which was intended, communication has taken place. Effective Communication, thus, is the process of sending a message in such a way that the message received is as close in meaning as possible to the message intended.

**Receiver oriented:** A manager may send a hundred messages, as Newstrom says, but there is no communication until each one is received, read and understood. "Communication is what the receiver understands, not what the sender says"

## BARRIERS TO COMMUNICATION

Several factors may disrupt the communication process or come in the way of effective communication. These can be listed thus:

### 1. Semantic Barriers

Many of our communication problems are semantic in nature, as the same word may convey a different meaning to different people. Studies of the Oxford English Dictionary show an average of over 25 different meanings for each of the 500 most frequently used words in the English language. The word 'productivity' for example, may mean effective usage of resources for managers but for workers it may mean doing more work to get the same amount of salary. For example, see how we make use of the word *make*: (i) A person asks *"what make of typewriter is that"?* meaning, brand, (ii) The production manager says, *"we make office machines"* meaning, manufacture, (iii) The Police Commissioner on the television ask *"did you make the notorious robber"* meaning, identify, (iv) At home the cook says, "I will make dinner" meaning, prepare, and (v) After an argument, the office manager suggests to subordinates that *they take coffee and make up,* meaning patch up. Take another word–'charge'. A manager may place an employee in charge of section. The company charges for services rendered. A person gets a charge out of an article in a journal. When two individuals attach different meaning to a word, a breakdown in communications can occur. Now, look at what happens when companies, too, do not understand the meaning of the words that they use in order to reach out to customers—of course in a different location.

- A U.S airline found lack of demand for its "rendezvous lounges" on its Boeing 747s. they later found that "rendezvous" in Portuguese refers to a room that is rented for prostitution!
- In China, Kentucky Fried Chicken's Slogan " Finger-lickin' good" was translated " so good you suck your fingers"
- The Chevrolet Nova car had trouble selling in Puerto Rico because it sounded like *no va* meaning "it doesn't go"

The use of jargon can also create a barrier to communication. The vocabulary and jargon employed by engineers, statistician skilled mechanics convey little meaning to unskilled and less-educated persons. Breakdowns in communication, thus, result when the sender does not tailor the message to match the knowledge base of the receiver. Further, some people have a limited inventory of words with which to express themselves. Others complicate the communication process through the use of empty and high-sounding words. It should be remembered that words are building blocks, and only the correct use of the blocks can create a structure.

## 2. Interpersonal Barriers

a. *Can't express effectively:* The old expression *"the mouth was in gear before the mind was operating"* reveals one from of breakdown in communication. Some people cannot communicate effectively because they cannot use words and their personality effectively. They might have instructed their subordinates to do a piece of work politely but the subordinates may feel that they have been 'told' to do the work. One's outward appearance, gestures, smile, animation, eyes, bodily posture, vitality and tone are all an expression of one's personality–an imperative tool to win over those with whom one is talking.

b. *Filtering:* Any attempt to alter and colour information to present a more favourable impression is called filtering. Since subordinates are evaluated on the worth of their performance, they try to filter information as it progresses up the chain of command. They short-circuit information and tell the boss what he wants to hear. Such attempts lead to message distortion and an incorrect impression of the real situation is created.

c. *Credibility:* Research has shown that we are more likely to accept information when we have a favourable attitude toward the sender. Credibility is based on a person's competence in the subject area being communicated, and is based on the degree of confidence in the person. All managerial efforts to motivate subordinates would fail if subordinates believe that managers are not credible and trustworthy. Those managers having a high credibility rating find it easy to send messages to subordinates and subordinates, in turn, are more likely to accept their messages, sometimes even blindly.

d. *Inattention:* Inattention is another barrier. We often hear but do not listen. This is more so in the case of highly repetitive material. For example, an employee may pay attention to one 'no smoking' sign but when such signs are put up all over the office, he no longer understands or 'listens' to it.

e. *Perceptual Differences:* Perceptual differences–differences in past experiences, educational background, emotions, values and beliefs—also affect each person's perception of a message or of words. Receivers will accept messages that are important to them. Messages that are against their values would be rejected or misperceived. For example, an accident that has taken place in an office may viewed thus: (i) the manager may regret the loss of a valuable employee: (ii) the safety people may resent the fact that their safety record has been tarnished: (iii) the fellow-employees may see an injured friend; (iv) the office doctor may see an injured employee to be treated and (v) the personnel manager may see the need to find a replacement for the injured person.

f. *Jealously:* Jealousy also plays an important role in reducing the effectiveness of communications. Competent individuals are viewed as a threat to the security of peers and subordinates. Individuals may try to diminish the worth of another person because they are jealous. If the jealous person is able to attract the attention of the manager, the competent person may find it difficult to communicate with the boss.

g. *Information Overload:* Managers are flooded with information from various corners. But there is no automatic thermostat to control and regulate the flow of information. Modern technology makes it possible for the managers to have the veritable mine of information on their finger-tips, no doubt. The effectiveness of communication is likely to be hampered when managers allow themselves to be inundated with bundles of data. Perhaps, that is the reason why managers are forced to ignore or just give a cursory review of too many messages. In this process, inevitably, many of the messages are either overlooked or misinterpreted.

h. *Emotions:* How the receiver feels at the time of receipt of information influences effectively how he interprets the information. For example, if the receiver feels that the communicator is in jovial mood, he interprets that the information being sent by the communicator to be good and interesting. Also, extreme emotions and jubilation of depression are quite likely to come in the way of effective communication.

i. *Time Pressures:* Managers are often subjected to time pressures; because decisions must be made within specified deadlines. Such time pressures can create communication problems. Formal channels get short-circuited in the process of expediting matters, leave some important people in dark, or messages transmitted may be incomplete, rendering communication ineffective.

## 3. Structural Barriers

a. *Hierarchy:* When an organisation grows, its structure expands, creating many communication problems. Messages have to pass through several hierarchical levels. It follows that something may be lost or added by transmission at each stage of the process. Messages are likely to be delayed and distorted.

b. *Status:* Open and free flow of communication is also affected by status relationship in the organisation. Superiors are reluctant to discuss important problems with subordinates because this may expose them completely. Subordinates, in turn, avoid situations which require them to reveal information that might present them in an unfavourable light.

c. *Specialisation:* Specialisation is another barrier. Too much fragmentation of work causes people to be more loyal to their particular departments than to their organisation as a whole. It tends to separate people even when they work side by side. Different functions, special interests, and job jargon can make people feel that they live in different worlds. The result can prevent employees from having feelings of a united family, make understanding very difficult, and lead to errors. Instead of working as one happy, hard-working team they begin to work disorganised groups. Factors like 'tunnel vision,' 'parts mentality' 'sectional interest' 'departmental loyalty' prevent employees from looking at organisational problems in a broader perspective and prevent them from listening to others' point of view in a patient manner.

## Supportive Communication

One of the easiest ways to improve interpersonal relationships between individuals is to use simple, clear language. Keep the message simple and short so that everyone is clear about what to do. Becoming an active listener would help clear the fog to a great extent. Active listening requires an ability to listen for feeling as well as for words. It is actually a state of mind that involves paying full and careful attention to the other person, avoiding premature judgement, reflecting understanding, clarifying information, summarizing and sharing.

**Box 8.5. Tips for effective listening**

1. Stop talking. You cannot listen if you are talking. Nature gave man two ears but only one tongue, which is a gentle hint that he should listen more than he talks. .
2. Show the speaker that you want to listen. Look and act interested. Do not read your mail while he talks. Listen to understand rather than to oppose.
3. Remove distractions and clear your mind before listening Avoid negative mannerisms. Fidgeting, tapping a pencil, playing with an object, or attempting to do another task while listening is a hindrance both to you and to the speaker.
4. Empathize with the speaker. Try to put yourself in his place so that you can see his point of view.
5. Hold your temper. An angry man gets the wrong meaning from words.
6. Ask stimulating, open ended questions. This encourages him and shows you are listening. It helps to develop points further.
7. Encourage the speaker with attentive eye contact, alert posture, and verbal encouragers such as 'yes' 'I see' 'that is fine' occasionally repeating the speaker's last words also helps
8. Put the talker at ease. Help him feel that he is free to talk. This is often called a permissive environment. Above all, do not interrupt him.
9. Delay judgment. Don't decide beforehand that you don't like the speaker or the subject. Give the speaker a fair hearing. Go easy on argument and criticism. This puts him on the defensive. He may 'calm up' or get angry. Do not argue; even if you win, you lose.
10. Summarize. Briefly highlight what the speaker has just finished saying to bring out possible misunderstandings.

More importantly, to be an effective communicator, you must be supportive of others. By supportive communication we are referring to any communication that is accurate, honest and that builds and enhances relationships instead of jeopardizing them. It helps communicators to handle negative feedback, resolve a difficult issue and strengthen relationships through straight forward and open communication based on mutual trust and confidence.

**Box 8.6 Why supportive communication?**

Positive interpersonal relationships developed through supportive communication have practical, instrumental value in organisations. Researchers have found, for example, that organisations fostering these kind of relationships enjoy higher productivity, faster problem solving, higher-quality outputs, and fewer conflicts and subversive activities than do groups and organisations in which relationships are less positive. Additionally, healthy interpersonal relationships produce bottom line advantages. Supportive communication, therefore, is not just a 'nice-person technique' but a proven competitive advantage for both managers and organisations. When handled properly supportive communication could go a long way in developing and sustaining healthy interpersonal relations at various levels in an organisation.

For example, suppose you send a very abrasive and insensitive message to your subordinate. The person is likely to take it to his heart, become distant and distrustful and begin to look at you as an uncaring person. Being attacked, he turns defensive and begins to spend more time on how to save his skin in case of a problem rather than focus attention on your message. In any case, a message that is not carefully drafted will not be understood easily and will only create further headaches for you. This leads us to an important question, that is: what can one do to become a supportive communicator? The following list could enhance our understanding on the subject to a great extent

- **Problem oriented, not person oriented.** Supportive communication puts the finger on the problem causing trouble. The focus is on the problem and the possible solutions rather than turning the blame on somebody. Person-oriented communication puts the blame on individuals and thereby adds fuel to the fire. If you say look Mr. Gupta you are a lazy guy is going to evoke a defensive reply: no I am not lazy. Instead it is better to focus attention on the problem itself by saying that look gentlemen we lost this account as on date—and seek support by asking them: what can we do about it? Communication tends to be far more supportive when it concentrates on the problem and the likely solutions than on one person's beliefs about the traits of another that caused it. The major problem with person oriented communication is that personality traits are not easily changed while behaviour can be changed.
- **Congruent, not incongruent.** Congruence occurs when what is said, both verbally and nonverbally, matches what the individual is thinking and feeling. There is general agreement among researchers that the best relationships are based on congruence. Incongruence can occur under two different circumstances. First, it can occur when there is a mismatch between what one is experiencing and what one is aware of. For example, a teacher may not be aware that he or she is experiencing hostility toward a student, even though the

student is can sense it. The second type of incongruence occurs when there is a mismatch between what one thinks or feels and what one is communicating. This is common in relationships where one party is less than honest while communicating with others. After a series of reprimands in front of colleagues for not meeting targets, if the boss were to come and console the affected person by saying that " I was making noise only to prevent others from going off the track—so don't take everything to heart" sounds very superficial. Such emotional blows expose the boss (X) in front of the subordinate (Y) in a completely naked manner. In future, Y is not going to trust X because the relationship itself has gone sour due to breakdown of mutual confidence in the past encounters. Congruence, it is worth noting here, also refers to matching the content of the words spoken to the communicator's manners and tone of voice. If X were to comment "what a great show by Y especially during the last couple of days" —it is not going to be interpreted in a positive manner. Problematic situations like these occur in organisations in a routine way simply because; people do not know how to communicate without being offensive.

- **Descriptive, not evaluative.** When we try to put others in a spot by saying that 'you are wrong' 'you are incompetent' 'your actions prove that you are an idiot' we are only turning things from bad to worse. Such evaluative statements only evoke strong negative reactions. The other person would immediately turn the tables on us and say: "No, I am not wrong" "you never told us to do this way" "I am more capable than you are, but you never gave me freedom to work on my own ideas" and so on and so forth. When the issue is emotionally charged, people tend to cross all limits of decency and indulge in a game of mutual recrimination and shifting of blame. Such mud-slinging tactics yield counter productive results, always. Many a time you might be trying to find a reason to suppress your own bad feelings and anxieties by putting the accusing finger on others. "you are dumb" implies "I am smart" therefore, I feel better. There is no use getting emotionally charged and join the race to get hold of the neck of someone in case things turn ugly. Such expressions are a poor reflection of your own personality and would always put you in a defensive mode. Because, evaluative communication is going to be self-perpetrating. If you blame me, I will blame you, and together we blame someone else and the game goes on and on without yielding any concrete results.

  An alternative to evaluative communication is descriptive communication. Descriptive communication is basically intended to reduce the tendency to evaluate or to perpetuate a defensive interaction. Descriptive communication involves three steps: First, describe as objectively as possible the event that occurred or the behavior that needs to be modified. This description should be objective in that it relies on elements of the behavior that could be confirmed by another person. Describing a behavior, as opposed to evaluating a behavior, is relatively neutral. Second, describe reactions to the behavior or its consequences. Rather than projecting onto another person the cause of the problem, the focus should be on the reactions or consequences the behavior has produced. Describing feelings or consequences also lessens the likelihood of defensiveness since the problem is framed in the context of the communicator's feelings or objective consequences, not attributes of the subordinate. Third, suggest more acceptable alternative. This helps the other person save face and feel valued by separating the individual from the behavior. The self-esteem of the person is preserved; it is just the behavior that should be modified.

- **Validating, not invalidating.** Validating communication helps people feel recognized, understood, accepted, and valued. Communication that is invalidating arouses negative feelings about self-worth, identity and relatedness to others. It denies the presence, uniqueness or importance of other individuals. Barnlund's (1968: 618) observation more than a quarter-century ago is even more true today: People often do not take time, do not listen, do not try to understand, but interrupt, anticipate, criticize, or disregard what is said; in their own remarks they are frequently vague, inconsistent, verbose, insincere, or dogmatic. As a result, people often conclude conversations feeling more inadequate, more misunderstood, and more alienated than when they started. Communication that is superiority oriented gives the impression that the communicator is informed while others are ignorant, adequate while others are inadequate, competent while others are incompetent. It creates a barrier between the communicator and those to whom the message is sent. Superiority-oriented communication can take the form of put-downs, in which others are made to look bad so that the communicators look good, or it can take the form of "one-upmanship" in which the communicator tries to elevate himself or herself in the esteem of others. One form of one-upmanship is withholding information either boastfully or coyly to trip people up. Boasting almost always makes others uncomfortable, mainly because it is design to convey superiority. Another common form of superiority-oriented communication is the use of jargon, acronyms or words used in such a way as to exclude others or to create barriers in a relationship. Doctors, lawyers, government employees, and mainly professionals are well known for their use of jargon or acronyms, designed to exclude others. Speaking a foreign language in the presence of individuals who don't understand, it may also be done to create the impression of superiority. Manager's communication validates the subordinate when it identifies areas of agreement and joint commitment. One way to express validation based on agreement is to identify positive behaviors and positive attitudes as well as negative ones during the process of coaching and counseling. The manager should point out important points made by the subordinate before pointing out trivial ones, areas of agreement before areas of disagreement, advantages of the subordinate's statements before disadvantages, compliments before criticisms and positive next steps before past mistakes. The point is, validating other people helps create feelings of self-worth and self-confidence that can translate into self-motivation and improved performance. Invalidation seldom produces such positive outcomes, yet it is a common form of management response to subordinates.
- **Supportive communication is specific (useful), not global (not useful)**. Generally, the more specific the communication the more motivating it will be. A department head who says to a faculty member, "You have trouble managing your time" is too general to be useful. A more specific comment might be "You spent an hour today photocopying articles when you could have asked the secretary to do it." Specific statements avoid global statements that might lead to defensive-ness. For example, the global statement "You have no consideration for others' feelings" is likely to be met with a defensive

statement "Yes I do, I am always con-siderate of others' feelings." A specific statement is much more effective: "By using sarcasm in your re-sponse to my question, you gave me the impression that you don't care about my feelings." The response is more likely to not be defensive: "I'm sorry. I know I am often sarcastic without thinking of how it affects others."

- **Supportive communication is conjunctive, not disjunctive**: Conjunctive communication is joined to previous messages in some way. It flows smoothly. Disjunctive communication is disconnected from what was stated before. Communication can become disjunctive in at least three ways (Whetton and Cameron, 2007). First, there can be lack of equal opportunity to speak. When one person interrupts another, when someone dominates by controlling "air time," or when two or more people try to speak at the same time, the communication is disjunctive. Second, extended pauses are disjunctive. When speakers pause for long periods in the middle of their speeches or when there are long pauses before responses, the communication is disjunctive. Pauses need not be total silence; the space may be filled with "umm," "aaah," or repetition of something stated earlier, but the communication does not progress. Third, topic control can be disjoined. When one person decides unilaterally what the next topic of conversation will be, the communication is disjunctive. These three factors-taking turns speaking, management of timing, and topic control-contribute to what Wiemann (1977) called interaction management. They have been found to be crucial in supportive communication. In an empirical study of perceived communication competence, Wiemann (1977) found that "the smoother the management of the interaction, the more competent the communicator was perceived to be." People who took turns, who did not dominate with pauses or excessive air time, and who connected what they said to what others had said in the first were judged as competent communicators.
- **Supportive communication is owned, not dis-owned**. Owning communication uses first-person words such as "I" and "me." Disowning communica-tion uses third-person words or first-person plural words such as "we think" or "one might say." The problem with disowning communication is that the communicator avoids investing in the relationship be-cause he or she has not taken responsibility for the message. A junior faculty member may perceive dis-owned communication from his or her department head as uncaring and aloof. It fosters ambiguity since the faculty member may feel that the department head's statements reflect someone else's viewpoint. Glasser based his approach to mental health (reality therapy) on the assumption that taking responsibility for one's statements builds both self-confidence and self-worth. The same can be assumed in the department head/ faculty member relationship.

Supportive communication requires listening, not one-way message delivery. The previous seven attributes of supportive communication focus on mes-sage delivery. However, just as important is listening effectively and responding to the other person's state-ments. "In any conversation, the person who talks the most is the one who learns the least about the other person." Therefore, a good department head must be a good listener. Listening is perceived as being important to effec-tive communication. Kramer reported that good listen-ing skills accounted for 40% of the variance associated with effective leadership. Indeed, people judged to be the most "wise" and the most sought-after for interaction are also the best listeners .About 80% of most people's responses are evaluative or judging. A goal of supportive communication is to suspend judgment and evaluation as a first response to a statement. This is neither easy nor automatic. When people are preoccu-pied with meeting their own needs (eg, I must win this discussion), have already made a prior judgment, or view the communicator negatively, poor listening re- sults. According to Rogers and Farson, good listening conveys that:

*I'm interested in you as a person, and I respect your thoughts and even if I don't agree with them, I know they are valid for you. I feel sure you have a contribu-tion to make. I think you're worth listening to, and I want you to know I'm the kind of person you can talk*

## WAYS TO IMPROVE INTERPERSONAL COMMUNICATION SKILLS

Communication skills help managers in selling their ideas quickly and effectively. They can move closer to the hearts of their employees easily. They can empathize with people and understand what the other side feels and thinks about various organisational policies, procedures and methods. They become better listeners and better communicators. In short, they are able to get along with people comfortably. In their own self interest, therefore, managers need to understand the nuances of the game. Some of the important ways of achieving this may be listed thus:

- **Listen and observe**. If you have really poor communication skills and can't seem to get any word across, be it at your work place or even with regards to your personal relationships, you must always remember you need to observe those people who communicate effectively. Look and observe those people around you who make easy and effective conversations. This should give you an insight and an understanding that should open up new ways for effective communication skills. To be able to communicate well, you need to listen to what others says patiently and attentively. You should take time before responding to views expressed by others.

  **Be positive**: Think about your positive points when you are about to start off on a great conversation. This will help you overcome the initial hiccups especially if you are going to give a speech before a very large audience.

  **Have a sense of Humour**: Having a sense of humor helps to make any conservation light and fun to be in! Develop your sense of humor and use it as an effective way to improve your communication skills. Do note one important thing in such cases. Always remember you must not hurt the sentiments of others in any possible way.

  **Read as much as you can**: It pays to read as much as you can before opening up your ideas, thoughts and feelings. A well read person's views are welcomed and even respected.

  **Be flexible**: Avoid thinking that what you say is always right. This may create a certain barrier beforehand in any conversation. Listen to the other viewpoints before you judge anything. This will help you to assess the situation better.

  **Rethink, reframe and refine your words**: Rethink about the ways you are framing your sentences. Ways to improve communication skills would also need you to frame your sentence in a better manner to avoid offending the person. Sometimes you may reply in such a way that it may seem to make the other person feel aggravated towards the way you speak. Remember, at work, even if you are displeased, sometimes an effective manner of speech can help you to get better results rather than yelling your head off about the same.

**Take care of your body language**: Sporting the right kind of body language can also help you to improve your communication skills. Having a good conversation can turn to be more effective when you combine it with the right posture. Maintain eye contact when you speak. Sit and stand in an erect position and have a firm handshake. All these factors are also very necessary for effective conversations.

**Be polite and courteous**: Polite and courteous replies would help you move closer to the hearts of your subordinates. You need to be careful about not hurting others' sentiments and feelings—always. You should also not rub people on the wrong side. And remember not to drag people into an argument. In an argument, even if you win, you lose.

- **Speak interestingly**: Another way to improve communication skills would be to get other people interested in your conversation as well. This will help them to open up and you can have a great time talking about various topics. Ask questions that would urge others to speak as well. Remember, that having good communication skills is not only about talking all the time, it is also about how you get others interested enough to participate in the conversation with you.

Good communicators endear themselves to people through their words, deeds, actions and body language. They have a special way of smiling at you, shaking hands with you, and even embracing you with love and affection sometimes. They are good at pleasing others through their excellent mannerisms. They choose words carefully, respond politely and encourage you, more importantly, to get a feeling that you are the most important part of the conversation. They talk less and do more. Yes, one of the ten commandments of communication, as stated by Keith Davis, also succinctly summarises this eloquently:

**Box 8.7 TEN COMMANDMENTS OF GOOD COMMUNICATION**

1. STOP TALKING.
   You cannot listen if you are talking.
   Said Polonious (in Hamlet), "Give every man thine ear, but few thy voice."
2. PUT THE TALKER AT EASE.
   Help him feel that he is free to talk. This is often called a "permissive environment."
3. SHOW HIM THAT YOU WANT TO LISTEN.
   Look and act interested. Do not read you mail while he talks. Listen to understand rather than to reply.
4. REMOVE DISTRACTIONS.
   Don't doodle, tap, or shuffle papers. Will it be quieter if you shut the door?
5. EMPATHIZE WITH HIM.
   Try to put yourself in his place so you can see his point of view.
6. BE PATIENT.
   Allow plenty of time. Do not interrupt him. Don't start for the door or walk away.

7. HOLD YOUR TEMPER.
   An angry man gets the wrong meaning from words. "He who angers you, conquers you."
8. GO EASY ON ARGUMENT AND CRITISM.
   This puts him on the defensive. He may "clam up" or get angry. Do not argue, "if you win, you lose."
9. ASK QUESTIONS.
   This encourages him and shows you are listening. It helps to develop points further.
10. STOP TALKING.
    This is first and last, because all other commandments depend on it.
    You just can't do a good listening job while you are talking.
    "Nature gave man two ears but only one tongue, which is a gentle hint that he should listen more than he talks!"

## REVIEW QUESTIONS

**1.** Explain the key dimensions of self-awareness

**2.** Write short notes on the following:
(a) the sensitive line, (b) the concept of self (c) Self awareness (d) Supportive communication

**3.** Managers who tend to take things lightly and do not get rattled by sudden turn of events seem to be doing well on their jobs. do you agree with this view? Why and why not?

**4.** What is the impact of values on behaviour? How do you, as a manager, propose to manage individual differences in values?

**5.** "To be a successful manager, you must be constantly learning in the $21^{st}$ century" do you agree with this view? Why or why not?

**6.** Explain the following concepts briefly:
1. Johari Window; 2. Transactional analysis

**7.** Comment on the following statement: " self understanding is a prerequisite to self-improvement and change"

**8.** Explain various ego states? What do you mean by transaction analysis?

**9.** What are the three ego states in transaction analysis? Give an example of each of the three major transactions. What are the strokes in transaction analysis. Give example of some you have received in the last day or two

**10.** Briefly summarize the four Selfs' in the Johari Window. What implications does each have for *interpersonal conflict* (this topic being discussed in the chapter on Group Behaviour and Managing Conflict)

**11.** Explain the following
1. Barriers to communication
2. Supportive communication
3. Ten commandments of communication
4. Nature of communication

## Case study: The Sales Girls

The Roopchand Departmental Stores, New Delhi, has a separate section to sell winter garments. This section consists of two groups: permanent clerks and temporary clerks appointed during winter season. Unfortunately, this section has always witnessed a tug-of-war situation between permanent and temporary clerks. The story begins thus:

The permanent clerks, by virtue of their long and fruitful association in the departmental stores, had developed intimate social relations among themselves. Usually, they take their lunch and tea together. They worked, like a well-knit group, in close proximity and not surprisingly, developed close relations even after the work is over. The slack period starting from April to September every year had given them wonderful opportunity to sit together, discuss about matters of common interest, peep into each other's minds and if possible solve their problems to mutual advantage. Presently, all of them are unmarried with the exception of two.

The temporary clerks were school girls who are normally appointed before the commencement of winter. Often, they have complained about their work in the winter garments section and two of the clerks even desired transfer to some other section after a short stay. The reasons are quite obvious. The permanent clerks bothered little about helping the newcomers. If the newcomer is not able to strike a deal with a customer, often, the permanent clerks joined hands in throwing arrows of uncharitable criticism before the section-in-charge. Being small in number, the temporary clerks could not resist the frequent onslaughts, which are at times irritating and insinuating. The temporary clerks had very little scope to let off steam.

In this heated atmosphere, the determination of commission on sales remained a contentious issue. The permanent clerks had through an informal understanding, agreed not to boost sales. They feared, inherently, that fluctuations in sales would lead to fluctuations in employment. At the same time, they could not tolerate the sight of a temporary sales person pocketing a fair share of commission. They always felt that the temporary ones do not deserve any commission, because they have not contributed anything on a continual basis for the development of the Department. Suffering from an inflated ego, they also believed that they had the right temperament and skill to boost sales. Thus, in every way, the temporary sales clerks are inferior to them. Recently an unhappy situation has developed when one of the temporary clerks is able make a substantial sale to one of her acquaintances. Now, the permanent clerks began to make a hue and cry regarding the commission payment. The poor sales clerk came to the assistant sales manager with tears after having been scolded bitterly by the permanent clerks for having sold a few sweaters in their absence.

The temporary clerks were always anxious to show good performance so as to earn a position in the department. To prevent this, the permanent clerks used to furnish false information about garments' quality, negotiable price etc. Whenever the temporary clerk sought the help of a senior in selling the garments to the customer, the latter would take over and claim the commission on sales herself. The temporary clerks were often assigned to insignificant tasks like arranging displays, rearranging garments, bringing garments from stores etc., and were prevented from striking it rich with customers. At every stage the temporary ones are taken for a ride by the senior clerks.

## Questions

1. How do you explain the behaviour of permanent clerks in the winter garments section?
2. Does the management derive any benefits from the increased cohesiveness of permanent clerks?
3. Is it realistic to find employees doing average or below average work and still consider themselves as top notch sales persons as in the above case?
4. What would you do if you were assistant sales manager in this case?

# UNIT 3: GROUP BEHAVIOUR AND TEAM DEVELOPMENT

# 9

# GROUP BEHAVIOUR

## UBIQUITOUS NATURE OF WORK GROUPS

Groups are an essential part of organisational life. They are found in all types of organisations. Sometimes, when they work with zeal, enthusiasm and commitment, accomplishment of goals becomes easy. Organisations scale to new heights. But most of the time, members of different groups seem to work to further their own narrow, self-interests with disastrous consequences. They spread rumours, indulge in gossip, spread juicy bits of news about others with reckless ease and do not hesitate to cut each other's throat, when confronted with choices not acceptable to them. The shouting brigade in every organisation, especially those with trade union links, provoke gullible employees to the point of breakdown, even on trivial issues—just to show their brutal strength. Organisations, therefore, require managers with excellent communication and interpersonal skills to handle such warring groups—who seem to be fighting always for space, resources, promotions and what not. Groups, of course, help people to move closer to each other. They offer an excellent means to share emotions, feelings, concerns. They can convert work into fun through camaraderie. When handled properly, to cut short a long argument, groups can inspire members to rise to the occasion and achieve the impossible!

### Group vs. Crowd

**A group is a collection of two or more interacting individuals (i. *mutual interaction*) with a stable pattern of relationships between them (ii. *regular face to face interaction over a sustained period of time*) who share common goals (shared interest) and who perceive themselves to be a group (*mutual awareness and collective identity*)** A collection of individuals that constantly undergoes a change—for example the people inside a bank waiting to collect a draft, cash etc—cannot be thought of as a group. Keeping this in the background, the important features of a group may be listed thus: (Homans; Schein ;Turniansky et al; Forsyth)

**Box 9.1 The Nature of Groups**

- ***Two or more persons:*** For a group to exist, it must have at least two members. The members are all dependent on one another. In a work situation, each individual is aware that the overall job cannot be achieved without assistance from others.
- ***Interaction:*** Each member must interact with one more member of the group on a regular basis. Some form of communication must take place i.e. either face-to-face, over a telephone, or through a computer network.
- ***Reasonable size:*** Groups could grow to any size. However, from an organisational point of view, we are concerned with groups of reasonable size. It is difficult for group members to interact with each other closely, when the size grows beyond a manageable number.
- ***Shared Goal Interest:*** Members of a group must have some common goals or shared interests. They need not agree with all the purposes of a group. If a group has a variety of goals or interests, each member of the group must share at least one of the group's interests.
- ***Stability:*** Groups must have a stable structure. Groups can change and often they do, but there must be some stable relationships that keep group members together and functioning as a unit.
- ***Collective Identity:*** Each member of the group must believe that he is a member of, is participant in some specific group. It is the awareness of each other that clearly differentiates a group from a mere collection of persons (passengers in railway compartment, students in a class, customers in a departmental store etc.).

A group is different from a crowd, which is nothing but a transitory collection of people who don't interact with one another, like a crowd gathering on the roadside watching an accident. An example of a work group would be a collection of 8 employees meeting to exchange information about various companies' policies on wages and working hours.

Generally speaking, members of an **effective group**

- Know each other well, and know why the group exists
- Communicate freely among themselves
- Have shared goals
- Receive help from one another and offer help to one another
- Put out fires within the group itself
- Constantly find out where they stand and try to improve their own and the group's functioning.

The team "**Group Dynamics**" is concerned with the interactions and forces among group members in a social situation. More specifically, it refers to the (i) interactive nature of the groups, as to how they are formed, (ii) what their structures and processes are, (iii) how they function and affect individual members, other groups and the organisation.

## Reasons for Formation

The reasons for group formation may be listed, thus:

- **Warmth and Support:** Groups provide warmth and support to individuals. Man needs others to feel fulfilled. When individuals are deprived of that warmth and support, they suffer. Aloneness leads to a degree of insecurity. In fact, the harshest punishment that can be given to a prisoner in the US Penal System is to be put in solitary confinement for a given period of time. Elton Mayo observed that employees who are isolated from each other because of plant layout find their jobs less satisfying than those group members who are able to socialise on the job.
- **Power:** In numbers there is considerable strength. What cannot be achieved individually could be obtained through joint, coordinated efforts. Membership in a union, for example, provides workers with the bargaining strength that they lack as individual employees.
- **Affiliation:** Regular interaction with members has a tonic effect on the psychology of members in a group. Exchanging smiles, cutting jokes, shaking hands with each other, participation in office politics, gossip keeps the environment lively and most members have a genuine hunger for such lively social interaction on a regular basis.
- **Security:** It is better to join a group rather than standing alone. Left alone, you can be pushed to a corner. Group or team members often collaborate to protect their interests from outside pressures or threats. Groups can also assist in solving work related problems and also to militate against stressful or demanding work conditions.
- **Recognition:** The work group is a primary source of recognition and esteem for many individuals. It gives an individual, recognition status and further opportunity to relate to others. Joining a high status group can help an individual acquire esteem in the eyes of persons outside the group whether or not he is a distinguished member of the group. Group membership provides opportunities for recognition and praise that are not available outside the group.
- **Proximity:** People tend to form groups with people who either live or work in close proximity to each other, generally belonging to the same work area. The proximity makes it possible for people to learn about the characteristics of others and offers an excellent opportunity to exchange thoughts, ideas and attitudes regarding on and off-the-job activities. This leads to mutual interaction (relieves boredom) and helps in establishing and stabilising perceptions of the work place.
- **Goal accomplishment:** Another reason as to why a person joins a group is his feeling that the group can help him accomplish goals. Organisational tasks demand cooperative effort of a number of people. The formal or informal group can be extremely useful in solving specific work problems or in preventing the individuals from committing mistakes on the job. "The variety of experience and expertise among members provides a synergetic effect which can be applied to the increasingly complex problems of modern organizations" (Mullins) After all, two heads are better than one, especially when you pool the knowledge, skills, experience together to accomplish a task.

## TYPES OF GROUPS

There are many different kinds of groups and many different ways of classifying them.. (Turner)

## FORMAL GROUPS

Formal groups are consciously created by managerial decision to accomplish the stated goals of the organisation. Organisations, in actual practice, are made up of a number of formal groups that exist at various organisational levels. Usually the head of the group plays an important 'linking pin' role that ties the formal group horizontally and vertically with the rest of the organisation. Formal groups may be permanent(command group) or temporary (work or task group).

**(i) Command Group:** It consists of a supervisor or manager and his subordinates who are a formal part of the organisation, i.e., those who have the legitimate power to give orders to others. They are relatively permanent formal groups that are presented in the chain of command on an organisational chart. They are officially created—with clear cut rules specifying who reports to whom— to carry out routine activities on an ongoing basis.

**(ii) Task Group:** It is a group put together by an organisation to complete a particular task or project— such as developing a new product, reviewing a promotion policy, examining a proposed grievance procedure— within a specified time frame. Unlike command groups, a task group consists of individuals with some special interest or expertise n a specific area, regardless of their positions in the organisational hierarchy. Being a member of a task group is not a full time assignment; it is a work assignment that temporarily takes individuals away from their command groups to work on a common problem. Task groups often disband once the assigned task is accomplished.

A task group is often called a committee, task force, or project group. A *project group* consists of individuals from many different areas or backgrounds. The group's purpose is to achieve its objective within specified time, cost, and quality limits, after which the group is disbanded Project groups are often employed in building spacecraft, skyscrapers, bridges, and ships. They are also pressed into service while designing new products and solving particularly complex problems. *Committees* are groups whose major responsibilities are to examine, analyse, and/or evaluate particular areas of organisational operations. Committees usually have only advisory authority.

## INFORMAL GROUPS

*Informal groups* are those in which membership is voluntary; they evolve gradually among employees with common interests. For instance, in many companies the female executives get together once or twice a month to discuss the particular challenges or problems they are facing in their jobs. A group of junior commercial loan officers in a bank might also constitute an informal work group. They might meet for lunch regularly to discuss common problems or to share work-related information. Employees may be members of several information groups. The following Table 9.1 brings out the differences between formal and informal groups clearly.

**Table 9.1. Characteristics of Formal and Informal Groups**

| *Characteristics* | *Formal Groups* | *Informal Groups* |
|---|---|---|
| Objective | Task accomplishment | Member satisfaction |
| Origin | Management | Individual members |
| Structure | Formal | Informal |
| Orientation | Task oriented | Relation oriented |
| Influence | Formal authority | Personality |
| Leadership | Formal leader | Informal leader |
| Control | Formal controls | Social sanctions |

Informal groups may be classified into three categories:

**(i) Friendship Groups:** Friendship groups are associations of people who like each other and who like to be together. They are formed because, members have something in common, such as social activities, political beliefs, religious values, or other bonds of attraction. Friendship group in organisations often extend their interactions to off-the-job activities, such as bowling leagues, softball teams, and bridge clubs.

**(ii) Interest Groups:** Individuals who may not be members of the same command or task group may affiliate to achieve some mutual objective. Employees grouping together to present a unified front to management for more benefits and waitresses pooling their tips are examples of interest groups. Also, the objectives of such groups are not related to those of the organisation but are specific to each group.

**(iii) Reference Groups:** A reference group is a special type of informal group that people use to evaluate themselves. Reference groups serve two important and related functions: social validation, which helps as justify and legitimate our attitudes and values; and social comparison, which helps us evaluate what we do by comparing ourselves to others.

## MODELS OF SMALL GROUP BEHAVIOUR

There are many ways of studying groups. Three of the widely employed models for analysing causal relationship in small groups are discussed below:

### Sociometric Analysis

Moreno's (1934) Sociometric analysis is one of the most descriptive measures of interactions in small groups. The sociometric test identifies certain types of intra group relationships. It tries to determine and depict the attractions and repulsions among individuals within a given group. Moreno simply asked group members to express their likes and dislikes of other group members. These preferences are charted on a sociogram representing the patterns of interpersonal attraction.

In Figure 9.1 each circle represents a separate person, the double-headed arrows denote mutual attraction between group members. The single headed arrows indicate one way attraction. From the diagram we can easily spot the 'star' i.e., person E. Note that person E is chosen by 8 out of 9 other group members. Person J could be described as isolate because, although, he is attracted to persons *G* AND *E*, no one reported being attracted to him. Moreno's Sociometric analysis proved to be extremely useful in data collection and has been used to study organisational effectiveness and morale to identify spontaneous leadership etc.

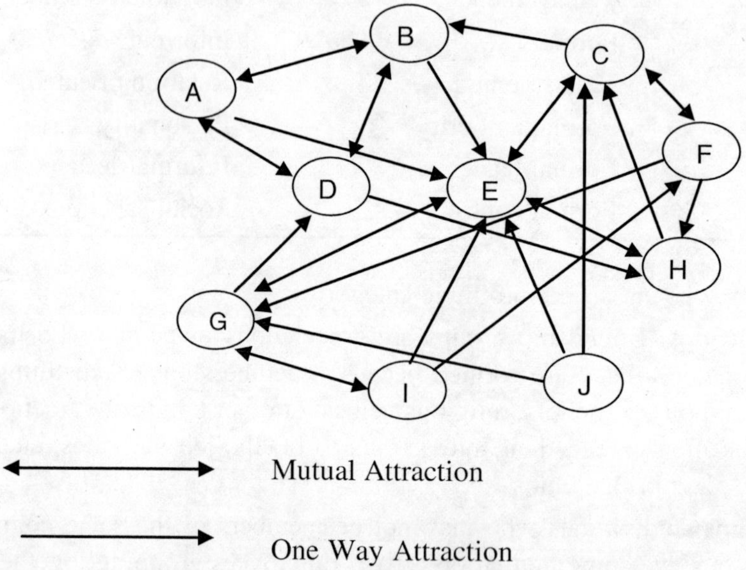


***Figure: 9.1. Sociogram of a ten-member group***

## The Bales System: Interaction Process Analysis

Robert Bales" has 'studied groups by observing their behaviour and recording (on a moving tape) which people interact with each other and how they do so. This is called Interaction Process analysis. This technique called as Interaction process analysis, is on observational method whereby interaction in groups is observed often after experimental conditions. Under this method, the observer notes each time a group member speaks; and classifies under one of the headings developed by Bales. Bales has tried to reduce all the possible interactions to 12 categories or six problems areas. In the words of Robert Bales "interaction process analysis is a way of classifying direct, face to face interaction as it takes place, act by act, and a series of way of summarising and analysing the resultant data in a useful manner".

**Table 9.2: Task Area**

| *Positive work acts* | *Key problems* | *Negative work acts* |
|---|---|---|
| Gives suggestions. | Control. | Asks for suggestions. |
| Gives opinions. | Evaluations. | Asks opinions. |
| Gives orientation. | Communication. | Asks orientation. |
| Positive human interaction | Socio-Emotional Area | Negative human interaction |
| Shows solidarity. | Reintegration. | Shows antagonism. |
| Shows tension release. | Tension reduction. | Shows tension. |
| Agrees. | Decision. | Disagrees. |

The six problem areas in the model can be noted by an observer as the group functions in a task:

(i) Arriving at a common definition of a situation (orientation).

(ii) Developing a common value system in terms of which alternative solutions are to be evaluated (evaluation).

(iii) Attempts of members to influence each other (control).

(iv) Arriving at a final decision.

(v) Dealing with tensions which arise in the group (tension management).

(vi) Working at the task of maintaining an integrated group (integration).

Bales model would be useful, for instance, in analysing the behaviour of committee members in the process of arriving at a difficult decision. It may reveal that certain members in the group are consistently negative in their behaviours, or that much of the group's behaviour is not task oriented etc.

## HOMANS MODEL

More than three decades ago, in the Human Group, George Homans developed a conceptual framework to aid in understanding the complex workings of group behaviour. His model, also called 'the A-I-S model', makes some commonsense notions about small groups and is based on three concepts: Activity, interaction and sentiment.

**(a) Activity:** Activities are the tasks that people perform, like walking to work, assembling a machine, inspecting a component, talking etc.

**(b) Interaction:** Interactions are the behaviour that occur between people in performing the above tasks. Interaction may involve two or more individuals. It may be verbal or non-verbal.

**(c) Sentiment:** Sentiments include feelings, values, opinions, and beliefs held by an individual or a group. Sentiments, unlike interactions and activities, are not directly observable in group interaction, rather, they must be determined subjectively by inference from ongoing group activity. Sentiments can be positive, negative or neutral.

### Required and Emergent System

Homans uses these three basic systems elements of activity, interaction, and sentiment to define and delineate two basic systems that exist within the group. Homans calls them the required system and the emergent system.

Required system: The required system/behaviour includes all activities, interactions, and sentiments that are necessary part of the group function. For instance, a student may have to frequently confer with his professor in order to complete the field assignment. Approaching the professor signifies an activity, having a dialogue indicates interaction and having continued discussions thereafter initiates the A-I-S chain. Together, these required activities, interactions, and sentiments form the required behaviour in the group.

Emergent system/behaviour. The emergent system includes activities, interactions, and sentiments that evolve as a result of the required group function. For example, it is quite possible that in working together within the required system, the members of the group will evolve their own social structure. This social structure may be characterised by status levels, norms of behaviour, friendships and hostile interaction patterns. The emergent system is made up of these elements.

## Background and Environmental Factors

According to Homans, the distinct features of a group's required and emergent systems will be influenced by a number of background and environmental factors. These factors include the physical aspects of the work to be finished, the organisational policies, and practices, the political, cultural and economic environment, the personal background factors of members. It is the interaction of these background factors (external system) influencing both the required and emergent systems that will ultimately determine levels of group output in three significant areas: productivity, satisfaction and personal growth. The Homans model is summarised in figure here.

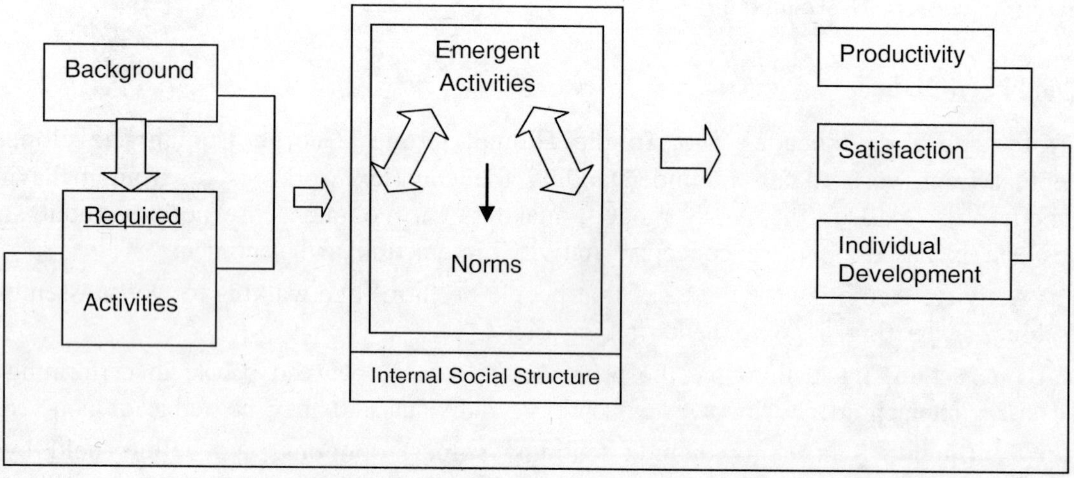


***Figure 9.2: The Homan's model of work group behaviour***

***Source'*** *A.N. Turner's, "A Conceptual Scheme for Describing Work Group Behaviour" in P.R. Lawrence and J.A. Seiler, Organisation and Administration, Homewood, Illinois, Richard D. Irwin, 1965, p. 158.*

As can be seen from the above diagram, the external system provides the raw material for forming the internal system, the set of emergent activities, interactions and sentiments and norms for behaviour in the group. The operation of the internal system leads to productivity, satisfaction and growth consequences. These results, then, feedback into stage I to affect the background factors.

## Implications

The Homan's model offers managers considerable insight into group behaviour and helps in predicting certain outcomes. For example, the model helps in predicting the emergent behaviour in a given situation. Emergent interaction is more likely between members whose given sentiments are similar, whose jobs force them to have a continuous dialogue, who are actually required by the management to interact and so on. Homans pointed out that interaction and inter-personal sentiments are closely related. Favourable sentiments emerge between members who interact frequently and frequent interaction develops between members who like one another. Unfavourable sentiments are directed against members who do not share or who violate the norms generally approved by the group. Managers, according to the model, can increase group cohesiveness by increasing the frequency of interactions among employees who like each other.

## FORMAL GROUPS: COMMITTEES

A committee is a group of people working together to solve a certain problem. It investigates, analysis, and debates that problem, and then makes a recommendation. Thus, a committee provides for exchange of ideas, thorough discussion of all aspects of the problem and stimulates committee members to give the organisation the best that is in them. It brings varied perspective and information to the problem-solving process, secures co-ordination and provides managers an invaluable opportunity to develop their administrative skills. No wonder, committees have become an integral part of the administrative structure of most modern business organisations. Managers, fifty per cent of lower-level managers, and over thirty per cent of non-managers serve on at least one committee.

### Advantages:

Committees are widely employed in organisations because of certain advantages:

**(i) Pooled knowledge and judgement:** A committee is an effective way of bringing the collective knowledge and wisdom of a number of members to bear on a problem. Every facet of the problem will be thoroughly explored and weighted in the larger interest of the company as a whole. More effort and time are devoted to each problem. There will be a fruitful exchange of ideas, opinions, knowledge and experience by a group of individuals.

**(ii) Group pressures bring about better quality decisions:** Another related advantage of committee is that the individuals members of the group exert pressure or censorship on ideas, suggestions, comments.

**(iii) Helps in consolidation of authority:** Often individual members lack enough power and authority to make or implement a decision. A committee permits management to consolidate authority that is splintered over several departments. The combined power and authority of a committee helps in securing action immediately.

**(iv) Helps in avoiding action and escaping responsibility:** Where a manager wishes to avoid action on a specific problem, it may be assigned to a committee. Again, committees are created to dilute authority and spread risk on important matters.

### Disadvantages:

Committees have their critics. Committees have come under blistering attack from different quarters. Sarcastic statements abound in number. A committee is a 'group of unfits engaged by the unwilling to do the unnecessary'. 'A camel is a horse that is put together by a committee'. Committees are an organised means of passing the buck. Obviously, committees have some serious defects that invite criticism almost spontaneously and restrict their widespread usage in organisations.

**1. Cost:** The cost of committee meetings is phenomenally high. Prolonged committee meetings consume executive's time and thus, entail a considerable waste of scarce resources. In addition, the time and expenses of travel, preparation of agenda, reports, etc., can quickly run the cost of such meetings much higher. Wasteful committee activities result from a number of factors–there may be too many committees in existence, a committee may be too large in its membership, a committee may be meeting too frequently (almost daily), a committee may be inefficient in its methods of operation. When poorly designed and managed, committees may fritter away time on trial subjects or subjects that could be disposed of by one person without much difficulty. No wonder, many people feel that committees are notorious time wasters where minutes are taken scrupulously but hours are spent indiscriminately.

**2. Indecisiveness:** Committee action is almost invariably slow. The very mechanics of assembling people and providing necessary discussion is time-consuming. Many a time managers may have to ignore important day to day matters to attend a meeting. In a committee meeting each person is expected to state views to listen to the views of other members (however inconsequential). To comment on the differences and to explain why he tasks the position he does. With poor leadership the committee might quite easily get bogged down in interminable debate and indecision. To make confusion worse and confounded, absenteeism, lack of preparation before meetings, and substitutions in membership, all show down decision-making.

**3. Compromising attitudes:** Nobody is happy with a committee decision because quite often, it represents a middle-of-the road plan which no one completely opposes but which no one really believes. Committee decisions simply represent the lowest common denominator of the thinking of the members on that committee. The reasons for this suboptimal behaviour may be that members may be reluctant to challenge a popular point of view, or take an extreme position; members may not approach problems with an objective and open-minded attitude as for instance, X may do a favour to Y by keeping silence in one meeting where Y has already taken a position and X may repay his debt of gratitude in later meetings; members may not be interested in embarrassing other members of the same committee; members may not be interested in ending up the tedious discussions without a solution. All too often a member says 'Let's agree on something; I have to get back to my desk'. As a result, a committee decision is watered down' and is not the best from anyone's view-point.

**4. Divided responsibility:** "That which is everybody's responsibility is nobody's responsibility." Committee members are jointly responsible for the decision arrived at. When responsibility is thus divided, holding an individual manager for performance becomes exceedingly difficult. No one feels anything personal at stake in matters entrusted to committees. This inevitably promotes slackness, inefficiency and evasion of responsibility for results.

**5. Dominance by few:** Committee meetings, usually, are dominated by the chairperson or by a strong personality. In such instances, there is a natural reluctance to disagree with the boss or the chairperson. Domination may limit the committee's effectiveness. 'Hidden agendas' may emerge as committee members, conscious of rank and status, worry more about creating favourable impressions than about the business of the committee. The chairman perforces the committee to come to a foregone conclusion on the basis of his own thinking and members may vie with each other in order to curry favour with the boss, rather than contribute meaningfully to committee decisions.

**6. Political decisions:** Committee members are often chosen to represent the narrow interests of departments in a forceful way, members have a proven 'track record' of speaking high of their achievements for departments. As a result, the broad interests of the organisation are totally discounted and members fight with each other for promoting departmental prestige and popularity.

## Conditions for Effective Functioning of Committees

Committees can be a useful agency of management, rather than a doubtful and much bedevilled administrative gimmick, if the following points/principles are observed.

**1. Committee Objectives:** A clear statement of the objectives, duties and authority of a committee will contribute greatly to its success. This clarifies the role to be played by each member within the established limits. A periodic review of committees and their objectives is also necessary to help avoid committees that are totally unnecessary.

**2. Committee Members:** Members must be carefully selected to assure objectives. Personal knowledge and experience that is useful to the functioning of the committee, ability to get along with people easily, skills in communication, etc., must be taken into account before conferring committee membership to individuals. To be effective, the number of members should not ordinarily exceed five.

**3. Agenda:** There should be adequate preparation for the committee meeting. Each member should be provided with factual data before the meeting commences. A right agenda should be prepared and served to members in advance. Without a clear-cut agenda, irrelevant discussions crop up simultaneously. A well-thought out agenda helps in considering all important aspects of the problem, provides a structure for discussion and enables the committee to proceed in a logical fashion to consider one topic after another.

**4. The Committee Chairman:** The committee chairman is the key figure to the proper functioning of a committee. He should possess leadership qualities and should be able to bring out the best from committee members. He should not try to force his own ideas through the committee. He should also have minimum human relations skills. He should be able to resolve differences of opinions, personal clashes, and bring the members to a common point of view.

**5. Conducting the Meetings:** The chairman should conduct the meetings according to the logical procedure. According to Allen, an effective procedure should include review of the facts by the chairman, analysis of the problem, suggested solutions, group decisions or recommendation. Members must come prepared and must participate in a meaningful way. To ensure adequate follow-up, minutes of the meetings should be prepare and distributed to members within a reasonable period.

## Stages of Group Development

Once a group is formed, it goes through certain phases to become a functioning group. When people are thrown into a group to perform a task, the group is not expected to function like a well oiled machine right away. It will take time for them to get acquainted, resolve any differences, and then develop productive relationships. B.W. Tuckman has suggested four phases of group development: (1) forming, (2) storming, (3) norming, and (4) performing. (Merwin E Shaw )

**1. Forming:** The first stage is called forming. During this period, group members discover those interpersonal behaviours that are both acceptable and unacceptable to others in the group. During this phase, each member relies on the others to provide cues regarding acceptable behaviour.

**2. Storming:** During the storming phase, there is often some degree of intragroup conflict as members attempt to develop a special place for themselves in the group and to influence the development of its norms ad roles. At this time, members also try to develop some form(s) of interpersonal relationships with others in the group. In the process, each person tries to make off certain domains of authority or power. This stage is often a period of jockeying for position.

**3. Norming:** During norming stage, the in-fighting is basically over and group cohesion starts to develop. Most group members have now come to accept their fellow members. A unity of purpose has developed and this serves to unite them. At this point the group's development has basically matured and the members understand how they are to interact with each other. People joining the group at this stage often find themselves having to go back through stages one and two (forming and storming) in an effort to integrate themselves comfortably into the group's environment.

**4. Performing:** The forth stage of group development is called performing. Here, group members agree on the basic roles each is to play. This concerns not only job behaviour but the ways in which each will interact with the others in getting things done. During this stage, task specialisation and personal needs and desires and brought together. The formal needs of the organisation are integrated with the informal needs of the member. The result is that group members are able to make their jobs more interesting and enjoyable.

As groups pass through these four phases their communication patterns change. The defensiveness and hostility that often characterise the early phases, give way to feelings of friendship, trust, confidence and openness.

The interaction patterns among group members have been the favourite hunting ground for researchers. The research findings, for the sake of convenience, may be examined under the following headings:

## 1. GROUP SIZE AND COMPOSITION

The size of a group can have profound implications on how the group behaves internally and with regard to other groups. It is an important factor determining the number of interactions of individuals in a group. In a small group, face-to-face interaction is quite easy and uncomplicated. Members can easily communicate with other group members. Research evidence confirms the fact that small groups are effective. On the other hand, in larger groups, members have a better chance of finding people they like to work with. The potential for greater variety of talents is also greater. But the disadvantages of size more than offset its advantages. Larger groups offer greater opportunities for differences between and among individuals. They are difficult to handle and demand a higher level of supervision. Absenteeism also tends to be higher. Larger groups are also prone to possible domination by aggressive members and have tendencies to split into coalitions or subgroups Also when the group size turns unwieldy, its goals may not be in sync with the goals of the larger organisation. Although it is not easy to pinpoint an ideal group size, a manager should not try to build a group around some ideal size.

How to achieve a happy balance in such a case? What is the correct size of a group? The problem of defining the size of a small group is, particularly a troublesome exercise. Interaction is a necessary ingredient of small groups. As such, the minimum size of a group is always two people (dyad). The upper limit is usually specified by some rule of thumb. Prescriptions in this connection vary from situation to situation. Generally speaking, the size of a group depends to a large extent on the group's situation and purpose. However, some studies have come up with definite numbers: for example, 7 is the ideal maximum for a decision making group and 14 is the maximum for a fact-finding group. (Thomas and Fink)

## Composition of a group

The productivity of a group to some extent depends on the composition of the group. The more homogeneous the group in terms of such features as shared backgrounds, interests, attitudes and values of its members, the easier it is to promote group cohesiveness. Homogeneous groups generally offer the following benefits:

**Easy to influence:** Group members who are alike, when compared to those who have little in common, find it easy to influence each other. They listen to each other and are ready to reciprocate in a friendly manner.

**Members find group experience satisfying:** We generally like the company of those who have the same opinions as we do and who are similar to us in many ways.

**Improved task performance:** Members of a homogeneous group find it easy to get simple as well as sequential tasks (where one is performed after another in a chain) turned into concrete performance, with active participation from others. This is because; members are generally very compatible and get along with each other quite admirably.

On the negative side, of course, with fewer hands, there will be fewer resources in terms of knowledge, skills and experience to apply to the team's tasks. A group that is very small may exhibit signs of lack of creativity and boldness because of peer pressure.

In heterogeneous groups, members have the necessary breadth and depth to deal with complex issues quite successfully. The varied skills, training and expertise that they bring to the table, help them examine the problem from different angles, discuss it thoroughly and come out with creative solutions. On paper, they look very sound from any angle but in actual practice such differences—in terms of interests, abilities, age, education, etc— may be the cause of disruption and conflict. With more members, there is less interaction, exchange of useful information and coordinating of activities. The larger the size, the more likely performance is to drop owing to **social loafing**. Also known as the Ringleman Effect, social loafing is the tendency of people to work less hard in a group than they would individually. This is because, in a large group, individual contributions are rarely looked into. The lazy and incompetent members would like to leisurely watch others carry the workload. To a large extent, as research studies indicate, people working in individualistic cultures (where people value individual accomplishments and success) such as USA exhibited social loafing tendencies (getting the most for themselves while doing the least than their fellow group members). In collectivistic cultures (where members place a high value on shared responsibility and collective good of all) such as China and Israel, members placed their group's interests ahead of their own (in fact members worked harder than they did alone while working in groups) (Earley P.C)

### *How to overcome social loafing*?

It is possible to overcome social loafing when you (Albanese et al)

- Identify each performer and make it difficult for him to get away easily
- Make work tasks more important and interesting
- Encourage individuals' interest in their group's performance
- Use threats to punish those who are slacking off

It always helps when group members work in close proximity to each other thereby enabling peer observation of individual contributions. In addition to offering member-to-member control, close proximity also reinforces the social needs of individuals and provides opportunities for feedback and helping behaviours. Unfortunately, punishing social loafers has unpredictable effects—sometimes it works, sometimes it doesn't work.

On the question of actual numbers, research evidence indicates that groups with an odd number of members find it easier to use majority voting rules to resolve disagreements. To speedily dissolve differences, not surprisingly, odd –numbered groups are preferred. But when careful deliberations are needed and the focus shifts to consensus building, such as in jury duty or very complex problem solving, even-numbered groups may be more effective unless an unfortunate deadlock results in.

## 2. STATUS AND ROLE RELATIONSHIPS

Status is the relative prestige, social position or rank given to groups or individuals by others All organisations have at least two status structures. The first is known as the formal status system (the prestige one has by virtue of his official position in an organisation) that follows the hierarchical structure of the organisation. In a college, a Principal has more status than a counter assistant, who in turn has a higher status than an attendant. Thus, in formal structures, status is closely related to the chain of command. The second status structure is called the informal system where the values ad norms of the group determine the status of a particular member. Status may be informally conferred by such characteristics as education, age, sex, skill or experience. Anything can have status value if others in the group evaluate it as such.

### How status develops in a group?

Three possible reasons could be advanced in support of the emergence of a status system in a work group: (i) The various jobs into which the work of the group is subdivided have different prestige value in the eyes of workers. Persons who are able to control the outcomes of a group tend to be perceived as high status. (ii) Again, people who contributions to a group are very important in determining the group's success also tend to have high status. (iii) Finally, people having certain pleasing characteristics that are positively valued by the group such as intelligence, pleasing manners, money etc seem to enjoy a higher status when compared to those who possess fewer valued attributes. A number of research studies have shown that people can quickly identify status –both formal and otherwise—differences within groups. (Webster and Hysom) Status symbols such as job titles, perquisites, membership in prestigious committees or assignments in important projects, luxurious working conditions etc convey the status of a person and his standing in a group. Status symbols reduce ambiguity and bring orderliness in social contacts. If you are enquiring from someone occupying a corner seat and in front of a small desk, you know for sure he is not the boss. Status rankings assure members of proportionate rewards and offer an easy and clear-cut identification mark to the member. Members can also get to know a lot about the informal status (the prestige accorded to individuals with certain characteristics that are not formally recognised by the organisation) enjoyed by a person by simply looking at his age, special skills, qualifications, experience, lung power, union membership etc –though not formally blessed with any distinct official rank.

## How Status Structures Influence Group Behaviour?

A peon with college education would find his job very uncomfortable in a place where illiterates are recruited for such positions. Unless able to play down the educational attributes, he is likely to be labelled as a city guy or the college kid. It will be difficult to gain full acceptance. **Status incongruence** (for example a supervisor getting lesser salary than his subordinates, air conditioned facilities given to clerical staff and not to officers, prestigious club membership offered to divisional heads but not to vice presidents etc) creates psychological tension and this state is unpleasant and dissatisfying. Employees expect the things an individual receives to be in sync with his official rank and status. When things do not move along such expected lines, the social order collapses causing serious disciplinary problems. It is therefore, highly important for employees to believe that the organisation's formal status system is congruent. Status congruency is said to exist, when all the status attributes are ranked equally by all members of a group. In other words, there is equity between the perceived ranking of an individual and the status accoutrements; he is given by the organisation. Status congruency provides for more consistent and predictable behaviour. Status incongruence can cause uncertainty and ambiguity. Low morale, high tension as well as high anxiety. (William F. Whyte)

## Managerial Implications

Status is an important cementing force in an organisation. Members, therefore, would like to preserve it at any cost. Loss of status has lot of negative implications. The damage does not stop at loss of benefits alone. "Loss of status is more than loss of its emoluments; it is more than loss of prestige. It is a serious injury to the personality." Therefore, it is highly important to achieve status congruency in the organisation. To meet this objective, it is necessary to distribute the rewards according to the perceived value of the skills, knowledge, experience etc demanded by the task. In this way, the status system is kept consistent with the reward system.

Managers must also try to demolish the barriers erected by status structures by seeking information and opinions from lower-status people. In addition, the behavioural problems arising from status incongruence can be avoided by:

- Selecting or promoting those people whose characteristics are all
- By changing the group's values about what leads to high status.

Apart from status equity, managers should also pay attention to the relationship between status and culture. The French for example are highly status conscious. In countries like USA and Australia status is more closely linked to accomplishments than official titles and family background. In India status counts a lot. Cultural differences, therefore, need to be carefully looked into before trying to strike rapport with people in a group, at least officially.

## Role Relationships

A role is a set of activities expected of a person occupying a particular position within the group. It is a pattern of behaviour that is expected of an individual when he interacts with others. Individuals play multiple roles adjusting their roles to the group in which they are part of, at the time. The expected role is more or less a formal role. It is what other people expect from an individual. The perceived role is how the individual thinks he or she should perform to fulfil the expected role. The enacted role is the behaviour that a person actually carries out. Much of what we do is determined by these roles.

## Characteristics

1. Roles are impersonal. It is the position that determines the expectations, not the individual.
2. An organisational role is that set of expected behaviours for a particular position vis-à-vis a particular job.
3. It is fairly difficult to pin down roles in exact terms. It is the most complex organised response pattern; the human being is capable of making.
4. Roles are learned quickly and can result in major changes in behaviour.

## Behavioural Problems

When an individual is confronted by divergent role expectations, and naturally, is not sure about which role to be played, behavioural problems result in. Role ambiguity (occurs when someone is uncertain about what is expected of him or her) may produce stress or anxiety in the role incumbent. Though some amount of ambiguity always exists, it is necessary to clarify roles. The degree of clarity can influence the quality of organisational life and emotional well-being of an individual. Lack of role clarity may lead to reduced performance. Since, it is not possible to achieve role clarity completely; a manager has to try to introduce the right amount of role ambiguity.

Whatever the consequences of role conflict (occurs when someone is unable to respond to role expectations that conflict with one another) on individual and group behaviour? The research literature is fairly extensive and in agreement. Numerous studies have shown that conflict produces greater levels of tension anxiety, insecurity and lower levels of satisfaction and productivity. To avoid role problems, managers must conduct proper analysis of job, design them properly and select the right type of persons and provide necessary training.

## 3. GROUP LEADERSHIP

A major responsibility in working with groups is the recognition of leadership forces. Of course, the formal leader of a group is appointed by the management and he can exercise legitimately sanctioned power. The formal leader possesses the power to discipline and or fire members of his work group. Informal leaders, on the other hand, tend to emerge gradually as group members interact. They emerge from within the group according to the nature of the situation at hand.

**Table 9.3. Formal Vs. Informal Leaders**

| *Formal leaders* | *Informal leaders* |
|---|---|
| 1. Represents the organisation | Represents the value of the group. |
| 2. Task oriented, gets the job done. | Group oriented welfare of the group. |
| 3. Attempts to dominate and impose. | Leadership role is based on group consensus and acceptance. |
| 4. Attempts to achieve goals by strict adherence to rules and regulations, (rules govern behaviour). | Prisoner of group values and norms, tries to achieve group goals without violating group norms. |

What factors encourage other members to accept a person as leader?

### Emergence of Informal Leaders

1. The member who talks and participates most actively in the group activities is the one most likely to emerge as leader.

2. The member who possesses more information enabling him to contribute more than members to solution of the group task tends to emerge as leader.

3. The member who respects group norms and values and attempts to fulfil group's social needs by encouraging feelings of solidarity tends to emerge as leader.

4. The member of the group who possesses the greatest technical knowledge, skills, qualities necessary to achieve in purpose, and accomplish the task of the group in a particular situation is likely to emerge as leader.

5. The member who is able to perceive the values of the group, organise them into an intelligible philosophy and sell the same success fully to other groups and non-members is likely to emerge as leader.

### Successful Leadership Behaviours

The primary function of an informal group leader (formal group leader) is to facilitate the accomplishment of group goals. He aids the group in accomplishing in goals. To survive, the group must gear its efforts to achieve its primarily goals. The cricket teem that fails to win a single match ultimately loses its cohesiveness, its sense of togetherness and disintegrates. The informal group leader personifies the values and aspirations of group. He initiates action, provides direction and compromises differences toward the accomplishment of goals. He differs from followers in ability to initiate and sustain interaction with a wide range of personalities. "He protects the weak and underchosen, encourages participation of less capable members, is tolerant of the deviate, and accepts rather than rejects a wide range of member personalities." He constantly evaluates, directs and motivates member behaviour toward overall goals. Thus, an informal group leader is an embodiment of the values of group, an initiator of group activities, a prisoner of group norms and a facilitator of group conflict.

## 4. GROUP NORMS

Norms are shared ways of looking at the world. They are the set of informal rules, shared beliefs, and values that guide member behaviour. Norms define the boundaries of acceptable and unacceptable behaviour and are the standard against which member behaviour is evaluated. As a code of conduct, norms define—sometimes explicitly and sometimes subtly—what members dare and dare not do either in the group on or the group's behalf. Infact, groups control their members through the use of norms. By securing *strict* compliance (because lack of conformity to group norms may often lead to verbal abuse, physical threats, ostracism or ejection from the group) norms ensure consistency in member behaviour of course, group norms are normally enforced only for actions that are important to group members( Feldman) Without norms, the activities in a group would be chaotic. It must, however, be noted that Not all norms apply to everyone. High status members often enjoy more freedom to deviate the 'letter of the law' than do other members. And, above all, not all norms are restrictive. Some norms are very loose and permit a great deal of leeway in behaviour while other norms, are much more restrictive on members' behaviour (like the norm laying down that no member shall speak anything about how the group deliberated on a sensitive issue before outsiders)

### Purposes of Norms

Norms serve the following purposes

- Group norms tend to reject deviant behaviour that fails to meet group goals or contribute to the survival of the group when it is under threat
- Norms summarise and simplify group influence processes. They summarise and highlight those things that the group feels it's important to control. Norms resolve interpersonal differences in a group and ensure uniformity of action.
- Norms help the group avoid embarrassing situations. Group members often want to avoid damaging other members' self-images and are likely to avoid certain subjects that might hurt a member's feelings. (G.Moorhead and R.W.Griffin)
- Norms showcase the core values and its distinct image to others. They, infact, regulate the behaviour of groups in significant ways,( known as prescriptive norms, reflecting the expectations within groups regarding what is supposed to be done) such as by encouraging employee honest and loyalty towards the company, establishing appropriate ways to dress

and specifying when it is acceptable to report late or remain absent from work. Of course, groups could also come out with other norms, known as proscriptive norms which specifically dictate behaviours that are inappropriate and should be avoided at any cost.

## How Norms are developed?

Norms usually develop gradually, but the process can be shortened if members so desire. If, for some reason, group members decide that a particular norm is now desired, they may simply agree to institute such a norm suddenly by declaring that 'from now on' the norms exists. (Feldman). However, certain key factors seem to influence the formation of norms in a group:

**Early behaviours:** Typically, initial behaviour, especially in newly formed groups, set standards for subsequent behaviour. in first few meetings, committee members may establish norms regarding attendance, discussion of sensitive topics, time for each member, how to deal with disagreements etc

**Imported behaviours:** Members often bring to the group standards of behaviour that were routinely followed in their former groups. When in doubt, such behaviours find ready acceptance.

**Critical events:** A sudden challenge to the group, such as criticism from another group, can create specific and vivid responses that form the basis for how members should react to similar situations in future.

**Explicitly stated standards:** High status members may declare that "this is how the show is going to run here" and may thus set the trend.

## Factors Influencing Conformance to Norms

Why members conform to group norms? Not every member conforms. Each group member, of course, has alternative choices before him: Generally speaking, a person characterised as intellectually average, unoriginal and low in ego strength and self-confidence and having dependent and distributed relationships with other people, would probably be a conformist. There can be complete conformity where the member accepts all the norms of the group (high conformist). Sometimes, he may accept all important norms but may reject other norms (selective individualism). At times, there maybe a case of rebellion where he decides to leave or is expelled from the group.

Thus, conformity to norms is not (automatic) usually blind, slavish and unthinking: nor is it only a function of the norms centrality. Conformity depends on the following factors.

**1. Personality Factors:** Research on personality factors suggests that the more intelligent are less likely to conform than the less intelligent. They prefer selective individualism. Authoritarians conform more than non-authoritarians. Again, people characteristics of the situation: In unusual situations where decisions must be taken on unclear items, there is a greater tendency to conform to the group's norms. Under conditions of crisis, conformity to group norms is highly probable.

**2. Situational factors:** Group size (increasing size increases conformity behaviour) communication patterns (decentralised patterns enhance conformity behaviour) degree of group unanimity etc.

**3. Intragroup relationships:** A group that is seen as being creditable will evoke more compliance than a group that is not.

**4. Compatible goals:** When group goals mesh with individual goals, people are quite willing to adhere to group norms of performance.

## Enforcing Norms

Norms quite often, can vary from very simple rules to very complex set of prescriptions and prohibitions. So it is always not possible to enforce norms quite easily. Group employs several specific functions in order to ensure that individuals with the group comply with its standards. Enforcement of "the letter of the law" is achieved through the following steps.

**Education:** Arouse a desire in members to remain in the group, show them how the group's standards contribute to the achievement of important goals. Increase each member's involvement in the group's work and ask the target person to give up individual gains in favour of the group's success. Present a right way of behaving to the members and admonish deviations.

**Surveillance:** Adherence to group norms is essential to group survival. Detect deviance from group norms. If conformity of members cannot be detected directly, develop a means for determining whether members have done what the group's standards require.

**Warning:** Make it known that any groupmate who does not conform to the group's standards will be removed from the unit. Issue a strict warning to the deviant. Provide a friendly and supportive contact to the deviate, to as to bring his behaviour back to compliance with group norms. Should he refuse to do so, stop the educational process and allow him to have a 'feel' of the negative consequence: razzing, argument etc.

**Sanctions:** This is the actual stage of enforcing discipline. Sanctions are imposed only when the deviant refuses to mind his ways. Sanctions take an ugly turn and many result in ostracism, physical violence, tempering with personal possessions etc.

## Implications for Managers

Among the manager's most important tasks, are learning the norms of the different groups, finding out which are critical and which are not, and determining the degree of conformity needed and degree of non-conformity allowed. Effective managers, of course, try to change norms that challenge the accomplishment of organisational goals.

## 5. GROUP COHESIVENESS

Generally speaking, people join a group because they expect it to satisfy their needs. Cohesion develops if these hopes are realised. Group cohesiveness is an important indicator of how much influence the group as a whole has over the individual members. It can be thought of as the strength of the 'glue' which holds the group together. It is defined as the degree to which members are attracted to one another and share the group's goals. Cohesiveness causes more harmonious behaviour in group members. A cohesive group is able to act as one body to achieve its goals. According to Shaw, members of highly cohesive groups are more energetic in group activities, are less likely to be absent from group meetings and are happy when the group succeeds and sad when it fails, whereas members of less cohesive groups are less concerned about the group's activities; the members are not dedicated to the group and its purposes; their loyalty and support are mediocre or variable.

## Features of Cohesive Groups:

Those that are high in cohesion are likely to be groups:

1. That have relatively few members.
2. Whose members have similar interests and backgrounds.
3. That have a high degree of status within the organisation.
4. In which members have ready access to one another so that interpersonal communication is easy to maintain.
5. That are physically remote or isolated from other groups in the organisation.
6. In which the leader rewards cooperative behaviour.
7. That are pressured or threatened by some common outside force and
8. That have a history of past success.

## What Makes a Group Cohesive?

There are numerous sources of attraction to a group. A number of factors determine the degree to which a group is cohesive:

**Size:** Other things being equal, small groups have a greater probability of being cohesive than larger one. In larger groups, the necessary interactions are inhibited, communication between members is reduced to a feeble walk and there is the danger of formation of subgroups. Small groups offer frequent interaction opportunities leading to better understanding between members.

**Location:** People who work closely together in the same geographical location have numerous opportunities to interact and exchange ideas resulting in highly effective and cohesive groups than do people who are geographically separated.

**Outside pressure:** A favourite topic of novelists is to describe the plight of two warring individuals who, through some quirk of fate, find themselves dependent on each other for survival or gain. External threats create higher bounds between members. When the members perceive that the group is threatened by an external force, they strive together to combat the collective threat. In the face of a common enemy, members forget their common differences and become cohesive.

**Status of the group:** A high status group that is successful in achieving its goals tends to have greater cohesiveness. Membership in such a group is highly rated than membership in a group widely denounced by all. It is better to be a "big fish in a little pond" or "a little fish in a big pond" than remain unnoticed as a "little fish in a little pond".

**Success:** There is nothing like success to increase group spirit and cohesiveness. A near universal finding is that cohesiveness generally increases with success.

**Other reasons:** Other reasons like compatible goals (goals of the group and the members are essentially alike and expressed in a clear language), attractive leaders (the group has a dynamic, energetic leader), collective power (people join groups to obtain personal power) also compel members to seek membership in well-knit groups.

## Effects of Group Cohesion

Research has generally shown that a cohesive group is more productive than a less cohesive group provided the group's attitude aligns with the goals of the organisation. For example if the group norm is a high level of performance, the more cohesive group is likely to influence each member toward high productivity. On the other hand, if cohesiveness is high but attitudes unfavourable, productivity declines. A highly cohesive group is like a 'time-bomb' in the hands of management. Where the group norms is not supportive of performance, cohesive groups are less productive. Resistance to organisational changes is greater and where proper leadership is not provided such groups can restrict output severely. "If management wishes to maximise productivity it must build a cohesive group and give it proper leadership."

## 6. GROUP THINK

Group think is an extreme form of consensus in which the group thinks as a unit rather than as a collection of individuals. It is a kind of consensus-seeking process that goes on in a cohesive group. When a group is too cohesive, new ideas maybe rejected too quickly. Members are imbued with feelings of "We know best". There is a tremendous desire for unanimity. Seeking consensus becomes an end in itself. Free exchange of ideas is inhibited. Some members in a group maybe timid or cowed down by dominating members imposing their ideas on others. At other times, the group members try to promote consensus at the possible expense of arriving at a more defective solution. Lack of critical thinking is at the heart of group think followed by the group's low-risk, conservative traditional and mediocre decisions Group members cease to think independently. Irving Jansis used the 'group think' to describe the unfortunate situation in which the desire to agree becomes so dominant in a cohesive group that it tends to override realistic appraisal of alternative courses of action. Members try to avoid being too harsh in their judgements of one another's ideas. They adopt a soft line of criticism. At their meetings, all the members are chummy and seek complete agreement on every important issue. As a result of little or no real criticism, the illusion of unanimity is created.

## Symptoms of Group Think

Group think is characterised by a "deterioration of mental efficiency, reality testing and moral judgement that results from in-group pressures" The following symptoms have been identified with group think.

**Table 9.3. Symptoms of Groupthink**

Illusions of group invulnerability: Members of the group feel that it is basically beyond criticism or attack.

Rationalising unpleasant and disconfirming data: Members refuse to accept contradictory data or to consider alternatives thoroughly.

Belief in inherent group morality: Members of the group feel that it is "right" and the above any reproach by outsiders.

Stereotyping competitors as weak, evil, and stupid: Members refuse to look realistically at other groups.

Applying direct pressure to deviants to conform to group wishes: Members refuse to tolerate a member who suggests the group may be wrong.

Self-censorship by members: Members refuse to communicate personal concerns to the group as a whole.

Illusions of unanimity: Members accept consensus prematurely, without testing its completeness.

Mind guarding: Members of group protect the group from hearing disturbing ideas or viewpoints from outsiders.

### Consequences of Group Think

Under group think conditions, the following consequences maybe identified:

1. Discussion is limited to only a few alternatives.
2. Once a decision is taken, re-examination is unlikely, even in the light of (valuable thought) new information.
3. Little or no time is spent trying to find ways to overcome the problems that have made rejected alternatives seem undesirable.
4. Little or no effort is made to obtain information from experts within the organisation.
5. Facts are ignored unless they are supportive of the group.
6. No contingency plans are developed by which to cop with foreseeable difficulties that could endanger the success of the group's chosen course.

### The Remedy for Group Think

When group think does occur, positive action must be taken if the group is to be effective in performing its task. As we have seen, concurrence-seeking will smoothen objective consideration and evaluation of alternatives. The following steps are recommended by Janis to overcome group think tendencies:

1. Encourage the group members to express doubts and criticisms of proposed solutions to problems. Permit critical evaluation of group ideas by members freely.
2. Allow key members to adopt an initial impartial stance on solutions.
3. Divide the group into subgroups to stimulate ideas. Then, have the subgroups confront one another to examine why they differ.
4. Periodically invite qualified outsiders to challenge group views.
5. Allow atleast one member to play a devil's advocate role to oppose the views of other group members.
6. After arriving at a tentative decision in a particular way, allow the group to hold a second chance meeting wherein members fully describe every possible doubt they have about the solution reached.

## 7. GROUP DECISION MAKING

Group decision-making is an activity that is based on the old adage that "two heads are better than one". It permits the coming together of people with heterogeneous characteristics who can understand the problems in a better way and hence, develop creative alternatives leading to effective group performance. Most decisions in organisation, no wonder, are made in a group context only. However, group decision-making is different in process and outcome from decision-making done by individuals in the following ways:

**1. Conformity:** Norms are established by a group as a means of achieving its goals. Over a period of time, these norms become standards of conduct accepted by participants in a small group. A group tries to enforce these norms ruthlessly and norm violators are punished in many ways. No wonder, decisions in groups move toward conformity. This point is well supported by research evidence. Solomon Asch brought together groups (of seven or eight people) consisting of one unsuspecting subject (USS) and other subjects who were actually participating to help the experimenter. In the experiment two cards were shown to the participants in which one card had one line and the other had three lines of varying length, one of which was identical to the length of the line of the first card. Asch coached the confederates to provide the wrong answer unanimously. Only the USS was unaware that the experiment was 'fixed'.

The USS was provided a seat where his turn for answering the question came only at the end. After a series of experiments, Asch found that subjects conformed in about 35 per cent of the trials. In other words, the subjects provided answers that they knew were wrong but that were consistent with the answers of other group members.

**2. Superiority:** The commonly said adage "Two heads are better than one" derives its strength from many sources. Groups have important problem solving abilities. A group, with its faculty drawn from many disciplines, has got the capacity to generate more ideas than individuals. Groups "have better learning and recall, make fewer mistakes and detect mistakes quicker. Group forecasting and judgment likely are more accurate." Heterogeneous people with characteristics can bring a greater amount of information and expertise to bear on a problem, generate more creative alternative solutions and make it more likely that the solution will be understood, accepted and implemented. A number of studies support the view that groups are superior to individuals in problem solving. After reviewing the literature in this area, B. J. Kolasa concluded thus, "the preponderance of expert opinion is in favour of superiority of the group in problem solving performance."

**3. Risky shift:** The average risk-taking score tends to be higher in groups. There is considerable evidence to show that in some situations, groups make riskier decisions than individuals. Why do groups make riskier decisions than individuals? Four explanations can be offered: (1) Taking moderate risks is something that is highly rated in our society. Moderate risk has a strong cultural value than caution. (2) Risk taking offers an opportunity for a group member to become the leader. Dominant and influential members generally occupy the leadership 'berths' in a group. (3) Groups are able to share information in an open environment. Members become more familiar with the problem being discussed. Initially, they encourage cautions, go-slow tactics and once the problem is familiarised, they are willing to take adventurous risky decisions. (4) If a project adopted by a group fails, buckpassing is easy and no one individual can be held wholly responsible. Group decisions dilute and thin out responsibility. So, whenever managers are forced to solve knotty problems, these are turned over to groups.

## Assets and Liabilities of Group Problem Solving and Decision Making

Every group brings to the problem-solving task some assets and some liabilities. If the assets are utilised and the liabilities avoided, groups are better decision-making units than individuals. According to Maier, the decision-making assets of the group are:

**1. Greater knowledge and information:** A group has more information than an individual. Because many individuals are involved, more data and information can be brought to bear on the decision. The group provides specialised inputs in defining variables and suggests alternatives that the manager acting alone, would be unlikely to come up with. The tremendous amount of information and knowledge so generated might help in improved decision making.

**2. More approaches to a problem:** A group can bring to bear a wider experience, a greater variety of opinion and a more thorough probing of facts than a single individual. Members not only bring new information to the problem but also generate more alternative solutions. "Since group members do not have identical approaches, each can contribute by knocking others out of ruts of thinking".

**3. Increased acceptance:** Participation in decision-making and problem-solving increases acceptance and commitment. Many studies have shown that when participation is given, people see the solution as 'their own' and acquire a psychological stake in its success.

**4. Better comprehension of the decision:** When a manager makes a decision individually he must relay it to those who carry it out. Failure to implement decisions effectively can often be traced to garbled communication. When those who must execute the decision have participated in making it, the chance of communication failure is reduced. People understand the decision better because they saw and heard it develop.

## Decision Making Liabilities

**1. Time consuming:** Groups are notorious time wasters. In the meetings, minutes are taken but hours are wasted. The time spend in discussion, quite often, within committee may exceed the importance of the issue itself.

**2. Pressures to conform:** Groups create pressures toward conformity. Other infirmities like group think attack work groups and prevent them from being more effective. A clubby feeling of 'we-ness' compels members to become chummy and compromise on the first satisficing decision that emerges. The final decision may be so extremely watered down or 'compromised to death' that the horse does not turn out to be a camel. The decision arrived at, may not satisfactory to any one.

**3. Individual domination:** Group members are not as alike as peas in a pod. In many groups a dominant individual emerges and slices out more than his share of influence on the outcomes, even though his problem-solving ability may be poor. Thus, quite a good number of decision arrived at in group meetings, are in fact product of excessive compromise, logrolling and one-person domination. Domination is counterproductive; it puts a damper on the group's best problem solvers.

**4. Conflicting alternative solutions:** When groups are confronted with a problem, the major goal is to obtain the best possible solution. But as alternative solutions are put forward, group members may begin to view and defend their own from a 'win or lose' standpoint, instead of examining objectively the merit of each. "The clash of ideas that develops in a group can breed resentment and hurt feelings".

**5. The problem of responsibility:** The group is composed of several individuals and hence, it is easy to pass the buck in decision making. Moreover, by spreading the responsibility for a decision, groups can occasionally come up with ill-conceived or irresponsible conclusions.

## IMPROVED PROBLEM SOLVING

Improved problem solving is an important function of leaders. From this standpoint, a leader has one major task: to manage discussion so that the group engages in true problem solving. According to Maier, true leaders must forego the temptation to sell their own solutions through dramatic monologues during group sessions and rely on the resources of the entire group. Improved problem solving demands the observance of the following points:

1. The leader must call for a meeting only when there is a good reason to have one.
2. Establish precise times for meetings to begin and end.
3. Rather than emphasising the answer to a decision problem, emphasise defining the problem (like the Japanese).
4. See that all group members participate actively, allow them to air conflicting views freely.
5. Try to elicit ideas from the group; do not supply them.
6. Discuss all the alternatives; look for a best solution rather than to sell a particular alternative.
7. While resolving conflicting views, spot the trouble shooters promptly and prevent blow ups.
8. Observe the following rules while conducting the meetings: control the garrulous; draw out the silent; protect the weak; encourage the clashes of ideas; watch out for the suggestion-squashing reflex; come to the most senior people last; close on a note of achievement.

### Improved Problem Solving Techniques

When posed with the need to solve a problem or make a decision a group has a variety of problem solving techniques from which to choose. Each has merits and demerits and since group decision making is such a critical process, careful thought must be given to the selection of a particular technique. Tailor the technique to the situation. The following techniques help managers make better group decisions.

**1. Ordinary group interaction:** This is the conventional method where the chairman calls the meeting, explains the problem, controls who speaks when and tries to obtain a consensus. The discussion is somewhat unstructured and lengthy, social pressures exert considerable influence. Suboptimal decisions are often reached just to end the meeting. In order to improve decision-making abilities of the group, the leader must solicit inputs from members, clarify them and try to resolve the conflicting views satisfactorily. Proper agenda, management of time, effective participation to all members–these factors also determine how effectively the decisions are arrived at.

**2. Brainstorming:** In its simplest from, brainstorming means to use the brain to storm a problem. Today, brainstorming is an effective instrument in the creativity training programmes and is increasingly employed in all organisations to improve the problem solving abilities of groups. In brainstorming session group members express themselves freely, regardless of how crazy or wild their ideas may appear to the other group members. The basic idea is to generate ideas spontaneously in a small-group setting. A group is assembled, presented with the problem and encouraged to produce as many ideas and solutions as they can. No criticism is allowed until the group members have run out of new suggestions. Any group member is free to 'piggyback' or 'hitchhike' upon the contribution of any other member of the group. The discussion is free; members are permitted to 'freewheel' as many alternatives as they can; even bizarre suggestions are welcomed; the climate is supportive and non-critical; refinements take place only at the end. Throughout the session, the manager's main function is to record the group's ideas only.

With such an excellent back ground it is small wonder that the brainstorming sessions have proven fruitful in generating a large number of potentially useful ideas. For example, the name of a new product could be developed through a short brainstorming session where the members may be asked to say aloud every name that comes to mind and at the end a long list of names can be prepared and the 'best' one can be picked up.

**3. The nominal group technique (NGT):** The nominal group technique restricts verbal interaction between members during the decision making process. The nominal group is a 'paper group'; it consists of a number of individuals acting independently whose actions are then added together. The essential ideas is to restrict inter-personal communication and the increase the deliberation and contributions of individual members. The nominal group-follows a highly structured procedure involving several steps.

(i) Member of the target group are selected and brought together.

(ii) The group leader outlines the problem.

(iii) Each group member writes down his ideas silently and independently.

(iv) Each member then presents a single (his best) idea at a time to the group, which is written on a blackboard or flip chart for all to see.

(v) A discussion is held to clarify and evaluate the ideas.

(vi) The meeting concludes with a silent, independent vote on priorities through a rank ordering or rating procedure.

(vii) The nominal group decision is the pooled outcome of the individual votes.

The NGT is widely employed in health, social service industry, education and government organisations these days. Although the research is not clear-cut, experiments have shown it to be equal to or superior to interacting groups. In fact finding, generating large number of ideas, avoidance of domination, minimising errors, reduction of conformance and satisfaction of group members.

## The Delphi Technique

Participants in the Delphi technique are physically dispersed and do not meet face to face for group decision-making. It does not require the physical presence of the group members. (The name Delphi indicates a shrine at which the ancient Greeks prayed for information about the future). The key to the Delphi process is the anonymous input. Communication between participants takes place through mail only. The anonymous input tends to eliminate the counter productive effects that status, intimidation, emotion, face-saving and argumentation can have in traditional interacting group decision-making procedures. The following steps characterise the Delphi technique.

### 1. First stage

(i) The problem is identified by the chairperson and a carefully structured sequence of questionnaires regarding the problem mailed out to members.

(ii) Each member anonymously and independently answers the questionnaire and mails his responses to the chairperson.

(iii) These suggestions are pooled and a feedback report is prepared by the chairperson.

### 2. Second stage

(i) The feedback report and a more advanced, second stage questionnaires are sent back to each member for reaction and reassessment.

(ii) Each member evaluates the feedback report, generates new suggestions, votes on the priority of the ideas contained in it.

(iii) The process is continued until a clear solution emerges.

The Delphi technique tends to take more time than other methods. It has the advantage of being able to involve people who are separated geographically in decision-making. The absence of face-to-face interactions insulates members from the undue influence of others. Like the NGT, the Delphi technique has an excellent track record. Many large companies employ the method to identify and solve problem.

## INFORMAL ORGANISATIONS

In a general sense organisations are collections of individuals, collectives with collective tasks to perform. The collective tasks are dissected into subtasks, and members are assigned to them, creating organisational positions. These positions prescribe the duties, activities and authority relationships of each organisation member. The classical organisation structure is built around positions and not around people. In reality, such a formal structure shows only one set of relationships, the officially planned relationships, between groups and individuals working together. Other important relationships exist, often, called the informal organisation exerting a powerful influence upon productivity and job satisfaction. They blend with formal system to make a workable system for getting the work done in a smooth way. Both formal and informal relationships are necessary for group activity. As pointed out by Davis, they serve to preserve the organisation from the self destruction that would result from iteral obedience to rules and regulations.

### Nature

The informal organisation can be viewed as a shadow organisation. It arises naturally, spontaneously from the interaction of people. It refers to unofficial and unauthorised relationships what inevitably occur between individuals and groups with the formal organisation. It exists within the confines of the formal authority structure. However, the interactions that occur informally are not prescribed by the formal structure nor can they be completely controlled by the formal structure. It is a by product of human nature and is affected by the formal structure.

## Formal and Informal Organisation Compared and Contrasted

**1. Origin:** Formal organisations are goal oriented. They are tightly built around the general principles of organisation and are the result of conscious thought processes. Informal organisation develops naturally. Informal structure reflects individual and group goals rather than organisational goals. Changes in formal organisation structure occur through collective agreements between members. In contrast, changes in informal organisations occur through administrative policies.

**2. Basic Structural Components:** Formal organisations have a definite structure reflected in the organisation charts providing a pictorial representation of authority relationships. These organisation charts are built around positions and exhibit officially blesses relationships. The organisation tends to be mechanical and impersonal. Informal organisations are built around people. They are structureless. Moreover, they are initiated by the workers themselves to serve the needs of workers. The basic purpose is to improve human relationships.

**3. Goals:** Formal organisations are wedded to well defined goals created by management. These goals may be to skim mercilessly an exploitative surplus from out of the GNP or to increase the market share of efficiency etc. Whereas the basic purpose of an informal organisation can be broadly defined as the social satisfaction of its members. It is the primary duty of every manager to provide meaningful goals to organisational participants so that there is no conflict between individual (informal) and organisational (formal) goals.

**4. Influence Processes:** In formal organisations, positions conferred on individuals are the centres of power and influence. Authority is equated with influence. People enjoying authority are supposed to be powerful. In contrast, influence in the informal organisation is attached to the person. The individual with the most influence is the person who is most able to satisfy the needs of the group. The stamp of approval from the relevant group is necessary to enjoy power and influence in the informal groups.

**5. Control Process:** Formal organisations are tied to a rigid system of rules and regulations. Control points are established to constrain behaviour, restrain the members from going off the track. Informal organisations are not glued to any rigid system of rules but are governed by group norms. Norms are standards of behaviour designed to regulate social behaviour along acceptable lines. Formal rules may be so much of a waste paper once they are not 'approved' by the informal groups.

**6. Communication:** Formal organisations depend on formal, official channels of communication. These officially blessed instruments employed scrupulously to convey the feelings of management to workers. Communication, thus, largely is a one-way traffic. The informal organisation designs its own channel of communication, popularly known as 'grapevine' for both organisational and social communication purposes. The grapevine can spread rumours and false information as rapidly as it can spread facts. It tends to outstrip formal channels on speed.

**7. Size:** Formal organisations can balloon to gigantic, unmanageable proportions depending on the degree of success enjoyed by them in the market. In contrast, informal organisations tend to be small and manageable.

## Reasons for the Emergence of Informal Organisations

Basically the informal organisation emerges because the formal structure does not satisfy all employee and organisational needs. Formal organisations fail to describe the dynamic relationships between members in the organisation. Informal relationships developed within any formal structure and managers do not have a choice. It is important for the managers to understand the informal organisation and channel its energies toward organisational goals. The informal organisation presents many opportunities for motivating employees, resolving conflicts and creating worker satisfaction.

**1. Psychological fatigue of routine tasks:** Simple and routine tasks in the office and in the factory can have an undesirable influence on the workers. Under such conditions personnel can become bored by their tasks and indifferent to their work and may experience psychological fatigue. Unable to relate their jobs to final output, workers suffer from feelings of meaninglessness, workers also feel powerless to control factors within the environment. Under such distasteful conditions, informal relations in the organisations serve to preserve the organisation from the self destruction that would result from literal obedience to formal policies, rules, regulations and procedures. Informal organisations fill the psychological void/vacuum created by dull, boring and monotonous jobs. It has the capacity to overcome deficiencies built into the formal structure.

**2. Desire to socialise with others:** Most people like to socialise in order to satisfy more of their social and ego needs on the jobs. "Formal organisations are systems of medieval torture which suppress and subjugate their victim—the individual. He lives in helpless conformity, stripped of his self-esteem in a phony and artificial environment. There is no challenge and chance for psychological fulfilment. Informal organisations provide social satisfactions. Affiliation with the informal groups is more than just friendship, it is a sense of belonging. It gives a man recognition, status and future opportunity to relate to others. Informal organisation acts like a 'safety valve' to release daily tensions and frustrations on their jobs. The informal organisations will lend a sympathetic ear to their troubles and will give an opportunity to ventilate their grievances.

**3. Source of protection:** Informal organisation offers a powerful protection against threatening and oppressive forces. Informal organisation increases the feeling of security; it restores some internal and external human values lost because of efforts to achieve efficiency by oversimplifying work. Informal organisation serves as a balancing function by giving satisfaction to individual members that the formal structure cannot give. It also assures members, a reasonable degree of stability in their interpersonal relationships. In an informal organisation the rules for behaviour are set by the members not by the management.

## Characteristics

**1. Goals:** The informal organisation has its own goals, objectives and authority patterns and these factors may or may not coincide with those of the formal structures.

**2. Membership:** Individuals in an informal organisation join on the basis of commonality of interest and willingness to be co-operative and to conform. Quite often, groups pressurise the members to conform to the group norms. These norms are established to achieve the goals of the group and to be accepted, forces members to conform group norms. It is reported that in the Bank wiring room study of the famous Hawthrone Studies, one of the inspectors failed to observe the group norms and in an attempt to punish him, the workers adjusted his testing equipment so as to render it ineffective. There is substantial evidence to support a statement, that when an individual takes a stand publicly, he is more likely to be influenced by group norms when he arrives at a conclusion in private. Individuals may than have overlapping memberships in multifarious informal groups.

**3. Leadership:** Informal leader will arise from the situation. That person with the greatest expertise relative to the situation at hand will emerge as a leader. As a result, a group may select numerous individuals to serve in specific leadership capacities depending on the situation. Informal leaders are selected normally, on the basis of respect, admiration, and the capacity to sit through the tasks successfully for the benefit of the groups. Informal leadership is a conditional offer. If the informal leader does something that is not approved by the group, the group will strip him off his position.

**4. Communication:** Informal organisation develops its own communication network, popularly known as grapevine. The grapevine has got a tremendous capacity to carry information with helpful and harmful effects to the organisation in an unpredictable way. According to Davis, the cluster approach adequately sums up the process of grapevine. In the cluster approach a message is communicated by an originator to two or three individuals, who in turn, each pass the message along to two or three others, who do the same thing. The grapevine is flexible and personal. It spreads the information faster than the formal communication channel. Unfortunately, what the grapevine possesses in speed, it usually lacks in accuracy. It can spread rumours and false information as rapidly as it can spread facts.

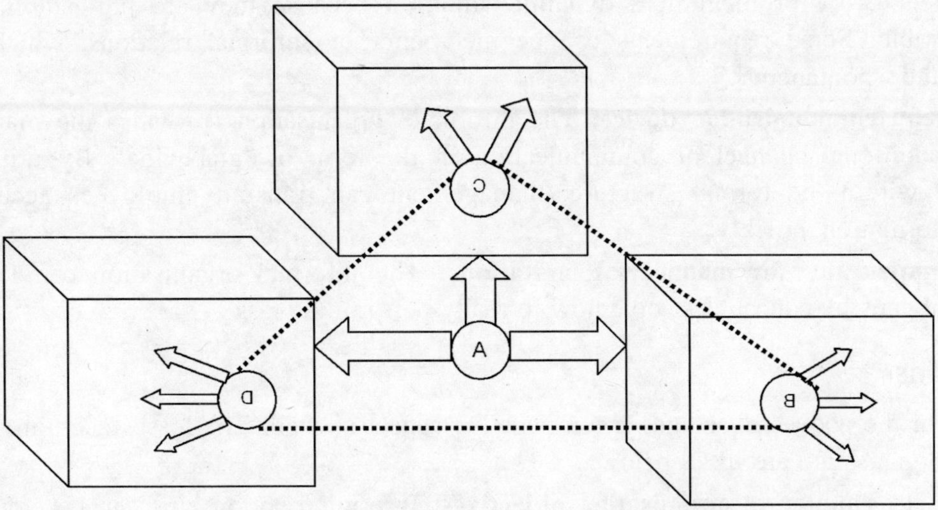


***Figure: 9.3 Communication Through clusters***

**5. Status system:** Status is important in organisations because it satisfies the basic human need for personal identification. It plays a very useful role in the interaction between the members of the group. Knowledge about another's status helps us to behave in a proper way; we are in a better position to structure, understand and predict the social interactions that are important to us. Status is determined by other external factors (education, age, personality, skills) and internal factors (location of office, secretaries, parking space etc.).

Members in an informal organisation can improve their communication depending on the status of the individual with whom they are communicating. For example students will be very careful about their mannerisms and words while talking to the principal (higher status). The same is not true when, they converse with their friends (equal status).

## Advantages and Disadvantages of Informal Organisation

The values of the informal organisation which can make a great contribution to organisational effectiveness are outlined below:

**1. Benefits to work groups:** The informal organisation protects the individual against arbitrary treatment by management against harsh work environments. As pointed out by Herbert, "the informal organisation allows human relationships and satisfactions to be superimposed over the Spartan structure created by technology and organisation, adding a human dimension to the formal organisation". The informal structure counteracts the cold and inhuman qualities of the formal structure by providing a means for developing friendships and being accepted by fellow workers. It provides satisfaction and stability to work groups.

**2. Supports formal structure:** The formal structure is viewed as one side of the "organisation coin" while the informal structure is viewed as the other. The informal organisation helps the formal organisation in many ways and without its support the formal structure would be like a "house built on sand". Informal systems "blend with formal systems to make a workable system for getting the work done". Formal plans and policies cannot meet every problem in a dynamic situation because they are pre-established and partly flexible. Some requirements can be met better by informal relations, which can be flexible and spontaneous."

**3. Useful communication device:** The informal organisation provides the management with an additional channel of communication in the form of 'grapevine'. By utilising the grapevine within the formal structure, management can transmit employees accurate and useful information quickly.

**4. Compensates for managerial limitations:** The informal organisation can fill in the managerial gaps by educating people how to really perform the task.

## Limitations

Each of the above advantages has a negative aspect as well. The losses accruing from the informal organisation are listed below.

**1. Works counter to organisation objectives:** Informal relationships can be employed to pressurise employees to restrict their output, exhibit a disinterest in organisational policies and procedures, cause insubordination, and in general, promote unauthorised actions that work counter to the formal organisation.

**2. Conformity:** Informal organisation exerts strong pressures for conformity. Conformity can make group members reluctant to act independently, creatively or assertively, for fear of losing group approval and membership. Sometimes, informal group leaders manipulate the group toward undesirable needs. They may block positive contributions from capable people. They may force members to restrict output, to exceed the time limit for coffee break, to indulge in intolerable activities, taxing the patience of the management. In this fashion the informal group can become "an instrument of neurotic sowers of conflict or non-responsible rabble—rousers using the group for their own selfish ends".

**3. Social costs:** Informal organisation, undoubtedly, is a safety valve for the frustrations and other emotional problems of workgroup. Studies have also noted the view that social interaction by alleviating monotony on the job, may actually contribute to production. But this is true up to a certain point. Allowing informal groups to engage in gossiping, joke telling and general horse play or idle conversation that satisfy some of the members' social needs, results in higher operating costs.

**4. Rumours:** Quite often, grapevine is susceptible for use in spreading destructive, distorted, inaccurate and incomplete information cutting across organisational lines with tremendous speed. Where the formal communication system is poor, such rumours prosper. When employees are not kept informed on matters that directly affect them, they may transmit incorrect information that undermines morale or leads people to make poor and mediocre decisions.

**5. Resistance to change:** Every group promotes certain cultural values, norms which it considers desirable. In course of time members zealously guard these values resulting in a perpetuation of the status quo. Any intended change by the management forcing alteration of shared values, real or perceived, is vehemently resisted. If the member perceive that a layoff is imminent, consequent to the introduction of such policies like rationalisation, automation computers etc., they try to stand like a rock resisting such changes with all their might. "Perception of threats are just as real in the formation and solidification of an informal organisation as an actual threat."

## Managing the Informal Organisation

The informal organisation is an unintended complement to the organisation. It emerges on its own, without conscious intent as a natural and human consequence of the host task organisation. It is an inevitable part of organisational life. Like it or not, managers must understand that the informal organisation exists and can't be worked away, banished or outlawed. Attempts to disperse with it without understanding its causes and processes can lead to harmful consequences. As such the manager must learn to accept it, deal with it and integrate it with the formal organisation. In dealing with informal organization, managers should be careful not to transgress the informal system resulting in reactive behaviour that blocks formal goals. He must recognise and respect the values, beliefs, norms and loyalties of the group and operate accordingly.

More specifically a manager should:

1. Let employees know that he accepts and understands informal organisation.
2. Consider possible influences on informal system when taking action.

3. Integrate the interests of information groups with those of the formal organisation.
4. Keep formal activities from unnecessarily threatening informal organisation in general.

## REVIEW QUESTIONS

1. What are the basic types of groups in organisation? Which type of group do you think is most significant? Why?
2. Discuss the nature of group dynamics which prevail in informal organisation and its impact on the effectiveness of organisation as a whole.
3. How is cohesiveness related to performance? What implications does this relationship have for improving performance in organisations?
4. What are the key components in Homan's group behaviour model? Explain the model.
5. What are the benefits that an individual member gains from group membership? What 'costs' are simultaneously incurred?
6. What we the social norms? In what ways might they make a manager's job easier? More difficult?
7. How does the size of a group affect its activities?
8. Describe the function of role playing in a group situation.
9. Discuss the forces that make for conformity in a group and those that make for differentiation.
10. Draw a sociometric analysis for a group with which you are familiar. Explain the patterns you have described.
11. What are the major functions of the informal group leader? Do you think informal group leaders can make effective formal leaders?
12. It was stated that the formal manager cannot control the activities of the informal organisation. Evaluate and discuss this statement.
13. Explain in detail how formal organisations and informal organisation can be integrated or encouraged to support each other more fully.
14. It has often been stated that most work within an organisation is done informally. Is this correct? Why or Why not?
15. What is meant by the statement that the informal organisation compensates for the formality of the formal organisation?

## CRITICAL THINKING QUESTIONS

- Think of a small work group that you belonged to recently. Assess the level of its cohesiveness. What factors contributed to or prevented its cohesiveness?
- "The actual process of interaction among the individuals represented in the formal plan cannot adequately be described solely in terms of its planned lines of interaction". Elucidate this statement.
- Have you ever been in a situation where informal group norms put you in role conflict with formal organisation standards? Discuss
- Are groups better than individuals in solving organisational problems? Explain.

- Why is it useful for a manager to understand group behaviour  why is it useful for an employee?
- "One cannot predict the effectiveness of an organisation structure or of a leader without understanding the group processes that exist in the situation". Explain whether you agree or disagree with this statement and why?
- Describe an incident of social loafing in which you may have been involved in the recent past. What might be done to overcome this effect?
- What kinds of issues must managers address when attempting to improve group effectiveness?
- is it always good to have a high level of conformity within a group?  Can managers affect the level of conformity within a group?  Why or Why not?

## Case 1: The New Employee

Bharat Kumar recently completed trade school as an apprentice plumber and had several months of experience through working summers.  He has just accepted a full-time job in the maintenance section of a chemical processing plant.  The first day on the job, the supervisor assigned him to work with Raj Kapoor who had been working in the section for over 10 years.

The two were assigned to do some repair work on a storage tank two miles north of the maintenance station.  As they drove to the area in a pickup truck, Kapoor stopped by a pump house to collect a bet on a ball game from the night before.  Bharat was eager to get to work his first day, showed his impatience with Kapoor talking with his buddies, and got a disapproving look.

Once on the job Bharat climbed quickly into the truck to get the tools, and Kapoor said, "What's your hurry? That job's not gonna run away".

Several times during the morning, Kapoor ridiculed Bharat for his enthusiasm.  After the morning break, as they got up to go back to work, Kapoor again asked why he was hurrying. When he sped back in the truck to get some materials from the warehouse, Kapoor said he acted as if he was being paid double time.  When they had to wait 45 minutes for an electrician to change some electrical connections, Bharat wanted to start on other work, but Kapoor told him to "hold tight and do one job at a time."

At lunch Kapoor ate in the cafeteria with three other buddies and played cards.  As Bharat looked around the cafeteria, he noticed that everyone was eating together in small groups, so he ate alone.

The afternoon went pretty much like the morning. Kapoor worked at a fairly steady pace all day as he kidded around with the  same group of pals, griped about the lack of support provided by other departments, commented on the "dumb supervisors," and played tricks on members of the gang. Bharat learned quickly that if he went along and followed Kapoor, there would be no trouble. But as soon as he tried to go it alone, he was sure to get a put-down or a wisecrack from Kapoor.

### Question

1. What group processes are taking place in this case ?

2. If Bharat conforms, why will he do so ?
3. What risks are there in his not conforming ?
4. Is it possible for Bharat to change the fair day's work norm ?
5. Is there anything the supervisor can do to capitalise on Bharat's enthusiasm and avoid his following the groups established work patterns? Should he?

## Case 2 : The Friendly Supervisor

Raju manages the customer relations department of a public utility company. The department is responsible for replying to customer requests for information and to customer complaints. There are seven typists in the department who handle the correspondence of customers dedicated by the staff.

Raju recently promoted Bobby to office supervisor. Bobby had been a typist in the department for ten years. She was considered the fastest and most accurate typist who had ever worked for Raju. Bobby had the best attendance record in the department, and Raju considered her his dependable employee. She was very well liked by all the typists, and they considered her to be a good personal friend.

As a supervisor, Bobby does a good job of handing out work assignments, but she does little else to supervise the typists. She does not like to criticise the typists and does not enforce office rules. No matter what a typist does, Bobby will not take any disciplinary action. She makes no attempt to check the work of the typists for compliance with quality standards or to see that work is completed on time. In fact, she spends most of her time typing to reduce the work load of the other typists.

Raju has been receiving an increasing number of complaints from the department staff about the poor quality of the typing and about the slow turn around the time for work. He has also received complaints about the typists taking excessively long coffee breaks and spending time on personal calls.

When Raju talked to the typists, they told him that Bobby frequently invites them to her house for dinner or to play bridge. It appears to Raju that the typists all like Bobby as a friend, but they are becoming concerned about her lack of supervision.

Raju mentioned to Bobby that she should focus her effort on improving the work of the typists. She replied, "These women are my friends, and I don't feel right about cracking down on them."

### Questions

1. Can an individual effectively manage a group and be a close personal friend with group members?
2. What should Raju do to ensure that the work of the typists will improve?
3. Should Bobby have been promoted to office supervisor?
4. If you were Bobby, what would you do? Would you quit the supervisor's job? Would you no longer be friends with the typists?

# 10

# Teams and Team Work

## TEAMS JAI HO!

What started as secret service outfits in Proctor & Gamble (P&G) in early 1960s (before that the pioneering work of Tavistock Institute in the late 1940s in the United Kingdom ) have acquired considerable strength, acceptance and admiration in corporate world with the passage of time. Not without reason of course. The results produced by teams are truly dazzling and even mind-numbing in some cases. For example, a General Electric Plant in North Carolina experienced a 20 per cent increase in productivity after team implementation. Wilson Sporting Goods reported saving $100 million per year for five years thanks to its teams. Colgate-Palmolive reported that technician turnover was extremely low—more than 90 per cent of technicians were retained after five years—once it changed to a team-based approach. Let us begin the journey and crack the mystery surrounding teams. In the 1960s P&G envisioned teams as a way to achieve a significant competitive advantage and for many years kept their idea secret. They had gone to the extent of asking their consultants and employees working as members of a team to sign nondisclosure agreements! P&G discovered that teamwork creates wonderful performance synergies and a competitive edge over the competition. Most organisations—including the likes of Monsanto, Caterpillar, AT&T, P&G, General Electric, FedEx, Honeywell, PepsiCo, Xerox, Ford, Maruti, Infosys, British Petroleum, 3M etc— today maintain a vast army of teams willing to stretch themselves to any extent, work with zeal and commitment in order to produce results beyond imagination. In fact, about 80 per cent of all Fortune 500 companies are using teams in some part of their organisation currently. At Mattel, a team of artists, toy designers, computer experts and automobile designers slashed 13 months from the usual toy design process, creating Top Speed Toy Cars in only 5 months. Ford uses teams to spot quality problems and improve efficiency and other manufacturers use teams to master sophisticated new production technologies. Roche, Pfizer, Merck and other pharmaceutical giants have been using multi-disciplinary teams to speed the process of bringing new drugs to the market place. Research evidence also suggests that companies are rather compelled to make use of teams over tasks demanding multiple skills, judgement and experience. Teams have found their way to success on most occasions because of their ability to quickly assemble things, deploy resources, refocus energies and disband operations—all at unbelievable speed. (Orsburn et al; J.R.Katzenbach; Charles C Manz)Introduction

**Box 10.1 Why teams?**

The world is changing fast nowadays. It is true that the world has been evolving and changing since time began, but what is so different today is both the pace and the effects of change, which impinge on everyone's life (Charles Handy, Age of Unreason). Competition is hotting up. New products, new technologies, new processes hit the markets with frustrating regularity. In order to survive, corporates are virtually compelled to economise on every front – go after modern technology, restructure operations, explore new markets, find new uses of existing products, innovate, experiment and find new ways of living and most importantly use human resources productively. While fighting with the various forces of change, corporations have realised the importance of teams which are more flexible and responsive to changing events than are traditional departments or other forms of permanent groupings. Corporations have benefited from the use of teams in the form of increased productivity, increased speed of operations, reduced costs, improved quality, reduced destructive internal competition, improved workplace cohesion etc.

## Differences between Groups and Teams

A group consists of two or more individuals, interacting and interdependent, who have come together to achieve a common goal. Members interact, share information and help each other in order to realise the goals. However, they do not necessarily engage in activities that would lead to a joint, well-coordinated, effort. Their performance is equal to the sum total of each member's individual contribution.

## Members

- Committed to goals they helped define.
- Possess complementary skills.
- Support one another willingly.
- Hold themselves collectively accountable for results.
- Trust and support other members.
- Offer suggestions and give feedback to other members.
- May disagree but work to resolve differences and reach consensus.
- In short, teams create the potential for an organisation to generate greater outputs with no increase in inputs.

On the other hand, a work team generates positive synergy through coordinated effort. The individual efforts result in a level of performance that is greater than the sum of those individual inputs. To be precise, a team may be defined as *a small group of people with complementary skills who work actively together to achieve a common purpose for which they hold themselves collectively accountable.* (Katzenback and Smith, 1993)

- A work team produces positive synergy through coordinated effort.
- Members put their complementary competencies (abilities, skills and knowledge) to best use in producing an overall level of performance that is greater than the sum of the individual inputs.
- The heart of any team is a shared commitment by its members for their joint performance. Teams focus on individual and mutual accountability—that is, they work together to produce an outcome (e.g. product, service or decision) that represents their joint contributions, and each member shares responsibility for that outcome.
- Team members also share a common commitment to purpose—typically positioning a firm at the top or serving customers in the best possible way, or producing quality products better than rivals etc. team members are passionate about such lofty purposes and remain heavily focused on activities that help them surpass common expectations. In fact, teams are said to establish 'ownership' of their purposes and usually spend a great deal of time, establishing their purpose.
- Teams usually set their own goals and choose the approach that helps them realize those goals without interference from management. This does not, however, mean that they are completely independent and free to do whatever they want. They still must be responsive to demands from higher levels while trying to manage the show in a very flexible manner. (see Greenberg and Baron, 2005). The differences between the two concepts may be summarised thus

**Table 10.1. Groups Vs Team**

| *Group* | *Point* | *Team* |
|---|---|---|
| A function of what its members do as individuals | Performance | Performance includes individualefforts and collective work products which are the result of joint, coordinated attempts. |
| Strong, clearly focused leader | Leader | Shared leadership roles |
| Individual accountability | Accountability | Individual and mutual accountability |
| Runs efficient meetings | Meetings | Encourages open-ended, active, problem-solving meetings |
| Random and varied | Skills | Complementary |
| Neutral (sometimes negative) | Synergy | Positive |
| Discusses, decides and delegates | Functioning | Discusses, decides and does real work together. |

As the table clearly indicates, a team is more than just a group of individuals working together. Teamwork has a synergistic effect in that the individuals working together achieve more than they could alone. Members share a common purpose which is clear to each team member. Teamwork, in any case, does not just happen, it needs continuous effort. The effort should also be enjoyable, full and should result in a feeling of personal satisfaction for every team member. Much of this job is done by the team leader who makes them realise that team interests are above personal aspirations. Another feature of the team is that it has a 'feel' about it, a sort or teamness. Members exchange feelings, opinions ideas freely, discuss openly and try to learn from each other. There is a pride, a sense of belonging to the team, which members find motivating.

## EFFECTIVE, HIGH PERFORMING TEAMS?

Effective, high performing work teams have a clear understanding of the goal for which the members have come together. Members have relevant skills and possess requisite knowledge. They know how to combine their capabilities in the service of team's goals. Effective teams are characterized by high mutual trust among members. Members believe in the integrity, character and ability of one another. They exhibit intense loyalty and dedication to the team. They are ready to do anything that is essential to keep the team's flag flying high. They are willing to expend extraordinary amounts of energy in order to realize team's goals in a unified manner. Members of an effective team are able to convey messages in a form that is readily and clearly understood by others. They share their feelings, thoughts, concerns with one another in an open and frank manner. The team leaders play the role of a coach, facilitator and a mentor. They clear the fog, show the way and put members on track through untiring efforts. They are also able to put out fires quickly and effectively. They do everything possible to boost up the morale of team members. They are also able to patiently explain the outcomes of outstanding team effort time and again. There is a conscious effort on the part of every one to turn the wok spot into a funny little world where members are willing to put their best foot forward, exploit their potential and produce outstanding results.( http://www.teambuildingportal.com/articles/effective-teams/team-effectiveness )

- Effective Teams Talk to one Another Rather than Behind Each Other's Back. Back-biting rare or non-existent in an efficient team and there is a high level of mutual trust. Trust creates a bond among the team members and this leads to rapport and solidarity. Tensions are therefore absent.
- Effective Teams Have a Healthy Respect for Each Other's Viewpoints. They actively listen and encourage one another and they participate and contribute during group discussions. Disagreements exist but do not snowball into interpersonal conflict.
- Effective Teams Know How to Deal with Conflicts. Conflicts or disagreements pertaining to task-related discussions are treated as a normal occurrence and the team members do not harbor any animosity towards one another once the team meeting ends.
- Effective Teams are True Partners in all Aspects Related to Teamwork. They are supportive and have an informal work ethic of sharing and fellowship. There are fully aware of their shared goals and shared responsibility and work towards jointly achieving their objectives.
- Effective Teams Want Team Success. They realise the need to focus on group goals and rise above personal ambitions. Team members are secure in their individual capabilities and understand the reason why the organisation constituted a team in the first place. They are able to work towards executing their role in line with the common goals of the team. They seem to realise that if they carry out their individual roles sincerely, personal recognition is bound to come their way. In other words, there is a good measure of 'team spirit' within the team.

## What Makes an Effective Team Member?

Effective team members need very special skills to succeed in a team environment. Not everyone has these skills. Most people can learn these skills with a combination of training and practical experience. Some people either can't or won't learn them and must be gotten rid of as soon as possible. The basic skills are:

- an ability listen well
- the ability to participate and contribute
- able to represent their own area of expertise
- gives up turf issues for the sake of the whole
- takes a multifunctional perspective on the issues
- can set aside his or her own ego
- is flexible, secure, competent, and inclusive

In addition to these basic skills, a good team member must develop good meeting skills as well:

- Stand up meeting facilitation
- Consensus building
- Probing and questioning for information and clarification
- Restating and clarifying issues
- Summarizing concepts and meeting segments
- Framing concepts and issues
- Identifying issues and solving problems
- Giving and receiving feedback supportively
- Generating ideas
- Observing and processing team effectiveness

## Team Advantages & Disadvantages

The advantages and disadvantages of teams also need to be considered before deciding to transition to teams.

**Table 10.2. Advantages and Disadvantages of Teams**

| *Team Advantages* | *Team Disadvantages* |
|---|---|
| • Team members have the opportunity to learn from each other. | • Some individuals are not compatible with team work. |
| • Potential exists for greater work force flexibility with cross-training. | • Workers must be selected to fit the team as well as requisite job skills. |
| • Opportunity provided for synergistic combinations of ideas and abilities. | • Some members may experience less motivating jobs as part of a team. |
| • New approaches to tasks may be discovered. | • Organization may resist change. |
| • Teams membership can provide social facilitation and support for difficult tasks and situations. | • Conflict may develop between team members or other teams. |

| | |
|---|---|
| • Communication and information exchange may be facilitated and increased. | • Teams may be time-consuming due to need for coordination and consensus. |
| • Teams can foster greater cooperation among team members. | • Teams can stymie creativity and inhibit good decision-making if "group think" becomes prevalent. |
| • Interdependent work flow can be enhanced. | |
| • Potential exists for greater acceptance and understanding of team-made decisions. | • Evaluation and rewards may be perceived as less powerful; |
| • Greater autonomy, variety, identity, significance, and feedback for workers can occur. | • "Free-riding" within the team may occur. |
| • Team commitment may stimulate performance and attendance. | • Less flexibility may be experienced in personnel replacement or transfer. |

*Adapted from Medsker, G.J., Campion, M.A., "Job and Team Design," in Salvendy, G., Handbook of Human Factors and Ergonomics, pp. 450 - 489, Interscience, 18 Apr 1997.

## TYPES OF TEAMS

In modern organisations, four different types of teams are commonly identified (Stewart et al)

### 1. PROBLEM-SOLVING TEAMS

It is a group of 5 to 12 employees from the same department, who voluntarily meet for a few hours each week to discuss and solve quality, cost, ways of improving efficiency and other work-related problems. (Quality circles come under this category). It must be mentioned here, that members in a problem solving team are there only to discuss work-related problems, share ideas and offer suggestions as to how work processes and methods could be improved. The recommendations of the team, emerging out of such regular meetings, are put forward before management for approval. Problem solving teams normally are the first step in a company's move toward greater employee participation. As the company matures, problems solving teams can take the shape of self-directed teams. .

### 2. SELF-MANAGING TEAMS

Self managing teams typically consist of 5 to 20 multiskilled workers who rorate jobs to produce an entire product or service or at least one complete aspect or portion of a product or service such as engine assembly, insurance claim processing et.c. These groups are empowered to make the decisions required to manage themselves on a day-to-day basis. Members here make decisions on scheduling work, allocating tasks, training for job skills, evaluating performance, selecting new teammates and controlling quality of work. Members are collectively held responsible for the team's overall performance. Self managing teams are permanent and formal elements in the organisational structure. They are large enough to offer a good mix of skills and resources. Members are trained usually to take up varied jobs, defending on situational requirements. This is made possible, partially, by multiskilling whereby team members are trained in undertaking more than one job on the team.

## Features

Self directed teams typically include the following elements

- The team includes employees with several skills and functions and the combined skills are sufficient to perform a major organisational task. A team may include members from the foundry, machining, grinding fabrication and sales departments, with each member cross-trained to perform one another's job. The team eliminates barriers among departments enabling excellent coordination to produce a product or service
- The team is given access to resources such as information, equipment, machinery and supplies required to perform the complete task
- The team is empowered with decision making authority which means that members have the freedom to select new members, solve problems, spend money, monitor results, adapt to changing conditions and plan for the future. The central idea is that the teams themselves, rather than managers or supervisors, take responsibility for their work.

## Self directed teams at GE/Durham

The jet engine building teams at GE are self directed work teams. Each team owns the engine it builds—from the beginning of the assembly process to getting the engine loaded on a truck for delivery. As a team starts to build each engine, it gets only one instruction from the top—that is, where engine is to be shipped from the plant. The team orders tools and equipment, chooses its own staff, conducts quality control checks and takes every other decision that is required to build the engine. As one employee expressed it: " I came from Northrop Grumman where I was working on a B-2 bomber. That plane, which used Stealth technology, was as high-tech as you can get. But someone else wrote the assembly process. Here, I write process—at the mechanic level. There I was on a 'team' but I also had a supervisor. He had a boss. And there were other bosses above him. In two years of working there, I never saw the plant manager. Everyday, my boss would just hand me my job. I had no input at all—none. I'm happier here." (C. Fishman, Engines of Democracy, Fsst Company, October 1999.

When it is truly empowered, a self directed team does more than simply take over administrative duties. It also has a strong commitment to the organisation's mission, the autonomy needed to control its own activities, belief in itself and a chance to see directly the impact of its efforts. (Kirkman and Rosen)

Self directed teams have proved to be effective. Several companies such as Federal Express and IDS have boosted productivity up to 40 per cent by adopting self directed teams. Volvo uses self-directed teams of 7 to 10 hourly workers to assemble four cars per shift. However, empowered self managed teams aren't necessarily right for every situation or organisation. A number of questions need to be answered properly before introducing self directed teams, dealing with issues such as specification of goals and expected results from the teams, access given to teams to draw needed resources, ability of members to carry out interdependent tasks, maturity levels of members to hire, select, train, evaluate and discipline teammates from time to time (J.D.Oshorn and L.Moran 2000)

## 3. CROSS-FUNCTIONAL TEAMS

It consists of a group of employees from about the same hierarchical level, but from different work areas who come together to accomplish a task. A task force or a project team comes under this category. These teams are created to deal with a specific problem and are usually disbanded when the task is completed or the problem is solved. A committee is (another cross-functional team) a formal organisational team usually relatively long lived, created to carry out specific organisational tasks. Roche, Pfizer and Merck and other Pharmaceutical companies have used cross functional teams to speed the process of bringing new drugs to the market place. Major automobile manufacturers including Toyota, Honda, BMW, Ford, GM, Daimler Chrysler, Mahindra & Mahindra, Tata Motor have relied on cross functional teams to create and manufacture new models. In the aircraft industry Boeing created cross functional teams that designed nd manufactured its latest aircraft, the 777. In all the above cases, cross functional teams have been used to speed design, production and services processes or to enhance creativity and innovation—of course, quite successfully.

However, cross functional teams are not easy to manage. Members from various fields with diverse backgrounds may find it difficult to get along, especially during the formative stages of the team. Unless members show maturity and tolerance, initial interactions may not yield fruitful results. Building trust among members and resolving issues to mutual satisfaction may take painfully long time. Experts have come out with useful guidelines to overcome these: hurdles: (Jassawalla and Sashittal)

- Work to see that each member believes that he or she has the opportunity to influence the group's decision making (stake building)
- Try to make sure that members' expectations and personal agendas are brought before the team and deliberated upon freely (transparency)
- Ensure that all divergent points of view are explicitly recognised and examined (improving quality of decisions)
- Facilitate the building of as much trust as possible within the group, so that no one feels that someone else will try to take advantage of them (Synergy building)

## 4. VIRTUAL TEAMS

IBM began to use virtual teams in early 1970s. Currently, about one out of three IBM employees participate as a member of at least one virtual team. A virtual team convenes and operates with members linked together electronically via networked computers. It uses computer technology and groupware (software that facilitates interaction among virtual group members) to tie together members from various locations working toward a common goal. Members need not be working in close proximity and may often be geographically dispersed—cross-organizationally or cross-nationally. Almost all meetings could take place via electronic communication( including wide area networks, videoconferencing, fax, e-mail etc ) Sometimes a company may also use virtual teams in partnership with suppliers or in many cases with competitors to pull together the best brains to complete a project or speed a new product to market. Leadership among team members is shared or altered depending on the area of expertise required at each stage of the project.

Virtual teams bring cost effectiveness and speed to teamwork where members are unable to meet easily face-to-face. There is the added advantage of objective information sharing and decision-making based on facts. Where members are well trained in the use of computers and are able to process and interpret data without any emotional considerations, virtual teams may yield positive gains.

On the negative side, virtual teams suffer from lack of social rapport and direct interaction. The information exchange may take place speedily but in the absence of direct contact, even straight forward ideas may be misinterpreted. The kind of getting-to-know-you socialization process that occurs with nonvirtual groups that meet face to face is missing. Without social rapport, it may be difficult to build trust and confidence among members. Interaction between members may be purely task oriented. Oft repeated issues like role ambiguity and social loafing may also crop up repeatedly in virtual groups.

The success of virtual teams, therefore, depends on several crucial elements (Brian Dumaine; Solomon, Jarvenpaa and Leidner)

- Careful selection of partners and team members; encourage team members to interact one on one, without feeling obliged to copy every email message to the entire team; encourage team mebers to discuss cultural differences freely.
- Strong management support of the team and its goals; be sure that someone is responsible for facilitating the communication process
- Utilization of best communication tools and procedures, better to use a variety of communication technologies ; pay special attention to the quality of the communication transmission (like low quality voice transmissions, poor video images etc)
- Development of trust among all members; to achieve this, it is better to hold an initial meeting on a face to face basis; whenever possible individual team members could pay a visit and meet members who are easily accessible; periodic meetings with members of course minimize the dangers emanating "out of site, out of mind" attitudes.
- Information sharing; also train team members to math their choice of technology to the task.

## Successful Team Requirements

The essential requirements of a successful team could be catalogued thus:

• **An Understandable Charter** - The charter is developed by the team and mutually agreed upon by the members. The charter should clearly define the mission or task and the boundaries within which the team is to operate. Has the team taken its assigned area of responsibility and designed its own mission, vision, and strategies to accomplish the mission? Has the team defined and communicated its goals; its anticipated outcomes and contributions; its timelines; and how it will measure both the outcomes of its work and the process the team followed to accomplish their task?

• **Effective Communication** - Good communication skills are vital to an effective team. This not only includes communication between team members, but also between the team and the organization.

• **Clear Roles and Responsibilities** - Clear roles and responsibilities need to be defined by the team, so that each member knows what is expected of him/her.

• **Time-efficient Processes** - Teams need well planned and structured meetings for efficient time management.

• **Interdependence** - Team member interdependence for task performance, shared goals, and rewards serves to increase group cohesiveness and efficacy.

• **A Sense of Accountability** - Both individual members and the team as a whole need to feel accountable for the team's actions, decisions, and performance.

• **Management Support** – A "champion" for teamwork in top management helps to create a climate for successful team work. Top management should increase delegation of authorities as the team matures and proves itself. (http://www.hf.faa.gov/webtraining/teamperform/Team019.htm)

## TEAMWORK

Teamwork occurs when group members work together in ways that utilise their skills to accomplish a common purpose.(Phillips) In such a scenario, members are prepared to listen and respond constructively to views expressed by others, give others the benefit of doubt, offer support and recognise the interests and achievements of others. Teamwork of this nature, of course, does not just happen. You cannot simply expect people to do a great job by assigning members to a group. To create a high performing team, a leader must invariably.(Dyer)

**Box 10.2. How to Create A High-Performing Team?**

- Communicate high-performance standards.
- Set the tone in the first team meeting.
- Create a sense of urgency.
- Make sure members have the right skills.
- Establish clear rules for team behaviour.
- As a leader, model expected behaviours.
- Find ways to create early "successes."
- Continually introduce new facts and information.
- Make sure members spend a lot of time together.
- Give positive feedback and reward high performance.

High performance teams, thus have strong core values, clear performance goals, the right mix of skills and creativity. Members in a homogeneous group (when members are alike in respect of age, gender, race, ethnicity, experience etc.) may score better than others in most cases because they find it easy to build social relationships quickly and begin interactions needed to work harmoniously together. Team diversity (in terms of demography, experiences, cultures) may create performance difficulties initially. However, once the members sort out interpersonal differences smoothly, they can put their varied backgrounds, experience and talents to effective use. Although it may take considerable time and effort to obtain teamwork from foundations of diversity, long-term benefits in creativity and performance can make it all worth while.(Watson)

## TEAM BUILDING

Team building is a broad title for activities designed to construct, develop and sustain groups of people who are working together to achieve common goals with a commitment to taking collective responsibility. (Watson) The process begins when someone notices that a problem exists which can be solved through collective efforts. Members then gather data concerning the problem, analyse these data, plan for improvements and implement the action plans. Everyone is expected to participate actively, and come up with solutions aimed at improving the effectiveness of the team. Team building, thus, is participatory and data based. Team building, as mentioned earlier, does not happen naturally in a group. Team members and leaders must consciously make efforts to build high performance teams. The important steps involved in this exercise could be listed thusLAdair, Robbins, Shaw, Thambain, Chhachhi)

### Members

a. ***Size:*** High performing teams tend to be small (generally 5 to 12). Large groups do not allow members to develop close understanding and rapport easily. As a team increases its size, it becomes harder for each member to interact with and influence the others.

b. ***Skills:*** Members must possess three kinds of skills. The most important one is the technical competence, followed by problem-solving and interpersonal skills. The right mix is important. Too much of one at the expense of others may affect performance.

c. ***Roles:*** For a team to be successful over the long run, it must be structured so as to both maintain its members social well being and accomplish its task. Two types of roles are worth highlighting here.

**Table 10.3. Roles of Team Members**

| ***Task-specialist Role*** | ***Socio-emotional Role*** |
|---|---|
| *People who play the task specialist role display the following behaviours:* | *People who support team members' emotional needs, play the following roles:* |
| • *Initiation:* Propose new solutions to team problems. | • *Encourage:* Are warm and receptive to other's ideas; praise and encourage others to draw forth their contributions. |
| • *Give opinions:* Offer opinions on task solutions; give candid feedback on others' suggestions. | • *Harmonise:* Reconcile group conflicts; help disagreeing parties reach agreement. |

| | |
|---|---|
| • *Seek information:* Ask for task relevant facts.<br>• *Summarise:* Relate various ideas to the problem at hand; pull ideas together into a summary perspective.<br>• *Energiser:* Stimulate the team into action when interest drops. | • *Reduce tension:* May tell jokes or in other ways draw off emotions when group atmosphere is tense.<br>• *Follow:* Go along with the team; agree to other team members' ideas.<br>• *Compromise:* Will shift own opinions to maintain team harmony. |

Some may even play a dual role, where the member contributes to both the team's task and supports members' emotional needs. Members who do not take an active part (playing a non-participative role) are held in low esteem by the team as a whole. Effective teams must have people in both task specialist and socio-emotional role. Humour and social concern are as important to team effectiveness as are facts and problem solving.

d. ***Behaviours:*** Team members must exhibit certain behaviours which help in developing close ties with others (S.R. Lloyd). These are listed below:

## Team Members: Ground Rules

- Speak respectfully to one another and about one another.
- Listen without interrupting.
- Express opinions, feelings openly, honestly.
- Make 'I' statements and not 'you' statements.
- Ask for help when needed, offer help when possible.
- Make commitments seriously and keep them.
- Support the team and each other.
- Focus on problems and solutions, not blame and accusations.

Not everyone could become a team player automatically. Members need to be picked carefully. If they lack team skills, training must be imparted. Workshops, counselling sessions, teaching classes could be held to help employees improve their problem solving, communication, negotiation, conflict management and coaching skills.

## Rewards

Members who indulge in social loafing (the tendency of individuals to extend less effort when working collectively than when working individually), as stated above, are not held in high esteem in a group setting. To avert this danger, successful teams make members individually and collectively responsible for teams goals. To encourage this, rewards are also designed to meet individual excellence as well as group targets. Selfless contributions to the team effort need to be adequately rewarded through promotions, pay raises, special allowances, etc.

## Leaders

The successful functioning of a team depends to a large extent on the 'soft skills' exhibited by the leader in the form of communication, conflict resolution, motivation, sharing and trust building.

- First, the leader should know his own strengths and how those strengths can help the entire group.
- Second, the leader should share power and information in order to empower team members and reach goals.
- Third, team leaders should enable members to find answers for themselves by asking questions and encouraging balanced participation.
- Fourth, team leaders should coordinate team activities and avoid wasting time on details that can be better handled through transfer of responsibility to the team.
- Fifth, leaders should accept the concept of continuous, on-the-job learning.

## Building Trust

The mere presence of a good leader does not guarantee the success of a team automatically unless members trust the leader. Trust, a belief in the integrity, character or ability of others, is essential if people are to achieve anything together in the long run.

The primary responsibility of creating trust in the minds of members rests with the leader/manager. The manager by virtue of his hierarchical advantage has greater access to key information. If the manager tries to get results through intimidation, members join together in cohesive resistance. Therefore, trust needs to be developed right from inception where team members would be more receptive and willing to accept managerial influence. Openness and honesty on the part of a manager, paves the way for sound relations between team members and the manager. A trusting manager is willing to be influenced by others and to change if facts demand such a change. When trust develops between the manager and the team members, members are willing to exercise self-control and self-direction.

**Box 10.3 How to Build Trust?**

| | |
|---|---|
| Trust | : A personal commitment to openness and trust<br>A willingness to change if necessary. |
| Information | : Full disclosure of relevant information, feelings and opinions. |
| Control | : Reliance on self-control rather than procedural control<br>Confidence that others will perform as agreed<br>Mutual commitment to success |
| Influence | : A willingness to be influenced by others concerning goals, procedures, and performance evaluation. |

*Source:* Reprinted from "Trust and Managerial Problem Solving," Dale E.Zand, Administrative Science Quarterly, 17, No. 2 (June 1972)

## Ways to Build Trust

Trust is a fragile thing and it grows slowly. A thoughtless remark, sometimes, may destroy years of hard work. According to Bartolome, managers need to concentrate on the following pointsLBartalome)

- Demonstrate that you are working for others' interests as well as your own.
- Support your work team wholeheartedly. When the team is under attack, you must demonstrate your loyalty to the team through your words and actions.
- Keep people fully informed about what is going on. Explain your decisions. Let them know the problems. If you hold back any of these, members begin to suspect your moves and withdraw support.
- Rewards must equal contributions. Learn to appreciate and give credit to people who show performance.
- In addition to cold facts, you need to share your feelings with team members. Such an interchange of opinions, helps you move closer to your team mates.
- If people share their concerns and feelings with you, do not try to betray their confidence by leaking it to affected parties.
- Learn to guide others through technical competence, team building and interpersonal skills.

## WHAT MAKES A GOOD TEAM LEADER?

Team leaders can make or break a team. It is the skill and capabilities of the leader or the tools and techniques put into practice that account for effective versus ineffective team performance. It is true that every team leader would talk about goals, clear paths, winning ways and extraordinary results. But these would not happen unless they establish their credibility, win the trust and earn respect from team members. In short, credibility is the name of the game. In any case, team members will not follow a person whom they do not trust, who is hypocritical or dishonest or whose motives appear to be in direct conflict with team objectives. if leaders fail to establish their grip over the team members through credible actions, the performance of the team suffers. Therefore, to effectively influence team members, leaders should have credibility. Credibility is developed in the following ways: (http://www.wright.edu/~scott.williams/LeaderLetter/chemistry.htm)

- **Demonstrating integrity**: having values and behaving in ways that are consistent with them; keeping promises and confidences.
- **Confidently expressing direction for the team:** being self-assured, but not dogmatic; being open to discussion, but not easily deterred.
- **Being positive and optimistic**: complimenting members' achievements; offering encouragement and assistance when performance is low; expressing optimism that the vision will be realized.
- **Finding and using common ground**: focusing on points of agreement when trying to influence others.

- **Managing disagreement**: presenting both sides of an argument when members are inclined to disagree with the conclusion.
- **Coaching**: showing the way and providing advice while granting a degree of autonomy to members.
- **Appreciating team members' perspectives**: inquiring about their agreement with decisions, the obstacles they encounter, the dissatisfactions they experience, their needs and the interpersonal problems they may experience.
- **Disseminating information**: sharing key information that only the leader can obtain.

***Articulate a vision.*** The kind of vision that energizes a team is a vivid picture of the future that's ambitious and exciting. To motivate a team to its highest level of performance, there must be passion. Perhaps the best metaphor here is falling in love. When we fall in love, a lot of our attention is directed toward the object of our affection, and our passion moves us to be creative and heroic. A leader's vision can produce similar passion, but the vision has to be **connected to the values** and priorities of the team members. When you articulate a vision for a team that you lead, make sure that you clearly make that connection. If your vision inspires passion, you can expect a high level of motivation and impressive performance. Thus, your vision should be **ambitious**. The vision should also be creative and original so that it's perceived as really interesting. Finally, as you describe your vision, use **colorful, emotional, and metaphorical language** to trigger the passion.

***Set goals***. After articulating a vision, break down the work to be completed into SMART goals. Smart goals are more concrete and manageable than a vision, and they point effort in a specific direction.

***Encourage constructive debate.*** Research on catastrophic group decisions (e.g., the Bay of Pigs invasion, the Watergate cover up, the space shuttle Challenger disaster) has identified a distinctive pattern in the teams that have made the poor decisions. One of the pitfalls of those groups is censorship of dissent. If team members pressure themselves or each other to suppress dissenting opinions in order to maintain harmony, the diversity of members' insights is wasted and lousy decisions can be made. Accordingly, effective team leaders understand that a moderate amount of task-focused conflict is constructive. If their teams are not debating issues, effective team leaders promote debate by playing the role of devil's advocate.

***Encourage role-making.*** It's neurotic and counterproductive for team leaders to think that only they should influence team members. Effective leaders don't perceive the role-making behavior of other team members as an inherent threat to their leadership. When nonleaders take the initiative to direct work activities or build relationships, effective leaders credit their initiative and shape their efforts to bring them in line with the vision.

***Promote cohesiveness.*** There are a variety of things that team leaders can do to promote cohesiveness:

- **Keep the size of the team to a maximum of about 12 members**, because people feel more attracted to small, intimate groups. Groups larger than 12 can be subdivided into teams.

- **Promote the perception that membership in the team is an honor**. Members feel more attracted to the team when it makes them feel special. One of the ways this can be achieved is by using a tough initiation.
- **Physically isolate the team** to promote intra-team interaction as an alternative to interaction with outside parties.
- **Have the group face challenges that require cooperation for success**. Through such exercises, members learn to pull together and rely on each other.
- **Stimulate competition with other groups** to emphasize the team's identity and the members' interdependence.
- **Reward the team, not individual members** to highlight interdependence and reinforce cooperation.
- **Focus on the team's successes**—success engenders cohesiveness. It's easy to feel attracted to a successful group. Who feels attracted to a team of losers?

## Managing effective teams Team Development

How to create and develop effective teams? The following tips should help managers in answering this question.(Hayward)

**Box 10.4 TIPS TO BUILD EFFECTIVE TEAMS**

**Tips**

1. Create a balanced set of roles.
2. Develop communication and process awareness.
3. Diagnose and manage stress.
4. Understand team preferences.
5. Define team goal.
6. Establish review mechanisms.
7. Share leadership and create equality of contribution.
8. Develop facilitation skills for effective meetings.
9. Confront issues and problems.
10. Decision making based on consensus.

***Balanced roles:*** People with different work preferences must gain entry into teams rather than like minded people.

***Open communication:*** Communication should be open, flexible and capable of building trust between people.

***Handling stress:*** Working with others in close proximity can itself be stressful. Additionally, we tend to react differently to various work pressures. The key skill which effective teams develop is the ability to recognise when either individual or collective stress is becoming a problem and to reduce it together.

***Team choices:*** These choices must be made explicit. Once the range is known, alternatives could be ascertained. Suppose someone from the team says, "I think teams are good in principle, but in practice they can be a complete waste of time." Once a response like this comes out, the team can begin to deal with it.

***Team goals:*** Teams make sense only when there is a common goal which requires collective action. Defining the team's purpose is vital. What are we trying to achieve and why? This, then, gives team members a focus for their energy and action. It is also helpful to set some short term goals to demonstrate gains, which sustain the team as it pushes towards longer term goals.

***Review mechanisms:*** For a team's success, there must be proper control over the team's activities and outcomes. A periodical review is needed to keep everything on track. If it is missing, team work will become just another 'flavour of the month'.

***Shared leadership:*** Teams need different forms of leadership at different times. Both the leader and the members must be willing to exchange roles, depending on the situation.

***Facilitation skills:*** Ensure that team meetings are well organised, allowing enough room for all to express their feelings and thoughts properly.

***Shake off the constraints of the past:*** All relevant issues affecting the functioning of a team must be discussed, debated and resolved.

***Consensus:*** Team decisions need to be based on consensus, so that all members can agree with – and be committed to – implementing important decisions. Consensus building does not imply 100 per cent agreement on the part of members. It only indicates the willingness of a member to support the decisions on reaching a certain stage or point.

**Table 10.4. Consensus Building Skills**

| | *Do We Always* | *Rarely Sometimes* |
|---|---|---|
| 1. | Ask each individual how he or she feels about the situation? | 1 2 3 4 5 6 7 8 9 10 |
| 2. | Ask for facts or explanations, try to uncover what different thoughts or words mean to everyone? | 1 2 3 4 5 6 7 8 9 10 |
| 3. | Clarify discrepancies of opinion with facts? | 1 2 3 4 5 6 7 8 9 10 |
| 4. | Modify our views when faced with compelling facts and opinions? | 1 2 3 4 5 6 7 8 9 10 |
| 5. | Identify similarities and differences among the points of view in the team? | 1 2 3 4 5 6 7 8 9 10 |
| 6. | Reinforce open-mindedness – the willingness to listen to other views and the need for cooperation? | 1 2 3 4 5 6 7 8 9 10 |
| 7. | Remain non-defensive when challenged and avoid emotional encounters? | 1 2 3 4 5 6 7 8 9 10 |
| 8. | List the positive and negative aspects or consequences of each point of view? | 1 2 3 4 5 6 7 8 9 10 |
| 9. | Make sure that each team member participates? | 1 2 3 4 5 6 7 8 9 10 |
| 10. | Define the level of risk associated with a decision and develop an approach? | 1 2 3 4 5 6 7 8 9 10 |

(Ask yourself how well your team practices these consensus skills. Rate each skill from 1 to 10 according to the scale. Identify which skills need improvement.

*Source:* M.D. Maginn, Effective Teamwork, American Media Publishing, Iowa, 1995.

## BUILDING TRUST AND BEHAVING ETHICALLY: ESSENCE OF LEADERSHIP

The inglorious actions on the part of leaders at WorldCom, Adelphia, Enron in 2001 and 2002 and more recently at Satyam Computers in 2009 have led many to question the credentials of many at the top—especially those who are known to be greedy and opportunistic, those whose public face is entirely different from their private face. The essential glue that holds social relationships together seem to have dried up, more or less, permanently.

Trust is essentially the belief in the integrity, character and ability of a leader. Those who follow the footsteps of a leader know for sure that the leader will not take them for a ride and do anything that would undermine that relationship. Trust is built around five basic principles" . Blind faith, undying loyalty, passionate commitment –all break down instantaneously, the moment subordinates lose their confidence and begin to question leaders with doubtful integrity and morals.

- Integrity: Honesty and truthfulness in expressions and behaviours
- Competence: technical and interpersonal knowledge and skills
- Consistency: reliability, predictability and good judgement in handling situations
- Loyalty: willingness to protect and save face for a person
- Openness: willingness to share ideas and information freely

Working with cross functional teams, leaders have to quickly earn respect from others through their expressions and behaviours. They have to live by their words and help people in tricky situations. They have to stand by people at all times and in all circumstances. When people commit mistakes and the leader is not there to lend a helping hand, trust gets broken and faith disappears. Earning trust thorough honest behaviour is essential to build long lasting relationships. You need to sustain trust through reliable and consistent behaviours—all the time. Like Herb Kelleher of Southwest Airlines who never indulged in downsizing, even when the entire airline industry was showing doors to thousands of employees. Leaders have to treat people with respect and have their ideas taken seriously and allow them to believe they can make a difference. They have to demonstrate a commitment to people, treat people with politeness, respect and dignity and create a strong role model for others to follow. To be a role model they have to live by their words. When they give themselves large salaries and bonuses while, at the same time, seek to cut costs by laying off employees—they are obviously not living up to expectations. The moral conduct of the leader and the means employed by the leader in realizing goals is scrutinized by people all the time. To get the best out of people, leaders have to lead from the front. They have to set high ethical standards for themselves and demonstrate those standards through their own behaviour—and encourage and reward integrity in others. Many leaders employ mentoring to coach, counsel and guide employee behaviours and actions along appropriate lines. Let's take a close look at mentoring now.

## Review Questions

1. Define the term 'work group' and 'work team'. Bring out the differences between the two. How are effective teams built?
2. When you are a member of a team, do you adopt a task specialist or socio-emotional role? Which role is important for a team's effectiveness? Discuss.
3. What do you mean by ' team building'? What can be done to improve team processes? How do teams contribute to the high performance workplace?
4. What does it take for you to trust someone? It is likely to hinder you as a manager? Why? What makes workplace teams effective?
5. "High performance teams have core values, clear performance objectives, the right mix of skills and creativity". Explain.
6. What are members of self-managing teams typically expected to do?
7. what type of team—self managing, cross functional or virtual—do you think is the most difficult to manage and why?Discussion Questions
8. Review the typical stages in a team's development. Think of a time when you were a member of a work group. Were those stages all represented? Did they appear in a different order? Did some of them emerge more than once? Explain.
9. Trust, a key ingredient of effective teamwork, is disturbingly low in the Indian workplace today. Do you agree or disagree? Why?
10. 'Individuals have a strong tendency to bend to the will of the majority, even if the majority is clearly wrong'. Discuss.
11. In a self managing team, 'Members are collectively held accountable for the team's overall performance'. Explain.
12. Quality circles, though popular in organisations around the world, are not to be viewed as panaceas for all of an organisational's ills. Discuss.
13. 'Diversity in team membership can be a valuable performance asset'. Comment.
14. How do you explain the emergence of problem solving and self directed companies throughout India? Do you think implementation of the team concept is difficult in these companies? Discuss.
15. Volvo went to self directed teams to assemble cars because of the need to attract and keep workers in Swede, where pay raises are not a motivator (high taxes) and many other jobs are available. Is this a good reason for using a team approach? Discuss.
16. As a manager, would you rather work with highly diversified teams or with more homogeneous teams? Why? What types would be best for which type of situations?

## Case study 1: Patel Mills

Patel Mills manufactures woolen clothes. Over the years, it has earned an envious reputation in the market. People associate Patel Mills with high quality woolen garments. Most of the existing employees have joined the company long back and are nearing retirement stage. The process of replacing these old employees with younger ones, drawn from the nearby areas, has already begun.

Recently, the quality of the garments has deteriorated considerably. Though the company employs the best material that is available, the workmanship has gone down. Consequently, the company has lost its customers in the surrounding areas to a great extent. The company stands, in the eyes of general public, depreciated and devalued. The production manager, in a frantic bid to recover lost ground, held several meetings with his staff but all in vain. The problem of course, has its roots in the production department itself. The young workers have started resisting the bureaucratic rules and regulations vehemently. The hatred against regimentation and tight control is total. The old workers, on the verge or retirement, say that conditions have changed considerably in recent years. In the days gone by, they say, they were guided by a process of self-control in place of bureaucratic control. Each worker did his work diligently and honestly under the old-set up. In an attempt to restructure the organisational set up, the managers who have been appointed afterwards brought about radical changes. Workers under the new contract, had very little freedom in the workplace. They are expected to bend their will to rules and regulations. Witnessing the difference between the two 'cultures', the young workers, naturally, began to oppose the regulatory mechanism devised by top management. The pent up feelings of frustration and resentment against management, like a gathering storm, have resulted in volcanic eruptions leading to violent arguments between young workers and foremen on the shop-floor. In the process, production has suffered, both quantitatively and qualitatively. The production manager in an attempt to weather the storm, is seriously thinking of bringing about a radical change in the control process that is prevailing now in the organisation.

## Questions

1. Analyse the problems leading to the deterioration in the quality of the manufacture in the company.
2. Critically evaluate the finding that old supervisors complain and new workers too, resist any type of control
3. What type of control system would you suggest to the company to improve the production?
4. Why has Mulye been accepted by the group? Do you agree with Shanker dada's statement?

# UNIT 4: ORGANISATION CULTURE AND CONFLICT MANAGEMENT

# 11

# Organizational Culture

## ORGANISATIONS HAVE A PERSONALITY OF THEIR OWN?

Like individuals, organisations have a personality of their own. Just as a human being has a personality—fun loving, warm, uptight, competitive or whatever—so an organisation has a personality too and that is its culture. Imagine for a second working at a company where for lunch you can enjoy roast quail or black bass, even a sampling of Spanish tapas. If you require a quick doctor's visit, the office is just down the hall. If your car is ugly-looking, you can have it washed in the parking lot. Likewise, you can pile your dirty laundry into one of the onsite washing machines. If you need a break, you can try the indoor climbing wall or start an impromptu game of volleyball in the gym. Well, all this is free!. You get $2000 for referring a new hire, a $5000 subsidy for buying a hybrid car. Working in 'high density clusters' each equipped with a high-powered Linux work station, each employee continues to enrich the company with new ideas, innovative suggestions and cost saving methods. This is the story of one of the best companies to work for, according to Fortune. The history of Google, the Internet search engine company that began in 1995, continues to dazzle stock market analysts, Wall Street pundits and academicians all over the world. Google designed its building so that staffers are constantly meeting each other in Google's funky lobby, in the Google Café where everyone eats together, in its state of the art recreational facilities and iin its 'snack rooms' equipped with bins packed with cereals, gummy bears, yogurt, carrots and of course make your own cappuccino. They also created many social gatherings for employees, such as TGF open meeting and a twice weekly outdoor roller hockey game, where staffers are encouraged to bring down the founders. Google founders Sergey Brin and Larry Page knew from the beginning that the company's most important strength would be its ability to attract the best software brains in the world and then to motivate them to give their best. Google never sleeps. The atmosphere is electrifying. Common offices, lobbies, cafes and so on bring staffers or Googlers into close contact with each other, which promotes collegiality and inspires them to share their new ideas with their colleagues in order to constantly improve search engine technology and find new ways to grow the company. Googlers can pursue new ideas without bothering about the monetary side .According to Larry Page, speed is the essence of success—that is rapid execution, response and delivery of results. They are fully empowered to take innovative decisions and break the cake of custom. The company knows that to have the next big idea, it requires the joint coordinated efforts of all its engineers to devote one fifth of their time to special projects of their own. Google's founders also gave them stock in the company, converting virtually all Googlers into owners. The firm operates round the clock, the staffers, though not bound by schedules, work really hard putting their heart and soul into the jobs. Google is always on the look out to generate that extra bit of fun and excitement in campus life. To this end, it has a chief culture officer (CCO) whose job is to keep employees happy and productive. The CCO takes special interest in hiring candidates (Known as Google-y) who are fairly flexible, adaptable and not focusing on title and hierarchy and has the potential to deliver results. the length of time Goggle takes to go from the first interview to a job offer is relatively long and usually one of the firms' two founders—Larry Page or Servey Brin—reviews each offer. Google can afford to be selective, being the best employer on the Fortune list. It wants to make sure that the new hires fit in with its unique culture—in every way!

(1. www.nytimes.com; 2. Fortune, October 2, 2006" Chaos by Design" http:/ /money.cnn.com;)

## WHAT IS ORGANISATIONAL CULTURE?

Simply stated, *it is the shared values, principles and traditions and ways of doing things that influence the way organisational members act.* It is all about the set of important assumptions, often unstated, that members of an organisation share in common. It speaks about the personality a company has and the style in which it does things. Celebrations are one way, for example, Southwest Airlines differentiates itself from the competition and provides a family-like environment that cares for its people; its customers, and its communities in a fun, loving way.

### Dimensions of organisational culture

Research suggests that the following dimensions of organisational culture separate companies from one another:

- Routine ways of communicating, such as organisational rituals and ceremonies and language commonly used
- The norms shared by individuals and teams throughout the organisation; like 'do not do too much ; do not do too little'
- The dominant values help by the organisation such as high product quality, low absenteeism, high efficiency etc.
- The philosophy that guides management's policies and decision making
- The rules of the game for getting along in the organisation; or the ropes that a new recruit must learn in order to be accepted as a full-fledged member of the group
- The feeling or climate conveyed in an organisation by the physical layout and the way in which managers and employees interact with customers, suppliers and other outsiders.

(J.Martin, Culture in Organizations, New York, Oxford University Press, 1996)

Important elements of the above definition may be stated thus

**Shared values and practices:** established by the founders, nurtured over time and perpetuated through repeated practice, these shared principles and values have actually stood the test of times. Members are well aware of what their organisation stands for, and how they should behave. The more clearly an organisation's shared perceptions and values are defined the more strongly people can associate with their organisation's mission and feel ain important part of it.

> FedEx stands for overnight delivery of packages entrusted to it. One of the folktales at FedEx is about a deliveryman who had been given the wrong key to a FedEx drop box. Instead of leaving the packages in the drop box until the next day when the right key was available, the deliveryman unbolted the drop box from its base, loaded it into the truck, and took it back to the station. There, the box was pried open and the content removed and sped on their way for on time arrival. (Thompson et al)

**Perceived meaning**: Organisational culture is the set of important assumptions, values, beliefs and norms that members of an organisation share in common. The common understanding of what to do or not to do has developed over time, based on what they have seen, observed or experienced. There are no rule books explaining appropriate employee behaviours in black and white. The values that make up an organisation's culture are often taken for granted. Everything has come through an implicit understanding of what the organisation stands for—in terms of a set of shared, enduring beliefs—and how the employee should act in a situation. Organisational culture captures the subtle, elusive and largely unconscious forces that shape a workforce.

> Here is the story of what an employee at Ritz-Carlton did to live up to the reputation of delivering unmatched service to customers – based on his own interpretation of the situation and instantaneously acting on his own, unmindful of consequences. a family arrived at the Bali Ritz-Carlton with special eggs and milk because of their son's allergies, but the food had spoiled. The manager and dining staff couldn't find replacements in town, so the executive chef called his mother-in-law in Singapore and asked her to buy the necessary products and fly with them to Bali! (Carmine Gallo, "How Ritz-Carlton maintains its Mystique." Business week, February 13, 2007

**It's the way we do things around here: The** key themes and dominant values of an organisation surface themselves in more than one way. The culture of an organisation manifests itself, over the years, to one and all without much of a difficulty. Thus McDonald's stands for QSCV—quality, service, cleanliness and value; Procter & Gamble stands for outstanding product quality; Sony Corporation "lives and breathes' new product development; 3M stands for innovation, Infosys Technologies stands for ethics etc. The organisation leader, of course, is primarily responsible for developing, sustaining and changing organisational culture.

> Some companies use unique ways to express themselves E*Trade Group, Inc the online stock and mutual fund trading company exhibits its lust for being different in a bit bizarre manner. CEO, Christos M. Cotsakos while trying to build an edgy, offensive and predatory culture once asked his newly hired vice president of international business development to **stand on a chair** and reveal something about himself to forty strangers in the company! To make people

move faster, he organized a day of racing in Formula One cars at speeds of around 150 miles per hour. To create a looser atmosphere around the office, he has employees carry around rubber chickens or wear propeller beanies. To bond the employees together, he organized gourmet-cooking classes. To convey the feeling "I care a damn for what others think" of E*Trade and to show that" this is the way we do business" (Louise Lee, "Tricks of E*Trade", Business Week E Biz, February 7,2000)

**Cultural products**: Cultural products include values, beliefs, rites, rituals, ceremonies, myths, stories, legends, sagas, language, symbols, heroes and heroines. Managers often make use of these products to shape the thinking and guide the actions of employees directly or indirectly.

**Descriptive**: Organisational culture is descriptive. It's concerned with how members perceive the organization, not with whether they like it. It describes rather than evaluates.

**Organisation Culture is different from Organisational Climate:** Organisational culture is the means through which members in an organisation learn and communicate what is acceptable or unacceptable; what is appropriate or inappropriate. It is based on the history and traditions of the organisation. The focus is on values and norms about employee behaviour. Organisational climate, on the other hand, **refers** to current situations in an organisation and the linkages among work groups, employees and work performance. Managers can easily manipulate organisational climate to bring about changes in the behaviour of employees.

**Culture has an important role in organisations:** It separates one organisation from the other.. Working for Southwest Airlines, for instance, is a unique experience, because the company is entirely different from other carriers. It gives members an identity. At Southwest Airlines top executives constantly reinforce the company's message that workers should be treated like customers and they continually celebrate employees whose contributions go beyond the call of duty. The funny, jovial atmosphere makes employees feel part of a large happy family and remain committed to their jobs. Culture has a mesmerizing impact on employee commitment. Consider 3M, one of whose corporate values is to be a 'company that employees are proud to be part of" As one executive puts it: "I'm a 27-year 3Mer because, quite frankly there's no reason to leave. I've had great opportunities to do different jobs and to grow a career. It's just a great company". It promotes social system stability. The more effectively conflict and change are managed within an organisation and the more that employees perceive the work environment to be positive and reinforcing, the more stable the social system within the organisation. At 3M, social stability is encouraged by promoting from within, by hiring capable college graduates in a timely manner and by offering displaced workers six months to find new jobs. Further, it shapes behaviour by helping employees make sense of their surroundings. The culture helps employees understand why the organisation does what it does and how it intends to accomplish its long term goals. Culture, in fact, clarifies and reinforces standards of behaviour. From an employee's standpoint, culture is highly useful because it reduces ambiguity. It clears the fog, puts the employee at ease –especially the new recruit—learn the tricks of the trade slowly and get going.

. **Multiple cultures:** Organisations contain not one but several cultures. An organisation may have one dominant culture and several distinct cultures. A dominant culture is a set of core values shared by a majority of the organisation's members. Most employees of Southwest

Airlines seem to subscribe to such values as hard work, company loyalty and delivering unmatched service to customers. At Hewlett-Packard, most of the employees seem to share a concern for innovation, product quality and responsiveness to customer needs. Such strong values guide the efforts of members on a day to day basis. On the other hand, subcultures, typically, are a result of problems or experiences that are shared by members of a particular department or unit. The marketing department, for example, can have a subculture that is uniquely shared by members belonging to that department. It will include the core values of the dominant culture plus additional values unique to members of the marketing department. Subcultures that come about as a result of the demographic characteristics of employees include those based on age, gender and ethnicity. Sometimes, units separated by distance develop subcultures of their own, based on distinct characteristics of the region and members working therein. Again, when two organisations merge, the subcultures of the original firms may become subcultures within the new organisation. . The presence of numerous subcultures would make it difficult to members to draw the curtain between appropriate and inappropriate behaviour. Many companies that have merged with or acquired foreign companies have to deal with language and custom-based cultural differences. Generally speaking, subcultures can weaken and undermine an organisation they are in conflict with the dominant culture (known as countercultures) and/or the overall objectives. Of course, they will keep the dominant culture going overboard and help whistle-blowers keep a healthy balance between diametrically opposite views advanced by numerous cultures prevailing within an organisation. A strong organisational culture can be a dangerous thing in the hands of owners or managers who do not behave ethically or legally. Subcultures would also encourage constructive conflict and more creative thinking about how the organisation should conduct itself, keeping societal interests in mind.

## STRONG Versus WEAK CULTURES

Not all cultures have an equal influence on employees' behaviours and actions. In strong cultures, employees are passionate about key values and exhibit tremendous zeal to uphold them. The Walt Disney culture, for example, encourages employees to show extraordinary devotion to customer service; the culture at Apple Inc encourages innovation. Employees in these companies don't need rule books to specify how they act, because these behaviours are conveyed as 'the way we do things around here'; they are rooted in their company's cultures. In strong culture companies, often, the values and behavioural norms are so deeply rooted that they don't change much when a new CEO takes over. Of course, they can erode over time if the CEO ceases to nurture them. Three factors are generally responsible for the development of strong cultures

- A founder or other strong leader who establishes values, principles and practices that are in sync with changing customer needs, competitive conditions and strategic requirements
- A passionate commitment to long held norms and practices that guide member behaviour and shape organisational actions time and again.
- A genuine concern for customers, employees and shareholders (Kotter and Heskett)

**Table 11.1. Strong versus weak organisation cultures**

| *Elements of strong cultures* | *Elements of weak cultures* |
|---|---|
| 1. Values widely shared | 1. Values shared by a few, usually top management |
| 2. Members know what is important | 2. Members not very clear about what is important |
| 3. Most employees can tell stories about company history/heroes | 3. Employees possess little knowledge of company history or heroes |
| 4. Employees strongly identify with culture | 4. Employees have little identification with culture |
| 5. Strong linkage between shared values and behaviour | 5. Little connection between shared values and behaviours |
| (S.P.Robbins and M.Coulter, Management, New Delhi, Pearson, 2008) | |

In weak-culture companies, members do not have any set of enduring values to rely upon, simply because they have never been preached or shared widely. Top management does not espouse these values nor show any commitment to a particular philosophy. A company, in the absence of any definable character of its own, simply becomes a place to work and make money. Members do not exhibit interest nor show commitment to the work and look at their jobs with scant respect. "There is neither passion about the company nor emotional commitment to what it is trying to accomplish" (Thompson et al)

Some cultures turn unhealthy because of the presence of certain counterproductive traits that could impact the work climate and company performance quite significantly. The following three traits are particularly unhealthy:

- A highly charged political environment where issues get resolved on the basis of which group has got the maximum political clout
- Hostility to change and a general weariness of people who champion new ways of doing things
- Members becoming averse to looking outside the company for best practices, new managerial approaches or innovative ideas.

In a fast changing environment, change-resistant cultures have no place. Every company, necessarily, must be open to new ideas and ways of doing things.

## HOW EMPLOYEES LEARN CULTURE?

Culture is passed on to employees in numerous ways. The most significant ones may be listed thus:

**Table 11.2. Cultural products**

- *Rites*: Relatively elaborate, dramatic planned sets of activities that consolidate various forms of cultural expressions into one event carried out through social interactions, usually for the benefit of audience
- *Ceremonial*: a system of several rites connected with a single occasion or event
- *Ritual:* a standardized detailed set of techniques and behaviours that manage anxieties but seldom produce intended technical consequences of practical importance
- *Myth*: a dramatic narrative of imagined events usually used to explain origins or transformations of something
- *Saga*: a historical narrative describing the unique accomplishments of a group and its leaders, usually in heroic terms
- *Legend*: a handed down narrative of some wonderful event that I based on history but has been embellished with fictional details
- *Story*: a narrative based on rare events, sometimes a combination of truth and fiction
- *Symbol*: any object and event, quality or relation tat serves as a vehicle for conveying meaning usually by representing another thing
- *Language*: a particular form or manner in which members of a group use sounds and written signs to convey meanings to each other
- *Values*: life directing attitudes that serve as behavioural guidelines
- *Metaphors*: shorthand of words used to capture a vision or to reinforce old and new values
- *Belief*: an understanding of a particular phenomenon
- *Heroes/Heroine:* individuals whom the organisation has legitimized to model behaviour for others

(H.W.Trice and J.M.Beyer, "Studying Organizational Culture through Rites and Ceremonials," Academy of Management Review 9, October 1984)

## STORIES

Every company has its own share of myths, legends and true stories about important past decisions and actions that convey the company's main values. The stories typically cover company's heroes who possessed the admirable qualities that have helped the company grow from strength to strength. Then there are stories of those who invented new ways of doing things at amazing speed, of those who ran that extra mile to meet customer expectations etc. As they are told and retold, members in an organisation get a fairly vivid picture of what they must do when confronted with novel problems. They inspire people to give their best. Companies with strong cultures are enthusiastic collectors of stories, anecdotes and legends in support of basic beliefs.

**Box 11.1 The story of Art Fry, who developed Post-It Notes**

The story of Art Fry, a 3M employee, is quite popular. According to the story, Fry became frustrated when the bits of paper he used to mark pages in a hymnal kept falling out. To solve the problem he needed an adhesive that would stick long enough to keep his pages marked without leaving a residue on the hymnal. When such an adhesive was found in one of 3M's labs, he suggested the idea of marketing the product that eventually became Post-It Notes. Subsequent market surveys yielded negative results and failed to capture the true potential of the product. Undaunted, Fry gave out samples to 3m secretaries and executives. Eventually, everyone—at 3M and elsewhere—was hooked on Fry's new product. Fry was elevated to the highest technical position later on. The moral of the story is that as an employee one should look for new ideas and when the idea is great, one must show monumental patience to turn it successful. (D.Hellriegel and J.W.Slocum, Organizational Behaviour, Bangalore, Thomson, 2006)

Reinforcing organisational folklore signifies many things to employees. For example, at Procter & Gamble there is a story about the outstanding brand manager who was shown the door for overstating the features of a product. The moral of the story is that ethical claims are important than making money. At AT & T there are numerous stories about field employees who made sacrifices to keep the phones working and operators who stayed on the line when people called in and asked for emergency help because they had suffered a physical calamity. The moral of such stories is that these types of sacrifices are all in the line of duty for telephone employees, who must view their primary responsibility as that of helping the customer (Luthans)

## RITES, CEREMONIES OR RITUALS

Rituals are repetitive sequences of activities that express and reinforce the endearing values of an organisation. Rites and ceremonies that sustain organisational culture include rites of passage (basic training, Indian Army), rites of degradation (firing an employee); rites of enhancement (company ceremonies) and rites of integration (such as office party). In many organisations, ceremonies are used to recognise special achievements and honour the retiring employee(s). one of the well known corporate rituals is Wal-Mart's company chant. Begun by the company's founder, Sam Walton as a way to motivate and unite his workforce—known as Wal-Mart cheer—has become a company ritual that stresses the importance of employees' to the company's success.

**Box 11.2**

**Wal-Mart Cheer**

Give me a **W!**

Give me an **A!**

Give me an **L!**

GIVE ME A Squiggly!

Give me an **M!**

Give me an **A!**

Give me an **R!**

Give me a **T!**
What's that spell?
Wal-Mart
Whose Wal-Mart is it?
*My Wal-Mart*!
Who's number one?
*The Customer! Always*!

## SYMBOLS

Symbols are the most basic observable way of expressing the culture of a company. They may take the form of logos, architecture, uniforms, awards and many other tangible expressions. Some companies use impressive buildings to convey their strength and importance, indicating that they are large and stable places. The way the company is furnished also provides useful insight into its culture. Offices where there are lots of plants and flower arrangement convey a friendly, person oriented culture; whereas those in which waiting areas are adorned with awards and trophies are indirectly revealing their passion for achievement.. Sometimes, the very design of the building itself is a symbol of an organisation's values. For example, Walt Disney hired famed Japanese architect Arata Isozaki to design the Team Disney Building, which houses Disney's "Imagineering unit", in Orlando, Florida. This building's contemporary and unusual design featuring unusual shapes and bright colours conveys the importance of imagination and creativity to the Walt Disney Company and to the people working in it. In GM, the executive suite on the top floor of their Detroit headquarters is isolated from the rest of the building and open only to top GM executives. Material symbols, thus, often reveal to employees who matters most, the degree of equality desired by top management and the kinds of behaviour that are expected and desirable.

**Box 11.3 Cultural symbols of McDonald's**

- Located in rectangular buildings with large windows to let the sun in and with neatly kept surroundings
- Large parking lots
- Rarely any visible litter
- Drive in window to facilitate speedy service
- Golden arch sign that towers over the building
- Bright colours and plants creating a homely atmosphere

## LANGUAGE

Organisations often develop special terms to describe key personnel, customers, suppliers, equipment, processes or products related to its business. The acronyms and jargon that get exchanged between members often mesmerize new recruits and compel them to listen carefully, go beyond the obvious and catch the real meaning. After a while, everything becomes part of their language. Once learned, everyone becomes part of a well-knit group exchanging notes, opinions, feelings, sentiments through the unique, special language.

## PRACTICES

How an organisation responds to problems, makes strategic decisions and treats employees and customers conveys a lot about what the top management is really looking for.

**Table 11.3. Infosys technologies ltd stands by its employees irrespective of the costs!**

- Take Sembi's own experience. In September 2001, he was working as a project manager at a client's site in Brighton, U.K. Two days after 9/11, while walking to office, he was heckled by four construction workers. "One of them told his American friend that I was from the same community as the terrorists who destroyed the Twin Towers. It was frightening," he recalls. Immediately, Sembi spoke to his HR people in Bangalore and a strong message went to the client that Infosys was "sensitive about racial discrimination". The catcalling subsided but Sembi was still scared, since his wife was pregnant and Asians were being routinely targeted. So in November, Infosys transferred Sembi to Bangalore, no questions asked. And this was no routine transfer. Remember, this was the time when people in his field were being sacked or " benched" (asked to hang around because there was not enough work to go around) without notice or warning.
- Many others have had similar epiphanic moments. Sonu Joseph, who was working at a telecom client's site in the US in 2001, would see people being sacked every day . "People were being handed pink slips and asked to leave the same evening. Obviously, I thought it'll happen to me sooner or later," she recalls. It didn't. she was brought back to Bangalore and continued working for the same client. Neither did it happen to her colleagues, even though telecom was the worst-hit sector, where IT spends were drastically slashed and getting new business was virtually impossible.
- The story is the same even when infosys was forced to dismantle large divisions. Geetha Kannan, an Infoscion since 1993, was part of an "elite" group that worked for e-business and dotcom clients and was 369-strong by 2000, when the New Economy was in full cry. These engineers were among the highest-paid in Infosys. Then came the tech crash in April 2000, and the dotcom dream died. Infosoys decided to shut down Kannan's hot-shot department. But everyone was absorbed elsewhere. Kannan herself was transferred to HR but, according to her, "This was the first indication that jobs are not going to be lost in this company." Literally thousands of such stories kept morale and loyality as high as ever. Mahesh Kamath, a civil engineer who joined Infy in May 2000, recalls how his two roommates were on the bench for months. "But they never looked frightened or scared."

(Business Today, Business Standard, Business World 2000-2008)

## TYPES OF CULTURES

Each organisation culture is unique. However, four general types of organisational culture that are useful for comparing organisations are bureaucratic, clan, entrepreneurial and market cultures. They are basically characterized by differences in formal control and focus of attention.

**Bureaucratic Culture:** In a bureaucratic culture, the behaviour of employees is governed by formal rules and standard operating procedures and coordination is achieved through hierarchical reporting relationships. To secure compliance, ensure discipline and obtain performance, the duties, responsibilities of all employees are clearly spelled out. Employees are made to follow the rule book, operating procedures and established practices. Bureaucratic cultures often are found in organisations that produce standardized products and/or services. Most government organisations find bureaucratic structure very useful because one can conveniently take shelter behind a mountain of rules and regulations, in case something goes wrong.

**Clan Culture:** In a clan culture the behaviour of employees are guided by tradition, loyalty, personal commitment, extensive socialization, and self-management. New hires are guided by experienced mentors and role models readily available within an organisation. Members understand the company's unique history and have a shared image of its style and functioning. They understand the importance of working together to produce results. There is lot of peer pressure to adhere to important norms of the company. Members share feelings of pride in membership and subscribe to the view that without teamwork, participation and consensus decision making, it is difficult to produce excellent results.

**Entrepreneurial Culture:** In an entrepreneurial culture, risk taking, dynamism and creativity are given lot of importance. There is commitment to experimentation, innovation and being on the leading edge. It suits a company very well in the formative years. Small and medium sized outfits also find it very supportive

**Market culture:** It is a culture characterized by hard-driving competitiveness and a profit orientation. The achievement of measurable and demanding goals such as sales growth, profitability, market share etc is given topmost priority. You have to push yourself to the limits-utilizing scarce corporate resources to best advantage. The relationship between individual and organisation is contractual. What you are supposed to deliver is agreed upon initially. Rewards follow performance, as per the agreement. The organisation expects performance (at the same time, does not guarantee job security) and the individual seeks rewards (at the same time does not promise loyalty). "Rather than promoting a feeling of membership in a social system, the market culture values independence and individuality and encourages members to pursue their own financial goals"

## CREATING AND SUSTAINING CULTURE

### The Role of Founder

The founders of an organisation have a major influence on the organisation's initial culture because of their values and beliefs. They usually pick up people who think and feel the same way they do; those who believe in the dream of the founders and are willing to follow their footsteps scrupulously and religiously. People, who turn out to be misfits, tend to leave the organisation. Those who stay on become more and more similar and tend to have values and interest similar to the founder's. With the passage of time, members buy into the founder's vision and perpetuate the founder's values in the organisation. The founder himself educates members as to how to get ahead to achieve his dreams. Through indoctrination and socialisation, members begin to embrace the values held in his esteem by the promoter and develop behaviours espoused by the promoter time and again. In fact, the founders' own behaviour acts as a role model that inspires employees to get along, internalizing their beliefs, values and assumptions. When the founder achieves success, his vision turns into a concrete reality and others try to emulate the same with passion and devotion. The promoter acquires a kind of cult status and becomes a powerful role model for others to follow.

Ray Kroc built McDonald's on four basic concepts: *quality, cleanliness, service* and *price*. He believed that McDonald's fast food concept would sweep the nation (United States) and pay rich dividends, and with this dream in view he bought the rights to franchise McDonald's units from Dick and Maurice McDonald brothers. To ensure that customers get the best product at the best price, Kroc required franchisees to attend McDonald's university where they are taught how to manage their business. The cultural values of McDonald's and the way to run the business are also taught to ensure that franchisees run the show in the same manner. Kroc's videotaped messages are passed on to new employees so as to make them learn and follow McDonald's philosophy. These included messages on cleanliness: "If you've got time to lean, you've got time to clean"; on competition: "If they are drowning to death, I would put a hose in their mouth" and on market expansion, "when you're green, you grow; when you're ripe, you rot". Kroc died several years ago, but the indelible impact that he left behind is still very much alive in McDonald's restaurants in every part of the globe till date.

**Table 11.4. The Man behind Microsoft's Culture**

Microsoft's founder Bill Gates is a workaholic who still often works 18 hours a day. He wanted Microsoft to stand for excellence, innovation and high quality. Exhibiting hard work, creativity and commitment, employees must put Microsoft ahead of competition. Gates expects his employees to put in long workdays because he demands this level of commitment from himself, and he expects them to do everything they can to promote innovation and quality because this is what he does. He used a product team structure to reinforce the team atmosphere and norms of "team spirit". Employees who do not subscribe to these values leave Microsoft and those who stay on are pressured to go that extra mile and complete their tasks to the best of their ability—creatively. Gates also established a culture for innovation by rewarding successful risk-taking and creativity with strong property rights. Many key employees receive stock options based on company performances, and all employees are eligible to get bonuses. The company does not believe in layoffs. And it is known to move closer to the hearts of employees as well as customers through excellent ethical standards. Microsoft's people, its structure, its property rights, and its ethics interact and fit together to make up Microsoft's culture

(E.H.Schein, "The Role of the Founder in Creating Organizational Culture" Organizational Dynamics, 12, 1983; Schein, Organizational Culture and Leadership, SanFrancisco: Jossey-Boss, 1992; G.R.Jones, 2007

## Keeping a culture alive

The founder, as the above examples show, sets the tone and keeps the spirit of an organisation alive through his own outstanding effort and innovative ways of thinking— while trying to position the organisation ahead of competition. To ensure success and to reinforce culturally acceptable behaviour, he has to establish policies and procedures—such as hiring those who believe in his dream, encouraging the new hires to give their best by offering requisite training, rewarding excellent performance, showing the door to those who lag behind or those who are declared as 'misfits', promoting a fun-oriented, family atmosphere to make everyone feel at home; empowering people to take actions independently, sharing the gains of success with employees etc. every attempt must be made to make people buy into the founder's vision and perpetuate the founder's values in the organisation. Consequently, the people inside the organisation become more and more similar, the values of the organisation become more and more parochial, and the culture becomes more and more distinct from that of similar outfits. Ultimately, it's the people— with strong work values and tremendous commitment to the ideals for which they work— who convert ordinary organisations into extraordinary institutions delivering value for money to customers all over the globe.

**Table 11.5. Role of founder in creating and sustaining an organisation's culture**

- Establish enduring values
- Create vision
- Reward performance
- Select people who fit in with culture
- Set excellent standards based on exemplary personal character and conduct
- Reinforce appropriate behaviour
- Inspire people to give their best
- Indoctrinate and Socialize so that new hires comfortably adapt to culture, internalize its core values, put the learned behaviours to good effect and produce results

## SOCIALIZATION

**Socialization** is a process through which a new recruit begins to understand and accept the values, norms and beliefs held by others in the organisation. HR department representatives help new recruits to "internalize the way things are done in the organisation". Orientation helps the newcomers to interact freely with employees working at various levels and learn behaviours that are acceptable. Through such formal and informal interaction and discussion, newcomers begin to understand how the department/company is run, who holds power and who does not, who is politically active within the department, how to behave in the company, what is expected of them, etc. In short, if the new recruits wish to survive and prosper in their new work home, they must soon come to 'know the ropes'

**Box 11.4 Orientation programmes as effective socialization tools**

Orientation programmes are effective socialization tools because they help the employees to learn about the job and perform things in a desired way. **Orientation** is the task of introducing the new employees to the organisation and its policies, procedures and rules. A typical formal orientation programme may last a day or less in most organisations. During this time, the new employee is provided with information about the company, its history, its current position, the benefits for which he is eligible, leave rules, rest periods, etc. Also covered are the more routine things a newcomer must learn, such as the location of the rest rooms, break rooms, parking spaces, cafeteria, etc. In some organisations, all this is done informally by attaching new employees to their seniors, who provide guidance on the above matters. Lectures, handbooks, films, groups, seminars are also provided to new employees so that they can settle down quickly and resume the work

## Socialization, in fact, is a three step process

***Pre-arrival stage***: The pre-arrival stage explicitly recognizes that each individual arrives with a particular set of values, expectations and attitudes. The employees undergo some kind of training wherein they will be taught how to behave in different situations, in work organisations.

***Encounter stage***: in the second stage, individual encounters the possible dichotomy between his expectations about the job, his co-workers and the organisation in general. If the expectations prove to be compatible with the needs of organisation, the individual is able to handle the job well and get along with his co workers smoothly. But where expectations and reality differ, the new hire must undergo socialization that will detach him from his previous assumptions and replace them with another set that the organisation deems desirable .**Reality shock** occurs when new hires perceive discrepancies between their pre-employment expectations and on the job reality. The larger the gap, the stronger the reality shock. Reality shock, of course, is quite common in many organisations. The employer might fail to put the new hire on a challenging assignment, as promised. Resources and information required to do the job satisfactorily may not be forthcoming. Of course, at the extreme, a new recruit may become totally unconvinced and disillusioned with the realities of his job and eventually resign. Proper selection would greatly reduce the chance of occurrence of the latter type.

***Metamorphosis stage***: Finally every new hire has to undergo the metamorphosis stage. If the new members work out problems during the encounter stage, then they have to go through changes in due course of time. When everything is complete, that is, when new hires internalize the learned behaviours—making them feel at home, understand how to handle the jobs and get along with people well— then socialization process is said to have come to an end. Successful metamorphosis will have a positive impact on employee productivity and commitment.

**Box 11.5 Socialization process at the Disney World**

Disney annually hires thousands of people and employs over 30,000 at Disney World. Employees who cannot afford housing are housed in a separate Disney gated complex. Initial applications from potential members are carefully screened. Those with a criminal record are lopped off from the list. All employees must follow Disney rules strictly( such as no mustaches, visible tattoos, dangling body piercing items and no hair colour outside of the normal colours) and observe norms scrupulously(such as taking the extra step to make sure guests have a good experiences) and behave in a certain way. To learn these rules, norms and behaviours, new recruits receive formal training at Disney University in groups of 45 and follow a tight schedule. During this training programme (Lasting a day and a half) new hires learn the

Disney language and four Disney values namely safety, courtesy, show or entertainment and efficiency. They also receive training in how to answer guests' questions no matter how simple or difficult the question. One the new recruits understand what their new roles are and how to enact these in line with what has been taught, they are given on the job training by an experienced member. This part of socialization process can take up two and a half weeks to complete during which the new cast members (that's how the new hires are addressed) wear a costume, learn to sing a song and begin to mix up with other cast members and guests. When are get along with this process smoothly, they are moved on to further socialization in other attraction areas such as Adventureland, Fantasyland and so on, depending on their competencies. (Hellriegel and Slocum)

Organisational socialization is thus, a process of learning and adjustment, where new hires get to know each other, understand policies and procedures, learn the tricks of the trade, move closer to other members of the organisation, adjust to the new environs and carry out work without violating norms or rubbing people on the wrong side. For some people, as research evidence indicates, the adjustment process is fairly rapid. In any case, new hires with diverse work experiences seem to adjust better than those with limited previous experience, because they seem to possess a larger toolkit of knowledge and skills to make the adjustment possible.

**Box 11.6 Perpetuating the Culture**

Once established, company cultures may be perpetuated:

- By Screening and selecting new employees that mesh well with the culture
- By systematic indoctrination of new hires in the culture's fundamentals
- By the efforts of senior management to reiterate core values in daily conversations and pronouncements
- By the telling and retelling of company legends and stories
- By regular ceremonies honouring members who display desired cultural behaviours and
- By visibly rewarding those who display cultural norms and penalizing those who don't.

(J.P. Kotter and J.L. Heskett, Corporate Culture and Performance, New York, Free Press, 1992)

## CHANGING ORGANIZATIONAL STRUCTURE

Organisational Culture, as stated previously, is generally stable. However, it is not immutable. Culture is something which evolves over a period of time—in response to changes in environment, particularly changes in composition of workforce, changes in top management, changes brought about by mergers and acquisitions, deliberate attempts to change the structure of an organisation, changes brought about by a crisis etc. In any case, there is growing evidence suggesting likely change in organisational culture due to the occurrence of any of the following (Kilmann et al and P.J.Frost et al)

**A dramatic crisis:** This is the shock that weakens the status quo and makes people start thinking about the relevance of the current culture. Examples include unexpected financial loss, the loss of a major customer or a dramatic technological innovation by a competitor.

**Leadership changes hands:** Senior managers working at the top level with an alternative set of key values may be perceived as being more capable of responding to the crisis than the old leaders were.

**Young and small organisations:** The younger the organisation, the less entrenched its culture. Likewise, it's easier for managers to pass on new values in a small outfit than in a large one.

**Mergers and acquisitions:** Another dramatic source of culture change is mergers and acquisitions –events in which one organisation purchases or otherwise absorbs another. Life in companies with incompatible cultures tends to be conflict-ridden and highly disruptive often resulting in arguments and considerable uncertainty about what to do. Culture clashes have led to the premature death of many companies in the past and unless such fires are put out quickly, even sound companies may begin to feel the pinch.

**Weak culture:** The more widely held the values and the higher the agreement among members on those values, the more difficult it will be to change. Conversely, weak cultures are more receptive to change than are strong ones.

**Responding to the revolution brought about by Internet :** Thanks to the revolution brought about by Internet, companies are compelled to be agile, fast paced and receptive to new solutions. The traditional brick and mortar models may have to be converted into click and mortar businesses. When structural changes occur, culture changes will have to follow suit.

## Moving closer to the Customer : Influence of the Leader

A leader can affect organisational culture in numerous ways. He can change the selection criteria for people. He can raise the bar considerably where merit becomes the only basis for hiring people. Only people with superior educational qualifications and experience could gain entry into a knowledge-based organisation. He can thereby put an end to extraneous considerations creeping into the selection process such as case, age, gender, ethnicity, regionalism etc. Likewise, a leader can change the socialization of organisational members including reformulating training programmes and introducing new managerial philosophies and values. Leaders can also change the meaning of work in an organisational culture. The dark three piece business suits that were the hallmarks of employee efficiency were to be discarded in favour of more casual dress when IBM failed to deliver results. To reiterate the point that IBM is not inflexible and is willing to shed clothes to change its image. Leaders can change other artifacts (surface manifestations of organisational culture) such as logos, symbols, buildings apart from dress codes in order to influence employee thinking and actions. In order to survive and flourish in a competitive world, leaders have to necessarily move closer to the hearts of employees and customers. Creating ***a customer-responsive culture*** is not easy but not impossible. Certain guidelines in this regard, advanced by research studies, may be listed thus: (Hoecklin; A.M.Francesco, Robbins et al)

- Selection of employees who are outgoing and friendly; who are willing to go that extra mile and serve customers to the best of their abilities.
- Not putting rules, procedures and regulations ahead of customer needs
- Empowerment of employees at every level so that they can do anything to please the customer—without fear of criticism or penalty for violation of rules

- Taking note of grievances of customers, paying critical attention to their suggestions, welcoming their suggestions and using such feedback to improve service
- Clarifying what the employee should do and should not do will put an end to employee anxiety and confusion—often over trivial matters. Show them the right way to carry out assigned tasks and encourage employees to think out of the box, especially in moving closer to the hearts of customers. If such behaviours are encouraged, even when the employee has crossed his limits, then the organisation need not worry about who does what. Everyone will rise to the occasion and deliver results, surpassing expectations.
- Create a feeling that every employee is the real owner of the company. Do whatever is necessary to bring about a radical change in the mindset of people—through stock options, excellent rewards, novel benefit plans, extra concessions. Make them feel that they are also entitled to share the fruits of organisational success. In such a scenario, employees may really be proud to initiate novel, often customer-friendly actions that may eventually take ordinary organisations to extraordinary heights.

## Ethical Behaviour and Influence of the Leader

It is usually the top managers who uphold the shared values and set the ethical tone. If they pursue and encourage a culture of" the end justifies the means," then you are virtually sending an open invitation to trouble. If managers at lower levels were to observe top level people sexually harassing others, falsifying expense reports, diverting shipments to preferred customers, misrepresenting financial health and other forms of unethical behaviour, they tend to take it lightly and perpetrate similar crimes without any fear. What the top managers do is far more important than what they do. If they begin to offer rewards to their friends, use company facilities for personal use and inflate their travel and medical bills—it conveys many things to many people. Likewise, if they do not punish the guilty and reward the efficient, the wrong signals catch the attention of many inside and outside the company.

The fall of mighty Enron Corp—once one of the most valuable companies in American—was a collapse of mind boggling proportions. Everything, in the end, traceable to unethical behaviour of people at the top. Managers who have espoused values such as growth at any cost, personal ambitions above team objectives, aggressive territorial invasion in place of doing what you know best have paid a heavy price in the end. At Enron, former chief financial officer Andrew Fastow and his wife pleaded guilty to falsifying the company's books so that they could siphon off tens of millions of Enron's money for their own use. Even though they knew Enron was collapsing, in the days before, its top managers decided to award themselves over $80 million in compensation for their"work". In 2002 a judge in Houston opened the way for representatives of its shareholders to go after this money and other money its top executives had extracted from the company. Enron, remember; too had an extremely detailed 60 page ethics code!

To be fair, the code of ethics must be prepared taking inputs from relevant stakeholders. It should not be a product of top management thinking. top managers should stand by what they say and serve as visible role models—in terms of exemplary character and conduct—for others to emulate. They must always communicate ways and means that are in sync with what has been stated in black and white. Seminars, workshops and other training programmes must be conducted frequently to encourage ethical behaviour on the part of employees. There is, of course, the debate whether ethics and ethical behaviour could be passed on to employees through formal teaching methods, since most people come to the workplace with their own set of ethical values and behaviours learnt and groomed since childhood. As research studies have indicated, repeated reinforcements (rewards for correct ethical conduct) and constant threatening postures (punishing the guilty for violating the ethical codes) would certainly help employees to put their behaviours on the paths espoused by top management. Ethics training certainly increases awareness of ethical issues in an organisation and makes each one realise what practices are and are not acceptable. In fact, top managers should encourage people working at all levels to report illegal, immoral or illegitimate organisational practices without any *fear*. Remember the famous memo sent by Sherron Watkins to her boss, Kenneth Lay of Enron: "I am incredibly nervous that we will implode in a wave of accounting scandals"? Watkins seven page memo has become the smoking gun in an unfolding investigation of alleged financial misdealing at Enron and Arthur Anderson.

## REVIEW QUESTIONS

1. Describe how culture affects your behaviour
2. What is the origin of organisational culture? Why do different organisations have different cultures?
3. How do new recruits learn the culture of an organisation? How can an organisation encourage newcomers to develop an institutionalized role orientation ?
4. How do strong cultures differ from weak cultures? What two factors determine the strength of the culture?
5. How do organisational cultures develop? What four steps commonly occur?
6. How do orgaisations go about maintaining their cultures? What steps are involved? Describe them
7. Describe how organisations use symbols and stories to communicate values and beliefs? Give some examples of how symbols and stories have been used in organisations with which you are familiar.
8. What is the role of leadership in developing, maintaining and changing organisational culture?
9. Discuss the role of organisation rewards in developing, maintaining and changing the organisational culture
10. What are the basic components of innovation and the stages through the process of innovation pro What is the difference between divergent and convergent thinking, and what is their relationship to the process of creativity?
11. Explain the basics of creativity. Elaborate the ways of improving creative abilities.
12. "R&D must be integrated to the corporate strategy" Explain why is it necessary to do so. What would happen when both are not welded properly?

13. Can a change made in one area of an organisation in technology for instance-not lead to change in other areas? Why or why not?
14. Define 'technology forecasting'. List the various techniques of technology forecasting.
15. Explain what you mean by In-house Development of Technology.

## CRITICAL THINKING QUESTIONS

1. In a field marked by rapid change, uncertainty and a high rate of technological obsolescence, is it advisable to make heavy R&D investments (especially in fields like pharmaceuticals, bio-technology, telecom software etc)? If yes, suggest a suitable strategy whereby the firm continues to get benefited from R&D investments at carefully spaced intervals, without losing its competitiveness.
2. Many pharmaceutical companies and software companies have invested in basic research, new product development etc and lost quite heavily in recent times. Mod-way they are forced to return back to their roots and start from the scratch all over again. In the light of this, is it advisable for mid-cap firms (or even large companies) to place their bets on R&D, innovation, new product development?
3. Do you think of yourself as a creative individual? What could you do to become more creative when it comes to the work you carry out?
4. Describe the culture of an organisation with which you are familiar. It might be one in which you currently work, one in which you have worked or one in which a friend or family member works. What values, beliefs, stories and symbols are significant to employees of the organisation?

## CASE STUDY 1: Culture at Google India

PALLAVI ROY,

Business Wolrd, April 2007

The first thing that hits you when you enter Google India's Hyderabad office is that it is a ***preppy kind of place*** — straight out of college sets in the film Kuch Kuch Hota Hai. You almost expect a 20-something to come skateboarding round the corner. The next moment, you spot the Roy Gilbert, director of online sales and operations, at work, poring over his computer. And just when you were least expecting it, a hijaab-clad girl walks into the cafeteria to take a break.

Sure, this is Hyderabad, the city of the Nizams, but not too many Indian workplaces can boast of the kind of diversity Google exhibits. *There are even ex-armymen and former school teachers among the workforce here*. The Bangalore office is one of their worldwide crucibles for R&D housing engineers who develop programmes that add to their search process.

At Google, all they look for in candidates is '**Googliness**'. Anything else they possess is either a bonus, or redundant. Gilbert says the company doesn't just look for someone smart and passionate. He says that the person has to be comfortable with technology and be optimistic about the future. **"Like someone who you would find interesting on a long train journey."**'Googliness' means a host of things. For instance, naming their printers after iconic but old Indian vehicle brands — the one on their first level is Bajaj Auto and that on the second is lovingly called Premier Padmini — just a quirk that gladdens the heart of the company's senior management. It also means creating a systems room that looks more like a 'hang loose' cyber café. And the graffiti that says 'I'm so boring without you' for a desktop minus the owner.

**Google SPEAKS**

**Psv. Jogeswari, team leader, AdWords: "We understand that every person doesn't have the same skills. So we give roles that you will be good at"**

**Abhinav K., software engineer, test: "Being a Googler is a lot of responsibility. In interviews, a candidate should feel good whether she is hired or not"**

**Antara Panda, software engineer, test: "People talk about a 70:20:10 time break up here. But we actually give our 120 per cent"**

**Aditya Dugar, AdWords associate: "I used to be a star in my earlier office and that felt so good! Here, everyone is so bright that everyone is a star"**

**Sujatha Narapaneni, admin. associate: "You are never asked to be like anyone else here. Which is why many bests can coexist"**

**Vinay Chandra, online ops specialist: "Sure, not everything is perfect here. But asking a rose-coloured question is not the way to get noticed"**

Most important, it means buying into 'Google Truths' like 'You can make money without doing evil' and 'There's always more information out there'. As long as its employees think like this, the management knows the future is safe.

The company's recruitment process ensures that it gets the people edge it needs. There is a battery of writing tests, interviews are rigorous, not in the sense of being a stress interview, but interviewers try and go deep into what makes the candidate tick. Then a detailed feedback on the candidate is given to an independent team in charge of hiring. In fact, the credo here is to hire someone who is better than you.

Just like at the headquarters of the 'Googler's' universe at the Googleplex in Mountain View, California, the employee count at Google India is also growing — almost as fast as its share price. Inevitably the company is faced with a growth conundrum — as you grow larger, you innovate less. Managing this growth without losing the nimble-footedness is a key organisational challenge.

To this end, the 20 per cent time that Google encourages is a win-win. It means that employees invest that much of their time on stuff that is not directly their work but adjacent to their work. They love it and the company gets ideas it can invest in for the future. Gmail came from there, as did Google Finance, from engineers in Bangalore. The Hyderabad centre mostly concentrates on two of Google's chief advertising and sales tools, AdSense and AdWords. So, if decoding search queries isn't the done deal here, having a felicity for language and generally being an interesting person gets one around.

Perhaps in keeping with this philosophy that Googliness is all you need, Google's management systems don't have a very spread out human resources function. Says Manoj Verghese, director (HR): "We don't keep HR as a separate function. In fact, we prefer our managers to be HR managers." But that might get tweaked as global headquarters in Mountain View decides to formalise its HR processes.

Google India might not have Michelin star-rated chefs cooking in the cafeterias. Nor are dogs allowed into the office yet (there are dog lovers campaigning for this but the going looks difficult because the company doesn't have its own campus here) like in their head office. But what is unmistakable is the kindred spirit they share with the office almost 18,000 km away. The essence of the charter that founders Larry Page and Sergey Brin set out has firm echoes in India. While the free chocolates and dry fruits at the pantry on every floor help, it is Google, the idea, which is the biggest contributor in making it the workplace it is.

### Discussion questions

1. Do you think the culture at Google would make employees give their best? Explain the reasons
2. Identify the dimensions of culture in Google that separate the company from similar outfits in the business world

## CASE STUDY 2: Microsoft 'S Culture Of Hiring The Best

The software major, Microsoft, considers human resources as a priceless corporate asset capable of delivering results that are beyond imagination. The intellectual talents of employees differentiate Microsoft from other software developers of the world. It looks for employees who are willing to learn, who are willing to forget what they have learnt outside and step into the company with an inquisitive mind. Employees who come with a learning attitude and with a strong will to gain a grip over current technological developments are given a warm welcome. Microsoft expects its employees to think in a flexible manner and adapt to the changing nature of the industry. Essentially, they need to be dynamic and willing to run ahead of times. In order to get the right people with a proper mix of skills, knowledge and experience, Microsoft spends lot of time and energies in reaching out to the right people

To attract potential candidates, Microsoft relies upon a variety of recruiting tools. The company advertises in newspapers, accepts applications on their Microsoft World Wide Web Page and recruits at college job fairs. In addition, the company relies upon innovative and creative hiring techniques that mirror its image and reputation in the market place. The company is flooded with over 15,000 applications from prospective job seekers almost every month. Each resume is logged into a computer database which recruiters sort through, deploying key word searches that highlight skills and competencies that Microsoft values most. Another novel feature about Microsoft hiring is the significant involvement of employees working at various levels. The needs of various jobs are being looked into from different angles, seeking feedback from employees. The whole exercise is meant to strike a fine balance between current position needs with prospective candidates' profile. Top management spends lot of time trying to get to the root of the problem—that is getting the right candidate without getting unduly influenced by the candidate's previous experiences, background and educational qualifications. At times, the highly visible founder and chairman, Bill Gates is known to call potential employees to let them know that the company is interested in bringing them on board.

The company's selection processes are equally creative. Instead of relying on the information provided by selection tests, it places heavy emphasis on reference checks or sometimes, drug tests. Rigorous interview sessions are meant to weed out the wheat from the chaff. Interviewers seek answers to specific questions aimed at testing candidates' willingness to think innovatively, learn and get along with others. For instance, an interviewer might pose questions like how much water flows through the Mississippi on a daily basis, or why manhole covers are round. The interviewers are not in any way looking for smart, intelligent or even answers but are only trying to assess an applicant's ability to solve problems by thinking differently.

Well, at the end of the day do these recruiting and selection practices deliver results for Microsoft? The answer is in the positive. The people who are inside the company seem to be a good fit for Microsoft. The attrition rate is much lower than the industry average, standing at about 7 per cent. The company's zeal to get candidates willing to go that extra mile seems to be paying off handsomely. The stunning results of the software major, quarter after quarter, are there for everyone to see. By pushing employees and recruiters to challenge interviewees to assess their true capabilities and potential, Microsoft continually recruits the best talent it can get. (Adapted from G.Bohlander et al, Managing Human Resources, New York, South Western, 2001)

## Questions

1. What are the costs and benefits associated with using such innovative hiring techniques?
2. How successfully would these practices transfer to other firms in the same industry? How successfully would these practices transfer to other firms in other industries?

# 12

# MANAGING CONFLICT

## INTRODUCTION

Conflict is a process in which one party perceives that its interests are being opposed or negatively affected by another party. It is, in fact, a basic part of life in groups and organisations. The very nature of an organisation guarantees the emergence of conflict. Firstly, organisations consist of people with divergent personalities, perceptions, and values. Secondly, these people are put on jobs with contrasting features that impart unequal degrees of status and frequently foster competition. Finally, organisations contain groups that often compete for scarce resources while trying to achieve assigned goals. In organisations, conflict can take many forms and can stem from many sources. If the fires are not put out in time, conflict has the potential to seriously disrupt organisational life.

### Meaning

Conflict is a *perceived* difference of values between two or more parties that results in mutual opposition. It implies both, opposing interests or goals; opposing or incompatible behaviour. It is a process in which A deliberately tries to offset the efforts of B by some form of blocking that will result in frustrating B in attaining his goals or frustrating his interests (Robbins). This definition reveals the following features of conflict:

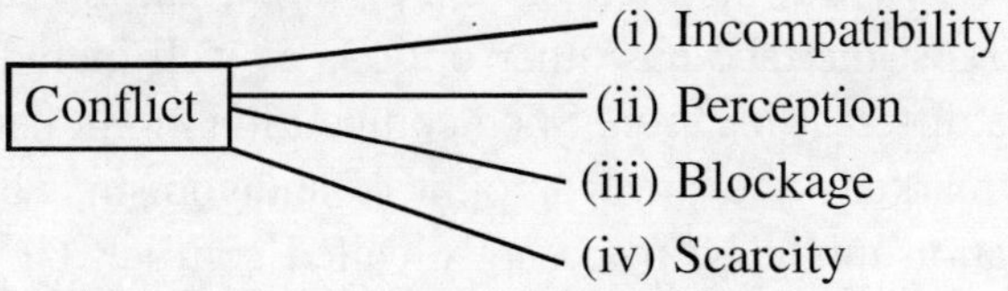


***Figure 12.1: Features of Conflict***

**(i) Incompatibility:** Conflict occurs when two or more parties pursue mutually exclusive goals, values or events. It is based on the assumption that there are two or more parties whose interests or goals appear to be incompatible.

**(ii) Perception:** Conflict arises out of two perceptions. If X perceives his goals to be incompatible with those of Y there is conflict if, however X has no opportunity to frustrate the goal attainment of Y, there is no conflict.

**(iii) Blocking:** Conflict refers to deliberate (blocking) behaviour. X deliberately tries to prevent Y from attaining his (Y's) goals. If interference is accidental, there is no conflict.

**(iv) Scarcity:** Conflict arises, basically because of scarce resources. Possibilities for conflict expand when there are limited resources such as office space, equipment, training opportunities , operating funds and pay allocations.

**(v) Latent or overt:** Conflict can exit either at the latent or overt level, but generally speaking, conflict is a term that is limited to overt acts.

**(vi) Verbal or non verbal:** Conflict behaviour may be verbal or non verbal. One can express opposition by words, by a shake of the head, by an indecent gesture, by writing a scathing memo, or by scratching the paint of a new car with a nail as it moves down the assembly line.

**(vii)Active or passive:** Conflict behaviour may be active or passive. One can sometimes counter the behaviour of another by tactics such as 'dragging one's feat' or withholding information. It is implicit in what has been said that perception of a loss or of a potential loss, accurate or inaccurate, can create conflict.

Conflict is not limited to interacting groups alone, since it can also occur within groups and between individuals and between organisations. Conflict occurs when two groups have mutually exclusive goals and their interactions are intended to defeat, suppress or inflict damage on the other.

## COMPETITION VS. CONFLICT

Conflict implies both, opposing interests or goals opposing or in compatible behaviour. Competition on the other hand, may involve considerable commonality of interests or goals, and only a limited amount of opposing behaviours. Competition occurs when two or more individuals or groups are structuring for a goal that can be achieved by only one. Fixed or limited resource base is one of the important features of a competitive situation. For example, the person with the maximum sales wins the sales contest; the bidder with the lowest quotation wins the contract; only one sales officer becomes the Head of Sales. In case of competition, the person who gets promoted, out of the two who applied for the post of Head of Sales is undoubtedly the winner. But the person who lost the race has other options as well including promotion into some other unit in the same or a different location. Such competition might be relatively friendly. However, if such a situation is marked by a great amount of antagonism, verbal battles and other negative behaviour, the situation might be more aptly called conflict. Competition, generally, has some ground rules that the parties have agreed to in advance. Parties are aware of how far they can gain or lose. Conflict, however, has few or no rules and when parties engage in a negative behaviour, they are not aware of how far the situation can escalate. The outcomes, definitely have the potential to negatively impact one of the parties and sometimes, the whole system as well. Competitive rules are generally framed by authorities, for example, Top Management framing promotion policies, or a Chess Federation developing contest rules and schedules. Conflict, on the other hand, is more spontaneous and is outside of certain pre-planned set or rules and regulations.

## Collaboration

As pointed out previously groups come into existence with a view to achieve some common goal(s) depending on how they approach the goal, conflict or collaborations takes place. If members feel that the goal is unshareable and can be achieved exclusively by only one, conflictful situations emerge. However, if they perceive that the goal is shareable and they can join hands to achieve it, collaboration is generated. Collaboration supplements what competition does. It performs several important functions.

It helps individuals to respect and accept each other in the workplace. It allows people to see the brighter side of people more closely. When people join hands to achieve goals, they can think through various creative ideas in an atmosphere of cordiality. They can generate and evaluate alternative solutions without dissipating energies in arguments and counter - productive criticisms. They get feedback from colleagues immediately and this helps in reinforcing workable solutions. They can also give feedback to collaborating partners that helps in building strong team ties. Members can work more productively, generating as many ideas (or solutions) as possible. They can multiply their contributions through such synergetic behaviours. Members tend to work with zeal, enthusiasm and confidence as they think they are part of a cohesive team. They can exchange notes freely without any fear of leg-pulling and ultra-initial actions. They will be keen to go beyond the four walls and take initiative in taking responsibility for the actions of the group as a whole. All people, additionally, get a chance to participate in organisational actively achievely and test their capabilities. The functions of competition and collaboration may be stated thus (Pareek 1982 and 1994).

**Table 12.1. Functions of Competition and Collaboration**

| Competition develops | Collaboration develops |
|---|---|
| • Sense of identity | • Mutuality |
| • Sense of responsibility | • Alternative ideas and solutions |
| • Internal standards | • Mutual support and reinforcement Excellence Synergy |
| • Individual creativity | • Collective action |
| • Individual autonomy | |

## CHANGING SCENARIO OF CONFLICT

Over the years, three distinct philosophies that refer to different managerial attitudes towards conflict have been identified: the classical, behavioural and interactionist philosophies.

(i) The **classical approach** viewed conflict as an organisational abnormality, a potentially dangerous process. Conflict induces mainly negative outcomes: anger, resentment, confusion, lack of cooperation etc. It disrupts the smooth functioning of organisational processes and creates chaos and disorder. Conflict is bad and must be avoided at all costs. The organisation structure with its clear policies, elaborate rules and well defined specifications of authority and responsibility should not permit conflicts. It will not occur if sound management principles are applied. By any chance if conflicts were to develop, they can be easily and quickly resolved by the management. Managerial attitude towards conflict was one of fear and disdain. Conflict, by definition, was viewed as harmful and was to be avoided, suppressed.

**(ii) Behaviouralists** also had a similar **jaundiced** view of conflict. They also believed that conflict, by definition, was harmful and should be avoided. Those who generated conflict were trouble-makers and were bad for the organisation. This view reflected a "popular pre-occupation with morals, human relations and cooperation, and the general value that peace is good and conflict bad". They, however, accepted the fact that conflict is a natural occurrence in all organisations.

(iii) The emerging view of conflict, called as **interactionist view,** reverses many of the cosy nostrums of human relations management. The interactionist view of conflict has a broader scope. It recognises that in some cases conflict may be helpful, facilitative and functional. The interactionist views may be summarised thus:

1. Conflict is not an organisational abnormality. On the other hand, it is a normal aspect of social intercourse. It is a fact of life that must be understood rather than fought.
2. Conflict is inevitable. It is an inherent structural component in all social relations.
3. Conflict is neither bad nor good for organisations. Perfect organisational health is not free from conflict.
4. Conflict is not always caused by trouble makers. It is rather determined by structural factors like the design of a career structure, the physical shape of a building etc.
5. Conflict is integral to the nature of change.
6. Conflict is not only inevitable but sometimes desirable.

A minimum level of conflict is optimal. In the words of S. P. Robbins, "While the behavioural approach accepted conflict, the interactionist view encourages conflict on the grounds that a harmonious, peaceful, tranquil and cooperative group is prone to becoming static, apathetic, and nonresponsive to needs for change and innovation.

## Positive (Functional) vs. Negative (Dysfunctional) conflict

In Negative conflict, individuals view others as adversaries. They are more concerned about protecting themselves. They are less, or not at all bothered about the basic human rights of others. They try to win at all costs and often see people as expenses and not as investments. They take criticisms to their heart and fail to elicit the true thoughts and feelings of others. In Positive conflict, individuals with differing points of view and personalities show mutual respect for each other's ideas, thoughts and feelings and consequently develop rapport and effective working relations. They support each other and communicate openly without playing 'games'. Rather than taking negative statements personally, they assert themselves to achieve positive results.

Most experts today view conflict as a potentially useful aspect of an organisation. It is said that an organisation void of constructive conflict is an organisation void of excitement, diversity and viability. Conflict prevents stagnation by stimulating interest and curiosity. It is the medium through which problems can be aired and solutions arrived at. It is the root of personal and social change. Conflict provides an adequate platform wherein people can "blow off steam," that is, it permits immediate and direct expression of rival claims. Without conflict, organisations would be only apathetic and stagnant. The following are some of the *positive consequences* of conflict:

1. **Major stimulant for change:** Conflict spotlights the problems that demand attention, forces clarification of their nature and channelises organisational efforts towards finding better solutions. It initiates a search for ways to polish and refine objectives, methods and activities.

2. **Group think is avoided:** Without strong vocal disagreement, group think could overpower a highly cohesive group, preventing it from making rational decisions based on facts. Conflict also counteracts the lethargy that often overtakes an organisation.

3. **Conflict fosters creativity and innovation:** It prevents stagnation; it stimulates interest and curiosity. In an atmosphere of open confrontation, people tend to put forward more imaginative solutions to problems. A climate to challenge compels individuals to think through their own ideas before airing them out. Conflict can help individuals to test their capacities to learn and develop. A scholar who exposes his theories and research to the scrutiny of his colleagues may be stimulated to a deeper analysis, when he is confronted with conflicting data and theoretical analysis by a colleague.

4. **Cohesion and satisfaction:** Inter-group conflict and competition drives groups closer together. Under conditions of mild inter-group conflict, group membership can be very satisfying to members. The whole purpose and internal unity of athletic groups, for example, would disappear if there were no conflict. In the face of a common enemy, group members close ranks and put aside former disagreements. For example, petty conflicts between cricket team members are generally put aside before the big game. According to Boulding, organisations, in many ways, are creations of their enemies and it is through a common hatred of the enemy that they establish their internal unity.

5. **A minimum level of conflict is optimal:** Conflict is necessary for the internal stability of organisations. The occasional flareup of inter-group conflict serves to balance power relationships between departments. It also helps individuals in reducing accumulated ill-feelings and tensions between them. A good fight clears the air.

The following are the **negative consequences** of conflict:

1. **Conflict creates stress in people:** Conflict exacts its toll on the physical and mental health of the combatants. Intense conflicts generate feelings of anxiety, guilt, frustration and hostility. Winners try to injure the feelings of the defeated. Losers feel defeated and demeaned. The distance between people increases. A climate of mistrust and suspicion develops. Discussion replaces cohesion. Losers indulge in non-cooperation and pay scant attention to the needs and interests of other group members.

2. **Diversion of energy:** One of the most dreadful consequences of conflict is the diversion of the group's time and effort toward winning the conflict rather than toward achieving organisational goals. Parties focus on their own narrow interests and tend to put their own aims above those of the organisation. Long term goals begin to suffer as short term problems become more important. Much energy is drained off in trying to put out the 'fires'. In extreme cases, sabotage and even illegal activities occur.

3. **Instability and chaos:** Under intense conflicts, collaboration across individuals, groups and departments decreases or vanishes. Tensions will continue to mount up and each new conflict will split organisation subunits further apart leading to communication breakdowns. In the heat of such an internecine warfare, the disputants squander away energy and resources that could be devoted to better use. The normal work-flow is disrupted; the moral fabric of the group torn apart and the whole system is skewed out of balance.

## STAGES OF CONFLICT EPISODE

According to Pondy, conflict can be more readily understood if it is considered as a dynamic process. "Process" here indicates a series of events. Each conflict is made up of a sequence of interlocking conflict episodes.

The model (Fig. 12.2) presents conflict as a series of stages namely, latent conflict, perceived conflict, felt conflict, manifest conflict and conflict aftermath.

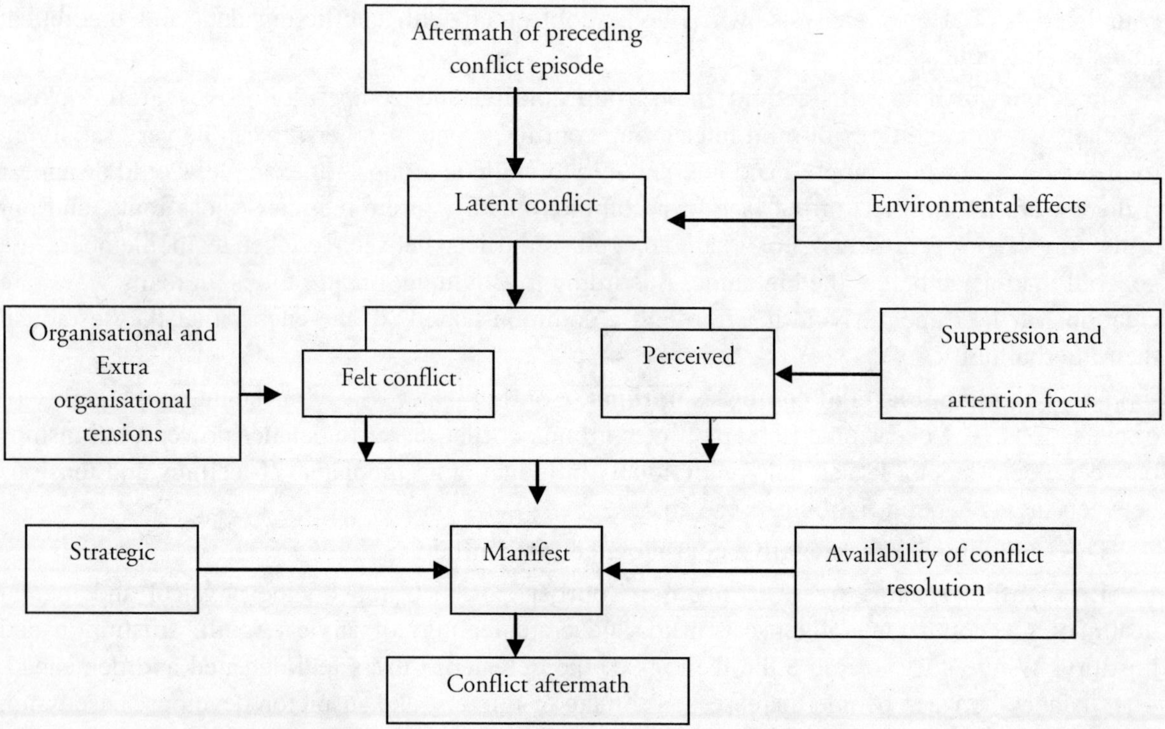


***Figure 12.2: Stages of Conflict Episode***

1. **Latent conflict:** Each episode of conflict begins with a "latent conflict". Important sources of organisational conflict such as competition for scarce resources divergence of subunit goals, competition for positions in the organisation, imply that role conflict are present, but the conflict has not yet emerged. Latent conflict provides the necessary antecedent conditions for conflict in organisations. Here, participants only anticipate conflict.

2. **Perceived conflict:** Here the basic sources of conflict like divergent goals competition for scarce resources do not exist. Conflict results due to the parties' misunderstanding of each

other's true position. Such a conflict can be resolved by improving communication between the parties.

**3. Felt conflict:** X and Y working in a departmental store are in serious disagreement over the interpretation of the policy "Customer is the King" and are arguing for hours together. If this episode does not make X tense or anxious and has no effect on X's relationship with Y then it can be safely concluded that conflict is not 'felt' by the parties. Even though people preceive that there is a basis for conflict, conflict will not arise unless the differences become personalized or internalized (felt).

**4. Manifest conflict:** This is the stage for open confrontation. It takes the form of conflictful behaviour, including open aggression, sabotage, apathy, withdrawal, letter perfect obedience to rules etc., all of which reduce organisation's effectiveness.

**5. Conflict aftermath:** The aftermath of a conflict may be either positive or negative for the organisation depending on how the conflict is resolved. If the conflict is genuinely resolved, it can lead to a more enduring and cooperative relationship between organisational participants; if the conflict is merely supressed but not resolved, the latent conditions of conflict may be aggravated and explode in more violent and serious forms. This legacy of conflict is called "conflict aftermath".

## Conflict and Organisational Performance

The relationship between conflict and organisational performance is illustrated through the following figure:

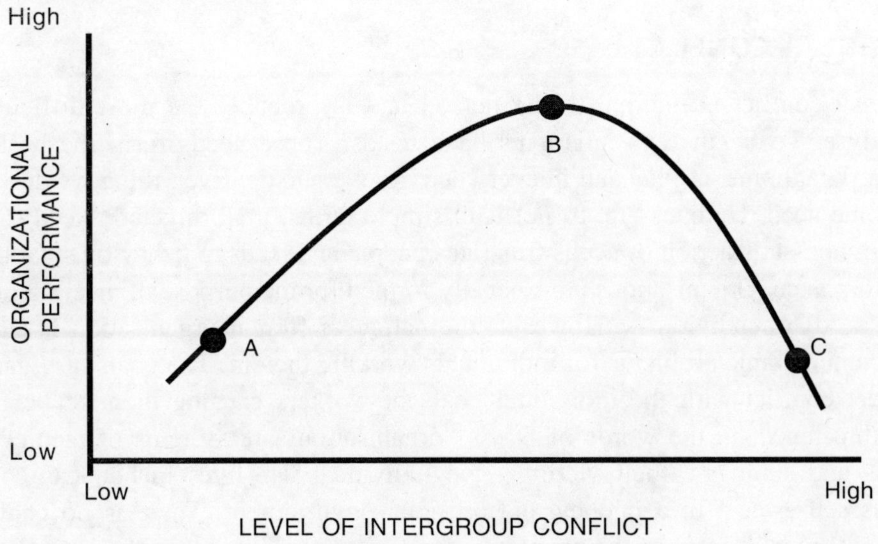


***Figure 12.3: Relationship Between Conflict and Organisational Performance***

Organisational performance, as can be seen, is low when the level of conflict is either extremely high or extremely low, while moderate levels of conflict contribute to high organisational performance. At point A, where conflict is low, performance suffers because of a lack of arousal and stimulation. Individuals find their environment devoid of any challenge. They do not search for new ideas and the organisation is slow to adapt to environmental changes. At point C, where conflict level is higher, performance suffers due to lack of coordination and cooperation. The organisation is in a state of chaos because of disruption to important activities. People spend more time defending themselves or attacking others rather than doing productive work. At point B, conflict is sufficient enough to provoke people to think creatively, act enthusiastically and achieve goals.

## TYPES OF CONFLICT

Conflict can be studied, generally, under the following heads Fig. 12.4:

Conflict

| Individual conflict | Group conflict | Organisational conflict |
|---|---|---|
| Intra individual conflict | Inter group conflict | Inter Organisational conflict |
| Inter individual conflict | Intra group conflict | Intra Organisation conflict |

***Figure 12.4: Analysing Conflict***

These can be broadly analysed under four headings namely: Intra Individual Conflict, Inter Personal Conflict, Group Conflict and Inter Organisational Conflict. (inter group, intragroup and inter organisational conflict have been combined under the Group Conflict broadly)

## INTRA INDIVIDUAL CONFLICT

Intra personal conflict is internal to the person and is probably the most difficult type of conflict to analyse. To begin with, all of us have needs. These needs form the basis for our behaviour at work, at home, at play and in every activity we pursue. Everything we do is directed at satisfying some need. Humans are, to put it in simple terms, goal directed. Need satisfaction spurs people on; non-satisfaction of needs frustrates people and leads to behaviour that negatively affects job performance. Organisations are basically formed for the purpose of meeting humanistic and economic needs of individuals. However, the nature of formal organisation is such that it tends to create innumerable problems for individuals working therein. The goals of organisational life are in direct conflict with the individual goals of workers causing them to be frustrated, alienated and threatened. In the words of Davis "organisations are systems of medieval torture which suppress and subjugate their victim – the individual. He lives in helpless conformity, stripped off his self-esteem in a phoney and artificial environment. There is no challenge for psychological fulfilment." Most of the people working in organisations are like inert instruments, mere appendages in the production process. There is little chance to be creative. As organisations grow, they tend to be less responsive to the needs of individuals. In addition to loss of freedom the individual is stripped off his identity also. The incongruity model developed by Chris Argyris postulates that there is lack of congruity between the needs of healthy individuals and the demands of the organisation.

The individual is caught in the web of his own making. He faces a conflict within himself. A smooth progression of the need-drive-goal motivational cycle does not occur. He is confronted with many puzzling questions: Whether to hang on the present job in spite of its in-built disincentives? Whether to tolerate the inhuman treatment meted out daily by the Boss? Whether to manipulate the figures to curry favour with the boss and prosper? To do or not to do? Basically intra-individual conflict can be related to two things: conflict arising due to divergent goals, or conflict arising from the multiple roles to be played daily.

## Goal Conflict

Goal conflict occurs when a goal that an individual is attempting to achieve has both positive and negative features or when two or more competing goals exist. Generally, three separate types of goal conflicts are identified:

**(i) Approach-Approach conflict:** A person wants two positive situations but can have only one. The person might be torn between lucrative jobs (mutually exclusive goals).

**(ii) Approach-avoidance conflict:** In this form of goal conflict, the person attempts to achieve a goal that has both positive and negative aspects. A Delhi University teacher may be offered an excellent job in a bad location. In pursuing a challenging goal like obtaining First rank in the University, many students must make personal sacrifices (time, energy, away from entertainments etc.).

**(iii) Avoidance-Avoidance conflict:** This type of conflict can be easily resolved because a person faced with two negative goals may not choose either of them and may simply leave the situation. This type of conflict may also exist when the person does not have the opportunity to leave. For example, a worker may dislike his present job, but the alternative of leaving and looking for another job may be even less attractive.

## Role

A role is a set of expectations people have about the behaviour of a person in a position. It is an expected mode of behaviour. An individual occupies many different positions in a variety of organisations and performs multiple roles. Professors may be teachers, researchers, consultants, wives or husbands, community leaders. In organisations such roles are formally prescribed and others are created by the informal activities of the organisation members. When we examine the concept of role, three types of roles clearly emerge; the expected role, the perceived role and the actual role. The expected role is what other people expect from an individual. For example, a college teacher is expected by his role partners (Principal, Colleagues, Students) to behave in a specific way. The perceived role is how the individual thinks he or she should behave to fulfil the expected role. The enacted role is the way the person actually behaves in an organisation. Thus in the complex theatre of modern life, most people play not to one audience but to several, and they play multiple roles simultaneously.

3. **The Role Episode Concept:** The role episode concept provides a useful framework for understanding the impact of roles on individual behaviour. Role senders transmit expectations to the focal person, who is a role taker. The sent role is received by the focal person, who behaves according to his own propensities as modified by the influence of the role senders.

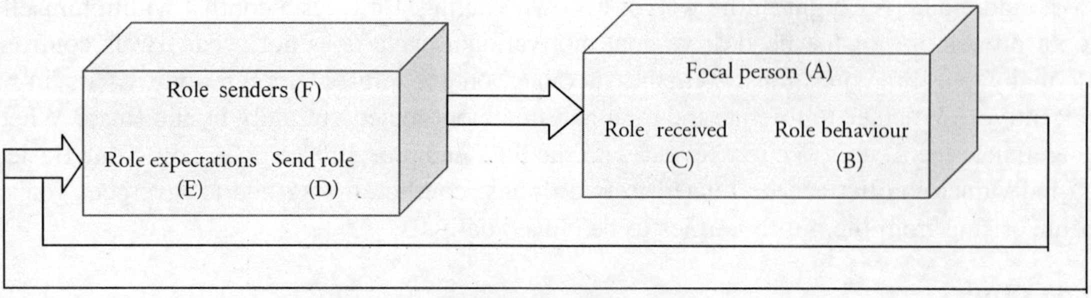


**Figure 12.5: The role episode concept.**
**Source: D. Katz and R.L. Kahn, The Social Psychology of Organisation, N.Y., John Wiley, 1966, p. 182.**

The focal person's actual behaviour (B) is a behavioural response to the received role (C). The sent role is related to but not identical with the expectations (G) of role senders (F). The received role is the focal person's perception of the sent role (D) and includes his own perception of what the role should be.

**4. Role Ambiguity:** Role ambiguity occurs when an individual is unclear regarding his job duties and responsibilities. As a result, the individual experiences difficulty in enacting the role. For example, a college principal's job may be the centre of a web of conflicting interest groups, none of which can be fully satisfied. He is, by definition, almost always wrong. If he spends much time in meeting the students, he is neglecting the faculty. If he spends much time with the faculty, he is being dictated by them. If he is off campus, he should be backminding the store. If he changes his mind on an issue he is wishy-washy. If he does not, he is pig-headed. Ambiguity provides enough scope for variations in work or role performance by individuals, thereby increasing opportunities for conflict. When employees experience role ambiguity, job performance is adversely affected because literally they do not know what they are expected to do. The following figure illustrates how role conflicts develop from divergence in role expectations:

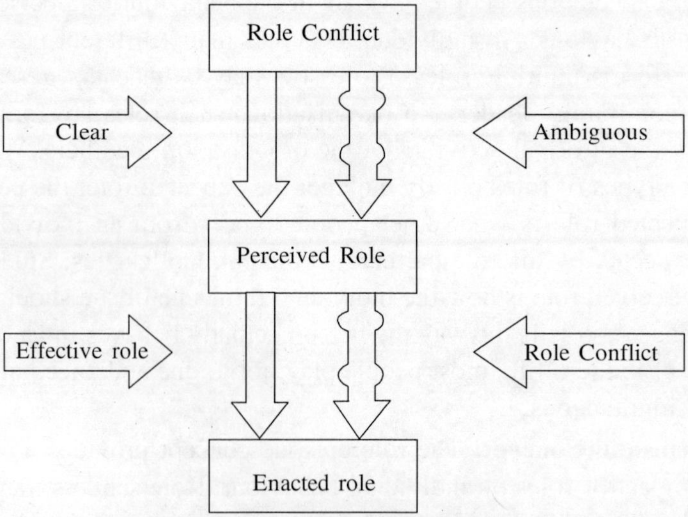


**Figure 12.6: Role ambiguity.**

## Role Conflict

Role conflict is the result of divergent role expectations. It exists when the expectations of a job are mutually different or opposite and the individual cannot meet one expectation without rejecting the other. For example, the supervisor, the man in the middle, is a bumping post, he has to take it from both ends. He has to perform strikingly different roles. He is both a boss and a subordinate. As a part of the management team, he should have the corresponding values and attitudes. As a member from the workers' group, he should have their values and attitudes. He is expected to wear both hats gracefully. Role conflict arises when roles are so that conflicting supervisors do not know which set of expectations they should follow, Again, managers occupying boundary positions, such as, marketing executives who have wide contacts with outsiders, work under role conflict. Some of their customer's expectations on product quality, delivery time and credit term may be inconsistent with company policies. This type of conflict is known as intra–role conflict. Several other forms of role conflict may be noted:

**(a) Person-role conflict:** This conflict arises when the expected behaviour is incompatible with a person's own basic values and attitudes. For example, a politician asks one of his supporters to play dirty tricks on an opponent and the supporter refuses on morale grounds.

**(b) Inter-role conflict:** This types of conflict is the result of facing multiple roles. It occurs because individuals simultaneously perform many roles, and such roles conflict with each other. Many professors who try to evaluate the performance of students (judge role) may find it uncomfortable to fulfil the demands of other role like the role of trainer, developer or teacher.

**(c) Intrasender role conflict:** This occurs when an individual is expected to perform a task within specified limits but it is not possible to behave in a manner consistent with role assignment. For example, if the librarian is asked to purchase rare, precious books from approved book sellers and the books are not found there but are found in roadside bookshops then intrasender conflict may develop.

**(d) Intersender role conflict:** If a building contractor asks a carpenter to do something that is different from the instructions of the architect, the municipal building codes or his union's work rules, that is called intersender role conflict.

## Results of Role Conflict

An individual confronted with role conflict will experience psychological stress leading to emotional problems. The likely end result will be a decline in performance. "Research shows that where a wide variance in a manager's role perception of his job and the employee's role expectations of that job there exists tends to be poor motivation and inefficiency." Role conflict is inversely related to job satisfaction and directly related to job tension and anxiety. Role conflicts can have a markedly adverse impact on satisfaction and even on mental or physical health. Sometimes for the focal person, the emotional costs of role conflict include low job satisfaction, low confidence in the organisation and high scores on the multi-item index of tension.

## Role Conflict Resolution:

Organisations using participative management tend to minimize role conflict. Persuasion and group pressures can be exercised to bring subordinates' goals closer to organisational goals. Role conflict cannot be completely planned and rules out. The management's approach towards resolving role conflicts should be to avoid situations where such conflicts arise. The important aspect will be matching situations and approaches. As pointed out y R.L. Kahn, a ceremony of confrontation and joint problem solving would seem to be a useful mode of (role) conflict resolution.

## INTERPERSONAL CONFLICT

Interpersonal conflict involves two or more individuals rather than one individual. Two boys fighting for one cinema ticket, two men vying for one women, two managers competing for the same promotion, two executives manoeuvring for a larger share of corporate capital–examples of conflict between individuals are legion and quite familiar. Such conflict situations are made-up of at least two individuals who hold polarized points of view, who are somewhat intolerant of ambiguities, who ignore delicate shades of grey, and who are quick to jump to conclusions.

### Reasons of Interpersonal Conflict

Interpersonal conflicts usually result in such cases where each person is jockeying to posses a scarce resource which maybe a material thing or an immaterial state such as status, prestige, fame, power or money. The most commonly cited reasons for interpersonal conflicts are:

1. **Personality differences:** Some people have difficulty in getting along with each other. This is purely a psychological problem and it has nothing to do with their job requirements or formal interactions.

2. **Perceptions:** Varied backgrounds, experiences, education and training result in individuals developing different perceptions of similar realities; the result being an increase in the likelihood of interpersonal conflict. The belief that somebody else is out to eat away our share of resources may create ill-feelings between us and that person. An individual who perceives conflict is likely (between managers and subordinates) to act in a manner conveying conflict intentions. Vertical conflicts develop usually because superiors try to control subordinates and subordinates tend to resist. The subordinates may resist because they believe the control infringes on their personal autonomy, "makes his behaviour more predictable to others and thus weakens his power position in the organisation".

3. **Clashes of values and interests:** Conflict that so commonly develops between engineering and manufacturing personnel shows how differences in values might underlie conflict. Members of the engineering department might place a premium on quality, sophisticated design and durability while members of the manufacturing department might value simplicity and low manufacturing costs. The typical reactions may erupt in such forms. "It is too expensive to do it your way". "But we'll lose our reputation for quality if we attempt it your way".

4. **Power and status differences:** Interpersonal conflicts arise from unequal distribution of power and status. As pointed out by Abraham Zalenznik, "Organisations are political structures." They operate by distributing authority and setting a stage for the exercise of power. Similarly, status inconsistencies lead to conflict.

For example, a conflict may result when low status waitresses try to give orders to high status cooks.

**5. Scarce resources:** Interpersonal conflict is almost automatic wherever there is scarcity. Conflicts over scarce resources are exceedingly common in organisations. Where the scarcity is absolute (the resource level cannot be enhanced), it is very difficult to manage interpersonal conflicts. For example, if three qualified individuals vie for superior positions in the organisation and there is only one such position, interpersonal conflict may develop to an unmanageable level.

## GROUP CONFLICT

### Intergroup conflict

(a) Intergroup conflicts over authority, jurisdiction and resources are exceedingly common. Every group is in at least a partial conflict with every other group it interacts with. Most of the departments in the organisation compete for the allocation of scarce resources and power. They differ in goals, work activities, power and prestige. The seeds of intergroup conflict are show in these differences. Research findings generally confirm the following sources of intergroup conflict:

**1. Incompatible goals:** Quite often, the goals of one group are incompatible with those of other groups. Differences in group goals can easily lead to group conflict. Goal incompatibility implies that goal attainment by one or more other groups. The achievement of one department's goal often interferes with another departments' goal. Quite often, this is due to high horizontal differentiation and task specialisation. The production department might perceive its goals as being potentially incompatible with those of marketing. Production department may pose such questions, "Why don't we have accurate sales forecasts? Is it possible to keep everything in inventory? And marketing people may pose a counter attack, "Why don't we have enough capacity? Why don't we ever have the right merchandise in inventory?" Such escalating differences are natural by-products of specialisation.

**2. Task interdependence:** Task interdependence refers to the dependence of one unit on another for resources or information. The relationship between mutual task dependence and conflict is not direct. But in general, it can be said that as interdependence increases, the potential for conflict increases. J. Thompson has identified three types of interdependence among groups: pooled, sequential and reciprocal. *Pooled interdependence* occurs when departments have little interaction with each other but are affected by each others' actions. For example, a branch in Delhi does not need to interact with a branch in Meerut. The only linkage between the two is that they share financial resources from a common pool and the success of each branch contributes to the success of the organisation. When interdependence is of serial from wherein the output of one becomes the input of another, then it is called *sequential interdependence.* Plant A's performance depends on plant B's performance. This type of mutual dependence specifies a one way traffic for the flow of materials and calls for careful planning. In such situations where one unit is unable to commence its work until the other unit completes its job, conflict potential is greatest. *Reciprocal interdependence* occurs when two or more groups are mutually interdependent in accomplishing the tasks. The output of departments influences one another in a reciprocal fashion. They mutually exchange information and resources. The relationship that exists between the nursing staff, surgeons, anesthesiology staff etc., is an example of reciprocal interdependence. Reciprocal interdependence forces employees to interact frequently. Employees are required to spend time coordinating and exchanging information and resources. Conflict is likely to crop up when agreement is not reached about the coordination of services to each other.

**3. Resource allocation:** Quite often resource allocation is a bone of contention between organisation members and groups. Recourses symbolize power, influence and are the means of accomplishing goals. As such, most of the departments in an organisation jockey for resources and power base. In their anxiety to achieve goals, groups try to cut a bigger slick out of the common pool. Generally, the more fixed the resources in terms of size, and the more parties competing for them, the more intense the conflict. Conflict may be minimized if the organisation is prospering and new resources are growing in allowing a greater share to each and every department.

**4. Competitive incentive and reward system:** When jobs can be performed independently, competitive incentive plans based on individual excellence can be successfully implemented. However, when tasks are interdependent, competition can hurt cooperation among members and performance may actually decline. When all students in a group received the same grade regardless of individual contribution, coordination and communication was better and the quality of the group project was better. But when students were graded according to their personal contributions to the group, they try to succeed at the expense of others and were more frequently in conflict. Similarly, intergroup conflict is more likely to occur when the reward plan is tied to individual group performance rather than to overall organisational performance. If departments are regarded and judged only for departmental performance, managers are motivated to excel at the expense of others.

**5. Line and Staff conflicts:** Today, line and staff differences are the most common type of intergroup conflict. This conflict is basically a clash of domain caused by dividing expertise, authority and roles. Dalton's study of line and staff conflict highlighted the following sources:

(i) Line managers dislike to take advice from younger staff specialists. They fear being 'shown up'.

(ii) Line managers label "staff" as agents on trial. The staff, in turn, views himself as an expert.

(iii) Line managers feel that staff oversteps its authority.

(iv) Line people resent staff's highly academic and untested ideas.

(v) Staff people feel that line managers are bull-headed and do not clothe staff with enough authority and resist new ideas.

**6. Differences in values or perceptions:** The differences in goals among the members of the various departments in the organisation are frequently accompanied by differences in attitudes, values and perceptions that can also lead to conflict. Young bank clerks with post graduate qualification may resent being given routine work, while the older, higher level (less educated sometimes) may view such task as a necessary part of training. Engineering people may value sophisticated designs while manufacturing people may prefer simple designs. Sometimes, status incongruence also promotes conflict. If members of a particular department perceive themselves as having higher status than the others for one reason or another conflict results in. For example, conflict was found to result when low status industrial engineers directed the higher status engineers in the implementation of certain tasks.

7. **Other reasons:** Additional sources of intergroup conflict may include:

**(a) Heterogeneity of members:** Personality differences such as background, education, age etc., lower the probability of interpersonal rapport and decrease the amount of collaboration between departments.

**(b) Communication distortions:** Inadequate or unclear communications stimulate conflict because important information is held back and parties do not know each other's jobs. This lack of knowledge can lead to unreasonable interunit demands. Sometimes, surprisingly, interdepartmental conflicts cropped up where departments possessed a great deal of knowledge about each other's activities. Complete knowledge may reveal each party's self interest more clearly and may exhibit the inequalities more prominently.

**(c) Participative decision-making:** Joint decision-making promotes conflict. It offers enough scope for the expression of existing disputes and allows more occasions for differences to develop. Higher interaction acts to strengthen disagreements more than facilitate coordination and cooperation.

**(d) Low formalisation:** Where formalisation is low, the potential for jurisdictional dispute increase. Conflicts between departments are likely to flourish in situations where they are not subjected to rules and regulations.

## Consequences of Intergroup Conflict

Groups experiencing conflict react in fairly predictable ways. The following table summarizes the changes which occur within the groups and changes which take place between the groups:

**Table 12.2. Reactions to Conflict**

| *Parties* | *Within the group* | *Between groups* |
|---|---|---|
| Winners | Members show 'We' feelings. | Negative sentiments against the rival group (enemy). |
| | Superiority complex develops. | We are good they are bad feelings. |
| | High morale. | More aggressive, overestimates its strengths and achievements. |
| | | More concerned for member needs and generally satisfied with itself. |
| Losers | Members indulge in mutual recrimination and shifting of blame. | Becomes a well-knit group. Enemy's win increase tension and conflict. |
| | Inferiority complex. | Initially resists admitting defeat. |
| | Low morale. | Search for a convenient scapegoat. |
| | Members lose cohesion. | Communication with winners breaks down. |
| | | Disintegrate. |

*Source:* Adapted from E.H. Schein's discussion in, Organisational Psychology (ed.), Englewood Cliffs, N.J. Prentice-Hall, 1970, pp. 96-99.

## INTRAORGANISATIONAL CONFLICT

The wellsprings of conflict in an organisation are many. But mainly three kinds of internal strains can be identified, (1) the horizontal strain, the competition between different functional subsystems, (2) vertical strain, the competition between various levels in the hierarchy for power, privilege or reward, and (3) line and staff conflict.

### Horizontal Conflict

Horizontal conflict refers to conflict between employees or departments at the same hierarchical level in an organisation. The source of conflict between departments consists of pressures toward suboptimisation. Each department may suboptimize by independently trying to achieve its own departmental goals. For example, production departments may prefer long economical runs whereas sales departments may insist on quick delivery. Again, when two departments are functionally interdependent, breakdowns in the performance of one department can lead to serious conflicts. Other reasons for intergroup departmental conflict have been discussed at length earlier.

### Vertical Hierarchical Conflict

Vertical conflict separates people in various levels of the occupational ladders in organisations. It refers to any conflict between levels in an organisation. It occurs usually in superior-subordinate relations. C.G. Smith identified three reasons for vertical conflicts, (1) inadequate communication between levels, (2) conflict arises essentially from differences of interests between position holders occupying different status in the organisational hierarchy, and (3) a distinct lack of shared perceptions and attitudes among members in various levels. Vertical conflicts arise because superiors attempt to control subordinates and subordinates tend to resist, forcing the superior to increase the dosage of impersonal rules to exact obedience and gain control. Impersonal rules rob the subordinate of the freedom of action enjoyed hitherto and as a result, "he perceives himself to be threatened by, and in conflict with his superiors, who are attempting to decrease his autonomy".

### Line and Staff Conflict

Controversy and conflict are inherent in the concept of line and staff. It is not an easy task to divide and distribute expertise, authority and roles in equitable quantities between the line generalists and staff specialists. The concept authorizes the splitting of various functions into two categories: hierarchical and non-hierarchical, that is, creation of low status and high status persons. The splitting of functions into hierarchical and non-hierarchical levels and the creation of low status and high status positions creates a discrepancy between expected and actual authority leading to resentment and frustration to all the parties involved. Line managers look upon staff specialists as 'unnecessary impediments in the otherwise simple and efficient administration of production operations.' Moreover, the staff specialist is cast in the role of a gatekeeper relative to the line manager and can often monitor information, resources and rewards flowing to him. To make confusion worse confounded, line and staff members have different time horizons, objectives and interpersonal orientations and approaches to organisational problems. For example, Dalton found that staff employees were usually younger, had a upper level of education and came from different social backgrounds than line employees. These different personal characteristics which are frequently associated with different values and beliefs, often exuberate conflicts between line and staff. The causes of conflict between line and staff are captured in the following table:

**Table 12.3. Distinction Between Line and Staff**

| *The line viewpoint* | *The staff viewpoint* |
|---|---|
| 1. **Unauthorised encroachment:** Staff oversteps its authority. Because line managers are ultimately responsible for results and profits, they tend to resent staff encroachment upon their duties and prerogatives. | Line does not use staff properly: The line manager prefers to run his own show. Staff's help is sought as a last resort. |
| 2. **Academic advice:** Staff does not give sound advice. The advice that staff offers, is not fully considered, well balanced, and soundly tested, Staff specialists are, in many cases cut off from the day to day operational relatives. | Line resists new ideas: Line management is often overly cautious and painfully slow in accepting useful ideas. |
| 3. Staff steals credit: But when things go wrong, staff people turn the tables on line officers. | Line does not provide staff enough authority: Even the best solutions offered by staff members, quite often are not supported and implemented by line managers. |
| 4. Staff fails to see the whole picture: Specialists have a limited perspective and fail to relate their ideas to the organisation's overall objectives. Staff is loyal to a narrow speciality, line is loyal to the organisation. | |
| 5. Empire building tendencies: Since specialists have fewer organisational levels to advance, each frequently tries to expand his own 'empire'. | |

## INTERORGANISATIONAL CONFLICT

The phenomena in interorganisational conflict is much the same as those arising within an organisation. The basis of interorganisational conflicts is essentially the same as the basis of intergroup conflict. Most commonly cited reasons for interorganisational conflicts like incompatible objectives, conflicts over status; prestige and money are present in interorganisational conflict also. As pointed out by March and Simon, "many of the phenomena of the intergroup conflict within the organisation are almost indistinguishable from the phenomena that we might consider under interorganisational conflict. The distinction between internal and external relations for an organisation is a cloudy one". In other words, interorganisational conflict is more extensive, more diffused than the conflict among persons of groups.

## Purposes

Conflict with outside organisations serves four purposes by:

1. Promoting closer bonds of unity among individuals within the organisation. "Organisations frequently organize themselves against something, and in the absence of a perception of conflict, their reason for existence is weakened or disappears, and they suffer from internal disorganisation or even dissolution".
2. Inducts new life into organisational objectives and values. A conflict usually simplifies the purpose of an organisation simply because the objective of winning or surviving the conflict comes to dominate over all others. A situation of conflict heightens the larger purpose of the organisation and so augments the internal rewards that come from a feeling of participation in these larger purposes.
3. Making organisational members aware of the strategy and tactics of the antagonist.
4. Acts are an agency of social control.

## Conditions

For conflict to exist between two organisations, the following conditions must be satisfied:

1. Two organisations that are ignorant of each other cannot be in conflict though they might be in competition. So each of the organisation must be present in the image of the responsible decision-makers of the other.
2. A decision on the part of either executive must affect the state of both organisations in value-significant direction. Two organisations that do not affect each other cannot be in competition and, therefore, cannot be in conflict.
3. A decision on the part of either executive must affect the image or the state or the other in a direction that he considers as unfavourable. Wherever two organisations are expanding into a common field, so that possession of part of the field by one excludes the other, conflict is possible.

## Types of Interorganisational Conflicts

Stagner and Rosen have identified five types of interorganisational conflict:

**1. Management-government:** Conflicts over political contributions, bribery, anti-trust actions, fair trade, consumer protection etc. (The government will generally monitor organisational activities and management performance in areas where government regulation of business is thought necessary.)

**2. Intermanagement:** Managements may compete against each other in ways that they believe will enhance their position in the industry. Disputes over patents and fulfilment of contracts, price wars may be included here.

**3. Interunion:** Unions may compete for members or jobs, as in jurisdictional disputes.

**4. Union-government:** The unions will be scrutinized by government agents for illegal activities like criminal activities discrimination, illegal strikes etc.

5. **Union-management:** If management and labour are to retain their institutional ideal ties, they must disagree and must adopt appropriate roles. Conflict is essential to survival for the union; lack of conflict would weaken it. Conflict between labour and management is expressed in many forms like strikes, peaceful bargains, grievances, debates, loyalties, sabotage and absenteeism.

## Conflict Management

Conflict may be harmful to an organisation, but there are times when it is useful. It is for this reason that managers must learn to recognize the differences between constructive and destructive conflict situations. The way conflict is managed rather than suppressed, ignored or avoided, contributes significantly to an organisation's effectiveness.

**Table 12.4. Distinction between Constructive and Destructive Conflict**

| *Constructive conflict exists when* | *Destructive conflict exists when* |
|---|---|
| 1. Problems are brought out, identified and clarified. | Too much stress is created for individuals. |
| 2. Group think is avoided. | Group decision-making is reduced to a 'feeble walk'. |
| 3. Organisational lethargy is dissolved; creativity is promoted. | Cooperation is replaced by in-fighting. |
| 4. More though goes into ideas; individual effort is stimulated. | Focus on short range goals at the cost of long range goals. |
| 5. Encourages group cohesiveness, and provides for a system of checks and balances within an organisation. | Goals are distorted and resolution of conflict is viewed as win-lose rather than win-win. |

***Source:*** Adapted from Samuel Deep, Human Relations in Management, California, Glencoe Publishing Co., 1978, p. 212.

Since conflict has constructive and destructive consequences, it must be analyzed and managed carefully. The manager should seek a level of conflict appropriate to the existing conditions. There are basically two approaches to deal with conflict in an effective way: to create and stimulate constructive conflict and to resolve destructive conflict.

## Conflict Stimulation Techniques

Conflict is not always negative. Conflict, like fire, can be a useful force when properly handled. Stimulating competition and conflict, sometimes, can have a galvanizing effect on the progress of organisations. An environment devoid of novelty, challenge can be unbearable to human beings.

As such there seems to be an optimal level of uncertainty, an optimum level of disruption, intellectual conflict or challenge for effective functioning of an organisation. Rather than always trying to minimize conflict, the effective manager must determine the most effective level of conflict stimulation for the organisation.

**When to stimulate?** Situations in which conflict is too low, generally involve, people who are afraid to 'rock the boat'. They passively accept things the way they are. There is too much lethargy, lack of disagreement as group members tolerate each other's weaknesses. What are those situations that require managers to stimulate conflict? Affirmative answers to one or all the following questions may suggest the need for conflict stimulation.

Is conflict stimulation needed?

(i) Are you surrounded by 'Yes' people?

(ii) Are subordinates afraid to admit ignorance and uncertainties to you?

(iii) Is there so much concentration by decision-makers on reaching a compromise that they may lose sight of values, long term objectives, or the organisation's welfare?

(iv) Do managers believe that it is in their best interest to maintain the impression of peace and cooperation in their unit, regardless of the price?

(v) Is there an excessive concern by decision-makers for not hurting the feelings of others?

(vi) Do managers believe that popularity is more important for obtaining organisational rewards than competence and high performance?

(vii) Are managers unduly enamored of obtaining consensus for their decisions?

(viii) Is there a lack of new ideas?

(ix) Do employees show unusually high resistance to change?

(x) Is there an unusually low level of employee turnover?

***Source:***

## Stimulation strategies

Considering the amount of controversy surrounding the term 'Conflict', the whole notion of 'Conflict stimulation' of often difficult to accept without reservation. The language of conflict stimulation is hard to digest and this partly explains the dearth of ideas on conflict stimulation techniques. Although writers often discuss ways of reducing conflict, relatively few write about the stimulation strategies. S. P. Robbins had offered certain guidelines in this direction, namely:

**(a) Communication:** Managers can manipulate messages in such a way as to stimulate conflict. Ambiguous or threatening messages encourage conflict. Information that a plant will close, that a department is to be wiped out or that a lay-off is certain can reduce apathy and force members to confront their differences to stimulate new ideas and force re-evaluation of current practices etc. Sometimes, a manager can also redirect messages and alter channels to encourage conflict. Intelligently planted rumours in the informal channels can also serve a useful purpose.

**(b) Bringing in outsiders:** A commonly used method of 'shaking up' a stagnant unit or organisation is to bring in people whose back-grounds, attitudes, values and managerial styles vary significantly from the prevalent norms. Introduction of heterogenous people into the organisation helps in disturbing the status quo (for example, suggesting innovative ideas, offering divergent options, demonstrating originality etc.,) bringing back life a stagnant organisation.

**(c) Restructure the organisation:** Changing the structure of an organisation is an excellent way of creating conflict. Breaking up old work groups and departments to reorganise them so that they have new entrants or responsibilities will create uncertainties that call for readjustments immediately. Conflict that develops during this period may ultimately lead to improved methods of operation as members try to adjust to new circumstances.

**(d) Encouraging competition:** The use of bonuses, incentive pay and awards for excellent performance will stimulate competition. Such incentives, when administered properly, foster a competitive spirit among individuals and groups. Conflict will be productive as one group struggles hard to out do the other.

## CONFLICT RESOLUTION STYLES

Conflict management style is often viewed in terms of a two dimensional model. Thompson suggested five styles: competitive, sharing, avoidant, collaborative and accommodating. The choice and use of the five conflict handling styles is likely to depend upon both, the nature of the individual and the situational factors.

The following figure is reflective of a useful two dimensional model for understanding and comparing the conflict resolution behaviours. These represent different combinations of assertiveness and cooperativeness. The two dimensions produce five types of conflict strategies:

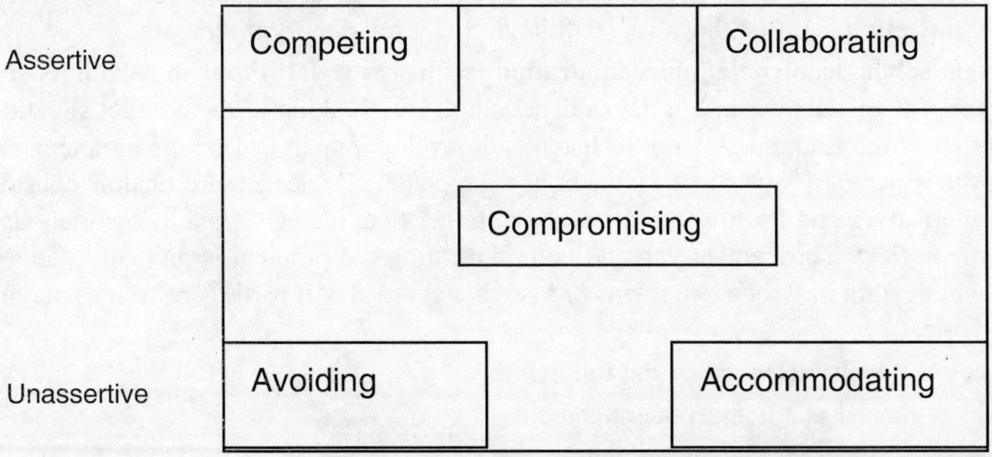


***Figure 12.7 Conflict Resolution Style***

***Source:***

1. **Competition (dominance):** The competitive style is high on assertiveness, and low on cooperativeness. This style is power oriented and is associated with direct physical aggression and heavy reliance on punishment to gain control over others. One party's gain in another party's loss. Parties use weapons like fights, arguments, intimidation to achieve their goals. Such a style generally creates forces which aggravate the struggle and does little to discover innovative, constructive solutions acceptable to all.

2. **Avoiding (withdrawal):** This strategy is associated with behaviours such as withdrawal, indifference, evasion, apathy, flight reliance upon fate and isolation. Parties to conflict fail to address important problems. They may detach themselves from the conflict believing that conflict avoidance is more mature and reasonable than childish arguments. It is only a method of avoiding

conflict. The person stays out of conflicts, ignores disagreements takes no position on the issues involved, and may even be hesitant to talk about the situation. As a result, the conflict is not effectively resolved, nor is it eliminated.

**3. Accommodating (smoothing):** The accommodative style is low in assertiveness and high on cooperativeness. Parties will be generous and self-sacrificing. The emphasis is on the common interests of the conflicting group and a de-emphasis on their differences. Implicit in this style is the belief by the individual or group that others will cut off their relationship if he or she expresses self-oriented concerns. So, better go along with whatever the other person requests, rather than get into difficulties of direct confrontation. "In a conflict issue that is associated with expressions of intense and aggressive feelings, the accommodative style may be very beneficial as a starting point." Smoothing is a more sensitive approach than the withdrawal approach. Smoothing can be used when a temporary solution is needed in the short run.

**4. Compromising Style (lose-lose):** This is a traditional method of resolving conflicts. There is no distinct winner or loser because each party is expected to give up something of value for a concession. It is commonly used where the conflict involves differences in goals, attitudes or values. It is effective when the sought after goal (for example, resource sharing) can be divided. In this style, the emphasis is on the process of compromise and bargaining. It is based on a simple give-and-take process and typically involves negotiation and a series of sacrifices. The amount given up by each party in conflict, however, will be in direct relation to its strength.

**5. Problem solving/confrontation/collaboration (with-win style):** Problem solving is said to be the opposite of conflict because it demands a complete rethinking of the conflict situation. Parties openly share information, attempt to listen and develop empathy. There is an attempt to depersonalise the issue. Parties debate the issue bringing together all relevant information, consider full range of alternatives and try to solve the problem rather than merely trying to accommodate different points of view. Through sharing and communicating the problem is mutually defined. Questions of who is right or wrong; who wins or loses are avoided. All parties are seen as playing a constructive role.

Problem solving is characterised by the following:

(i) Conflict is viewed as a non-zero sum game.
(ii) Other party is seen as a mutual problem solver.
(iii) Parties purpose joint outcomes.
(iv) Issues are looked at objectively.
(v) Open, honest sharing of information.
(vi) Flexibility.
(vii) Tries to solve the conflict in a way that will benefit both the parties.

## Choosing Conflict Modes

A survey of Chief Executives produced guidelines for using the five conflict handling modes. Careful review of Table 13.4 shows that the executives had given substantial thought to the question of conflict resolution. We advise the aspiring young manager to benefit from the obvious experience and wisdom summarised in the table:

**Table 12.5. Uses of the Five Conflict Modes, as Reported by a Group of Chief Executives**

| *Conflict-handing Modes* 1 | *Appropriate Situations* 2 |
|---|---|
| Competing | 1. When quick, decision action is vital-e.g., emergencies.<br>2. On important issues where unpopular actions need implementation–e.g., cost cutting, enforcing unpopular rules, discipline.<br>3. On issues vital to company welfare when you know you're right.<br>4. Against people who take advantage of noncompetitive behaviour. |
| Collaborating | 1. To find an integrative solution when both sets of concerns are too important to be compromised.<br>2. When your objective is to learn.<br>3. To manage insights from people with different perspectives.<br>4. To gain commitment by incorporating concerns into a consensus.<br>5. To work through feelings that have interfered with a relationship. |
| Compromising | 1. When goals are important, but not worth the effort or potential disruption of more assertive modes.<br>2. When opponents with equal power are committed to mutually exclusive goals.<br>3. To achieve temporary settlements to complex issues.<br>4. To arrive at expedient solutions under time pressure.<br>5. As a backup when collaboration or competition is unsuccessful. |
| Avoiding | 1. When an issue is trivial, or more important issues are pressing.<br>2. When you perceive no chance of satisfying your concerns.<br>3. When potential disruption outweighs the benefits of resolution.<br>4. To let people cool down and regain perspective.<br>5. When gathering information supersedes immediate decision.<br>6. When others can resolve the conflict more effectively.<br>7. When issues seem tangential or symptomatic of other issues. |
| Accommodating | 1. When you find you are wrong–to allow a better position to be heard, to learn and to show your reasonableness.<br>2. When issues are more important to others than yourself–to satisfy others and maintain cooperation.<br>3. To build social credits for later issues.<br>4. To minimise loss when you're outmatched and losing.<br>5. When harmony and stability are especially important.<br>6. To allow subordinates to develop by learning from. |

***Source:*** Kenneth W. Thomas, "Toward Multi-Dimensional Values in Teaching: The Example of Conflict Behaviours", Academy of Management Review, 2 (1977), 487.

## Conflict Management Strategies

As pointed out previously, conflict can produce functional as well as dysfunctional effects. If allowed to continue it will have a disruptive influence over the entire organisation, resources will be wasted, people go off the track, targets may be missed and the entire organisation may have to pay for such costly lapses in the long run. There are, therefore, very strong reasons for attempting to resolve conflicts in a rapid and effective manager. Fortunately, a number of tactics for achieving this goal seem to exist. These approaches to conflict management include the following:

**Ignoring the Conflict:** If the conflict is not too severe and the consequences are not very serious, managers tend to ignore it and pretend that it does no exist. Some managers think conflicts speak badly about an organisation, so they ignore the conflict and hope it will eventually resolve itself. Because the sources of conflict are neither identified nor resolved, this strategy fails to put out the fires in time. Eventually, the situation may go from bad to worse.

**Physical separation:** If the warring fractions or parties are physically separated, the likelihood of open hostility and aggression is reduced. Parties, however, may continue to indulge in sabotage and occasional acts of aggression unless the source of conflict is eliminated. Physical separation may work when the two groups are not required to interact while achieving targets. If they need to interact, however, separation may not sole the issue.

**Withdrawal:** Another way may be to withdraw from a conflict it when it takes place. The withdrawal may be from the situation (fighting for resources, for promotion etc.) or from the relationship with the other group (one party may severe connection with the other as in the case of Proctor and Gamble and Godrej Soaps Ltd).

**Dominance:** The simplest conceivable conflict solution is elimination of the other party — to force opponents to flee and give up the fight, or slay them. Quite often, managers use positional authority to fire a lower ranking subordinate they consider to be a trouble-maker. Conflicting parties are told to maintain a calm composure, an appearance of grace and drop their fight and get on with the job. Positional authority enables a manger to serve as situational authority which enables a manager to serve as a 'conflict sponge' to absorb the antagonistic feelings of the disputants. Sometimes, managers try to alleviate conflict through "physical separation". Groups are not allowed to interact with each other. Separation helps in attaining a temporary solution and provides enough time for more fundamental conflict resolution afterwards. It has the distinct advantage of preventing more damage being done and of preventing the creation of further rationale for fighting. Individuals in organisation, with rare exception, recognise and accept the authority of their superiors as an acceptable way of resolving conflicts. Although, they may not be in agreement with these decisions, they abide by them. Stagner, after conducting research on executive decision-making in major corporations in America, found the (power of) Chief Executive to be the most widely employed arbiter of disagreements. However, it is always not possible to effectively resolve interdepartmental conflicts through the use of positional authority. The 'dominance approach' does little to prevent recurrence of conflict in a more violent form in later stages.

**Appeal procedures:** A conventional method of resolving disputes in an organisation is that the people in disagreement ask for a higher authority to help them arrive at a solution by resolving the problem satisfactorily. A formal procedure for redressing grievances is demanded through an appeal made to "one's boss's boss". For if, the faculty members could not decide on the allocation of work load, they may refer their disagreement to the principal of the college for a final, binding decision.

**Compromise:** This is a traditional way to putting out fires. Here, there is no clear winner or loser and the decision arrived at is probably not ideal for either group. For example, management may offer to increase wages by 4 percent, while the union may be seeking 8 per cent. A compromise figure of 6 percent may result in a reasonable settlement of the conflict. Compromise can be used very effectively when the goal sought (e.g. money) can be divided equitably. If this is not possible, one group should be prepared to give up something of value as concession. Compromise may also involve third-party interventions as well as total group or representative negotiating and voting.

**Liaison group/intermediaries/integrators:** To arbitrate differences between two warring fractions, a full-time integrator can be appointed who can speak the language of both the parties. The integrator has to use expertise and persuasion to achieve coordination and get people together. He must understand each group's problems and able to rally both groups toward a mutually agreeable solution. Lawrence and Lorsch found that many organisations have reduced interdepartmental conflicts by setting up special liaisons between the conflicting departments. One advantage of the liaison person is that he is perceived as not having a vested interest in either group or department. Sometimes, third party consultant mostly human relations experts, can also be appointed to change attitudes and reduce conflicts.

**Member relation:** Inter organisational activities, sometimes, help in reducing conflict. Exchange of people between interdependent departments creates an atmosphere where the new comer can exchange his views with others. It helps him see the big picture and his role in it. As group members understand each other better they tend to lessen some of their perceptual distortions. Role reversal or empathy helps them in "shaking up" their narrow perspectives, departmental loyalties and misunderstandings created by the organisational boundaries.

**Reduce interdependence:** The potential for conflict is very great in situations where two departments have to work in an interdependent fashion and share scarce resources. As a result of this mutual dependency there are more occasions for disagreement and conflict. One way to resolve conflict is to reduce interdependencies by moving from reciprocal to sequential or from sequential to pooled interdependence. Departments maybe provided with resources and inventories that are independent of those provided for other departments (known as "decoupling") However, decoupling is an expensive proposition; it increases costs because of duplication of effort and equipment. To avoid this, large 'buffers' (inventories) are created. For example, department A might send its output into the buffer inventory and department B might be allowed to process goods from this inventory independently. Sometimes, formal integration departments may also be created to facilitate coordination and smoothen work flow.

**Procedural and Structural Changes:** Conflict can occur because a procedure is illogically structured. When a credit manager and a sales officer were both about to be tired because of an irreconcilable personality conflict, it was found that the processing of credit applications too late in the credit procedure was the cause of their difficulty. The credit manager was forced to cancel too many deals already made. When the credit check was placed earlier in the procedure, most of the conflict disappeared. In another case, the HR manager and the Production manager were found to be hostile to each other over a recruiting procedure which did not allow the production manager to review applications at early stage of the hiring sequence and to offer comments. When the procedure was changed, many of the difficulties were resolved.

In some firms, one may find sales and distribution being handled by separate departments, each reporting to a senior manager. The division often creates conflict. Individuals in sales expect quick delivery in response to customer requests. But the distribution department, to keep costs down, wants to make deliveries in full trucks and at fixed intervals. To resolve such situations, it may be useful to combine both departments under a Marketing Head who has experience in both sales and distribution.

Changes in physical layout also could be used effectively to reduce or eliminate conflict. People can use desks as barriers and buffers. Some offices have dividers to separate employees. However, if a manager wants to encourage a problem–solving atmosphere, a more open office arrangement may be used. When known antagonists are seated in conference directly across from each other, the amount of conflict increases. When they are seated side by side, the conflict tends to decrease.

**Superordinate goals:** A superordinate goal is a common goal that appeals to all the parties involved and cannot be accomplished by the resources of any single party separately. Superordinate goals demand interdependence and cooperation between departments. It is believed that the possibilities for achieving harmony are greatly enhanced when disagreeing parties are brought together to work towards overriding goals which are real and compelling to all concerned. For example, national leaders use the ploy of claiming that their countries are about to be attacked in order to bring about (at least) a temporary unification on the opposing factions in their own countries.

**Identifying a common enemy:** The classical study by Sherif and Sherif illustrates how groups in conflict temporarily resolve their differences to combat a common enemy. The Sherifs and their colleagues stimulated conflict by encouraging rivalry between groups at a boys' camp. When the conflict had become very intense, they experimented with two effective methods: One was creation of superordinate goals and the other was to present a common 'threat' or 'enemy'. In the latter case, a camp truck was rigged to breakdown on the way to a camp out. Neither group could know how the truck was to be repaired independently. The boys got a rope, and both groups pulled together to start the truck. In the words of Boulding, "A strong enemy is a great unifying force; in the face of a common threat and overriding common purpose of victory or survival, the conflicting claims of the group fall into the background and are swallowed up into the single, measurable, overriding end of winning conflicts." The threat of Hitler, for example, produced an alliance between the Western powers and Russia that fell apart as soon as the common threat disappeared.

**Integrated problem solving:** Another conflict management strategy tries to find a solution that incorporates the requirements of both parties. Both parties work together to define the problem and identify mutually satisfactory solutions. They freely exchange task-related information. A minimum level of trust between parties is essential for this strategy to produce results. Since it takes time for parties to resolve issues through healthy interaction, there should be no pressure for a quick settlement of contentious issues. Problem solving in a healthy approach for it recognizes that usually neither party is completely right or wrong. Creating a concession is not interpreted as a sign of weakness. Neither party feels that it has to win every battle to maintain self-respect. For conflicts resulting from misunderstanding or language problems, the problem solving or confrontation method has yielded good results. For solving more complex problems (e.g. conflicts where parties have different value systems), the method has not been very successful.

The important conflict management strategies followed in organisations may be summarized thus (Table)

**Table 12.6. Conflict Management Strategies**

| *Conflict management strategy* | *Type of strategy* | *Appropriate situations* |
|---|---|---|
| Ignoring the conflict | Avoidance | When the issue is trivial. When the issue is symptomatic of more basic, pressing problems. |
| Imposing a solution | Avoidance | When quick, decisive action is needed. When unpopular decisions need to be made and consensus to be appears very unlikely. |
| Smoothing | Defusion | As a stop-gap measure to cool down temperaments and regain perspective.When the conflict is over nonwork issues. |
| Appealing to superordinate goals | Defusion | When there is a mutually important goal that neither group can achieve without the cooperation of the other.When the survival or success of the overall organisation is in jeopardy. |
| Bargaining | Containment | When the two parties are of relatively equal power.When there are several acceptable, alternative solutions that both parties would be willing to consider. |
| Structuring the interaction | Containment | When previous attempts to openly discuss conflict issues led to conflict escalation rather than to problem solution.When a respected third party is available to provide some structure and could serve as a mediator. |
| Integrative problem solving | Confrontation | When there is a minimum level of trust between groups and there is no time pressure for a quick solution.When the organisation can benefit from merging the |

| | | |
|---|---|---|
| | | differing perspectives and insights of the groups in making key decisions |
| Redesigning the organisation | Confrontation | When the sources of conflict come from coordination of work.When the work can be easily divided into clear project responsibilities (self-contained work groups), or when activities require a lot of interdepartmental coordination over time (lateral relations). |

## CONTINGENCY APPROACH TO CONFLICT MANAGEMENT

Derr has argued in favour of a contingency approach to conflict management consisting of three strategies: collaboration, power play and bargaining

**Collaboration** is the result of a constructive rethinking on the part of people involved in a conflict. They begin to share information openly, attempt to listen, develop empathy, depersonalise the issue, gather relevant information, consider available alternatives and try to put an end to the problem—through a win-win approach. .

**Power play**: When the parties to a conflict are not able to resolve differences on their own, some form of power intervention or dominance comes in. Higher level managers may step in and say "All right, you guys, that's the end of it, no more." In addition to the universal decree that conflict will go no further, the command may be accompanied by threats such as termination or transfer to a different group. Higher-level managers may also establish rules and procedures to contain the conflict to an acceptable level.

**Bargaining**: {In some cases, people use the word bargaining taking a short term view like you bargain for a carpet in a shopping mall and negotiate a long term housing loan from a housing finance company) The terms bargaining and negotiation are used interchangeably in this text) In the third strategy – bargaining – the opposing parties exchange offers and concessions directly or through representatives. The principal difference between dominance and bargaining lies in interdependence. In dominance, the dominator does not need the loser any longer, in bargaining, both sides recognize that they are mutually dependent and they must work together after the conflict. The two parties are aware that each is trying to influence the other, and that agreement is a function of the power they bring to the situation and their bargaining skill.

## NEGOTIATION

### Basic Assumptions

Negotiation is the process of bargaining between two or more interdependent parties to reach a solution that is mutually acceptable. It is usually a give and take process. There is no room for threat or coercion. Both parties have come to the table not to shake hands but to arrive at a solution that is mutually beneficial. Both expect the outcome to be a win-win solution. There is also an implicit belief that each party is willing to listen, to make sacrifices in order to get meaningful outcomes that are fair and equitable. Parties are willing to shift their focus and attention on protecting self interests in the interest of a joint, mutually agreeable solution. Another important assumption surrounding the negotiation process is that both parties have equal strength. If one party tries to dominate the other by showing brutal force, negotiations fail inevitably. The possibility of one party throwing its weight on the other is ruled out, at least on theoretical grounds at the beginning of a negotiation process. Parties are also aware of the fact that other options to come to an agreement exist but they have come to the table believing in the process of give and take to be a superior alternative. (Saiyadain2007)

## Essential Features

Negotiation is the process that takes place when two or more parties, each of whom is seen as controlling some resource which the other desires, confer to reach an agreement on mutual exchange of the resources. For negotiation to happen, transactions between a minimum of two individuals or groups must take place. Parties, having a conflict of interest, present their proposals and counter proposals for division and/or exchange of resources in a mutually helpful manner. A fair share of the pie is all that the parties want. The focus on narrow self interests and individual issues gets diluted as parties begin to focus on finding a solution through joint effort. Negotiation, thus, is a process of building on common interests and reducing differences in order to arrive at an agreement, which is at least minimally acceptable to all parties concerned. Parties get together with a view to resolve differences and find solutions. People conduct negotiations to get workable agreements. To this end, parties put forward their proposals and counter proposals. Feelings, attitudes, beliefs and values gain the upper hand while proposals find their way into negotiation chambers. People do not always act in perfectly rational and expected ways. People with superior power may try to bulldoze others into submission. Weak hands may get united and come out with outrageous demands—as in the case of labour-management negotiations. It all depends on the bargaining strategies that are pressed into service to meet the specific goals of negotiating individuals/groups.(Lewicki; Raiffa; Rubin)

## Distributive Bargaining

*Distributive bargaining* is all about the pieces to be cut from the pie (a zero sum game where either side gains at the expense of the other). The method seeks to find the size of the slice for each party that reflects each side's power and ability to harm the other, without totally disrupting the relationship. Each side tries to inflate its projected power and readiness to absorb injury while attempting to find the other's true minimum position.

In a soft approach, one of the parties may give in to the other or compromise in which case both give up something of value in order to reach an agreement. Each party may decide to split the difference between the original positions equally. Still, parties may not be happy because they are still deprived of what was originally demanded. Most labour management bargaining falls in this category In a typical labour management dispute regarding wage hikes, workers may demand minimum wage of say 8000 for unskilled labour and 12000 for skilled. Management may start with 5000 for unskilled and 8000 for skilled. When we split the difference between the two equally unskilled may get 6500 and skilled 10000, still away from the original demand.

Confusion, obfuscation and deception are inherent and necessary in this process. Closely associated with distributive bargaining is the commonly used *positional bargaining* approach. This strategy typically involves successfully taking, and then giving up a sequence of positions (e.g. what happens when one haggles in an open market).

## Bargaining Zone model for Negotiations

Bargaining zone is the range between one party's minimum reservation point and other party's maximum reservation point. X, an MBA from a premier management institute may be willing to work for a minimum monthly salary –minimum reservation point, or the lowest outcome of negotiations that is acceptable (also called resistance point)—of Rs. 35,000 but may quote Rs. 45,000 as her preferred salary(called as the initial offer point) The recruiting firm might actually offer initially Rs.30000 but has a maximum reservation point of Rs. 40000 per month in mind. The bargaining zone, accordingly, is Rs. 40,000-45000. 40,000 is the resistance point beyond which recruiting firm will call of negotiations, likewise a monthly salary of Rs. 30000 is the resistance point for X below which he will not take up the offer. At this point, parties are not willing to make further concessions. Both parties start off with an initial offer, knowing fully well that the scene will change quickly. As negotiations proceed further each will come to know the resistance point of the other. To what extent they can push forward without breaking off negotiations—each party will come to know during negotiations and this knowledge helps them settle down to work out a solution accordingly.

## Integrative Bargaining

In contrast to the distributive bargaining approach, there is the *integrative bargaining* approach that uses problem solving techniques to find win-win outcomes. This process does not reject conflict because the parties still must look out for their own interests. Rather, it transcends conflict by shifting from bargaining to problem solving. The focus shifts from reducing demands to "expanding the pie" (resources); from how the small pie is to be sliced toward how to bake a larger pie, so that both sides can increase their welfare. Ideally, the new satisfactions are bigger than the original demands so that whatever concessions the parties must make are perceived not as defeats but as "sacrifices to the common cause".

In a conflict bargaining situation, such mutually satisfying agreements do not come by easily. Usually the person who does not demand is taken for a ride. People tend to 'walk over the fool' who leaves himself vulnerable. Bargaining often tends to concede small initial concessions and keeping this in mind, parties in a conflictful situation should proceed cautiously. In general, a combination of a 'cautious trust' showing readiness to extend cooperation and a firmness preventing partners from exploiting the cooperativeness seems to characterize persons who hammer out joint agreements in competitive situations. For integrative bargaining to flourish, certain conditions, however, should be present. These include parties, who are open with information, and candid about their concerns, a sensitivity by both parties each the other's needs the ability to trust one another and willingness by both parties to maintain flexibility. Effective bargaining, above all requires cool rationality rather than emotional game-playing.

## EFFECTIVE NEGOTIATION SKILLS

Negotiation requires demands preparation, hard work and the ability to foresee the moves of the adversary and respond appropriately. One needs to have a game plan before one undertakes the journey. Such a game plan, inevitably, would involve the following steps:

### Preparation

**Set realistic goals and the bargaining zone**: At the outset you should be clear about what you want to achieve. This may mean three things: the best achievable outcome, the lowest—still acceptable—outcome and a realistic outcome which would compel you to settle for—as indicated in the bargaining zone model. When you are not losing much, you can be generous. You may infact try to help the other party feel satisfied with the outcome. When you happen to lose lot of ground, you need to be firm and willing to say 'quits'. In negotiations, firmness and clarity of thought are the essential prerequisites. If you get confused or get angry too early, you may end up losing the grip over the issue completely. those who have very little tolerance for ambiguity end up losing in a big way.

**Assess the adversary**: Research evidence suggests that people having a similar background in terms religion, caste etc or subscribing to the same ideology tend to cooperate with each other. Cultural differences may come in the way of understanding each other's moves. . If you are able get sufficient information about the other party's objectives, needs and interest in advance, you will be able to respond better..

**Tactics**: Where to negotiate may be the first question to be answered. A neutral local location is preferable, because most negotiators prefer to conduct the show in places where they have a grip or feel comfortable. You need to pay attention to secretarial help and also seating arrangements, too, at this stage. Next issue is about the timing. Provide a time frame for everything. There must be sufficient time for critical analysis, discussion, and agreement. Always avoid starting negotiations on the spur of the moment. To be effective, the negotiators need a common understanding of what is to be discussed and why. The subject, scope and purpose, therefore, need to be agreed upon before negotiations kick off.

### Discussion

**Give the mike to the other party**: The very beginning is perhaps the most important element of any negotiation because it sets the tone for all that follows. It is a good idea to allow the other party to open the discussion. Before negotiations begin, you can come out with a brief sketch of the issue in question. Based on the opening moves made by the adversary, you can find whether the mood is cooperative or competitive. To this end, pose lot of questions. The more information you can get from the other side the better. Look for factual errors, faulty logic, statistical misrepresentation, hidden agenda etc.

**Your sales pitch**: the convention is that you always demand more than you expect to get and offer less than you expect to give. Your opening position must leave enough time and space for you to manoeuvre subsequent moves to your advantage. As a matter of abundant precaution, you should resist the temptation of accepting the early offers made by the other party—however attractive they might be. At the same time you cannot be too liberal or too conservative in advancing your initial offers. When you turn extremely generous, people try to extract more juice out of you to maximize their own gains. When you hold up everything, it may take painfully long time to reach the comfortable zone where both parties are willing to settle the issue.

**Clarification and justification:** After the initial offers get exchanged and parties begin to look at each other more closely, the period of clarification and justification begins. both must try to explain, amplify, clarify, bolster and justify original demands in an accommodating and nonconfrontational style. Both must try to inform and educate each other with lot of clarity, empathy and understanding.

**Frequency and size of Proposals:** Frequency refers to the number of times proposals are advanced and size refers to the quantity/value of the proposals. You can straightaway make a large initial concession followed by several small concessions. Another way is to come out with several small concession followed by one big concession at the final stage. Alternatively, you can make uniform concessions throughout where size remains the same but the frequency is large. Better to avoid a high frequency of offers and counter offers, because that would confuse the parties and compel them to think about the next offer that's in the queue. When parties exhaust their gun powder after an emotional battle lasting several hours or days, they tend to make a concession, change their stand a bit and impatiently shout at the other:" Take it or leave it.". skilful negotiators drop names of influential people, use their expertise in coming out with novel solutions, and pinpointedly present the benefits of reaching an agreement or the prohibitive costs of not moving towards a solution. If the other party is equally tough and is not afraid to face the music and resists every move with a powerful counter move, then parties end up shaking their head in frustration.

When negotiations breakdown, both parties may quit the field and a deadlock may raise its ugly head. **Deadlock** or stalemate can arise due to a variety of reasons:

## Both parties have widely divergent objectives

One party interprets firmness as rigidity and impatiently declares its unwillingness to make further concessions—even to keep the negotiation 'alive'

As a deliberate tactic during a negotiation to force the other party to reconsider its position and make concessions

You can overcome such painful outcomes by advancing a last minute offer unilaterally aimed at closing the deal, or seek third party intervention as in the case of labour management negotiations. When both parties fail to resolve issues to mutual satisfaction—third party intervention in the form of government officials , judiciary, general public etc step in to close the deal.

When parties realise that the outcomes are really beneficial to both parties, they may try to dissolve their differences and overcome last minute hurdles and move towards reaching an agreement. After all, the basic purpose of negotiation is to reach an agreement, not to score points in arguments. However, quick settlements may not put out fires easily. They may often favour someone who is skilful and experienced and the party that is at the receiving end may start the battle all over again.

### Post-negotiation

Both parties must come out of the negotiation room in a positive frame of mind. The sacrifices made, the concessions extracted and the agreement reached and in fact every outcome that is likely to emerge out of the room should be mutually agreed upon and beneficial to all. It is not a" tough guy" or "nice guy "approach but a kind of **win-win approach** where both parties have worked together to find ways that are mutually rewarding in the long run. Once the agreement comes in black and white, an action plan should take care of every aspect that has been agreed upon in terms of commitment of resources, careful monitoring and evaluation.

## REVIEW QUESTIONS

1. Some people feel that conflict is necessary for organisational activity. Explain why?
2. Bureaucracies are mechanisms that simultaneously resolve and stimulate structural conflicts. Do you agree or disagree? Discuss.
3. Discuss the benefits and wastes of interdepartmental conflicts. At what level of conflict do these benefits and wastes appear?
4. Is conflict at the organisation level inevitable? Why or why not?
5. Identify the various types of conflict.
6. How could a manager stimulate conflict in his department?
7. Under what conditions might conflict be beneficial to a group?
8. What are the components in the conflict process model?
9. While short notes on:

   The process of negotiation

   Conflict resolution styles.

   Line and staff conflicts.

   Inter-Group conflict.
10. Explain what you mean by distributive bargaining and constructive bargaining. Why isn't integrative bargaining more widely practiced in organisations?

## DISCUSSION QUESTIONS

1. Would you consider an argument in which you disagreed with someone on which movie to go to a conflict? Use the conflict model to explain why or why not/
2. How do the traditional assumptions about organisational conflict differ from the modern assumptions? What implications do these new assumptions have for the management of organisational conflict?
3. Identify an organisational conflict situation of which you are aware the trace the causes?

## Case Study: 1. Aditya Financial Services Limited

Aditya Financial Services Limited (AFS) is a medium sized finance company, with headquarters in Bangalore. During the last decade, the company has achieved phenomenal success partly due to the adoption of liberal policies by the Government towards Financing Companies and partly due to favourable customer response. The Chairman of the Company, Bangarappa, having tested success wants to carve out a niche for himself in the market in the near future. Consequently, about 5 years ago, he has established branch offices in all parts of South India and wants to peep into the Northern Region also, in the next five years.

To meet the challenge, AFS decided to revitalize some of its marketing activities through centralized advertising campaigns, offering attractive discounts to promoters of Fixed Deposits etc. Among other things, AFS wanted to enlarge the Marketing department to include contact calls on potential large depositors, small investors and trading communities.

AFS hired its first marketing manager, Raja Ram, an ambitious and hard working young man, from one of the highly successful investment companies in Andhra Pradesh. Raja Ram did an excellent job by setting up a separate Marketing Department and setting it organised. Then, after three and one half years on the job, Raja Ram, obviously attracted by the lucrative terms, left to head the Marketing Division of another investment company.

AFS then hired Shyam Kumar, a thirty year old MBA of IIM, Bangalore. Shyam Kumar had worked in the Marketing Department of another savings and investment company in Madras. He is married, has no children, and wants to build up his career quickly.

Unfortunately, the road to prosperity is not smooth. Time and again, he is confronted with puzzling questions from different quarters. It is true that he has been given the credit for having developed four major investment plans, which, when implemented according to his suggestions, would yield fruitful results. For some inexplicable reason, the branch managers have not shown any enthusiasm to translate his plans into action. Only two branch managers have cooperated. Others did not evince any interest.

The Branch Managers are:

| | |
|---|---|
| Armugum B. | 25 years old, B. Com ; Holds Diploma in Marketing, Madras University; 4 years with AFS. He refused to cooperate. |
| Raja Rao. P | 34 years old, MBA, Andhra University: 6 years with AFS. He cooperated. |
| Nijalingappa. E | 46 years old, M.Sc., Bangalore University; 7 years with AFS, He cooperated. |
| Gopalakrishnan Nair | 55 year old, B.A., Kerala University: 14 years with AFS. He agrees to cooperate and than forgets. |
| Rajasekhar S. | 26 year old, MBA., Madras University; 4 year with AFS. He is reluctant to accept the proposals. |

**Questions**

1. You work for AFS and Shyam Kumar has asked for your advice on how to increase his effectiveness with the branch managers.
2. Please advance your suggestions briefly.

## 2. IT's The Same Story Everywhere

Prakash hails from a hard-working, immigrant family. Right from his childhood he wanted to achieve something and acquire power for himself. Unfortunately, he could secure only a low-paid job in the assembly line in a large manufacturing firm. It is a charmless job having no promotional opportunities. Since he had to support a large family, he needed a well-paid job and all his efforts in this direction had gone waste. To blow on his steam and to relieve himself from wordly woes, he started living in a "fool's paradise" and spent most of his days in day-dreaming. Not surprisingly, he fell a prey to drinking and other vices. After exhausting his meagre financial resources, he would get depressed and start worrying about his family.

It has been a vicious circle and he wants to come out of it. Unable to bear with this miserable situation, one fine morning, he wanted to seek advice and counsel from his supervisor. But since his relationship with his supervisor is not-too intimate, he sought help from his union leader. The union leader has listened to Prakash's woes patiently. He told Prakash in a sympethetic tone: "There is no use working in this company. We have innumerable problems, and not a single problem is solved by management so far. The working conditions are pathetic. Our salary is too low. And let's not talk about our benefit plans. After our contract finishes let's unit together and fight with management for better salary and working conditions".

**Questions**

1. Analyse the nature of role conflict experienced by Prakash in this case.
2. What type of conflict resolution strategy is the union leader suggesting in this case?
3. How do you advice Mr. Prakash?

## 3. Student Novelist

Mr. Ram Sharma was a doctoral student in the Department of Telugu, in one of the reputed Universities in Andhra Pradesh. Unlike other students, he joined the Ph.D. Programme at the age of 36 years. He was nearly 10 years older than most of the other students in the department. He did not receive any fellowship from any financial agency. However, he was rich enough to stand on his legs during the programme.

Sharma's background was quite well known. After obtaining M.A. degree in Telugu, he joined as a lecturer in one of the colleges in Hyderabad. During his leisure time, he used to write short-stories. At the age of 26 year, he could publish his first novel which was highly acclaimed by the public. Thousands of the copies of the book were sold. His second novel was published after two years. With this, he could establish himself in the market firmly. This novel, too, had enjoyed phenomenal popularity. His third novel was the best-seller. The copy rights of the book were sold for a hefty sum.

Mr. Sharma, however, was not happy with his achievements. He had developed an aspiration for academic excellence. He wanted to become a professor in a University and loved constant interaction with young brains so as to share his thoughts and feelings. To this end, he wanted to complete the Ph.D. programme by joining the **University Department** as a full-time research scholar.

Life was not easy in the Department. His professors could not relish neither his ideas nor his popularity. He had to struggle a lot while collecting information for his doctoral programme. He had to cross several hurdles and impediments thrown in his way by faculty members. One professor, after a heated argument with Mr. Sharma burst out" "You don't deserve a place here. You've no talent. You may be popular as a novelist but you don't deserve the doctoral degree, I'll see that you never get it".

Sharma's frustration knew no bounds. He wondered why all faculty members are tossing brickbats against him. It is true that he is a popular novelist. But that has nothing to do with his academic pursuits. Like any other student, he is humble, sincere and hardworking. It is now clear to him that his success in the department is critically dependent on his relationship with professors alone.

## Questions

1. What is the actual conflict that Mr. Sharma was undergoing?
2. Analyse the situation in terms of inter-personal conflict.
3. How can Mr. Sharma overcome the problem to obtain his degree?

13

# MANAGING CHANGE

## INTRODUCTION

Everything in this world is subject to change. Technologies change rapidly. Competition springs up surprises almost every day. New products hit the markets in quick succession turning even successful products into obsolete ones. Economic shocks occur every now and then. Regulatory mechanisms may hit companies from any corner. Workers and unions might come up with a new charter of demands without giving any notice. Too much is changing too fast for an organisation or its managers to be complacent. Today, as never before, organisations are facing an environment that is undergoing rapid changes and the primary job of managers is to help organisations respond and adjust to the changes taking place. To be successful and to play a long innings, organisations have to adapt and change continually in order to stay ahead of others in the competitive race (M.Beer)

- Organisational change may be defined as *'the adoption of a new idea or behaviour by an organisation' (Daft).* It is a way of modifying an existing organisation—any alteration of people, structure or technology.
- The purpose of undertaking such modifications is to increase organisational effectiveness, that is, the extent to which an organisation achieves its objectives.
- Organisational change is largely structural in nature as it brings about modifications in organisational structure, methods and processes.
- Most managers agree that if an organisation has to be successful, it must change **continually** in response to significant developments such as customer needs, technological breakthroughs, economic shocks and government regulations. It is not sufficient today to simply react to change.
- Managers need to anticipate change and ideally be the creator of change. Managers who undertake ***appropriate changes*** at a right time achieve success and put their organisations ahead of others in the race.

- World –class companies, in fact, turn in extraordinary performance by putting things in place in sync with changing conditions. They change continuously, driving for progress via adaptability, experimentation, trial and error, entrepreneurial thinking and fast action. They do not focus on beating the competition, they focus primarily on beating themselves.

**Box 13.1 How Samsung had to destroy its own products to change for better!**

Remember how Samsung changed over the years. It is a pretty interesting story. In early 1970s Samsung began selling black and white televisions in Korea. 20 years later Samsung chairman Kun-Hee-Lee visited Los Angeles to find where the company products stand in comparison to rivals. Sony, Nokia and Motorola products were going off the shelves in a brisk manner and Samsung products were pushed to a corner. Even sales clerks labelled the company products as low quality knockoffs, suitable only for the bargain bin. Back home things were no better. To celebrate the company's survival skills for over two decades, Lee distributed mobile phones to friends and colleagues. Many complained that the phones were defective. Humiliated, Lee ordered that $50million worth of inventory be destroyed in broad day light in front of employees. As workers watched smashing of phones, fax machines and other electronic products, there is a growing realization that the company must innovate and change. It must focus on innovation and not imitation. Over the years it has changed for better and better and is occupying a place of pride in most countries where its products are being sold currently. Bill Breen, "The Seoul of Design" Fast Company, 2005

## THE DILEMMA OF CHANGE

### 1. Stability Verses Change

Organisations desire change in order to remain competitive, in order to remain in harmony with the ever-changing environment. Organisations also want to achieve internal stability because of the predictability and certainty it provides. As such, organisations sit on the horns of a dilemma with reference to change.

Organisations handle the stability-change dilemma depending on the amount and type of innovation required. The organic organisation is, for example suitable when frequent technological changes are required. The organic organisation is always oriented towards change rather than stability. Mechanistic organisations, on the other hand, are oriented towards technological stability. Organisations, thus, resolve the stability-change dilemma by structuring in an organic way when the organisation needs new ideas and frequent changes, and by structuring in a mechanistic way whenever possible, to obtain efficiency. The point is that to resolve the dilemma, organisational change process must be managed. To the extent change is planned, uncertainty and unpredictability is reduced.

### 2. What Type of Change?

Changes can be seen in a variety of ways. This poses another major dilemma.

**Evolutionary Changes:** Some changes are evolutionary in nature and do not greately violate the traditions and status quo expectations. They are usually piecemeal, take place one by one.

Because they are adjustments within the status quo, they seldom promote great enthusiasm, arouse deep resistance, or have dramatic results. Since they do not constitute significant departures from the past practices, they are unlikely to provoke resistance. One limitation of such changes is that they are very slow and organisation may fall behind the requirements.

**Revolutionary Change:** Changes sometimes may be cataclysmic. The revolutionary changes result in over turning the status quo arrangements, cause violations, rejections or suppression of old expectations. The revolutionary churnings generally pose strong resistance and sometimes only an exercise of power can order the implementation of such changes. Revolutionary changes are rarely introduced except where situation becomes highly intolerable having no other acceptable options.

**Box 13.2 Changing everything all at once: The Proctor & Gamble Way**

When Dick Jager assumed office as CEO he was greatly concerned about the sagging performance of the company. In an attempt to shake up the company, Jager changed the company's processes for developing new products, conducting market tests and making decisions about which products to promote. He closed several plants in quick succession and cut thousands of jobs. Managers who survived this kind of onslaught were moved into new jobs. New financial measures were adopted for assessing company's progress. Jager's reactive attempts to bring about radical changes didn't succeed. Meanwhile, the stock fell 50 per cent—a year after he began to make these changes—and Jager had to go. Sad to relate, many felt that Jager tried to change everything all at once—without adequate preparation and careful planning.( New York Times, June 9, 2000)

**Planned changes:** A new and scientific way of viewing change is "the planned alteration in the existing organisational system" Planned organisational change, is the intentional attempt by an organisation to influence the status quo itself. Planed changes are made by the organisation with the purpose of achieving something that might otherwise be unattainable, or accomplishable with great difficulty. Through planned changes organisations reach new frontiers and progress more rapidly toward a given set of goals and objectives.

**Box 13.3 Starbucks Way of Retaining its Customers**

Starbucks the coffee house giant, is demonstrating its proactive stance by examining various ways to retain its current customers and attract the next generation of young coffee drinkers. It has gone so far in its consumer assessment methods—as to hypnotize a group of 20+ year olds to try to find out what they really think about Starbucks. Among the early results of such assessment is the company's establishment of Starbucks Express, which allows customers to e-mail their orders to the stores they patronize, which then will have their coffee waiting for them in personalized cups when they arrive. (S.Holmes, "Planet Starbucks", September 9, 2002

Planned change has two important goals. First, it seeks to improve the ability of the organisation to adapt to changes in its environment. Second, it seeks to change employee behaviour. To survive in a competitive world, the organisation must respond to changes in an intelligent way (stimulate innovation, empower employees, create work teams, find new products etc.). It must also make employees learn new ways of doing things by changing their behaviour.

**Box 13.4 Features of planned Change**

- It is deliberate, systematic and intentionally undertaken.
- It takes place in all organisations at varying speeds and degrees of importance.
- It takes place in all parts of an organisation.
- It challenges the status quo and sets the organisation on a new path
- It can have positive as well as negative impacts. When viewed positively, employees accept and undertake change enthusiastically. If employees look at it in an unfavourable way, they tend to oppose it vehemently
- Planned change may focus on organisation's technology, products, markets, processes, people etc.
- Planned changes are difficult to bring about, costly and time consuming.

## 3. Proactive change versus Reactive change

Proactive change takes place when some forces to change lead an organisation to conclude that a particular change is desirable. Reactive change occurs when these forces to change make it necessary for a change to be implemented. For instance, introduction of a new employee-benefit scheme is proactive as the management strongly believes that it enhances satisfaction and motivation to employees. The change (introduction of scheme) would be reactive if the benefit plan was introduced because of demands made by employees. Thus, proactive change is the change initiated by an organisation because it is identified as desirable (i.e., it is not forced on the organisation). On the other hand, reactive change is the change implemented in an organisation because it is made necessary by outside forces.

There is no close agreement among the researchers about the extent to which organisation change occurs. Perrow describes change as "glacial", whereas Griener considers change as 'revolutionary', rather than 'evolutionary', But change is 'real' and organisations must cope with it or fail to survive. The following summarises the major types of organisational change (D.A. Nadler)

**Box 13.5 Major Type of Organisational Change**

***Anticipatory Changes:*** They are systematically planned changes intended to take advantage of expected situations.

***Relative Changes:*** They are those changes that are forced on the organisation by unexpected environmental events or pressures.

***Incremental Changes:*** They involve subsystem adjustments needed to keep the organisation on its chosen path.

***Strategic Changes:*** They alter the overall shape or direction of the organisation. For example, adding a night shift to meet unexpected demand for the company's product is an incremental change. Switching from being a software trainer to being a software developer would be a strategic change (NIIT for example)

## THE PROCESS OF PLANED CHANGE

According to Kurt Lewin, individual behaviour is the result of an equilibrium between driving and restraining forces. The driving forces push one way; the restraining forces push the other.Driving forces are those forces affecting a situation that are pushing in a particular direction; they tend to initiate a change and keep it going Restraining forces are forces acting to restrain or decrease the driving forces The performance that emerges is a reconciliation of these two sets of forces. An increase in driving forces might improve productivity but it might also increase the restraining forces. For example a manager may believe that not giving any relaxation time to employees during lunch and tea breaks might bring more discipline and improved performance (driving forces). But the employees may turn hostile, develop distrust and offer greater resistance (restraining forces). Therefore, the natural tendency of the manager would be to explain and go slow in a step-by-step manner till he is able to secure compliance to such an order. Driving forces generally activate their own restraining forces. Decreasing the restraining forces – as explained above – is a more effective way to encourage change. Lewin's model reminds us to look for multiple causes of behaviour rather than relying on a single cause. The equilibrium also reveals that organisations have forces that keep from falling too low, as will as forces that keep it from rising too high.

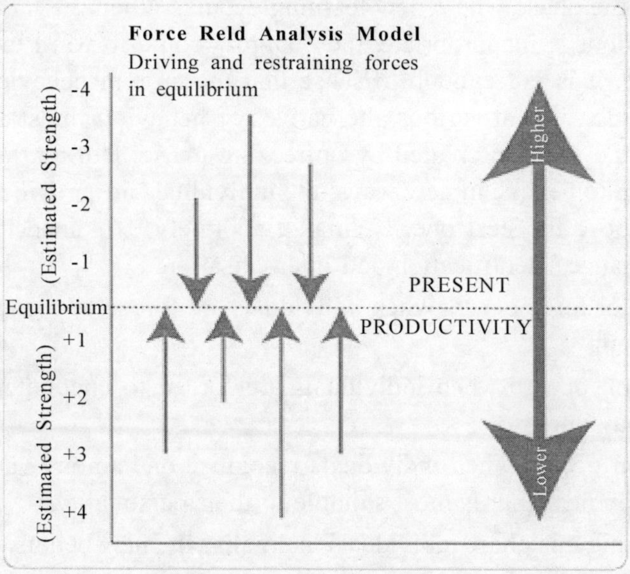


***Figure: 13.1 Kurt Lewin's Force Field Analysis***

To initiate planned changes, managers have to remove or weaken the restraining forces and work toward creating or strengthening the driving forces that exist in organisations. Lewin also studied the process of bringing about effective change. Usually, individuals experience two obstacles to change: (i) they are unable or unwilling to alter long established attitudes and behaviour for various reasons (ii) they may try to do things differently but return to traditional ways after a short time. To overcome this, Lewin proposed a three step sequential model of the change process.

- Unfreezing involves making the need for change so obvious that the individual, group, or organisation can readily see and accept it. The following elements are vitally necessary during this unfreezing phase:
  i. The physical removal of the individuals' is being changed from their accustomed routines, sources of information and social relationships.
  ii. The undermining and destruction of social support.
  iii. Demeaning and humiliating experience to help individuals being changed to see their old attitudes or behaviour as unworthy and think to be motivated to change.
  iv. The consistent linking of reward with willingness to change and of punishment with unwillingness to change.

  Untreezing is, thus, the breaking down of the existing mores, old taboos and traditions–the primitive ways of doing things, so that the people are ready to accept new alternatives. It involves, discarding the orthodox and conventional methods and introducing a new dynamic behaviour that is most appropriate to the situation.

  The essence of this unfreezing phase is that the individual is made to realise that his beliefs, feelings and behaviour are no longer appropriate or relevant to the current situation in the organisation.
- Changing: It is the phase where new learning occurs. When the individuals are convinced that their behaviour is inappropriate, they happily come forward to accept the change. In order to change, it is not enough to sense that the current behaviour is inadequate. The necessary condition is that various alternatives or behaviour must also be made available in order to fill the vacuum created by unfreezing phase. During this phase of 'changing' individuals learn to behave in new ways; the individuals are provided with alternatives out of which to choose the best one. Kelman elaborately explained this 'moving' phase in terms of compliance, identification and internalisation.
  (a) Compliance or force occurs when individuals are forced to change either by rewards or by punishment.
  (b) Internalisation occurs when individuals are forced to encounter a situation that calls for new behaviour.
  (c) Identification occurs when individuals recognise one among various models provided in the environment that is most suitable to their personality.
- Refreezing: During this phase individuals internalise the new beliefs, feelings and behaviour learned in the 'changing' phase. That is to say a person accepts the new behaviour as a permanent part of his behaviour repertoire. He has to practice and experiment with the new method of behaviour and see that it effectively blends with his other behavioural attitudes. It is very important for the manager concerned with the introducing change to visualise that the new behaviour is not extinguished soon Refreezing is appropriate when it permanently installs behaviours that maintain essential core values, such as a focus on important business results and those values maintained by the companies that are "built to last".

## FORCES FOR CHANGE

Organisational changes do not occur spontaneously. (They occur when the forces encouraging change become more powerful than those resisting change.) These forces to change can be either internal (emanating from within an organisation) or external forces (coming from outside an organisation).

### Internal Forces

**Increased Size:** Increased size is followed by major shifts in internal structure (increased specialisation, growing complexity etc). As organisations prosper and grow in size, they generate more resources. These resources help them seize new opportunities, enter new markets, experiment with novel ideas etc. They tend to be more flexible and open to change.

**Performance Gaps:** When there is a gap between set targets and actual results in terms of market share, profits and employee productivity – it's time to change, innovate and go ahead. If companies do not change hats and switch gears quickly, they may go off the track and reach a dead end too soon. Like success, thus, disappointing performance can be a stimulus for change.

**Employee Needs and Values:** Effective organisations have to tune their policies and procedures in line with employee needs and values. Attractive financial incentives, challenging assignments, vertical growth opportunities are all part of the same game. If employees change their attitudes toward financial rewards and expect more freedom and autonomy at work followed by flexible schedules, organisations, too, must follow suit.

**Change in the Chief Executive:** One of the frequently cited reasons for major changes in an organisation is the change of executives at the top. No two managers have the same styles, skills or managerial philosophies. Managerial behaviour is always subjective so that a newly appointed manager might favour different organisation design, objectives, procedures and policies than a predecessor. The newly appointed manager or the newcomer usually begins by examining the structure below him to see whether it corresponds to his ideas. If it is not so, he indulges in making sweeping changes. Thus, the filling of the top vacancies where the new person comes in from outside, presents a strategic opportunity for re-examination of the entire structure and explanation of the changes to the people who are affected. The point to note here is that the managerial differences cannot be overlooked, for inevitably they will influence task performance.

### External Forces

**Technology:** The pace of technological change is increasing and literally wiping out businesses every day. Advancements in technology can dramatically affect organisation's products, services, markets, suppliers, distributors, competitors, customers, manufacturing processes, marketing practices and competitive position. New products could hit the market with electrifying speed. New markets could sprout up from nowhere. The emergence of Nano car from Tata Group could alter the thinking of automobile industry forever—especially toward cost-effective, fuel-efficient cars. Technological changes can reduce or eliminate cost barriers between businesses, create shorter production runs, lead to shortages in technical skills and could even turn the customers against the company if it fails to meet expectations. No company, unfortunately, is insulated against emerging technological developments. (F.R.David).

**Box 13.6 Technology as a source of Competitive Advantage**

The technology of an organisation's input, conversion, and output processes is an important source of a company's competitive advantage. Why is Microsoft the most successful software company? Why is Toyota the most efficient car manufacturer? (Though it suffered a loss recently) Why McDonald is's the most efficient fast-food company? Each of these organisations excels in the development, management and use of technology to create competences that lead to higher value for stakeholders.

Organisations with out dated technology are either shown the door or decimated quickly. Furthermore, technological change in recent times has become increasingly diverse and complex. Its pace is stepping up, making the executives more and more concerned with the adequacy of organisation structure (and new forms of organisation) to meet and match the needs. New technology will affect organisations in ways we cannot yet predict. It is not entirely without reason that mass customization is gaining popularity among leading firms too. You can now buy clothes cut to your proportions, supplements with the exact blend of the vitamins and minerals you like, CDs with the music tracks you choose and textbooks whose chapters are picked out by your professor. Companies are able to make these bold moves because they are able to organise around a dynamic network of relatively independent operating units. The Internet and the World Wide Web are changing the way companies and individuals communicate market, buy and distribute faster than organisations can respond.

**Box 13.7 IT comes to the rescue of many retail giants**

At Wal-Mart the electronic cash register indicates the goods sold, their prices and the inventory on hand. If the system recognises that a store is low on Tide detergent for example, an order is send to the nearest distribution centre to send more Tide to that store. If the distribution centre reports shortage of Tide, the system automatically generates an order to be placed with P&G for additional supply of Tide. Other retailers and even grocery stores, now-a-days use scanners linked to computers that provide instant inventory information.

Experts are unanimous in their opinion about IT and its impact on organisations. They are of the opinion tat IT(Hellriegel and Slocum)

- Changes almost everything about a company—its structure, its products, its markets and its processes
- Increases the value of invisible assets, such as knowledge, competencies, and training
- Democratizes a company because employees have more information and can talk to anyone in the company
- Increases the flexibility of work by allowing more people to work at home, on the road, or at hours that suit them, and
- Allows companies to unify their global operations and to work a 24-hour day spanning the world.

## Competition

Competition in virtually all industries is intense and sometimes cut-throat. Most companies are fighting a do-or-die battle for survival. The rising oil prices, stock market crash, internet bubbles, collapse of banks and financial institutions, crashing real estate markets, rising unemployment, corporate crimes and scandals have complicated matters further especially after 2007. Cash-hungry companies are finding it difficult to experiment with new ideas. Companies with heavy debt burden find it very tough to carry out business in the traditional way. Customers have begun to question the way a shampoo is priced, a car is manufactured and service warranty is written for say, an air conditioner. Any company that is not able to run the race in terms of price, quality, speed, efficiency etc is shown the door without any mercy. To survive in this economic jungle, companies are trying every trick in the book to woo customers away from competitors through cost-effective, high-quality innovative products and services. To this end, factories are organized around products—working with self-managed teams taking appropriate decisions at the shop floor level itself while actually doing the job, instead of relying on top management. Quality, speed and flexibility are the new corporate mantras. *Lean manufacturing* is the order of the day. Lean manufacturing is based on a commitment to making an operation both efficient and effective; it strives to achieve highest possible productivity and total quality cost effectively, by eliminating unnecessary steps in the production process and continually striving for improvement. New alliances are formed, sometimes even with rivals just to withstand economic shocks and stay afloat. Cooperative agreements between competitors, not surprisingly, are gaining popularity in recent times.

## Social and Political changes

Cultural, social, demographic, political and environmental changes have a significant impact upon virtually all products, services, markets and customers. Social trends keep changing, thanks to the ever-changing consumer tastes and preferences and the heightened competition in the market place. People share information in Internet chat rooms. The percentage of women in the workforce is rising steadily. Work force diversity in terms of race, religion, region, educational background, age, skills etc is something that every company must look into carefully and adjust its antennae accordingly. Consumers keep chasing discount stores in order to maximize their return as well as satisfaction. There is, of course, the growing realization that business cannot survive without consistent support and continued blessings from government. Many new legal provisions in the corporate sector get introduced every time, affecting the organisations. For example, changes in patent laws, antitrust legislation, tax rates and lobbying activities can impact firms significantly The increasing global interdependence among economies, markets, governments, and organisations makes it imperative that firms consider the possible impact of political variables on their internal policies and strategies. In short, organisations cannot afford to be rigid and inflexible in the wake of environmental pressures, they must be dynamic and viable, so that they survive.

**Box 13.8. U.S Government's anti trust case against Microsoft**

Do you want to know the impact of government on business? Simply ask Microsoft's CEO Steve Ballmer and founder Bill Gates about the U.S Government's influence on their company. For over three years, the U.S Government pursued an anti trust case against Microsoft, alleging that the company enjoyed a monopoly on fundamental aspects of the personal computer business. Now the dust has settled down. However, it had a damaging impact on the company for so long and it surely will compel changes in the way the industry operates in the years ahead.

### Certain Other Forces: The Domino Effect

Another main source of change is the change itself. Domino effect is one in which one change touches off a sequence of related and supporting changes. For example, creation of a new department may cause the introduction of new managerial positions, changes in assignments within other departments, reallocation of tasks etc. Other departments might have to realign their structure, tasks, missions and staffing. Most of the managers fail to consider the potential domino effects. Such an oversight might lead to the problems of coordination and control. Before any significant change is made, the possible consequences of that change must be evaluated and examined to see whether undesirable chain reactions occur.

## RESPONSES TO CHANGE

The response to change depends on the perception of the employees about change. Perception, in turn, depends on attitudes. Different individuals react differently to a given change depending on their attitudes. It should, however, be noted that though people react individually and differently to change, they sometimes unite through social actions to make a uniform response (in such situations as slowdown or walk out). Therefore, one important task of a manager introducing change is to study and understand employees' attitudes so as to create a positive response. A manager can understand human attitudes by studying the factors on which these attitudes depend. According to psychologists, a person's attitude depends on three sets of factors—psychological, personal and social factors. Evaluation of change in the light of these factors leads to one of the four basic reactions–rejection, resistance, tolerance and acceptance. A comprehensive view of these attitudes and reactions is presented in the following figure.

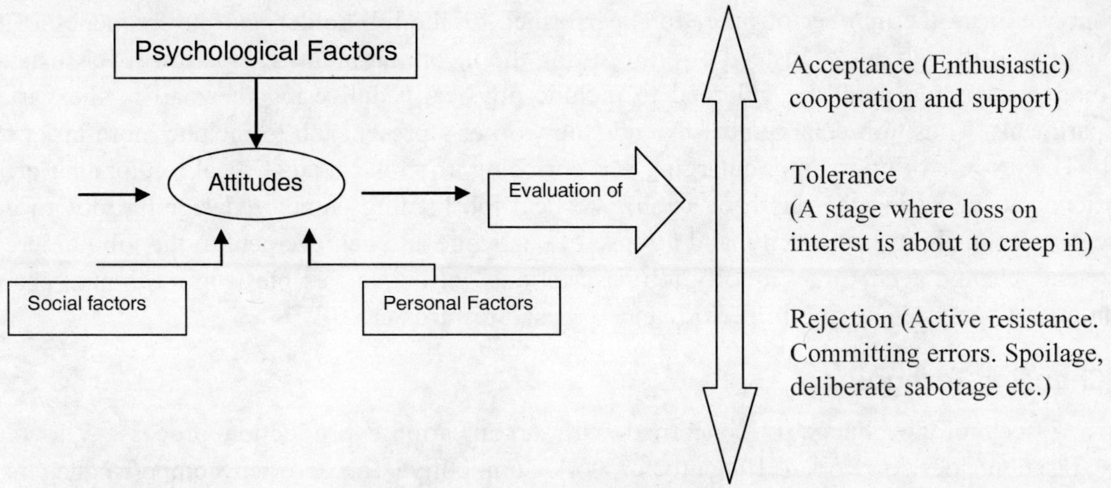


***Figure 13.2: Reponses to Change***

If an employee perceives himself as capable of adjusting to change without an overwhelming degree of personal sacrifice, and if he views the outcome of the change as largely beneficial, he may psychologically adopt a positive attitude toward the change. On the other hand, if the worker feels incapable and insecure and fails to notice many personal benefits forthcoming from change, his psychological attitude may be negative and in opposition to change.

## TYPES OF PLANNED CHANGE

The next question is what can a change agent or manager change? The options fall into four categories: Structure, Technology, Task and People.

### 1. Structural change

Structural change is change aimed at increasing organisational effectiveness through modifications in the existing organisational structure. The structure focused change efforts may include:

(i) Changing the number of organisational levels.

(ii) Altering the span of management.

(iii) Changing from one base of departmentation to another base (functional to product type)

(iv) Altering the line and staff, and functional authority relationships.

(v) Bringing in more rules and procedures to increase standardisation etc.

A manager's strategy here, sometimes, is reorganisation. Reorganisation involves entirely a redesign of the structure of the organisation. It also calls for remarkable changes in the departmentation, span of control and coordination. Reorganisation has proved to be an effective and most widely used strategy in the case of serious problems.

### 2 Redesigning Tasks

Here change efforts focus on increasing the scope or diversity and depth of the job. By job scope we mean the number of operations performed by the job holder and the frequency of the operation of the job cycle. Instead of only sorting the incoming mail by department for instance, a mail sorter's job could be enlarged to include physically delivering the mail to the various departments. Thus, job enlargement extends the worker's present job to include more tasks of a job. The process of upgrading, enlarging and enriching a job is called vertical job loading or job enrichment increasing the depth of a job). Vertical job loading entails redesigning jobs to give greater responsibility, autonomy, and a sense of challenge and achievement to the job holder. To this end, change agents may modify job descriptions, introduce flexible working hours, change compensation system, bring in performance – based rewards etc.

### 3 Changing Technology

A technology change is concerned with organisation's production process – how the organisation does its work (efficiently or not) Competitive forces often compel managers to introduce new equipment, tools or operating methods. Many steel plants in India (including TISCO, Essar Steel, Jindal Steel, SAIL) have significantly modernised their plants in recent years to compete more effectively. Efficient handling equipment, furnaces, and presses have been introduced to reduce the cost per tonne of steel. Computerisation and automation have changed the face of automobile manufacturers, process industries etc., everywhere now. Technology-focussed changes comprise of:

(i) Changing problem-solving and decision-making procedures.

(ii) Introduction of computers to facilitate managerial planning and control.

(iii) Converting from unit production to mass production technology.

(iv) Introduction of sophisticated management information systems

### 4. Culture/People change

People change emphasises increasing organisational effectiveness by changing attitudes, skills, perceptions, expectations and values of organisation members. Managers generally initiate such a change when the performance gaps occur due to employee-related problems. Competitive wages performance-based bonuses, creating promotional avenues, offering training programmes, are all steps intended to bring about positive changes in the attitudes of employees. OD interventions are basically meant to change people and improve their working relationships.

### CULTURAL CHANGES

A strategic change often requires changing the culture of an organisation. A culture change refers to a change in employees' values, norms, attitudes, beliefs and behaviour. Fuji - Xerox, for example, took several steps to implement such cultural change. It created a new set of "heroes", individuals and teams who were publicly congratulated whenever their behaviour reflected Fuji's new values of quality, team work and customer focus. Leaders, often, play a great role in coaching the values that they want to emphasise. For example Wal-Mart's founder Sam Walton embodied the values of hard work, honesty, neighbourliness and thrift "that he wanted Wal-Mart employees to follow. Although one of the richest men in the world, he drove a pick-up truck, a preference he explained by asking, "If I drove a Rolls Royce, what would I do with my dog?" Much the same way, the Chairman and Managing Director of Infosys Technologies, N R Narayana Murthy leads the company by example, setting impossible targets, putting in 70-90 hours each week, sharing wealth with all employees, and sticking to personal values that he often preaches (e.g., not using company resources for personal use, sharing information with all, never violating laws, having a simple down to earth life style - sending children by bus, not employing a domestic help, not allowing his IIT gold medallist wife to set foot in his office, travelling economy class and staying in budget hotels etc). He believes that "leadership is about making what seems impossible. It's about changing the perception of what reality is". (Business India, 1999).

**Box 13.9 Embedded Mechanisms to Change a Company's Culture (Schein)**

- Tell your employees what you pay attention to, measure and control – whether it is controlling costs or top class customer service or market leadership. At Xerox the key themes include respect for the individual and services to the customer; at Proctor & Gamble the overreaching value is product quality; at McDonald's the focus is always on - quality, service, cleanliness and value.
- React properly to critical incidents and organisational crises. For example if you value the contributions of your employees, do not lay off people when profits fall suddenly.
- Deliberately role model, teach and coach the values you want to emphasise. For example Wipro's Azim Premji puts emphasis on benchmarking, upgrading, innovation at all levels. A notorious workaholic, he is extremely unassuming and values honesty, integrity and open communication in daily life. Stories of Premiji refusing to give in to graft are legion in India which has recently acquired the notorious label of the third most corrupt country in the world (Out look June 19, 2000 and Business India, Dec. 11 - 24 - 2000). In actual practice, companies with strong cultures are enthusiastic collectors and tellers of stories, anecdotes and legends in support of basic beliefs; 3M tells innovation stories; P&G, Johnson and Johnson, IBM, Tata Steel tell quality stories etc. Communicate your priorities by the way you allocate rewards and status. For example when the top management at General Foods decided to reorient its strategy from cost to diversification and sales growth, the compensation system was linked to sales volume rather than just increased earnings as in the past.
- Make your human resource procedures and criteria consistent with the values you espouse. In order to build productive, high - performing team members, the leader has to scrupulously follow certain guidelines like; (i) setting demanding targets, (ii) selecting people with requisite skills and capabilities, (iii) empowering members so that they can stand on their own, (iv) training people continuously and forcing them to learn the art of working in teams etc. After taking charge of IBM which is viewed as traditionally bureaucratic and highly politicized, Louis Gerstner changed IBM's HR policies and procedures - new incentive plans, promotion and appraisal criteria etc - to support IBM's new performance-oriented strategies (Dessler).

Culture is something which is created by the actions of leaders; it is institutionalised by leaders; and when it becomes dysfunctional, leadership is required to change it. According to Sachein, what a CEO needs most is an understanding of how culture can help or hinder the organisation in attaining its mission and the skills to make the appropriate changes.

## RESISTANCE TO CHANGE

Resistance to change may be individual or organisational. People resist change for a variety of reasons: fear of losing job, obsolescence of skills, disturbs the status quo and social relationships etc. Organisations, too, resist changes because of resource constraints, difficulty in bringing about structural, technological changes etc. Let's examine these in greater detail.

### A. Economic Reasons

**1. Fear of economic loss:** Employees often feel insecure about loss of employment and economic benefits such as:

(i) fear of technological unemployment

(ii) fear of reduced work hours and consequently less pay

(iii) fear of demotion and thus reduced wages

(iv) fear of speed up and reduced incentive wages.

Machines, computers and Robots have destroyed thousands of jobs in the recent past. Employee fears in this regard, therefore, seem genuine and well-founded.

**2. Obsolescence of Skills:** Change may render existing employee skills and knowledge obsolete. What they have been doing for ages together might be under threat. If employees feel that they do not possess requisite skills that are currently in demand, they resist changes quite seriously.

### B. Personal Reasons

**1. Fear of Unknown:** Change is resisted often because of its unknown consequences. Whenever people do not know exactly what happens they are likely to resist it with all their might. For example, a bank employee may resist posting to a rural branch because of the anxiety of unknown area. Female clerks in Indian banks often refuse promotions because promotion requires relocating. In all such cases, employees do not know how a change will affect them and worry about whether they will be able to meet the demands of a new procedure, technology, or location.

**2. Status quo:** People like status quo because they have adjusted to the demands of a job over a period of time. Change would render all such experience, knowledge and learning somewhat useless. When introduced, change would require people to learn new or even difficult ways of doing things. This means loss of expected rewards, convenience and comforts. This kind of emotional turmoil forces them to embrace status quo arrangements passionately. Why to rock the boat and invite trouble?

**3. Self interest and Ego-defensiveness:** Employees typically resist a change they believe will take away something of value. A proposed change in job design, structure or technology may lead to a perceived loss of power, prestige or company benefits. Many impending changes threaten the self-interests of some managers in the organisation. A change may diminish their power and influence within the company, so they fight it. Again, a sales person's suggestion to expand sales by offering seasonal discounts may be turned down by the branch manager who thinks the sales executive might steal the credit (different perceptions).

## C. Social Reasons

**1. Social Displacement:** Change often causes social displacement of people by breaking informal groups and friendly relationships. Employees get emotionally upset when friendships breakdown. They dislike new adjustments, new groupings and new relationships brought forward by change efforts and resist vehemently.

**2. Peer pressure:** People may resist change because of peer pressure. As individuals they may like computerisation, but refuse to accept it for the sake of the group. Any change that upsets group norms is likely to be opposed. even if it is known to have a positive impact.

## D. Organisational Issues

**1. Threats to Power and Influence:** Some people consider change as a potential threat to their position and influence in the organisation. Novel ideas and the new use of resources can disrupt the power relationships and therefore, are often resisted at organisational level. Specially people who are occupying the top place in the organisation resist some changes because any change might threaten their existing power. That is to say people resist change on the ground that it might affect their position-power.

**2. Organisation structure:** Some organisational structures have inherent forces acting against change. In a bureaucratic structure, for example, jobs are narrowly defined, lines of authority are clearly spelt out, the information flows from top to the bottom. In such an organisation novel, innovative ideas do not find favour and are screened out. The structural inertia favours stability and status quo rather than change and innovation.

**3. Resource Constraints:** Organisation many a time operate under some, resource constraints. If the resources with which to operate are available in abundance there will be no problem of introducing change. But the necessary financial, material and human resources may not be available to the organisation to make the needed changes.

**4. Sunk Costs:** The plight of some companies is such that heavy capital is blocked in the fixed assets. If an organisation wishes to introduce change then, difficulty arises because of these sunk costs. Sunk costs are not restricted to physical things alone; farther, they can be expressed in terms of people also. For instance some members in the organisation retain their jobs by virtue of enough seniority, though they do not significantly contribute to the organisation. Unless they are motivated properly to higher performance, the payments for their services (for example, fringe benefits, salaries, and other payments) represent the sunk costs for the organisation.

## Overcoming Resistance to Change

Some of the approaches, at the individual as well as group level, designed to reduce resistance to change, may be listed thus:

**1. Education and Communication:** One of the easy ways to overcome resistance to change is to help employees understand the true need for a change as well as the logic behind it. Tell them clearly as to what is going to occur and why to dispel their fears. To this end, A manager should specifically explain:

- What the change is
- When it is to be introduced
- How it will be implemented
- Why the change is required
- What is the basic purpose of change
- How the change is going to help them etc.

When employees realise the need for change and understand the logic behind it, they tend to accept it easily. However, it is a very time consuming approach. Managers have to explain everything patiently in order to gain acceptance from employees.

**2. Participation and Involvement:** Participation is another key concept in gaining acceptance. If people participate in what is happening, they will be more likely to go along. They get a chance to express their opinions freely, get their doubts clarified and understand the perspectives of others. As a result, uncertainty is reduced; self interests and social relationships are less threatened. Involving users and potential resisters in the change process has other benefits also. It helps managers identify potential problems and understand the differences in perceptions of change among employees. After a series of discussions, any change effort that is likely to be made is going to be accepted wholeheartedly. People generally support what they help create. People who participate will be committed to implementing change. However, it is a time consuming and costly exercise.

**3. Facilitation and Support:** Change agents can offer a range of supportive efforts to reduce resistance. Compassionate and sympathetic listening may be used to reduce employee's fears and anxieties. Managerial support can also come in the form of special, new-skills training; job stress counselling and compensating time-off. The approach, obviously, rests on the belief that prople have the ability to solve their own problems with the help of a sympathetic listener. The role of the manager as a facilitator is one of understanding and perhaps advising rather than passing judgement. This requires a somewhat permissive and friendly atmosphere.

**4. Negotiation and Agreement:** Sometimes management can neutralise potential or actual resistance by exchanging something of value for cooperation. It can offer rewards to those who go along with the change. It can also agree to protect those who will potentially be damaged by the change. Every attempt can be made to see that people do not lose their face in the change process. Unions and their representatives who bargain for their members should be allowed to air their opinions freely so as to have a clear picture of what they stand for. When management is able to strike a deal by offering something of value, an agreement is reached. Negotiation as a tactic works when resistance comes from a powerful source. Its costs can be quite high when the field is wide open to several contending groups. As commented by Robbins "there is the risk that, once a change agent negotiates which one party to avoid resistance, he or she is open to the possibility of being blackmailed by other individuals in positions of power".

**5. Manipulation and Cooptation:** Manipulation occurs when managers selectively withhold undesirable information, create false rumours, distort facts to get potential resisters accept the change. In Cooptation the change agent seeks to buy off the leaders of a resistance group by giving them a key role in the change process. This method, however, is not a form of participation because the change agent does not really want advice from those coopted. In this sense, cooptation would prove to be a non-productive, self-defeating exercise. People who feel that they have been tricked, are not being treated fairly, or are being lied to, are likely to respond negatively to a change. Once the coopted members discover the tactics, the change agent's credibility may nose dive.

**6. Coercion:** In coercion managers use formal power to force employees to change. Resisters are told to accept the change or lose rewards (threats of transfer, loss of promotions, negative recommendations) or even their jobs. This approach may not pay in the long run because employees feel like victims, are angry at change agents and may even sabotage the changes. In critical situations where an urgent response is required, coercion works.

**7. Group Dynamics:** Forces operating within groups can be used to overcome resistance to change. A group can be very effective in changing members' attitudes, values and behaviour especially in those areas as are related to the purpose of the group. In a group where members share perception that change is required, change can be easily implemented. The source of pressure for change lies within the group. Likewise, open communication with group members helps in resolving knotty issues amicably and implement the change smoothly.

**Table 13.1. Group Dynamics as a Means of Overcoming Resistance to Change**

Darwin Cartwright has mentioned the following characteristics of group that are essential for the manager to consider when he uses 'group' as a means of overcoming resistance to change:-

- Strong sense of belonging: When there is a strong "WE FEELING' prevalent in the minds of individual members, group can be effectively used as a change agent.
- Group prestige: If the group is attractive to the members, it becomes easy for the group to exert influence on individual members. Group pride often creates a dynamic quality of give-and-take within the group itself. That is, a deep sense of what each member has to offer and a willingness of each member to adapt to the needs of the whole. The more cohesive the group is, the more it becomes desirable for the organisation to use group as a change agent.
- Attitudes, values and behaviour: Group will be generally more successful in changing members' attitudes, values and behaviour especially in those areas as are related to the purpose of the group. For instance, a union leader can exert influence over rank and file members regarding the strikes and lockouts etc.
- Individual prestige: If a particular group member has a status or prestige to other members, he can greatly influence them. Prestige is not so being popular as being respected. Prestige does not necessarily accompany authority. For instance, official leader and the actual leader of the group may be different personalities.
- Deviations from group norms: Usually, members follow certain group norms. Any change

efforts that deviate from the established norms encounter strong resistance. In group interaction therefore, the idea of homeostasis must be taken into account.

- Shared perception: In a group where members share perception that change is needed, change can be easily implemented. The source of pressure for change lies within the group.
- Shared information: Any effort to bring change requires frank and open communication in order to succeed without arousing undue amount of resistance. Shared information brings shared perception in its wake, and plays an important role in the change process.

## MANAGEMENT OF CHANGE

In large scale organisations, changes seldom occur without a bit of chaos. Usually change agents try to minimise it by imposing some order on the change process. Change becomes orderly when it is planned and implemented in a systematic way. The process of planned change comprises the following steps.

**1. Identify the Need for Change:** First of all, the manager should identify the forces demanding change.

These forces thus, may be internal or external. Internal forces include:

(i) employee turnover.

(ii) change related role conflicts.

(iii) mounting problems from its growing size.

(iv) any other internal changes (for example, introduction of new department due to expansion in sales, production etc.).

External forces demanding change, on the other hand include:

(i) technological changes

(ii) new marketing strategies

(iii) new production techniques etc.

The above forces may not demand change but some may require immediate and careful attention of management. The minor forces, therefore, must be isolated and the focus must shift to the major ones. Feedback information, control mechanisms generally help in identifying where major gaps have occurred between the desired performance and the actual performance in key areas. A performance gap is the difference between what the organisation wants to do and what it actually does. A careful examination of performance reports would help the manager put the finger on the problem causing trouble.

**2. Diagnose the Problem:** This step involves the identification of the root cause. "Most organisational problems have multiple causes, seldom is there a simple and obvious cause and seldom does only one perspective need to be considered." Several techniques may be used, therefore, for diagnosis, e.g. interviews, attitude surveys, team meetings, questionnaires etc. Where the problem can be traced to a single department, the focus of diagnosis is limited to that area. If the problem has wider implications and affects a large number of departments, organisational analysis is required. Organisational analysis includes exhaustive study of organisational goals, principles, practices and performance at a macro level. After such an exhaustive analysis, the change agent would be a position to identify the areas where modifications have to be made. It must be realised here that a change in one part may affect other parts of the organisation (as shown in Figure 13.2 through the arrows connecting the type of change). A new product may require changes in technology, and a new technology may require new people, skills or a new structure.

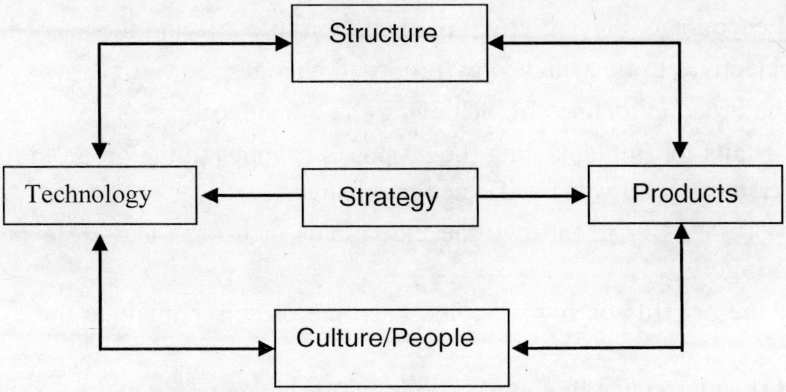


***Figure 13.3: Types of organisational change***

**3. Plan the Change**: This is a crucial step in the management of change. It involves answering three important questions (i) when to bring the change (timing) (ii) how to bring the change (methods) and (iii) who will introduce the change (Change agent). While introducing change, reactions from people must be carefully assessed. People affected by change must be consulted; the likely impact should be explained patiently; sufficient time to pick up new skills should be given and adequate rewards to those who follow change should be indicated. As a rule, individuals should get information that will help them answer the following change – related questions (Kotter).

- Will I lose my job?
- Will my old skills become obsolete?
- Am I capable of producing effectively under the new system?
- Will my power and prestige decline?
- Will I be given more responsibility than I care to assume?
- Will I have to work longer lours?
- Will it force me to betray or desert my old friends?
- In addition, selection of an appropriate method is essential to bring about changes in technology, products, structure, strategy or people.

Changing structure involves reorganisation of the departments, re-specification of span of control, decentralisation etc. Changing task includes job enrichment, job specification and specialisation and job redefinition or any other changes concerned with the task of employees. Changing technology involves introduction of new lines of production, installing new control system, instituting new selection and recruitment etc. Act finally, changing people comprises of training, meetings, development activities etc.

The question as to who will bring the change involves the selection of a change agent. Who initiates necessary steps for bringing about change. These may include (Schein).

1. Make clear the need for change or provide a climate in which group members feel free to identify such needs.
2. Permit and encourage relevant group participation in clarifying the needed changes.
3. State the objectives to be achieved by proposed changes.
4. Establish the broad guidelines for achieving the objectives.
5. Leave the details for implementing the proposed changes to the group in the organisation or to the personnel who will be affected by change.
6. Indicate the benefits or rewards to the individuals or groups that are expected to accrue from the change.
7. Materialise the benefits on rewards, i.e., keep the promises made to those who made the change.

**4. Implement the change:** While implementing any change programme, managers encounter three programmes (Nadler and Tushman) – resistance, power and control. As explained previously, there is the problem of resistance to change. Again change may undermine the balance of power in the organisation and disrupt the existing control system.

**Table 13.2. Implementation of change: Action steps**

| *Problem* | *Implication* | *Action Steps* |
|---|---|---|
| Resistance | Need to motivate | • Invite participation from peoplel Offer appropriate rewards<br>• Encourage open communicationl Explain why change is essential |
| Control | Need to manage the transition | • Use multiple and consistent leverage points<br>• Develop organisational arrangements for transitionl Build in feedback machinations |
| Power | Need to shape the political domain | • Assure the support of key groupsl Use leader behaviour to get support of changel Use symbols and language |

***Source:*** D. Nadler, "Concepts for Management of Organisational Change."

Regardless of which approach is used (to change technology, design, task or prople) the ability to sustain change depends primarily on how well the organisation reinforces newly learned behaviours during and after the change effort. A combination of money, pats on the back, and stimulating job/growth opportunities help create a climate that reinforces new behaviours. Where the rewards are perceived to be fair, employees commit themselves to the 'new ways of doing things' wholeheartedly.

**5. Follow up and Feedback:** Management of change is incomplete without proper follow-up. Organisation must evaluate the effects of change. Objectives must be present and be compared with the performance to see the degree of success in change. End results should be operationally defined and measurements must be done both before and after the implementation of change. This enables change agent to compare the performance after the introduction of change with the one prior to it. The change agent must make sure that the change is implemented in such a fashion as to maximise the benefits to the organisation by the effective changes.

## Review Questions

1. What is change? What are the most frequent causes of change?
2. Discuss the change and its effects on employees and organisations.
3. How individual employees react to change?
4. Explain Kurt Lewin's force-field analysis?
5. "In our rapidly changing technological society, resistance to change is a normal result of psychological, economic, or social factors or a combination of these three." (Jack Halloran) Comment on this statement.
6. What are the six management strategies for dealing with human resistance?
7. Discuss how a manager manages change effectively.

## Critical Thinking Questions

1. A company has recently purchased equipment that, when installed, will do the work of one hundred employees. The workforce of the company's is very concerned and is threatening to take some kind of action. If you were the human resource manager, what would you try to do to satisfy all parties concerned? Why?
2. Carefully planned change often is assumed to be effective. Do you think unplanned change can sometimes be beneficial to an organisation? Discuss.
3. Why does an OD intervention without proper 'unfreezing' have only limited chances of success?
4. Explain force-field analysis. Suggest three situations in which it might be useful in helping you analyses a change situation.
5. Is most organisational change forced on the organisation by external factors or fostered from within? Explain through contemporary examples.

## Case Study 1. Unwanted Promotion

Kartar Singh joined Laskhmi Bank, Meerut branch as a clerk other obtaining the post graduate degree in chemistry from Delhi University in 1986. He did his work with due diligence and was generally rated as a hard-working, ambitious young man. He obtained the professional qualification, CAIIB, in 1992. Thereafter, he has applied for the officers' post under the promotion quota. He could not get the promotion as his scores in the written test were low. Meanwhile, he is transferred to the Delhi University, campus branch, Delhi. His attempts to scale the career ladder did not succeed and after several frustrating trials, he consciously decided to joint the ranks of the union as an active member. He became the president of the local branch of Bank Employees' Union in 1995. Through his interpersonal skills, he moved closer to most employees in the bank and is able to put out the fires between people quickly. Of late, he is considered a tough union activist to bargain with and management has developed a kind of negative attitude towards his career moves. In 1996 when the opportunity came, he was not considered for promotion as his interview score this time was found to be not satisfactory! The branch managers' confidential report about his union activities, it is rumored, is said to be the major obstacle to his promotion. Meanwhile, Kartar Singh started a business of dealership in automobiles using a dummy name. He has also succeeded, to a large extent, in diverting the deposits of nearby business community to other banks. Based on the recommendations of the new branch manager, management has decided to promote Kartar Singh to the office cadre in 1999. Kartar received the appointment order for the officer's post from the head office recently. The colleagues, along with the Branch Manager planned on evening tea party, congratulating his achievement. To their surprise, Kartar expressed his unwillingness to accept the offer and refused the promotion straight away, citing medical reasons.

### Questions

1. Comment of the promotion policy of the bank, using inputs from the above case.
2. Do you think management's action of selecting Kartar as an office after 13 years' of service is in the right direction? Why? Why not?
3. Why did Kartar refuse promotion?

## Case Study: 2. Quality Control Equipment

Mr. Chandrasekhar is the supervisor of 25 unskilled workers working in a grocery warehouse. To reduce the costs, the management has decided to install mechanised materials—handling equipment. Since the workers lacked training and knowledge about productivity and cost reduction effects of this equipment, the supervisor had to struggle a lot to introduce the change by involving all of them in it. Ultimately, the new equipment was installed with the active cooperation of his workers.

A few months afterwards, Mr. Chandrasekhar has been asked to install a sophisticated quality control equipment among a group of technical workers. Since this group consisted of educated employees, who are in a better position to understand the company's problems, he expected little opposition to the proposed change. Accordingly, he did not exert himself much before introducing the new equipment as he had done earlier in the case of unskilled workers. Contrary to his expectations, the group resisted tooth and nail the introduction of the new system until it was given up. However, the mistake proved to be very costly to Mr. Chandrasekhar. He lost his job.

### Question

1. How do you explain the behaviour of the two groups in accepting or rejecting the change contemplated by the management?
2. What should have been done by the supervisor to avoid resistance by the technical group of workers to the proposed change?

# 14

# Empowerment and Participation

## INTRODUCTION

In 1985 there were 23 people in Swedish Car-maker Volvo's quality department. Most employees believed that quality was the responsibility of the quality department. To break this traditional belief top management empowered rank and file workers with the authority needed to improve quality. Channels of communication were made more flexible and open. Quality has become everyone's job. By 1988, wastage had been considerably reduced, leading to considerable savings in manufacturing cost. The number of people in the quality department dropped to 12 and their responsibilities shifted from inspection to teaching, coaching and empowering (Krantz, 1989). Pick up any popular business periodical, and you are likely to find interesting profiles of managers whose roles have changed considerably. They are being called coaches, advisors, sponsors and facilitators. The dividing line between the roles of managers and workers has become very thin. You will find in progressive, pro-active organisations decision-making authority being pushed to lower levels where workers are given a free hand to decide about schedules, procedures and work-related issues – all by themselves. In early 1980s managers encouraged workers to participate in work-related decisions. Now managers let employees make decisions at all levels of an organisation without seeking approval from 'upstairs'. Simply stated, managers are asking employees to take charge of what they do. The idea behind empowerment is quite simple. People who do the job for years together are in the best position to learn how to do that job the best way. So, when there is a chance to improve it, people should go ahead and carry out improvements without getting the stamp of approval from the manager.(Krantz; Dobbs; Dwivedi)

Empowerment, thus, is the authority to take decisions within one's area of operations without having to get approval from anyone else. Here the operatives are encouraged to use their initiative to do things the way they like. To this end, the employees are given not just authority but resources as well so that they not only take decisions but implement them quickly. This empowerment means giving the employees the authority to make decisions and providing them with financial resources to implement these decisions.(Thomas; Randoph; Rothstein)

**Box 14.1 How to empower employees?**

"An empowered organization is one in which individuals have the knowledge, skill, desire, and opportunity to personally succeed in a way that leads to collective organizational success." - Stephen Covey Empowerment is the degree of responsibility and authority given to an employee. By empowerment, the employees are supported and encouraged to utilize their skills, abilities and creativity by accepting accountability for their work. Empowerment occurs when employees are adequately trained, provided with all the relevant information and the best possible tools, fully involved in key decisions, and are fairly rewarded Employee empowerment entails identifying how much responsibility and authority an individual can effectively handle without becoming over-burdened or distressed. Empowerment includes supervisors and employees working together to establish clear goals and expectations within agreed-upon boundaries.(http://retention.naukrihub.com/why-employee-empowerment-fails.html)

## EMPOWERMENT, DELEGATION AND POWER

Empowerments is the process of enabling or authorizing an individual to think, behave, take action, and control work and decision making in autonomous ways. It is a way of boosting up the self confidence of subordinates by allowing them to think and act independently. It means offering freedom for people to do successfully what they want to do, rather than getting them to do what you want them to do. Where people are empowered, they are enabled to direct their work and make decisions about the areas of their job for which they are responsible. They do not have to seek permission from anyone. Empowerment is a "pull" strategy, managers design a work situation so that it energizes and provides intrinsic encouragement to employees rather than a "push" strategy where managers induce employees to respond in desirable ways through incentives and influence techniques.

**Box 14.2 What is empowerment?**

To empower means:

- to enable
- to help people develop a sense of self-confidence
- to help people overcome feelings of powerlessness or helplessness
- to energize people to take action
- to mobilize intrinsic motivation to accomplish a task(Whetton and Cameron)

It is necessary to draw the curtain between empowerment and delegation here. In delegation, the subordinate gets the freedom to carry out work according to the broad limits set by the superior. A broad set of rules are established by the superior before hand, keeping organisational rules and regulations in mind. Within such a framework, the subordinate is allowed to function. However, there is very little room for improvisation when the need arises.

Empowerment, it must also be noted here, is not just giving power to someone. Like empowerment, power connotes the ability to get things done. But power and empowerment are not the same thing. The source of empowerment is internal. The source of power is external. For example, you cannot empower me; you can only create the circumstances in which I can empower myself. In an organisation only few people enjoy power, whereas empowerment is something that every one can think of and actually attain. Even without any power, political acceptance, or even social support or title one can attain empowerment. Mahatma Gandhi, Nelson Mandela are shining example of individuals who, despite the absence of attributes of power, maintained complete empowerment in dismal circumstances. Sad to relate, one can only get more power at the cost of someone else in an organisation. My power gets in the way of your power. X gains recognition at the cost of Y –paving the way for an unstoppable tussle to gain the upper hand in sharing scarce organisational assets and resources. This is not the case with empowerment. Conflict and controversy are inbuilt in the concept of power. Every individual in an organisation can be empowered without affecting any other individual's position or stature. Each one of us could get empowered to accomplish what we choose. Empowerment, in a way, is more likely to lead to cooperation and collaboration than to conflict.

**Box 14.3 Why empowerment?**

When Xerox Corporation's dominance in the photocopier market was challenged by Japanese competitors more than 15 years ago, Xerox responded by harnessing the full power of its work force. A change in the management style of the employees that allowed them to participate in management decisions was the key to Xerox's comeback. Since Xerox has implemented policies of employee empowerment, they have posted impressive results. In 1989, Xerox won the Malcolm Baldrige National Quality Award; and, from 1993 until 1994, their return on assets rose 3.5 points (Profile: Xerox Corporation Ohio Consumer Business Unit, Training & Development, 1996).

It is vital to have a work force with potential, but how do you get your employees to perform at their highest ability? A work environment consisting of empowerment will help keep top employees and will attract new, high quality employees. Empowering employees can be the key in turning an average employee into an exceptional one. Empowered employees are usually happier; and, therefore, more likely to stay (Blanchard, O'Connor & Ballard (2003). The difference between mediocre and excellent [employees] depends on how the employee is managed" (Blanchard, et. al. (2003). The job of an empowering manager is more similar to that of a coach than that of a traditional manager. The manager's mission is to unlock the potential of every person within the organization. Motivated, empowered employees are more productive. They are able to use their own innovation to streamline inefficient processes and policies, saving both you and your customers' money. Empowerment, to cut short a long argument, unleashes an individuals potential and enhancing his abilities to nurture growth in the organisation, it gives authority to an individual to take action and take control of his work by making decisions on his own. The organisation should therefore make an enabling environment which helps the employee to undertake their tasks in an empowered manner by removing any barriers that limit the process of empowerment.

## DIMENSIONS OF EMPOWERMENT

There are five dimensions of empowerment, namely:

- a sense of **self-efficacy**,
- a sense of **self-determination**,
- a sense of **personal consequence**,
- a sense of **meaning,** and
- a sense of **trust**.

When managers are able to foster these five attributes in others, they create a condition that is highly empowering.

### 1.Self-Efficacy

When people are empowered, they have a sense of **self-efficacy**. Self-efficacy is defined as having a core belief or conviction about one's abilities, efficiency and effectiveness. Self efficacious people have the initiative, a high level of confidence, considerable amount of self esteem, think analytically, and are action oriented and persistent. A person with high level of self efficacy has the "I can do it" and "I will do it" attitude and this is good. It is this certainty that makes them self motivated and able to handle a task and overcome obstacles and challenges with little help from outside. They set goals and execute the actions required and find the resources, ideas and solutions. They make good leaders, innovators and entrepreneurs.

| *People with a strong sense of self efficacy* | *People with a weak sense of self efficacy* |
|---|---|
| • View challenging problems as tasks to be mastered.<br>• Develop deeper interest in the activities in which they participate.<br>• Form a stronger sense of commitment to their interests and activities.<br>• Recover quickly from setbacks and disappointments | • Avoid challenging tasks.<br>• Believe that difficult tasks and situations are beyond their capabilities.<br>• Focus on personal failings and negative outcomes.<br>• Quickly lose confidence in personal abilities (Bandura, 1994). |

Additional research notes how feelings of self-efficacy can be a significant factor in overcoming addictions and recovering from injuries to name a few. Bandura suggested that three conditions are necessary to feel a sense of self-efficacy:

- a belief that they have the ability to perform a task
- a belief that they are capable of putting forth the necessary effort
- a belief that no outside obstacles will prevent them from accomplishing the task.

### 2. Self-Determination

**Self-determination** refers to feelings of having a choice. People feel self-determined when they can voluntarily and intentionally involve themselves in tasks, rather than being forced or prohibited from involvement. Their actions are the result of personal freedom and their autonomy. Self-determination is associated most directly with having choices about:

- the *methods* used to accomplish the task
- the amount of *effort* to be expended
- the *pace* of the work
- the *time frame* in which it is to be accomplished

research shows that a strong sense of self determination is associated with less alienation in the work environment.

## 3. Personal Consequence

**Personal consequence** is the conviction that through one's own actions, a person can influence what happens. Therefore, a sense of personal consequence refers to a perception of impact. By expending effort, people with a sense of personal consequence know that their efforts will produce impacts. They know that their actions influence the outcomes. Whatever obstacles that they encounter in producing results, they are sure, they can overcome. They know for sure how to bring the environmental forces in sync with their own wishes. Instead of passively reacting to events, they take full control of the forces that come in the way of making things happen in a desirable manner. In other words, people with a sense of personal consequence know how to produce an effect—a desirable result— that is planned by themselves. Research has shown that people who are intrinsically motivated (they have taken up a task that they like or passionate about— not because there are incentives or rewards associated with it) maintain a sense of control over themselves and their situations. Prisoners of war for example many a time refuse to eat certain foods, do not work in a certain place or develop secret communication codes in order to have a sense of personal control. To maintain their physical and mental well being, they need to take charge of their lives. When they allow situations, events and people to guide their destinies, they would eventually be compelled to hang their head in shame for failing to deliver results. Loss of personal control even in small doses sometimes may throw a person into a state of depression, stress, anxiety, low morale, loss of productivity, and burnout. However, it is not always possible to control the outcomes of everything that we carefully plan. Complete control of the outcomes in one's life is not possible. Nevertheless, empowerment helps people to increase the number of personal outcomes that they can take control. This, of course, requires the person to identify the areas where he can exercise such a control effectively and then commit himself to those tasks with total devotion and commitment

## 4. Meaning

Empowered people value the purpose or goals of the activity in which they are engaged and care about what they produce. They invest psychic or spiritual energy in the activity, and they feel a sense of personal significance from the involvement. **Meaning** refers to a perception of value in the activity. When their actions create lasting benefits to a large majority, empowered people are excited to commit themselves to such tasks. It gives them a sense of personal worth and meaning for their existence. Their own ideals and standards, in such cases, are in sync with what they are actually doing. Such purposeful actions produce outcomes that will eventually have a beneficial impact on the general public and make the world a better place to live. Involvement in activities with very little meaning, usually, produces boredom and monotony. Hefty pay cheques also do not guarantee success simply because people do not find any worth in expending their energies on such unexciting tasks. When employees are put on tasks that do not excite them, that do not engage them productively, that do not generate any enthusiasm that only leads to dissonance and annoyance. It creates a sense of disengagement from the work and employees find themselves totally lost in an economic jungle—just trying to make their way in order to survive. Self estrangement results from lack of meaning, vigour and stimulation result from meaningful work. People Research has found that workers engaged in meaningful work are more committed, and involved in the work. They exhibit more passion and excitement.

### 5. Trust

Empowered people have a sense of trust. They are confident that they will be treated fairly and equitably and those holding authority or power positions will not harm or injure them and they will be treated impartially. **Trust** means having a sense of personal security. Trusting individuals are more self-determining, more self-assured, and more honest in their communication, maintain high personal ethics, and are willing to learn. Trusting people are willing to try to get along with people and to be a contributing part of a team. They have less resistance to change and are able to handle stressful situations better than those with low levels of trust. Trusting others allows people to act in a straight forward manner. They are less inclined to play the organisational roles in a self serving manner. They are reluctant to play politics and go in search of hidden agendas. Their behaviour is likely to be open, honest, and congruent than deceptive or shallow. When trust exists in an organization or in a relationship, almost everything else is easier and more comfortable to achieve.

Research findings associated with each of the five dimensions of empowerment indicate that both personal and organizational advantages result when people feel empowered. People (free riders) who don't want empowerment exist when they do not value the outcome assigned (absence of a sense of value), or they believe that someone else will produce the result without their input (absence of a sense of personal consequence), or they don't believe that they have anything to contribute (absence of self-efficacy).

## HOW TO DEVELOP EMPOWERMENT?

Research suggests that at least nine specific prescriptions for fostering empowerment; producing a sense of competence, choice, impact, value, and security. Let's examine these in greater detail:

### 1.Articulating a Clear Vision and Goals

Having a clear vision of where the organisation is going and how the individuals can contribute is essential to build an environment of empowerment. Using word pictures, stories, metaphors and real life examples would go a long way in achieving this. Empowerment is enhanced also when specific behavioural goals are identified that help guide individuals' behaviour as they work on their tasks. Locke and Latham (1990) identified the attributes of the most effective goals and the acronym **SMART goals** best summarizes these attributes:

**Box 14.4 SMART GOALS**

- ***Specific goals***- those that are identifiable, behavioural, and observable.
- ***Measurable goals***-those that have outcome criteria, assessed objectively, and degree of success can be determined.
- ***Aligned goals***- those that are congruent with purpose and vision of the organization.
- ***Realistic goals***-goals that are not so far above the capacity of the individual, challenging goals.
- ***Time-bound goals***- time for accomplishing the goals is specified.

Clear goals help to legitimize the presence of an organisation in its environment. People know what it stands for and will accept its existence and continuance. It helps people to remain focused on a common purpose. Activities can be kept on the right track. Goals specify desired outcomes as well as accountability.

## 2. Fostering Personal Mastery Experiences

The most important thing a manager can do to empower other people is to help them experience personal mastery over some challenge or problem. By accomplishing results, by defeating an opponent or by resolving a problem, one gains a sense of personal mastery over events and situations. A manager should encourage people to expand their vision, exploit their true potential, and assume full responsibility for results by meeting challenges head-on — putting resources to best use. It is like getting the best returns by putting our talents to judicious use. To facilitate this, a manager should break up a large task into smaller tasks. The key is to start with easy tasks and progress by small steps to more difficult tasks until the person experiences a sense of mastery over the entire problem (small-wins strategy). Now the big question is how happy you are right now? Are you doing things that you are passionate about? That are close to your heart and that mean a lot to you? If the answer is in the affirmative, then you are in control of your life. You cannot be fulfilled in doing what you hate. No matter how much you are being paid, the totality of the satisfaction you derive in doing what you are not passionate about is a life without fulfillment. The ability to take full responsibility of your own life is an evidence of your self-leadership on display and this makes you highly effective as a person. (http://ezinearticles.com/?Achieving-Personal-Effectiveness-Through-Personal-Mastery&id=2525499)

**Clear vision:** Achieving personal effectiveness, as mentioned above, requires a clear-cut vision. Know what you want out of life and vividly picture yourself achieving it. This calls for a purposeful living because if you do not know where you are going, any road can take you there. Success and progress towards achieving your goals in life begin with knowing where you are going. Many people go about their lives trying to do everything and then end up being a master of none. Having a clear-cut vision of your life is an indisputable first step of becoming highly effective because it makes you to be mentally focused in one direction.

**Put first thing first**: The first step in putting first things first is to identify the "first things" in your life by prioritizing your projects and tasks. The second, and often the hardest step, is to actually put the "first things" first: to live your priorities. Once you have a clear-cut vision as outlined above, then you must align your priorities towards achieving it by not engaging in unnecessary activities that will steal your time. Remember that you can do almost anything, but you cannot do everything. Whenever you start a task, you are automatically giving up everything else you could have done during that time. The best practice of putting first things first means taking conscious control of your choices and choosing to spend more time on the projects and tasks that are important and valuable, and less time on the ones that are not as important or valuable.

**Thinking outside the box:** is a cliché or catchphrase used to refer to looking at a problem from a new perspective. The catchphrase has become widely used in business environments, especially by management consultants and executive coaches, and has spawned a number of advertising slogans. Anyway, you should know that you cannot do without thinking, and not just ordinary thinking, but creative thinking that produces creative ideas.

**New perspective**: To be highly effective, you must learn to see problems from a new perspective that it does not stifle your creativity. A creative mind thinks outside the box and it does not see limitations. It cannot be caged by problems or setbacks. Thinking outside the box is an individual choice, and it begins by thinking differently in every situation that confronts your way.

**Personal development:** Committing to lifelong self-improvement is one vital key of becoming highly effective. As they say, "knowledge is power". What you don't know is greater than you until you discover it. Personal development is about adding value to life. It exposes ignorance and ushers you into the realm of knowing. Commit to learning all you can and be the best in your profession. For example, if you are an accountant, learn all you can and study to become a chartered accountant. Aim to always be at the top, and become an expert in whatever you do.

## 3. Modeling

Another way to empower people is model or demonstrate the correct behaviour that they can follow and overcome seeming insurmountable barriers. Look at what happens when a barrier is broken and a record is established. Once John Thomas broke the seven-foot high jump mark and Roger Bannister broke the four minute mile record, a host of other athletes quickly exceeded that standard. Till the barrier is broken it was considered an impossible job. "It took someone to demonstrate that the standard could be exceeded in order for others to experience the empowerment necessary to replicate the accomplishment themselves" (Whetton and Cameron) While acting as role models, managers must lead by example, by setting a shining example of exemplary character and conduct—whether in following rule, adopting operating policies, dealing with customers or putting resources to best advantage. . You cannot expect your people to work overtime, while you are relaxing on the beach. You have to treat people with respect and dignity, so that your subordinates emulate the example and treat customers well. As far as work is concerned, past examples of successful accomplishment of a difficult or hazardous job could be used to clear misunderstandings and put people on track. Above all, your people have to see you in office in order to learn from you. You cannot expect to act as their role model when you are not in the office most of the times. A manager has a responsibility to make the company grow in a positive environment. By following the company policy, being punctual, showing good leadership, being tidy, organized and enthusiastic not only will you motivate staff but you will prove yourself as someone who works hard and brings the best out of others. You will be a positive role model for others.

## 4. Providing Support

Empowerment flourishes in an environment of praise, appreciation and recognition. Managers should encourage employees through rewards, awards, incentives, recognition; express approval of them, back them, and reassure them of their full support and cooperation. Employees must feel proud to be working in a climate of trust, mutual support and cooperation. They must be encouraged to give their best and live up to their true potential. There are several ways to motivate people to peak performance and make them feel part of an organisation that supports their initiative, drive, enthusiasm and effort. A manager can write letters appreciating their effort. He can offer constructive feedback about what he liked and how performance could further be improved. He can create exciting opportunities for people to grow, putting emphasis on their creative talents. To this end, he could even tell them to go on their own putting resources to good use, the way they like—instead of monitoring everything from close quarters. Regular ceremonies could be organised to celebrate the grand success achieved by ordinary workers in the organisation. In short, he could do everything possible to make them feel like real super heroes of the organisation by announcing special rewards, awards, medals, or recognitions of various other kinds. Recognising talent, allowing people to find creative ways of doing things, picking up star performers for praise, and creating a healthy, positive environment where everyone can try out something new and come out with solutions that are different—in short, will ignite people to lead enriching, fulfilling, productive and meaningful lives. In course of time, the employees begin to develop a feeling of how invaluable their services have become for the success of the organisation.

## 5. Emotional Arousal

Emotional arousal means replacing negative emotions with positive emotions such as excitement, passion, and anticipation. To empower people, managers should help to make the work environment fun and attractive. However, emotional arousal doesn't simply mean tooting horns, listening to ceremonial speeches or artificially creating excitement through high decibel campaigns. When people do something that is connected to values that they hold dear and close to their heart, that is the result of emotional arousal. When aroused emotionally, whatever the employee does it remains close to his or her own basic beliefs. You are after all doing something worthwhile, something to live and die for, something to uplift the spirits of mankind, something to proudly showcase things that the world would love to see. Managers could increase workers' sense of empowerment by holding frequent social gatherings. This helps in building rapport and understanding between workers. Light-hearted, funny messages could be used to relieve the tension of workers. Managers can use superlatives while offering feedback to workers. Money alone does not put workers on the track. The atmosphere must be tension free and friendly. There must be excitement all around. Humour, jokes, fun and recreational activities must fill their hearts all through the day. Cheerleaders must enable workers to catch every moment of joy built around the work-spot and help them fill their lives with truckloads of excitement.

**Box 14.5 Empowerment: The Burger King Way**

Nation & World: Sunday, October 07, 2001

More than 100 members of Burger King's marketing department walked barefoot over an 8-foot strip of glowing, white-hot coals as part of a corporate bonding experience at the Ocean Reef Club in Key Largo, Fla. Firewalking was supposed to show them that by reaching beyond their limits, they could achieve things they never thought possible. Instead, about a dozen employees suffered at least first- and second-degree burns on their feet. "We certainly didn't intend for that to happen," Burger King spokesman Rob Doughty said.

One woman was taken to an emergency room Wednesday night and the company brought in a doctor to treat the others, whose feet were blistering. Some were in such pain they used wheelchairs the next day when they went to the airport to leave for another team retreat.

Everyone who participated was required to sign a waiver acknowledging there was the possibility of getting burned.

"You're walking over hot coals, and something can happen," said Robert Kallen, owner of The Achievement Group, which ran the event for Burger King. "The majority of the people get through it without a nick or a blister. When you see over 100 people and only 10 to 15 people have blisters, I don't term that unusual.

"I wish it didn't happen," said Kallen, who has been firewalking since 1992 and operates his company from Philadelphia and Miami Beach. "Some people just have incredibly sensitive feet."

Despite the injuries, Burger King executives termed the event a success.

"It was a great experience for everyone," said Dana Frydman, vice president of product marketing for Burger King and of the event. Although Frydman was injured, she has no regrets.

"It made you feel a sense of empowerment and that you can accomplish anything," said Frydman, who was in Memphis on Friday for the second half of the retreat. She said the pain in her feet had subsided. "It's really about mind over matter."

Still, Burger King said it will no longer have firewalking.

## 6. Providing Information

If we want people on the front lines of companies to be responsible for making good business decisions, they must have the same information that managers use to make good business decision. People without information cannot make good business decisions, nor are they motivated to risk making decisions in such a void. On the other hand, people with information are almost compelled to take the risk of making business decisions to the best of their abilities. If we want people to take the risk of being accountable in making important decisions, they must feel they can trust management and the organizational systems. What we have learned from experience is that sharing information is one of the most effective and simplest ways to kick start the enhancement of trust. If a leader is willing to share the power that information represents, people hear – more clearly than any words can express – that this leader is reducing the barriers and including people into the circle of influence and involvement. Another factor that pushes information sharing to the forefront of the journey to empowerment is the need people have for direction, both individually and in teams, during the early stage of the change process. Most people start the empowerment journey as enthusiastic beginners. They need a leadership style with high direction, and if they do not get it, they must feel safe enough to ask for the information and direction they need to start moving down the road to empowerment. In any organizational change effort, people initially have a variety of information concerns that need to be addressed. Information sharing at this time will help people answer these kinds of ( http://www.masetllc.com/news/pdfs/1005-1.pdf)

**Questions**

- What is the change and why is it needed?
- What is wrong with the current situation in our company?
- What exactly needs to be changed, and what outcomes must be expected?
- How much do we need to change and how fast must we change?

Addressing the information concerns that people have during this first stage of change can provide them with the direction they need to focus their energy in positive ways. Particularly, this focusing leadership style should help people understand the desired outcomes and provide them with an image of what things would look like if a culture of empowerment was realized. Information sharing helps people understand the need for change. And when people understand the need for change, they develop willingness that helps drive the process. Information sharing is the key tool to drive continuous improvement. In an empowered company, people want the ongoing challenge of getting better and better at their work. They recognize that continuous improvement is the means for keeping the company healthy and competitive. But they also recognize that it is the means for success, satisfaction and fulfilment in their jobs and careers. Information sharing is, quite simply, the lifeblood of an empowered organization. Without it, a company can never become or say fully empowered.

## 7. Providing Resources

Managers should provide the resources needed to accomplish the task. Moreover, employees should be given the training and development needed as well as the space, time and equipment required. Also, managers should ensure people have access to communication and interpersonal networks that will make their jobs easier. Finally, individuals should be given discretion to spend monies or commit resources to activities that they consider important. Empowerment is created when the manager can not only provide need-to-have resources but also some nice-to-have resources. As rightly pointed out by Whetton and Cameron, "when individuals feel that they have what they need to be successful and that they have the freedom to pursue what they want to accomplish, performance is significantly higher than when these types of resources are not available."

## 8. Connecting to Outcomes

Workers can experience more empowerment when they can see the outcomes of their work. Japanese companies routinely send teams of workers to interact with end users of products manufactured by them with a view to get valuable feedback. The interaction with end users often led to unique ideas that led to further improvements in the products that the workers produced. When workers actually saw the outcomes of their effort, and how it made an impact on the lives of end users, they felt greatly empowered. A related idea is to provide employees with the authority to resolve problems on the spot. According to Whetton and Cameron, when workers are allowed to accomplish the whole task (increase task identity—that tis the opportunity to accomplish a whole task) they would be highly motivated and satisfied. Having task identity implies that individuals can plan, implement, and evaluate the success of their efforts. The effects of what is accomplished can be assessed as well as the outcome. This, in a way, means that " If I am able to do a whole task and this has greatly enhanced the work unit's performance as a whole, I feel greatly empowered.". Clarifying the connection between individuals' work and their outcomes fosters empowerment by helping others develop a sense of self-efficacy and a sense of personal consequence.

## 9. Creating Confidence

Empowerment creates a sense of confidence among workers in the trustworthiness of the manager. When managers share information and resources, when they show the right ways of doing things, when they offer a friendly atmosphere full of fun and excitement, there is no reason for workers to turn suspicious and remain on guard. They also begin to open up, do things with confidence and face challenges head on. This kind of confidence helps drive out uncertainty, insecurity and ambiguity in the relationship between the workers and the manager. In creating a sense of confidence and trustworthiness five factors are very important:

- ***Reliability***- managers' behaviour must be consistent, dependable, and stable. Their actions should be congruent with their words and behaviours.
- ***Fairness***- managers must be fair. Managers must make clear the standards by which workers will be judged and ensure that those standards are applied in an unbiased way.
- ***Caring***- managers must show a sense of personal concern and validate the point of views of others. Caring managers focus on the mistake or the behaviour, not on the individual's personal characteristics.
- ***Openness***- managers are straightforward and honest and are open in their relationships. Others do not worry about a hidden agenda.
- ***Competence***- employees need to believe that the manager has the necessary ability, experience, and knowledge to perform tasks and solve problems.

Successful managers often do everything possible to earn the confidence of workers. by putting their heart and soul into everything they do. Their ethical behaviour, honest actions and trust worthy words and friendly moves would, in the final analysis, help them earn the trust and confidence of workers. When trust exists, workers indulge in experimentation, go that extra mile, take a few risks and do everything possible to take the organisation to commanding heights—without any fear of criticism or retribution.

## Review of Empowerment Principles

The following Table summarizes the list of actions in relation to the nine prescriptions for empowerment. Research suggests that empowered individuals are most inclined to empower others.

**Table 14.1. Empowerment Summary**

1. **Articulate a Clear Vision & Goals**
   - Clarify impact on the ultimate customer
   - Create a picture of desired future
   - Foster attributes of recreation in work: clear goals, scorekeeping, effective
   - Feedback systems, out-of-bounds behaviour
   - Use word pictures and emotional language to describe the vision
   - Identify specific targets and strategies that will lead to the vision
   - Establish smarter goals.
   - Associate vision & goals with personal values
2. **Foster Personal Mastery Experiences**
   - Break apart large tasks
   - Build history of success with simple tasks first
   - Highlight/celebrate small wins
   - Incrementally expand job responsibilities
   - Give increasing responsibility to solve problems
3. **Model Successful Behaviours**
   - Demonstrate successful task accomplishment
   - Point out others who have succeeded
   - Facilitate interaction with other role models
4. **Provide Information**
   – Provide all task-relevant information
   – Provide technical info and data
   – Provide cross-unit & functional data
   – Provide access to info/people with senior responsibility
   – Provide access to info from its source
   – Clarify effects of actions on end users
5. **Provide Resources**
   – Provide training & development
   – Provide technical and admin support

- – Provide time, space, equip, $, people
- – Ensure access to relevant information
- – Find a coach and/or mentor
- – Provide more budget authority

6. **Provide Support**
   - Praise, encourage, express approval, reassure
   - Send letters or notes to family/co-workers
   - Regularly provide feedback
   - Foster informal social activities to build cohesion
   - Supervise less closely and allow some time slack
   - Hold recognition ceremonies
7. **Connect to Outcomes**
   - Measure effort, effects and outcomes
   - Create opportunities for task identity by allowing completion of a whole task
   - Provide immediate, direct feedback
   - Directly connect with customers or other users of team's output
8. **Arouse Positive Emotions**
   - Foster activities to progress through storming stage
   - Periodically send light-hearted messages
   - Use superlatives in giving feedback
   - Highlight compatibility between personal values and organizational values, mission, purpose, goals
   - Be reliable and consistent
9. **Create Confidence**
   - Be competent and show expertise
   - Be open and honest
   - Be caring and show personal concern
   - Be fair and equitable

## Inhibitors to Empowerment

Empowerment requires consistent support and continued blessings of top management. If it is being carried out in a mechanical manner, just for the ornamental purpose, it is bound to fail. Managers have to take it seriously and invest their time, energies for bringing about a radical change in outlook of all. Giving decision making powers to others and watching the proceedings from a safe distance is not an easy task. Of course, they can always establish boundaries for empowerment so that no one tries to misuse it or exceed the brief given to them. Without such limits empowerment may not yield fruitful results. Once the limits are established managers have to provide full information to the empowered and allow them to experiment and learn from the mistakes and grow gradually. Quality decisions do not happen by chance; they happen only when there is support from 'upstairs' and the employee is fully equipped with relevant facts and necessary resources for taking informed decisions. Employees should not be elevated with a view to showcase their failures. Without the initial support and encouragement from the top, employees do not get emboldened and live up to their full potential. The whole exercise is not meant to pull them down and show to the world that managers only can deliver results and lower down the order there is no talent available. To ensure that employees feel truly empowered, at least some of the ideas and suggestions given by them have to be implemented otherwise they will end up feeling that only managers can get their ideas realised. At the same time, empowerment does not mean that managers should wash off their hands and indulge in abdication of their responsibilities. In the hands of the untrained, unprepared empowerment could prove to be a disastrous experiment. Between the two extremes, the answer lies somewhere and with experience both management and workers would be able to find who can do what and convert promises into concrete realities. (Block; Argyris) According to Whetton and Cameron, many managers and employees are reluctant to accept empowerment, but they are even more reluctant to offer empowerment. One reason for this is the personal attitudes of managers. Reasons offered in opposition to empowerment can be classified into three board categories: attitudes about subordinates, personal insecurities, and need for control.

## Attitudes about Subordinates

Some managers are reluctant to empower subordinates because they are obsessed with negative thoughts and feelings about the capabilities and competencies of their own subordinates. They have a feeling that their subordinates are::

- Not competent enough to accomplish the work
- Aren't interested in taking more responsibility
- Are already overloaded and unable to accept more responsibility
- Would require too much time to train
- Shouldn't be involved in tasks typically performed by the boss

## Personal Insecurities

Some managers visualise a threat in empowering others fully. Empowerment results in loss of power, dilution of their authority, sharing of secrets that could put them in a spot and so on and so forth. They are gripped by the fear that they would certainly lose those rewards that come with successful task accomplishments—if they empower others. The reasons for such insecure feelings could be traceable to the following:

- Managers' fear of losing power or their position
    - Managers have an intolerance for ambiguity
    - Managers prefer to work on the task by themselves
    - Managers are unwilling to absorb the costs associated with subordinates making mistakes

In sum, these managers' rationale is "I'm willing to empower people, but when I do, they either mess things up or try to grab all the glory".

## Need for Control

Managers who are reluctant to empower others have a pronounced desire to be in control of everything. After all they are finally accountable for results. So why invite trouble by handing over the baton to some one who is not fully prepared, fully trained, not as experienced as I am and not as fully competent as I am. As a manager," I need to oversee everything from close quarters and be ready to answer all questions. The subordinates can never math my skills, can never be sure of what is going on and will never be able to receive the brickbats when the time comes." They have a feeling that direction from 'upstairs' is the name of the game and is absolutely essential to ensure success at every stage .They also point out the fact that innovative ideas such as work teams, suggestion systems, job enrichment programs, and other fix-it activities have been tried in the past and none of these types of programs worked.

## Delegating work

All managers are necessarily compelled to share work with others, because they cannot accomplish results doing everything under the earth. Therefore, they have to delegate a portion of their work to subordinates, establishing certain broad limits within which the subordinates could operate. It all depends on how empowered the subordinate is in carrying out a task. Delegation normally refers to the assignment of a task. It is work-focused. Empowerment may involve nonwork activities, emotions, and relationships. Empowerment involves the way people think about themselves. Therefore, empowered delegation is a means by which managers can assign a task while simultaneously empowering employees. A competent delegator who can simultaneously empower others has several important advantages for managers. Table 8.6 outlines the advantages of empowered delegation as:

- The manager gains more discretionary time.
- Subordinates gain more capabilities and knowledge, thereby increasing their effectiveness.
- Demonstrates trust and confidence.
- Enhances worker commitment.
- Improves the quality of decision making by involving more people.
- Enhances efficiency and timeliness of decisions
- Improves coordination of work.

When competently administered, empowered delegation can produce all five dimensions of empowerment: a sense of competence, choice, impact, value, and security. Empowerment and delegation must be linked in the accomplishment of work. All aspects of delegation are being discussed in the next chapter in greater detail.

## CONDITIONS NECESSARY FOR EMPOWERMENT

There are four basic conditions necessary for empowerment to gain credibility and acceptance at various levels in an organisation. These are discussed below (JH Dobbs, 1993).

a. ***Participation:*** Workers must be encouraged to take the initiative. To this end, the bureaucratic hurdles that come in the way must be removed. Proper training should be given to employees so that they can participate more actively and make things happen.

b. ***Innovation:*** Management must encourage employees to try out new ideas and make decisions that help in finding new and improved ways of doing things. Even when employees fail in their attempts to break the mould of custom, the words of encouragement must come the same way, so that they begin to feel that failures are stepping stones to success. One day, with such a supportive management, they are sure to ride the tidal wave of success.

c. ***Information:*** Employees must have free access to information and resources that they need to nurture their talents. If they need additional training in putting the classified information to use, it should be offered readily.

d. ***Accountability:*** Empowered employees should be held accountable for results. This step is not intended to identify their black spots and single them out for punishment. The intent, instead, is to see that they are giving their best efforts, working toward mutually-agreed goals and behaving responsibly towards each other. When employees exhibit such behaviours, they are encouraged to go the same way at their own 'comfortable pace'.

A wide variety of companies, nowadays have undertaken interventions to empower employees at various levels, such as quality circles, autonomous work groups quality of work life councils, etc. These are discussed briefly in the next section.

**Table 14.2. What managers could do to empower employees?**

- Actions must speak louder than words: Managers play a pivotal role in the empowerment process. They must be committed to allow employees morc decision-making powers though they may like to define the scope of it. Managers must also be willing to give up control on some aspects. As team leaders, managers must convey through their words, expressions and body language how much they value each team member and respect them for their contribution. They should let them know about the mission, vision and goals of the organisation. They should share with them strategic plans so that they feel they are a part of it and can contribute to its achievement.
- Trust people: Managers should learn to trust their people to do the right thing and make the correct choice, because when they have trust and confidence in their employees, they will be willing to empower them. Though the employees may not be able to always make precise decisions, the manager should accept them with the optimism that they may still work.
- Give challenging work: Empowerment also means delegation and managers must be careful not to pass on only the regular work but give them exciting and challenging work and make them part of important meetings and decisions. They should also provide constant feedback so that the team knows how they are doing. It is also one way of acknowledging their good work.
- Seek answers from employees: When employees come up with problems, instead of readily giving them a solution, managers should ask them on the possible solutions. Empowering employees is presuming that employees know how to solve problems and giving them enough freedom to do so. They should not be told how to do things but rather allowed to do it on their own.

- Allow employees to play a bigger role: However, many managers are reluctant to empower their subordinates thinking it will undermine their own authority. They may believe that employees are not competent enough to take independent decisions. Such managers should be assured that their responsibilities are not decreasing but are changing. They can also be given a bigger role in the performance evaluation of their team to alleviate the feeling of insecurity.
- Make employees feel that they are the real owners: An empowerment initiative will succeed only if employees start feeling a sense of ownership to the company and have the power to make a positive change. When employees are confident in the knowledge that they are important to the success of the business and the management has complete trust in them, they are ready to put their heart and soul into work. The result is happy and productive employees who will lead the organisation to success. (Hema Gopalakrishnan, Participative management indicates employee empowerment" Feb 18, 2009, The Hindu)

## MOTIVATING EMPLOYEES THROUGH PARTICIPATIVE SCHEMES

The word 'participation' means sharing the decision-making power with the lower ranks of the organisation in an appropriate manner. Participation has a unique motivational power and a great psychological value. It promotes harmony and peace between workers and management. When workers participate in organisational decisions, they are able to see the big picture clearly, i.e., how their actions would contribute to overall growth of the company. They can offer feedback immediately based on their experiences and improve the quality of decisions significantly. Since they are involved in the decisions from the beginning, they tend to view the 'decisions' as 'their own' and try to translate the rhetoric into concrete action plans with zeal and enthusiasm. Participation makes them more responsible. They are willing to take initiative and contribute cost-saving suggestions and growth-oriented ideas. The feeling of being treated as equals, forces them to repose their confidence in management and accept plans of rationalisation, expansion, etc., without raising serious objections. Since they are treated with respect now, they begin to view the job and the organisation as their own and commit themselves to organisational activities wholeheartedly. Bilateral decisions help in bringing out radical changes in organisational systems, plans and procedures more easily. Employees do not feel threatened by such moves, as they understand and appreciate the reasons behind such 'strategic shifts'. (Mhetras; Virmani)

The implications of workers' participation in management have been summarised by the International Labour Organisation thus:

- workers have ideas which can be useful.
- upward communication facilitates sound decision making. Workers may accept decisions better if they participate in them.
- workers may work more intelligently if they are informed about the reasons for and the intention of decisions that are taken in a participative atmosphere.
- workers may work harder if they share in decisions that affect them.
- workers participation may foster a more cooperative attitude amongst workers and

management thus raising efficiency by improving team spirit and reducing the loss of efficiency arising from industrial disputes.

- workers participation may act as a spur to managerial efficiency.

## PARTICIPATION: Definition and Objectives

The concept of workers' participation in management (WPM) is a broad and complex one. Depending on the socio-political environment and cultural conditions, the scope and contents of participation may change. In any case, a common thread running through all interpretations is the idea of associating employees in managerial decision-making. The view expressed by The International Institute for Labour Studies (Bulletin 5) is worth quoting here. WPM has been defined as, "the participation resulting from practices which increase the scope for employee's share of influence in decision-making at different tiers of organisational hierarchy with concomitant assumption of responsibility".( Sheth; Tarie)

In the words of Gosep, workers' participation may be viewed as:

- an instrument for increasing the efficiency of enterprises and establishing harmonious industrial relations;
- a device for developing social education for promoting solidarity among workers and for tapping human talent;
- a means for achieving industrial peace and harmony which leads to higher productivity and increased production;
- a humanitarian act, elevating the status of a worker in the society;
- an ideological way of developing self-management and promoting industrial democracy.

The major **objectives** of the scheme of workers' participation are:

- to improve the quality of working life by allowing the workers greater influence and involvement in work and the satisfaction obtained from work; and
- to secure the mutual cooperation of employees and employers in achieving industrial peace; greater efficiency and productivity in the interest of the enterprise, the workers, the consumers and the nation.

Participation has a *tonic effect* on the psychology of a worker. He develops of sense of belongingness, a feeling of togetherness, a feeling of being a member of a large family. It gives him a sense of importance, pride and accomplishment. He begins to express his thoughts, opinions and feelings openly without any fear. He gets an opportunity to mingle and exchange notes with others on various on the job and off the job related matters. He gets a platform for meaningful interaction and democratic exchange of notes. When he begins to think that he has a stake in the company and all other co workers have a common purpose to achieve, his devotion to work would improve and he will commit himself to the task on hand with greater motivation and commitment.

Workers participation should, however, be distinguished from collective bargaining. Collective bargaining is essentially based on power-play, pressure tactics and to a certain extent non-sharing of information whereas participative management is based on mutual trust, joint sharing of information and mutual problem-solving.

## Forms of Participation

The word 'participation' is a glamorous term. Workers welcome it because it enhances their status in the company. Employers use it to exhibit how 'progressive' they are. Unions want it because it brings about a new power equation between labour and management. Irrespective of these interpretations, participation is welcomed at all levels, because it has a 'tonic effect' on the psychology of an individual. The term 'workers' participation' in management, is generally interpreted in four different ways:

i. It is a way of sharing information with workers. Management keeps the workers informed about what is going on within the organisation. The final decisions are taken by the management. Workers are allowed to express their opinions regarding various organisational matters.

ii. It is joint consultation prior to decision-making. Workers are taken into confidence, invited to share the information, participate in discussions, suggest alternatives to solve an issue and enjoy a greater say in the decision-making process.

iii. Mere sharing of information and influencing decisions through discussions in a limited way will not enhance the status of workers. To be meaningful, participation should mean active involvement of workers, where they are treated as members of a decision-making team with equal voting rights. It is a kind of joint decision-making where workers are formally involved in resolving work – related issues.

iv. In the final analysis, workers' participation may involve workers in all strategic, policy and operational issues, treating them as active members or even partners with equal voting rights. Workers' participation here implies self management or self control.

Mhetras (1966) while reviewing the progress of joint management councils of thirteen enterprises belonging to different industries spread over in eight states identified five levels of participation. Box 14.6 reveals the picture more clearly:

**Box 14.6: Five Interpretations of Participation: Mhetras'**

***Informative participation:*** It refers to sharing of information with workers regarding economic position of the firms, state of the market, production and sales programme, work methods, balance sheet, expansion plans, etc. Here the workers have no right to scrutinise the information provided by management.

***Consultative participation:*** This involves a higher degree of sharing of views of the workers and giving them a chance to express their views on various issues concerning work, workplace, working conditions, market standing, financial status, etc. Here the joint council of workers and management works as an advisory body only. Management may or may not accept the suggestions.

***Associative participation:*** Here the council is not purely advisory. The management is under a moral obligation to accept and implement the unanimous decisions of the council.

***Administrative participation:*** Here there is a greater degree of sharing authority and responsibility of managerial work, allowing workers a little more autonomy in exercising administrative and supervisory powers in respect of welfare, safety, benefits, rewards, etc.

***Decisive participation:*** This is the highest form of participation where decisions are taken jointly on matters relating to production, safety, welfare, etc.

In view of these different views it is difficult to define the term. It can only be described as a system of communication and consultation where workers are kept informed about the affairs of the undertaking and through which they express their opinions and contribute to management decisions.1

**Box 14.7 Participation Has A Tonic Effect on the Psychology of Workers?**

Participation cuts at the very root of industrial conflict. It tries to put an end to conflicting interests between the parties by substituting it with cooperation, homogeneity and common interests. Both labour and management begin to look at ways and means to put out fires, realise the importance of reaching organisational targets and share the fruits of progress. Participation improves behavioural climate and enthuses workers to work with zeal, enthusiasm and commitment. Participation allows the individual worker to assert himself and find meaning in the work place. He begins to take pride in what he does. If an individual knows that he can express his opinions, feelings and thoughts freely, a personal sense of gratification and involvement develops from within. Information sharing takes place at a broader level and the quality of decisions, too, certainly improves. When everyone participates and the ideas are being tossed around freely and discussed thoroughly, everyone begins to feel the responsibility. They now understand the reasons behind every move and begin to feel a sense of commitment and responsibility. After all they have to deliver what they have promised in a group setting. Consequently, the resistance to change is reduced quite dramatically!

## How to ensure effective participation?

In order to make workers' participation in management a success, certain conditions should be satisfied:

***Managerial attitude:*** There is an urgent need to offer training and education to workers and employees to make the participative culture a success. The employers should be willing to share information and shed a portion of their hard-earned authority in favour of workers. Workers are uninformed and lack experience. The employers, therefore must make conscious efforts to bring them up to a certain level before drawing them to the negotiating table. To earn their respect and trust, management must involve workers by: (1) identifying a clear cut agenda where the roles of participants are clearly defined, (2) developing guidelines for decision-making by the joint management councils, (3) defining the roles of office bearers as against trade unions, (4) Keeping employees informed of all decisions arrived at, their implementation and the outcomes and (5) evaluating the progress of joint councils from time to time.

***Union cooperation:*** The workers participation scheme, to be effective, must be based on mutual trust and confidence between unions and management. Unions must believe that participative forums are not meant to cut their roots. To this end, management must try to define the boundaries clearly. To be fair, they must give due representation to members from the recognised union without playing favourites. In a multiple union situation, this issue assumes added significance in that the employer can influence the election of representatives to the participative forums by aligning with their own 'yes men' from the ranks and file. Not all unions agree now to the election of representatives through secret ballot (INTUC opposes this; HMS, CITU, AITUC support the move)

**Meaningful participation:** If participation relates to only tea, towels and toilets as the Indian experience clearly shows – it does not serve any purpose. To be useful, participation should cover a wide range of issues where workers can openly represent their cases and seek quick solutions on the spot. Further, the participative forums should not be mere consultative and advisory bodies, dealing with peripheral, insignificant, routine issues relating to labour welfare. Workers must have a real 'say' in all important work-related matters including grievance handling and then only will they begin to participate in these participative bodies with zeal and enthusiasm.

**Workers' attitudes:** Workers must have complete faith in the efficiency of the system. To encourage a participative culture among workers, seminars, conferences, workshops must be held highlighting the usefulness of participation. Workers must have a sense of job security and freedom from reprisals resulting from their participation. The overall working environment must be congenial enough to inspire the workers to give of their best to the organisation.

**Table 14.3. Pre-requisites for the success of workers participation in management**

- **The overall climate** in the organisation should be favourable to workers' participation. There should be an attitude of mutual co-operation, confidence, and respect for each other. Management, in particular, should be genuinely receptive to the labor's ideas so that the latter can perceive that their ideas are useful.
- There must be **sufficient time to participate** before action is required; because participation in emergent situations is hardly advisable.
- The **subject of participation** must be relevant to the enterprise; it must concern something in which both the parties are interested, otherwise the parties are likely to become indifferent to the process of participation.
- The workers' representatives should have the **ability** such as intelligence and knowledge, to participate. It is not appropriate to ask workers to participate in technical aspects of the machinery; but they can participate successfully in problems relating to their work. The contributions made by the workers should be worthwhile and should benefit the workers in the long run. It should be in the interest of the management as well! Now maintaining that balance is not that easy but that is what experience is all about!!
- There must be **effective system of communication**. Both labor's representatives and management's representatives must be able to understand each other and express themselves without any inhibitions. The whole idea after all is to be able to speak out one's mind and listen to the counterpart's point of view!
- Participation **should not adversely affect the status or authority** of the participants. Managers will not participate, if their authority is threatened. Workers will hesitate in participating if they think that their status is being adversely affected. In fact for worker's participation to be effective, both the management and the labour should get rid of their ego problems and share their ideas. In fact, no relationship can continue for long if there are ego clashes. Both the parties should make efforts to come closer rather than moving away.
- The **financial cost of participation** should always be lesser than the benefits-both economic and non-economic-of participation. We all can understand the economic aspect but as far

as the non-economic part is concerned, it will depend on the organisations. What I can tell you at this point of time is that the pains and pleasures should be matched! The pleasures should be much more as compared to the pains.

- Participation should be **within the framework of overall policy** of the enterprise. Every decision has to be in line with the Vision and Mission statements of the organisation. (www.thecodexpert.com)

## Indian Experiences

In some of the organisations, the scheme of workers' participation in management (WPM) has proved to be a 'hit'. Let us briefly examine these experience. (Saraf; Sahu)

***TISCO:*** In 1982 TISCO celebrated the first silver jubilee of workers participation scheme. Right from its inception, TISCO firmly believed in achieving success through employee involvement and participation in organisational work. To regulate employer-employee relations, two forums are consistently put to use; i.e., wage related issues through collective bargaining forum and safety, welfare, working conditions, cost saving efforts, etc., through participative forum. Since 1957, WPM at TISCO has been functioning at three levels – Joint Departmental Council (JDC), Joint Worker Councils (JWC) and Joint Consultative Council. There are over 40 joint-departmental councils operating at the base level – one to discuss production and productivity related issues and another to discuss safety and welfare matters. The Joint Worker Councils review the working of JDCs and likewise the Joint Consultative Councils review the functioning of JDCs and JWCs, at periodic intervals. These councils consist of representatives of labour and management in equal number. WPM has succeeded in TISCO because the management stood behind the scheme firmly right from the beginning. The presence of a single, strong union has also created a congenial atmosphere for improving relations between labour and management greatly. Management has created special task forces to oversee that the councils' functions do not overlap. Special training is being offered to prepare workers for participative 'give and take' sessions. Spurred by these encouraging initiatives, workers have also come out with highly useful, cost-saving suggestions arrived at improving overall productivity from time to time. Generally over 70 per cent of these suggestions are actually implemented with great success!

**BHEL:** In 1966, BHEL, Tiruchirapalli had no single union, several splinter groups existed. A works committee was formed consisting of elected representatives of workers and management. The committee functioned quite successfully integrating the units' activities with the larger interests of the community. In 1978, BHEL, Bhopal introduced the Management Employees' Communication Meeting (MECOMs) which has become an answer to the prime need of employee expression. BHEL has also pioneered the quality circle movement in India in 1981. It has multifarious quality circles now covering a large number of employees, undertaking and implementing quality improvement programmes from time to time.

**Maruti:** Right from inception in 1981, the top management at Maruti realised the importance of treating workers as human assets. To promote a healthy work climate, Maruti had undertaken several pioneering initiatives:

- Minimise distinctions between employees.

- Encourage teamwork and employee involvement in quality circles, transfers, etc.
- Hold regular meetings with unions to clarify matters.
- Free and fair exchange of facts, information, opinions at various levels.
- Encourage employees to advance suggestions and reward the practicable suggestions immediately.
- Employee participation in equity, etc.

## REVIEW QUESTIONS

1. "Empowerment means providing freedom for people to do successfully what they want to do, rather than getting them to do what you want them to do" Explain through examples.
2. Why do managers hesitate to empower their subordinates? How can managers be encouraged to practice empowerment more freely—in the larger interests of an organisation?
3. Write short notes on the following:
   - self efficacy
   - self determination
   - modelling
   - emotional arousal
4. Briefly explain the fundamental principles of empowerment.
5. In what ways managers could empower their employees?
6. Explain what you mean by empowerment, delegation and power clearly. Why do you think empowerment is needed to get effective and efficient results from subordinates?
7. Do you think empowerment is the essence of managerial effectiveness? Why or why not?
8. In the midst of rules, routines and traditions that often come in the way of empowerment, explain how modern organisations can practice empowerment?

## CRITICAL THINKING QUESTIONS

9. "With more information, people tend to experience more self determination, personal control and trust" Is this true? Why or why not?
10. Why do a majority of people, in most organisations, feel that they alienated from their work, unengaged and not flourishing? What can be done to overcome such sinking feelings and thoughts?
11. Participation In India has not been a resounding success. Do you agree? Why or why not?
12. What steps should be taken by management in order to encourage participation of employees in decision making at all levels

## CASE STUDY: Smart Beginning

Miss Kalyani hails from a sophisticated family. She is twenty-three year old and will be receiving her M.A. degree from Bhopal University at the end of this semester. She has spent the past two summers working for a large dress-making company STYLES, designing clothes for women while the permanent employees of the organisation took their vacations. Having undergone training in USA for about six months when her father was posted there, she had no problems in designing clothes for women and her designs were appreciated and readily accepted by both management and customers. It is small wonder, then, that she has received and accepted an offer to join STYLES on a permanent basis upon her post graduation, as a chief designer in the design department.

STYLES is a large dress-making company taking care of the development of latest designs for gents, ladies and children in Madhya Pradesh. In the headquarters office (Bhopal) alone, where Miss Kalyani will be working, they employ 800 employees. The company believes strongly in the personal development of all its employees and takes every care to meet employee expectations.

The job Kalyani will be assuming requires her to direct the activities of 12 designers. Their job requires a certain amount of training so as to develop attractive designs for women and children. Their designs have to be approved by the chief designer before they see the light of day.

Kalyani's group is composed of all females ranging from 19 to 50 years of age, with a median of 23. For the most part they have high school education, well-supported by a certificate in dress designing awarded by a reputed design institute in Madhya Pradesh. The salary range is Rs 800-3000 per month. Miss Kalyani will be replacing a long time employee, Mrs Vanaja, who is retiring after 27 years with Styles, the last fourteen years as a chief designer. Since Kalyani had spent a few weeks in Styles group last summer with most of the group members, she expected no problems from any of her soon-to-be employees, except possibly from Mrs Vimal. Mrs Vimal was well into her fifties, had been a designer for over a dozen years, and as the 'grand old lady' carried a lot of weight with group members. Miss Kalyani concluded that without Vimal's support her job could prove very difficult.

Miss Kalyani is determined to get her career off on the right foot. As a result, she has been working hard on how to win over Vimal and other group members.

## Questions

1. What strategies do you advise Kalyani to pursue?
2. What if, Vimal revolts along with her teammates?

# 15

# MANAGING ACROSS CULTURES

## HOW TO MANAGE RESOURCES IN A GLOBAL WORLD

The world is shrinking in all major respects. People, goods, capital and information are moving around the globe like never before with faster communication, transportation and financial flow, the barriers between nations have disappeared and the world is becoming a borderless market. In the 21st century, global companies seem to virtually dance all over the place. They are not constrained by national borders. BMW builds cars in South Carolina. McDonald's sells hamburgers in China. Coca Cola has over 80 percent of its sales outside of its home market. Nestle has 50 per cent, Proctor and Gamble 65 per cent and Avon 60 per cent. They source and coordinate resources and activities in the most suitable areas, to offer cost-effective products and services to customers all over the globe. Businesses can hire, source and sell wherever they want now. For many of these global corporations, with the entire world as a market, national boundaries have become virtually irrelevant. It is not without reason that IBM dropped its organisational structure based on country and reorganised into 14 industry groups. In a border-less world, success in business increasingly depends upon offering products and services that are competitive on a world basis, not just on a local basis. If the price and quality of a firm's products and services are not competitive with those available elsewhere in the world, the firm might be racing towards extinction. Global competition, whether you accept or not, has become a reality in all but the most remote corners of the world.

**Box 15.1 Clearing the fog**

**Domestic Company:** A domestic business acquires essentially all of its resources and sells all of its products or services within a single country (e.g. Hindustan Times).

**Multinational corporation:** It has significant operations in two or more countries simultaneously but are based in one home country

**Transnational corporation:** It maintains significant operations in more than one country simultaneously and decentralizes decision making in each operation to the local country.

**Global Corporation:** A global business is one that transcends national boundaries (stateless, boundaryless firm) and is not committed to a single home country. it has a management structure in which internal arrangements that impose artifical geographic barriers are broken down.

**Globalism:** It refers to global competition characterized by networks of international linkages that bind countries, institutions and people in an interdependent global economy.

**Global management:** It is the process of developing strategies, designing and operating systems and working with people around the world to ensure sustained competitive advantage.

## OPPORTUNITIES

Globalisation offers numerous opportunities in terms of market size, revenues and profits. But only for those companies that are able to adapt to local laws, customs, traditions, cultures and get along smoothly. A global company may have to incur heavy losses, if mistakes occur due to ignorance, negligence or over confidence. For example Coca-Cola had to withdraw its two-litre bottle in Spain after discovering that few Spaniards owned refrigerators with large enough compartments to accommodate it. Hallmark cards failed when they were introduced in France. The French dislike syrupy sentiment and prefer writing their own cards. Without the global thrust, therefore, business would be easier and safer. United Airlines discovered that even colours can doom a product. The airline branded out white carnations when it started flying from Hong Kong, only to discover that to many Asians such flowers represent death and bad luck. The factors that compel corporations to undertake a global journey may be listed thus:

***Homogeneity of Demand:*** Factors such as the rising income levels, growing awareness of new products and services available in other countries, fascination toward items that are not available in domestic markets (luxury cars, tennis rackets, cellular phones) have compelled many a firm to look at international markets quite seriously. They are forced, in away, to realize the fact that people's desires for products and services are becoming steadily more homogeneous. Homogeneity of demand means that irrespective of where customers are physically located, buyers are likely to prefer the same kind of product or service with certain similar characteristics. Where tastes, preferences, desires for a certain product converge – manufacturers find a great opportunity to come out with products that would meet the expectations of customers world wide (e.g. Sony Walkman, Hollywood movies, Nokia's Cellular phones, Levi's jeans, soft drinks such as Coke and Pepsi etc.).

***Spread Research and Development Costs:*** Firms in industries that face escalating R&D costs, are compelled to spread their operations globally. Commercial air craft manufacturers, for example, are forced to secure orders from different national airlines before building a single place (a new model or line of air craft could suck up to $4 billion!). The large markets provided by international expansion are attractive in other cases also (e.g. computer hardware, biotechnology, electronics, medical equipment, fibre optics, semiconductors) because they expand the opportunity to recover a large capital investment and large scale R&D expenditures.

***Increased Market Size:*** Firms can expand the size of their potential market, quite dramatically, by moving into global markets. Faced with limited growth opportunities in their home-country, soft drink manufacturers such as Coca-Cola and Pepsi have entered the international arena to take advantage of new growth opportunities. Over 80 per cent of Coke's revenues come from overseas markets (mostly Asia) now. Coke's strategic mission speaks about placing the soft drink "within an arm's reach of desire" no matter where the customer might be. The secret behind Coca-Cola's enormous popularity and market success lies in the company's continuous desire to innovate new products and enter new markets, no matter how prohibitive they may seen initially. Thus, Benetton decided to expand outside its European base because it had a firm belief that its brand value could be extended to other geographic markets. Likewise, Wal-mart's market in the United States became saturated; it sought to apply its competitive cost advantage to distributing branded products to Latin America and Asia.

***Rising Economies of Scale:*** Firms need a large customer base to achieve economies of scale. Global markets offer exciting opportunities for firms to exploit the latent demand there and expand their production volumes to profitable levels. For example Japanese automakers such as Toyota, Honda, Nissan are able to penetrate international markets, offer their products at commercial prices (due to economies of scale and experience curve effects) and maintain their low cost position, compared to their rivals, quite successfully.

***Favourable Government Policies:*** Support from the government in the form of subsidies, preferential tax treatment, export incentives could spur domestic firms to expand their operations globally. Generous loans, subsidies etc. have helped South Korean firms such as Samsung, Daewoo, and Lucky – Goldstar (LG) to invest huge sums in new technology and build global-sized plants for export. Low corporate and personal tax rates generally encourage an inflow of capital. Ireland and Puerto Rico offer two compelling examples. Each offers corporate tax rates that are considerably lower than those in many industrialized nations and has attracted considerable foreign direct investment as a result.

***Exploit Local Advantages:*** One of the important reasons that have prompted many firms to beyond their national boundaries is the prevalence of low-cost labour and resources in various parts of the world. Countries such as India, Taiwan and Israel are becoming important engineering, manufacturing, and development centres for key skills such as software and computer design. Availability of cheap labour, cheap land prices, low energy costs etc. in countries such as China, India, Indonesia and other South-east Asian countries has encouraged many Japanese, Korean and American companies to build factories there. The resultant savings in costs would help such firms to compete quite effectively in international markets.

## RISKS

Globalization, thus, can help a multinational company achieve numerous benefits. The MNC can overcome the limits of domestic growth (maturing, stagnating, slowing down etc). It can develop new insights, identify new product opportunities and exploit them profitably. It can recover the huge investments needed for new products and processes quickly. It can build a powerful image world-wide. It can learn from new markets and transfer the knowledge so gained within the firm. However, globalization is a double–edged sword. Coordinating operations across multifarious markets may be difficult. There could be several other factors impacting the firm's operations negatively (Kotler).

***Failure to Understand Foreign Customer Preferences:*** The MNC may not understand foreign customer preferences and fail to offer a completely attractive product. For example, take the case of Wal-mart which made significant mistakes in some Latin American countries. Wat-mart executives learned that giant parking lots do not draw large numbers of customers in a country where the shoppers do not have autos. The lots were so far away from the bus stops used by many Mexicans for travelling and shopping that potential customers did not come to Wal-mart stores because they could not easily get their goods home. Wal-mart committed another blunder of stocking its shelves with footballs in Brazil where soccer rules. By failing to do its homework properly, Wal-mart lost nearly $50 million. Perhaps most damaging was the company's insistence on doing things 'the Wal-mart Way' (bringing stock-holding equipment that did not work with standardized local pallets in Latin America, installing a computerized book keeping system that didn't take Brazil's complicated tax system etc.) has alienated some local suppliers and employees. In the end the company had to pay a lot of tuition to learn what it had to learn. Wal-mart encountered difficulties in translating the warehouse club concept to Hong Kong. As a young accountant eyed a 4-pound jar of peanut butter, he said "the price is right, but where would I put it?" or take another example. When Coors Beer tried to translate a slogan with the phrase, "Turn it Loose" into Spanish, it came out as 'Drink Coors and Get Diarrhea!" (The New Mexican) .

***Failure to Appreciate the Level, Intensity and Complexity of Competition in Global Markets:*** MNCs that are used to a highly competitive domestic market experience more complexities in international markets. Caused not only by the number of competitors encountered but also by the differences among those competitors. For instance a US firm venturing into a European country may have to live with competition from European, Asian, Latin American, African, Australian firms. Firms from some of these countries may have low labour costs, others may have easy access to financing and low capital costs and still others may have access to new, high technology. Adapting to the vast differences in the way these firms act and react is not an easy job (Hitt).

***Failure to Understand Host Country's Rules of the Game:*** The MNC may fail to understand the host country's business culture or does not know how to deal effectively with foreign nationals. It may underestimate foreign regulations and incur heavy costs. Host governments have myriad laws concerning libel statutes, consumer protection, information and labeling, employment, safety and wages. Global firms must learn these and regulations and abide by them. When it first established operations in China, Anheuser Busch was unaware that employers were required to provide employees with lunch. When it provided lunch, the firm was startled to find that many more people were eating at the plant than were working there (an accepted informal norm there!). If managers lack requisite skills to counter threats from political, economic and legal forces in the host country, the firm may be out of the business scene completely. For example in Mexico city government inspectors made a surprise visit to Wal-mart's safer centre and charged that more than 10,000 of the store items were improperly labeled or lacked instructions in Spanish (Daft).

***Failure to Understand Political Risks:*** Another frequently cited problem for international firms is political instability which includes riots, revolutions, civil disorders and frequent changes in government. Civil wars and large-scale violence have taken place in Malaysia, Thailand, Sri Lanka and Indonesia. Companies moving into former Soviet Republics have faced continued instability due to changing government personal policies and political philosophies. Violent protests have occurred in several cities in India against Kentucky Fried Chicken in the recent past. Foreign Managers in Russia are under constant attack and they often keep bodyguards for protecting their lives (Ron Kainen).

## COMPLEXITIES IN GLOBAL OPERATIONS

Managing a global corporation in the 21st century could be truly challenging. Global operations have:

- More functions
- More heterogeneous functions
- More involvement in the employee's personal life
- More complex external influences, such as from societies and governments
- More cultural differences (with completely different languages, foods, values, beliefs and ways of doing things).
- Different approaches to management, since the population of expatriates and locals varies

**Box 15.2 Types of organisation members found in global corporations**

- ***Host country nationals (HCNs):*** Also called local nationals, they are the employees from the local population. A worker from Bihar employed by an American firm operating in India would be considered a host country national.
- ***Parent or home country nationals (PCNs):*** Also called expatriates, they are the people sent from the country in which the organisation is headquartered. An American manager on assignment in India is an expatriate.
- ***Third country nationals (TCNs):*** TCNs are from a country other than where the parent organisations' headquarters or operations are located. If the American firm employs a manager from Great Britain at facilities in India, he would be considered a third country national

Organisations that operate in the global marketplace often employ all three types of employees. The use of host country nationals, however, is increasing because they are usually the least expensive to employ. They need not be relocated or undergo training in the culture, language or tax laws of the country where the company carries out its operations. Both expatriates and third country nationals, on the other hand, would have to be relocated and undergo training relating to local languages, customs, traditions, business norms and practices etc.

## INTERNATIONAL OB: MANAGING ACROSS CULTURES

*International OB describes and explains behaviour in cross-cultural and geographically-dispersed organisations located anywhere, in any part of the globe.* Though there is **McDonaldization** of the globe—that the cultures of the world are relentlessly and inevitably becoming more similar—some important cultural differences can not be wished away. As countries get industrialized, modernized and globalized slowly but steadily, the way we study, understand and interpret cultural differences may also change. There are solid economic arguments, as indicated previously, backing up the movement of capital, resources, and jobs to low cost countries in recent times. The knowledge of other cultures and the behaviour in their organisations certainly helps a global company to move ahead with confidence. It can profit through collaborations and strategic alliances with local outfits, exploiting local resources and enjoying significant cost benefits. It can facilitate borrowing ideas from other cultures to improve organisational performance. (Francesco and Gold 2006)

**Box 15.3 Exodus of jobs to India and China**

- 3.15 million (U.S) jobs, according to Forrester Research will be lost in service sector offshore outsourcing by 2015 and third world countries would be the biggest beneficiaries of this overseas exodus. Well educated, skilled and English speaking programmer from India, for example, would deliver results at about $20,000 a year compared to $80,000 per year payable in USA. Over 100,000 people work for Intel, Dell, IBM, Yahoo and AOL in Bangalore, India in chip design, software call centres and tax processing offering significant cost savings to companies in USA. In China—the world's low cost manufacturing hub—jobs are on the upswing for back office support for financial services and for telecom and retail companies in Asia. Such employees communicate to people in Hong Kong and Taiwan in local languages
- Toy companies such as Mattel and Hasbro have significant production operations in China where the average worker earns US $120 per month. Such low labour costs enable these companies to offer high quality toys at low cost. (Forrester Research Report; and J. Fox "Where your Job Is Going?" Fortune, Novmber 24, 2003)

The next decade will see most companies operate in a boundaryless global market arena Communications will be instantaneous, placing a premium on information. Governments will be forced to democratize everything so as to catch up with the rest of the world. Businesses will be compelled to think about profits, efficiency and growth all the time. Highly skilled labour will be available in many parts of the world. New competition can threaten the very survival of a company at any time, from anywhere in the world. Accordingly, managers must think globally if their organisations are to flourish in the long run. They must face the challenges posed by globalisation head on and be able to work with individuals from diverse cultures.

**Box 15.4 Attributes of the Global Manager**

A global manager has the international awareness and cultural sensitivity required to work well across national boundaries. Often multilingual, the global manager thinks with a world view, appreciates diverse beliefs, values, behaviours and practices and is able to map strategy accordingly.(Schermerhorn, Hunt, Osborn)

- Adapts well to different business environments
- Respects different beliefs, values and practices
- Solves problems quickly in new circumstances

- Communicates well with people from different cultures
- Speaks more than one language
- Understands different government and political systems
- Conveys respect and enthusiasm when dealing with others
- Possesses high technical expertise for a job.

## CULTURE AND INTERNATIONAL OB

One of the important challenges for organisations is preparing people to be expatriate employees working in a nation other than their home country. Without this preparation, such employees may not be able to take on and successfully complete an overseas assignment. As an example, let us see how people behave in the Arab world. Arabs talk with their hands and with profuse facial expressions. When talking, Arabs stand much closer together; kissing on the cheeks is the common way for men to greet each other; they use right hand always for public matters (the left hand, considered the 'toilet hand', should not be used for giving or accepting anything from the other person) and they always insist on a personal, one-to-one meeting for concluding deals. In such meetings, foreigners should be careful to present their business cards, printed in both Arabic and English, with the Arabic side face up. Westerners should accept offers of hospitality to visit an Arab's home and the invitation must be returned. No alcohol should be offered to Arab guests, or consumed in their presence. Arabs are habitually late for appointments (like Indians) as they believe that such things are in the hands of Allah (they call it insha-Allah ;) Contrast this with another example from China. Chinese, generally, do not like to be touched, even to shake hands, Westerners should know that Chinese do not like loud, boisterous, or aggressive behaviour. Chinese prefer to meet others in groups. They are more retiring, reticent and shy. They prefer to conclude deals through a third party. Appointments with Chinese take a lot of time. They do not like to conclude anything in a hurry. Patience and persistence are required to strike deals with the Chinese. They are punctual and expect others to arrive promptly for each meeting. Cultural differences such as these make executive life in a foreign country much more difficult. Sometimes, a small mistake may cost a huge fortune. In their own self-interest, organisations must take every precaution to offer requisite training and consultancy assistance to executives to be sent abroad.

**Box 15.5 Puzzles Confronting the Expatriate Manager**

The following questions must be looked into carefully before sending managers on a foreign assignment:

- What is the host country's business culture like? What is the management style? Do I have the skills I will need to handle relationships with my employees?
- Will this assignment be good for my long-term career growth? Can I expect to be promoted when I return? How will I be treated if I do not succeed in my overseas job?
- What is the country like? What are the customs? Will I be able to adjust to the culture?
- Will my family be able to adjust to the new situation? Will my spouse be able to find suitable employment? Will my children be able to adjust to going to school in another country? How good is the educational system there?

- How will we learn enough of the new language to communicate effectively?
- Where will we live? How will the new housing arrangements compare to our current home? What will happen to our current home when we leave for the new assignment?
- What are the tax and other financial issues I will have to address as an expatriate? Who will advise me on these topics? Will the Company pay me in a way that protects my income from high foreign tax rates?
- How will our medical needs be taken care of?

L. Grant, "That overseas job could derail your career," Fortune, 14.4.97; S. Taylor R.N. Nappier, "Working in Japan", Sloan Management Review, Spring 1996)

To survive, cope and succeed, managers generally require training in three areas: the culture, the language and practical day-to-day matters (Tung; Selmor et al; Mendentall et al) Research studies show a high rate of expatriate failures, ranging from 25 to 50 percent mainly due to the culture shock that usually occurs 4 to 6 months after arrival in the foreign country. According to Harris and Moran the cultural differences between countries could be examined (areas where training is to be offered to expatriate managers) along the following dimensions (Hodgetts; Barlett and Ghoshal, Ricks; Thiederman, Briscoe)

1. ***Sense of self and space:*** People in a number of cultures prefer to stand close when conversing. Both Arabs (as indicated previously) and Asians fall into this group. An interpersonal distance of only six inches is very disturbing to a Northern European or an American who is used to conversing at arm's length. Cross-cultural gatherings in the Middle East often involve for example, an awkward dance as Arab hosts try to get closer while their American and European guests shuffle backwards around the room to maintain what they consider to be a proper distance. Japanese and Chinese emphasis group cooperation, whereas Americans and Canadians value independence and creativity. In Japan, bosses often sit together with their employees in the same large room. The heads of some of the biggest Japanese firms ride the public subways to work in the morning so that they can be with their workers. In contrast, North Americans prefer private space. In India, usually one finds the boss occupying a large territory in any Public Sector or Private Sector organisation.

2. ***Language:*** Foreign language skills are the gateway to the cross-cultural understanding. Words and gestures mean different things to different people. Consider the following example. Ford introduced a low cost truck 'Fiera' into some Spanish speaking countries. Unfortunately, the name meant 'ugly old woman' in Spanish. Needless to point out, this name did nothing to boost sales. Ford also experienced slow sales when it introduced a top-of-the-line automobile 'Comet' in Mexico under the name 'Caliente'. The puzzling low sales were finally understood when Ford discovered that 'saliente' is slang for a 'street walker'! Such ethnocentric actions (applying home-country procedures and evaluation criteria without any variation) inevitably fail to deliver the goods because of the cultural mismatch. Proctor & Gamble, too, failed to do its cultural homework when it ran a series of advertisements for Pampers in Japan. Japanese customers were bewildered by the ads, in which a stork carried a baby, because storks have no cultural connection to birth in Japan.

3. ***Dress and appearance:*** Garments and body decorations vary by culture. Anyone disrespecting the turban in India may be roughed up badly. Formal dress for business meetings may be essential in some cultures but not in others.

4. ***Food, eating habits and perceptual problems:*** Different cultures may have different ways of preparing and eating food. Beef, a favourite of many Americans, may be a prohibitive term (leave alone eating the same) in the Hindu culture. Some may eat with their hands; others prefer to use chopsticks or a full set of cutlery. A US manager who sees the wife of a Latin American host enter the door of the kitchen assumes that the woman is putting the finishing touches on the meal. Unknown to the manager perhaps is the fact that the woman actually is supervising the cooking of the food and is checking to see that everything is in order.

5. ***Time and time consciousness:*** The sense of time varies across cultures. To Americans, time is money. They are obsessed with making and keeping appointments. They live by schedules, deadlines and agendas. In other cultures (Latin American, Mediterranean, Arabs, Indians etc.) such as Mexico, people have no problem with loosely scheduled meetings and late coming. Consider the following example. An American company eager to do business in Saudi Arabia sent over a sales manager to 'to get something going'. The sales officer began calling contracts soon after his arrival on a particular Monday. After many disappointing appointments, the salesman ran into an old friend who gave him an introduction to some basic rules of Saudi etiquette and how to do business with the Arabs. The officer learned that he had repeatedly insulted his contacts by his impatience, refusal of coffee, the 'all business-like talk' attitudes and aggressive selling. Even individual acts such as handing papers with his left hand and exposing the sole of his shoe while sitting on the floor were offensive to Saudi sensibilities.

6. ***Relationships:*** Cultures specify human and organisational interactions by age, gender, status and family relationship, as well as by wealth, power and wisdom. In Hindu culture all family members generally live under one roof (self, spouse, children, parents etc.). Here monogamy (one wife) is the rule but in other cultures polygamy (one husband, several wives) or polyandry (one wife, several husbands) might well be accepted. In some cultures, elderly people are respected and their advice is accepted without question. Other cultures might dismiss them as unwanted. In some countries, women must wear veils and remain without identity but in others they are treated with respect even when their faces are exposed to view. Women drivers, for example, are an ordinary sight in most parts of the world, but not in conservative Islamic Saudi Arabia. In late 1990, when fifty Saudi women broke with cultural tradition and drove automobiles through the capital city of Riyadh, 'religious leaders went on the offensive and the government cracked down hard. All the women involved who had government jobs, were fired, and they all lost their passports for two years, as did their husbands.

7. ***Values and norms:*** Material wealth might be the dominant value in some cultures. People are ready to do anything in order to acquire wealth. In other cultures, people may value means as important as ends. Sharing wealth with others may be a way of life in some cultures. Customs regarding gift giving, birth, death, marriage, treating elders with respect, showing exemplary manners also differ from culture to culture.

8. ***Beliefs and attitudes:*** Religious beliefs and attitudes vary among cultures. Hindus let things happen. Most North Americans try to control events by taking charge of things all by

themselves (Internals). Some religions teach reincarnation whereas others believe they pass this way only once and, hence, want to achieve and enjoy as much as they can. Some religions teach sacrifice and caring for others. Other religions emphasise individual success leading to overall community welfare. In some cultures, work is valued as an act of service to God; in others, it is not valued properly and hence, employees working therein do not recognise the importance of quality and commitment.

9. ***Mental processes and learning:*** Across cultures, one can always find profound differences in the ways people think and learn. Some people emphasise logical thinking and proceed cautiously, weighing pros and cons from various angles. In other cultures, people may go after ideas, take risks, face innumerable difficulties that come in the way with courage and finally emerge victorious. Some cultures emphasise abstract thinking and conceptualising, whereas others favour rote memorisation. The Japanese, Korean and Chinese languages emphasise learning through word pictures whereas the English prefer to do the same through words.

10. ***Work habits and practices:*** The attitude toward work may vary greatly across various cultures. In some there is a strong focus on work values and ethics, whereas in others it is missing. You may be praised profusely for turning out good work in some cultures; in others, you may be pulled down at every stage for not meeting expectations (called management by objections) Europeans favour power and status; Americans prefer to be informal and value initiative and achievement greatly; Japanese emphasise consensus and teamwork in workplace more than anything else. These orientations and preferences greatly affect the manner in which expatriates are supposed to react to different events and situations in various countries. Any mistakes on their part would attract punitive action from 'upstairs' and they may be fired not because they lack technical competence but because they have not been able to get along with people –understanding the peculiarities in human behaviour in various settings. Careless defiance or accidentally overstepping of cultural norms, traditions or taboos by outsiders (in this case expatriates) could lead to grave personal insult and jeopardies important business dealings. Fortunately *cultural sensitivity can be learned* through various techniques.

(a) ***Documentary programmes:*** Trainees read about a foreign country's history, culture, institutions, geography, and economics. Videotaped presentations are often used.

(b) ***Culture assimilation:*** Cultural familiarity is achieved through exposure to a series of simulated intercultural incidents, or typical problem situations. This technique has been used to quickly train those who are given short notice of a foreign assignment.

(c) ***Language instruction:*** Conversational language skills are taught through a variety of methods. In most multinational companies, executives learn various languages in a routine way, so that they can be useful to the company in case of short-term foreign assignments.

(d) ***Sensitivity training:*** Experiential exercises teach awareness of the impact of one's actions on others.

(e) ***Field experience:*** Firsthand exposure to ethnic subcultures in one's own country or to foreign cultures heightens awareness.

(f) ***Business basics:*** This covers negotiating cross-culturally, working with various types of clients, making presentations etc.

(S. Oden Wald, "A Guide for Global Training", Training and Development, July 93.)

## CULTURAL VALUES AND INTERNATIONAL OB

Because values address what ought or ought not to be, differences in values often lead to clashes and negative judgements about others. Managers' personal values help shape their perception of a situation, influence the way they analyse a particular problem and find a solution. The followers' personal values, in turn, will also influence their manager. How they accept authority—their power distance—their loyalty and commitment etc will differ across cultures, as revealed by Hofstede's study.

**Table 15.1. Values across Cultures: Hofstede's Study**

Hofstede's study of thousands of IBM employees in 50 countries about their work related values revealed interesting differences among countries in terms of five value dimensions:

**Power distance**: The degree to which less powerful members of society accept that influence is unequally divided is the measure of its power distance. Managers operating in countries ranked low in power distance are expected to be generally supportive of equal rights and equal opportunity for example, managers in Canada and United States typically support equal opportunity. In countries like Mexico, France and India where power is somewhat centralized, decisions are made at the top.

**Uncertainty Avoidance**; The extent to which members of a culture feel threatened by risky or unknown situations is the measure of its uncertainty avoidance. In the United States and Canada employees and managers ranked low on uncertainty avoidance, sharing a relatively high tolerance for uncertainty, compared with their counterparts in Japan and France. In France and other cultures with high uncertainty avoidance, individuals often try to make the future more predictable by following established rules and procedures that foster tradition.

**Individualism**: Individualism is the tendency of people to look after themselves and their immediate family only. Collectivism is the tendency of people belonging to groups or collectives and to look after each other in exchange for loyalty. In countries like Japan group incentives and strong seniority systems prevail in organisations whereas in United States and Canada individual merit and incentive pay systems are valued greatly. High individualism culture often provokes managers and employees to move from company to company more frequently. They do not believe that their organisations are primarily responsible for their welfare; nor do they expect decisions made by groups to be better than decisions made by individuals.

**Masculinity**: It is a situation in which the dominant values in society are success, money and things. Femininity, on the other hand, is a situation in which the dominant values in society are caring for others and the quality of life. Countries with a high masculinity index, such as Mexico Japan, Austria, and Italy place great importance on earnings, recognition, advancement and challenge. Countries with a low masculinity index such as Norway tend to give great importance to cooperation, a friendly atmosphere and employment security.

**Long-term/Short-term Orientation**: People in cultures with long term orientation such as China, Hong Kong, Japan, stress the importance of thrift, ordering relationships by status and persistence. In the United States, Canada, France practices such as thrift, gift giving, seniority etc are not highly valued and practiced.

Values of managers, thus, may differ from culture to culture. These differences influence managerial decisions significantly. To arrive at sound decisions, today's managers must not only be aware of their own values, but also of others inside and outside the organisation.

## COMMUNICATION ACROSS CULTURES

For the global manager, dealing with people of diverse cultures, legal systems and business practices can be really frustrating, especially when he or she is inexperienced and untrained. Managers who fail to understand cultural differences tend to look at things in a very narrow way. They believe in the inherent superiority of their own group and culture. They tend to look down on 'foreign' cultures. Instead of accepting cultural diversity as a natural phenomenon, they view and measure alien cultures in terms of their own culture. ***Ethnocentrism*** is a cultural attitude marked by the tendency to regard one's own culture as superior to others. Sending home country executives abroad - thinking that they will be able to deliver the goods – may be an appropriate strategy in the initial stages of expanding company operations world-wide as these officials know what to do immediately. At Royal Dutch Shell, for instance, virtually all financial controllers around the world are Dutch nationals. Often the other reasons advanced for ethnocentric staffing policies include: lack of qualified host country managerial talent, a desire to have a unified corporate culture, tight control and the keenness to transfer the parent company's core competencies (say, a specialised design skill) to a foreign subsidiary more expeditiously. However, a policy of ethnocentrism is too narrow in its focus and may evoke strong negative reactions from local executives whose upward mobility is blocked. There is also no guarantee that the expats will win over the hearts of local employees and offer positive contributions. On the other hand, cosmopolitan managers are sensitive to cultural differences. They respect the unique practices of others and make concessions for them when communicating with representatives of different culture groups.

**Cross cultural communication** occurs when people from more than one culture communicate with each other. Language is obviously the most important problem confronting a global manager dealing with a multicultural workforce. The way he receives and interprets information from various sources could be another problem. Inability to read non verbal cues correctly could complicate matters further.

**Language**: The soft drink Fresca was marketed in Mexico without a change of brand name. the company later discovered that *fresco* is slang for *lesbian* in Mexico. A Romanian hotel posted a notice for its English-speaking guests that the elevator was not working. The notice read: "The lift is being fixed. For the next few days, we regret that you will be unbearable" When GM's theme "Body by Fisher" was translated into Finnish it read "Corpse by Fisher" When Braniff Airlines translated its "Fly Leather" slogan for its Latin American campaign, it became "Fly Naked" Not surprisingly, many global companies—IBM, Motorola, Coca-Cola, Pepsi—are spending heavy amounts in order to impart language training to their employees before sending them abroad.

**Gestures**: many American managers communicate a relaxed atmosphere by 'putting their feet up'. The manager with his feet on the desk is saying " I'm relaxing, and you can, too" However, people from other cultures may consider this rude (Germans consider it uncivilized) or even insulting.(outrageous insult to most Arabs) in the Arab world, one should always use one's right hand, the use of left hand (known as toilet hand) is insulting.

**Traditions**: McDonald's hasn't even tried to market Egg McMuffins in Brazil because of the deeply ingrained tradition of eating breakfast at home. Coke withdrew its two-litre bottle from the Spanish market after discovering that compartments of Spanish refrigerators were too small for it

**Rules of etiquette**: If business people are traveling together on a train in Japan, the most senior executive sits next to the window, facing the direction in which the train is moving. In a taxi, the "top" seat is behind the driver and most junior seat is next to the driver. In elevators, the senior person stands at the rear in the centre facing the door and the most junior person stands near the button.

**Meaning of distance**?: the distance at which we stand from someone as we speak has meaning. In the United States, standing very close to someone you are talking to generally signals either familiarity or aggression. The English and Germans tend to keep a distance while talking. Whereas the Arabs, Japanese and Mexicans stand close when conversing.

**Cultural context**:: In low context cultures such as Australia, Canada and United States messages are expressed mainly by the spoken and written word. Members in high context cultures such as Asian and Middle Eastern cultures convey only a limited part of the message through words. The rest must be inferred or interpreted from the context, which includes body language, the physical setting and past relationships.

**Stereotyping**: Due to stereotyping, cross cultural communications may fail. Stereotyping is the tendency to oversimplify and generalize about groups of people. It occurs both within and between cultures and thus it influences communication in virtually all organisational settings. If you may believe that technical people are unfit for positions requiring social interaction, you are bound to encounter frequent problems while dealing with technicians.

With necessary training and exposure to tricky situations described above, global managers might be able to avoid the culture shock. To survive in an borderless world, managers must leave their headquarters-country bias and begin to think in global terms. More specifically, as suggested by Adler and Bartholomew, the multinational managers must:

- *Understand* the world wide business scenario from a global, rather than a single country perspective
- *Learn* about many foreign cultures' perspectives, tastes, trends, technologies and approaches to conducting business
- *Be skillful* at working with people from many different cultures simultaneously
- *Be able to adapt* to not only living in other cultures but also using cross cultural skills on regular multicultural business trips and in daily interaction with foreign colleagues and clients worldwide.
- *Interact with* foreign colleagues as equals, rather than from within clearly defined hierarchies of structural or cultural dominance and subordination.

## NEGOTIATION ACROSS CULTURES

Negotiation approaches differ considerably because of culture. A wide variety of tactics could be used in international negotiations to arrive at a solution acceptable to all. As a measure of abundant precaution it is advisable not to identify the counterpart's home culture too quickly based on name, physical appearance, language, accent, location etc. The counterpart may belong to more than one culture in a negotiation situation; all aspects of culture are not equally significant. In any case, it is better not to overestimate your familiarity with your counterpart's culture (Hodgetts and Luthans) The Americans tend to approach negotiations with a factual and objective frame of mind. They often make early concessions to show their flexibility and reasonableness. They tend to get things resolved quickly so as to meet deadlines, which are very important from their point of view. The *Arabs* on the other hand, use an emotional route to resolve issues through negotiation. Deadlines are not important. They look at everything subjectively. They also yield ground and make concessions, of course, after starting off with an extreme initial position. The British negotiators may appear polite and reserved but they could be tough and ruthless when the situation demands. They tend to avoid 'games' The *Germans*, on the other hand, are risk averse and seek more compromises. They are logical, examine issues thoroughly and are serious and honest. The *French*, in contrast are friendly, humorous and hard to impress. They take time to reach decisions and are difficult to negotiate with. It is difficult to extract anything from them. By nature, they are very secretive. The *Japanese* are very cautious in their approach, not very emotional and get very uncomfortable when others lose control. They confront their counterparts with lot of questions. Decisions are made by consensus. *The Chinese* take time to resolve things over the negotiation table. They require the development of good interpersonal relationships prior to reaching any agreement. They are reluctant to commit everything to writing, and anticipate that any agreement reached will be subject to modification as future circumstances may demand. The *Russians* generally move forward in negotiations on professed ideals. They are not known for generous concessions. Any concession offered by an opponent is being interpreted as a weakness and almost never reciprocated. For them, deadlines do not matter.

Looking at the vast differences in the approaches—due to differences in socio-cultural, political and economic diversity— taken by participants from different countries, one can safely conclude that negotiating for scarce resources—money, time, people, facilities, equipment, rewards, and so on—is not an easy job. The effective management of negotiation requires an understanding of the perspectives, values, and agendas of other parties and the use of a problem-solving approach (discussed in chapter 17 elaborately) To move towards consensus and settlement of an issue, negotiators must believe in the **win-win approach** where there are no winners and losers. They can utilize negotiation as an opportunity and try to get what they want without demanding too much nor yielding ground greatly. It is not a kind of tough guy or nice guy approach but an approach where both parties work together to find ways to satisfy both parties at the same time. Experts have suggested ways and means to clear the fog in this respect"

- *People,: separate the people from the problem*
- *Interests: focus on interests, not positions*
- *Options: generate a variety of possibilities before deciding what to do*
- *Criteria: insist that the result be based on some objective standard.*

This kind of principled negotiation 'permits you to reach a gradual consensus on a joint decision efficiently without all the transactional costs of digging in to positions only to have to dig yourself out of them. And separating the people from the problem allows you to deal directly and empathetically with the other negotiators as a human being, thus making possible an amicable agreement" (Fisher and Ury) Effective intercultural communication is going to be a vital skill—especially in the 21st century—for international managers and domestic managers of multicultural workforces. Without appropriate cultural sensitivity, global managers may not be able to satisfy all parties and build lasting relationships.

## MOTIVATION ACROSS CULTURES

Thanks to globalization, managers can hire, source and sell wherever they want. Indians wear clothes made in China, work on computers whose parts come from Thailand and watch movies filmed in USA. Global companies have a vast army of employees with diverse cultural, religious, educational background from all over the globe. Work activities are increasingly pushed to countries that offer significant cost advantages to parent organisations. To remain competitive, every company is compelled to shift focus to profits, efficiency and growth relentlessly. The challenges before a global manager, especially while trying to motivate people to peak performance are truly challenging. Knowledge workers demand everything under the sun in terms of pay, rewards, benefits, and comforts of various kinds. Companies want to deliver excellent results through cost-effective methods. They want tremendous amount of commitment of employees toward quality, service and efficiency. To work effectively with a group of diverse people, global managers need to understand how the culture, geography and religion of employees have shaped their values, attitudes and beliefs and get along. Motivation theories may be of very little use, as research has indicated, because the subject of motivating people is essentially culture-specific. (Luthans) The important issue here is to understand the basic meaning of work and the cultural dimensions that contribute to the possible differences in motivation of people across cultures.

***The Meaning of Work***: The meaning of work and what people find rewarding varies with culture. For most employees all over the globe, work is tied to economic necessity. People commit themselves to work to earn rewards and buy comforts. The level of commitment may vary as we run through the research data covering the Americans, the Japanese, and the Germans etc. What work provides in addition to money, in terms of achievement, honour, social contacts etc is always not very clear. The Thais, for example, call work ***ngan***, or "play" and they tend to introduce periods of play during working hours. The Chinese take work seriously. Seven day work weeks with long hours and few days off are quite common. Same is the case with Koreans.(R.M.Steers, Made in Korea). Koreans' hard work was attributable to loyalty to the company, group-oriented achievement and emphasis on group harmony and business relationships. For the Americans time is money. Work is the most important and dominant part of life. They believe in doing as much in as little time as possible. They also like to find out what is expected of them and by when their tasks are to be accomplished. In Middle East religion plays a major role in influencing attitudes toward work. Arabs are serious about their work and that favouritism, give and take and paternalism have no place in the Arab workplace. (Deresky). The role of religion also may not be discounted here. For example, the Hindus believe in just letting things happen. The Americans, in contrast, believe in taking charge of things and events. They also do not believe in reincarnation. The best way to help others is to achieve success individually. In other cultures the opposite is stressed. Such differing religious values influence the way, directly or indirectly, managers guide the efforts of others in organisations. Some employees might be interested in their own self pursuits and interests and might be working just to collect the weekly pay cheques. They may not be interested in making their work more challenging or interesting or in winning performance contests. The intra-country and inter-country differences in terms of what attitudes people have toward their work, what aspects of work in their life context are meaningful to them etc make it difficult for global managers to base their judgement on some generalizations.

***What Motivates people in a specific Country?:*** Opinion, expectedly, is divided here. For the Germans and the Americans, interesting work would pave the way for self-actualization. People from China, Israel and Korea gave maximum weightage to achievement as satisfying self-actualization needs. A Gallup opinion poll found that Chinese wanted to work hard and get rich whereas the Europeans and the Americans placed a premium on self achievement over wealth. A study by Ronen concluded that need clusters-proposed by Maslow—is constant across nationalities and that Maslow's need hierarchy is confirmed by those clusters. Another conclusion is that managers around the world have similar needs but show differing levels of satisfaction of those needs derived from their jobs. In countries like Japan, Greece and Mexico where uncertainty avoidance characteristics are strong security needs topped the list of need hierarchy. Countries with nurturing characteristics such as Denmark, Sweden, Norway, Finland placed social needs on top. Anglo-American countries like the United States, Canada and Great Britain valued high achievement as a powerful internal motivating element. This was not the case with managers in Chile and Portugal(Hofstede) Variables other than culture—such as country's stage of economic development—might be at play .

***Factors influencing motivational approaches in a multicultural environment:*** A study of the managers in the American, Japanese and the Arab world indicated the following (Farid and Harris)

- Management Style: The Japanese managers used counselling and persuasion to motivate people. The American managers used professionalism and friendliness, and the Arab manager used coaching and personal attention as tools to achieve the same purpose.
- Control: The American managers loved taking charge of the situations; the Japanese got motivated through group harmony and consensus, whereas the Arab manager tried to control others through a parenting relationship
- Emotional Grip: The Americans seized opportunities and were committed fully to realize targets, putting aside emotions and sentiments. The Japanese were ignited by the love of their company. The Arabs were motivated by the inner self and the authority structure.
- Recognition: The Americans were passionate about recognition; the Japanese loved group identification and the Arab found their status in hierarchy
- Threats: Demotion means loss of reputation and status in the Arab world. Fear of being excluded from the group is the greatest threat to the Japanese. The threat of being fired is being taken by the Americans seriously.

- Rewards: Rewards obtained by the group as a whole would excite the Japanese managers. Rewarding the individual is frowned on in Japan because it encourages competition rather than the desired group cooperation. The American values culturally appropriate rewards based on individual excellence. The Arabs value rewards for the family as well as individual. Employees in collectivist cultures such as Japan, Korea and Taiwan, in any case, would not respond well to typical American merit based reward system to motivate employees. In Taiwan, recognition and affection are important. Company departments compete for praise from top management at their annual celebration. In China the reward system is entirely different. The low wage rates are compensated for by free housing, schools, and medical care. They believe in 'more work, more pay'. One objectionable aspect of the Chinese reward system is being illustrated by the example of a plaque award titled:" Ms. Wong—Employee of the Month" given in a Chinese retail store. We tend to take it as an award of excellence, but in fact the award was given to Ms. Wong, the worst employee, to shame and embarrass her!(Wall Street Journal)

## LEADERSHIP ACROSS CULTURES

The past decade has been characterized by unbelievable changes, cut-throat competition, a stunning explosion of new technologies, mind-numbing chaos, tremendous turbulence and high levels of uncertainty. Organisations are being reengineered and restructured and network, virtual and modular corporations are emerging. The economic world, not surprisingly, consists of global companies, boundaryless corporations and virtual outfits. As we step into the next decade, the organisations that we will be living in, moving with and competing against are likely to be vastly different from what we know today. We find corporations increasingly flooded with people with diverse backgrounds, from all over the globe. **Multiculturalism** and **Diversity** related issues are going to confront global managers wherever they go. Multiculturalism deals with broad issues associated with differences in values, beliefs, behaviours, customs and attitudes held by people (from different national cultures) working in an organisation. Diversity exists in a group or organisation when its members differ from one another, along one or more important dimensions such as age, gender or ethnicity. Virtually all organisations in the 21$^{st}$ century are becoming more diverse and multicultural. Factors such as globalization, the entry of women and minorities into the labour force, the hunt for talent across the borders to hire the best, the favourable laws encouraging companies to hire people based on merit etc have brought about a sea change in the composition of labour force in corporations all over the globe. Confronted with these realities, the corporate world, now-a-days, is looking for not merely transformational leaders, charismatic leaders but leaders who are capable of delivering results, resolving cross cultural differences in a competent manner.(Howard et al)

***Leadership style in sync with cultural expectations:*** In the changed scenario, leaders cannot choose their styles at will; they are constrained by the cultural conditions that their followers have come to expect. Korean leaders, therefore, have to adopt a paternalistic style to keep their employees in good humour. Arab leaders, in contrast, who exhibit kindness and generosity, are labeled as 'weak'. In Japan silence pays; hence Japanese leaders are expected to be humble and speak infrequently! Dutch leaders who single out individuals for public praise may be, indirectly, sending an open invitation to criticism from all quarters. (Peterson et al). Effective German leaders are characterized by high performance orientation, low compassion, low self protection, low team orientation, high autonomy and high participation. Arabs worship their leaders—as long as they are in power. Malaysians expect their leaders to behave in a manner that is humble, modest and dignified. The French expect leaders to be cultivated—that is highly educated in the arts and in mathematics The Leadership Theories inevitably contain the American flavour, since most of these have been developed there, reflecting things such as centrality of work, democratic value orientation, responsibilities of followers in place of spirituality, religion and superstition. Leaders, however, cannot afford to ignore national culture, because it comes in the way of getting positive responses from subordinates.

***Universal traits associated with transformational leadership will help?***

Cross cultural studies covering leadership have spelt out the elements that need to receive attention from one and all such as: vision, foresight, providing encouragement, trustworthiness, dynamism, positiveness and proactiveness. According to the GLOBE research team, "effective business leaders in any country are expected by their subordinates to provide a powerful and proactive vision to guide the company into the future, strong motivational skills to stimulate all employees to fulfill the vision, and excellent planning skills to assist in implementing the vision".

***Effective leaders must be global business and organizational savvy.***

From their recent research involving 125 global leaders in fifty companies Morrison et al concluded that effective leaders must be global business and organisational savvy. They explain global business savvy as the ability to recognize global market opportunities for a company and having a vision of doing business worldwide. Global organisational savvy requires an intimate knowledge of a company's resources and capabilities in order to capture global markets, as well as an understanding of each subsidiary's product lines and how the people and business operate at the local level.

In the end, we can only conclude by saying that effective leadership is crucial to the ability of a company to achieve its goals. The challenge is to decide what is effective leadership in different international or mixed-culture situations.

## HR POLICIES ACROSS CULTURES

Differences in economic systems among countries also translate into inter country differences in HR practices. In free enterprise systems, companies tend to focus on HR policies that value productivity, efficient workers, cost cutting measures in line with market situations. In socialist systems, HR policies tend to shift toward preventing unemployment, even at the expense of efficiency. In India for example, public sector companies like NTC, DTC, ITDC, IDPL, HFC continue to protect the lives of workers even though the units were declared unviable long back.

In countries like India and Pakistan, the loss of man-days due to disturbances is alarmingly high. Labour productivity is very low. Portuguese workers average about 1980 hours of work annually, while German workers average 1648 hours. In UK and Germany, the severance pay is relatively high. Such labour cost differences could influence hiring and firing decisions. Likewise, industrial relations factors also influence HR policies. In Germany codetermination is the rule. In India, powerful unions especially in Banking, Insurance, Post and Telegraphs, Railways, Coal, Steel and Mining sectors significantly influence the shape of HR policies. In some states like West Bengal and Kerala, there is support from the Governments too (for various political reasons). In the United States, on the other hand, HR policies in most matters such as wages and benefits are being decided by the employer alone, of course in consultation with labour unions. The laws governing labour also impact HR policies and there are wide variations in the way labour is subjected to regulation in different countries. Even within the relatively unified European community, there are substantial differences in matters like minimum wage laws and length of workday etc

Inter-country differences in cultures, economic systems, labour costs, labour and industrial relations systems, thus complicate the task of selecting, training, and managing employees abroad. A large percentage of expatriate assignments may fail, but the batting average can be improved if attention is being paid to international assignee selection, training, appraisal and developmental aspects.

## International Recruitment Policy

Companies operating outside their home countries, essentially, follow three ways of hiring executives: (Tung; Foster)

1. ***Ethnocentrism:*** It is a cultural attitude marked by the tendency to regard one's own culture as superior to others. Sending home country executives abroad - thinking that they will be able to deliver the goods – may be an appropriate strategy in the initial stages of expanding company operations world-wide as these officials know what to do immediately. At Royal Dutch Shell, for instance, virtually all financial controllers around the world are Dutch nationals. Often the other reasons advanced for ethnocentric staffing policies include: lack of qualified host country managerial talent, a desire to have a unified Corporate culture, tight control and the keenness to transfer the parent company's core competencies (say, a specialised design skill) to a foreign subsidiary more expeditiously. However, a policy of ethnocentrism is too narrow in its focus and may evoke strong negative reactions from local executives whose upward mobility is blocked. There is also no guarantee that the expats will win over the hearts of local employees and offer positive contributions. In fact, failures of US expats range from 10% to 15%. European and Japanese expat failures are equally alarming, the costs of each such failure running to several thousands of dollars.

**Box 15.6 Reasons for Expatriate Failures (Thakur)**

- ***Transfer anxieties:*** Foreign assignments might have been pushed ahead without adequate preparation and advance planning. The expat might, as result, find the task insurmountable, feel the pressure unbearable and return empty-handed.
- ***Career problems:*** A foreign posting creates, for the expatriate a number of career problems (i) being 'out of sight, out of mind' and being bypassed for promotions (ii) the danger of coming home a stranger with few familiar faces to greet his/her arrival (iii) the likelihood of being tempted by the foreign life style and losing the desire to return.

- ***Personal problems:*** As Negandhi reported, expatriates may encounter serious adjust problems such as: personal discomfort and uncomfortable living conditions, homesickness; education, medical, health problems of family members; social aloofness, cultural mismatch.
- ***Other concerns:*** These include: (i) the foreign posting might be looked at as a short term obligation (ii) the expats performance might be evaluated against a short-term criteria, (iii) the expat may begin to feel the pinch due to lack of continuity in plans empowering him to conduct the show for a reasonable period (iv) business environment of the host country might be too restrictive, unfriendly and even unbearable.

Too often expats are selected on the strength of their domestic track record. They are posted abroad without requisite cross-cultural training. The family factors stand completely discounted in the selection process. The rate of failures could be drastically reduced if these issues are properly addressed.

2. ***Polycentrism:*** In the polycentric corporation, there is a conscious belief that only host country managers can ever really understand the culture and behaviour of the host country market; therefore, the foreign subsidiary should be managed by local people. The home-office headquarters, of course, is staffed by parent-country nationals. Hiring nationals has many advantages. It eliminates language barriers, expensive training periods, cross-cultural adjustment problems of managers and their families. It also permits the firms to attract talented locals by offering an attractive compensation package. Many western MNCs have found that the key to success on foreign soil is to employ local people. Analog Devices Inc., has achieved global success in a highly technical field by picking up local managers, training them extensively and then empowering them to hire and manage more local talent. Likewise, global sales of Bausch & Lomb improved dramatically after putting the local managerial talent to good use.

3. ***Geocentrism:*** Geocentrism assumes that management candidates must be searched on a global basis, without favouring anyone. The best manager for any specific position anywhere on the globe may be found in any of the countries in which the firm operates. Such a staffing policy seeks the best people for important jobs throughout the organisation, regardless of nationality. It helps to build a stronger and more consistent culture and set of values among the entire global management team. 'Team members here are always interacting, networking and building bonds with each other, as they move from assignment to assignment, around the globe and participate in global development activities'. Colgate-Palmolive is an example of a company that hires the best person for the job regardless of nationality. It has been operating globally for more than 55 years, and its products are household names in more than 175 countries. Fully 60 percent of the company's expatriates are from countries other than the Unites States and two of its last four CEOs were not US nationals. Moreover, all the top executives speak at least two languages and important meetings routinely take place all over the globe.

## International Selection Criteria

International postings are complex and carry a lot of in-built pressures along with them. It would be erroneous to assume that the job requires the same set of skills in different locations. The local dynamics might be different, the cultural and social pressures might be too complex. If the spouse and children join the expatriate, there are additional issues to be resolved - from learning a new language, to shopping in new environs, to children finding new friends and attending new schools. For an expat to succeed, therefore, the selection process must be rigorous and must invariably include criteria such as:

***General and technical criteria:*** Research findings consistently indicate that MNCs place heavy reliance on relevant technical skills during the expatriate selection process. In addition, the expatiate manager should be a good communicatior, and possess management talent, maturity, emotional stability in ample measure.

***Language skills:*** Most researchers argue that knowledge of the host-country's language is an important factor affecting the performance of an expatriate. Where the expatriate is expected to communicate with host country subjects frequently, language skills come to occupy the centre-stage. Tung and Anderson's study indicated that the respondents (mostly Americans) greatly valued the ability to speak local language, regardless of how different the culture was from their home country.

***Cross-cultural suitability:*** Expatriate managers must be able to adapt to change. They must have the ability to translate their technical or managerial skills into meaningful action plans in a foreign environment. They should get along with local people easily without upsetting host country customs, traditions and other cultural niceties. The expatriate managers should as a rule, have good interpersonal skills and extra-cultural openness - including a variety of outside interests, tolerance for ambiguity and non-judgemental behaviour.

***Motivation for a foreign assignment:*** The candidate for foreign assignment must believe in the importance of the job and possess a certain amount of idealism or a sense of mission. Applicants who are not happy with their current situation at home and are looking to get away, rarely succeed as overseas managers.

***Family situation:*** Several items including the adaptability of spouse and family, spouse's positive opinion, willingness of spouse to live abroad, stable marriage comprises this factor. This factor was found to be the most important of the above list, contributing to the expat's success or failure on a foreign locale.The first key to finding a successful expatriate is a selection process that accurately determines who is culturally flexible and adaptable, has a supportive family situation, and is motivated to accept the overseas assignment.

## Selection Process

The selection process varies widely from country to country. Asian companies use extensive testing procedures and screening techniques. Europeans do not test as much as Asians but considerably more than Americans. Testing in the US is not favoured because of its negative impact on equal employment and affirmative action efforts. In most global corporations, however, adaptability screening is usually followed. The screening, carried out by a professional psychologist or psychiatrist, tries to assess the family's probable success in handling the foreign transfer, and to alert the couple to personal problems (impact on children's education etc) the foreign move may involve. Many companies more or less have realised the importance of preparing managers to work in foreign cultures. In fact, several companies try to give future managers exposure to foreign cultures early in their careers. American Express Company's Travel related services unit gives American business-school students summer jobs in which they work outside the United States for up to 10 weeks. Colgate-Palmolive selects 15 recent graduates each year and then offers up to 24 months of training prior to multiple overseas job stints. The overall US selection and training practices, however, continue to lag behind those of Japan and Germany. In Japan, for example, expatriates are selected a year or more prior to their posting so that they and their families receive extensive cultural and language training. Not surprisingly, the overseas success rate for the Japanese is significantly higher than that for Americans.

## International Training and Development

Careful selection is only the first step in ensuring the foreign assignee's success. The expatriate may then require proper orientation, cross-cultural training, assistance in career planning and development, etc., in order to handle the assigned jobs in a competent way.(Earley; J.D.Lein et al)

A. ***Orientation:*** International positions require an extensive orientation to familiarise the employee with culture, language and other unique aspects of the assignment. Familiarisation trips could also be arranged for the prospective expatriates so that they can actually visit the country of their posting and live like natives there for a while. The orientation programmes, generally cover areas such as:

### Pre-arrival orientation

(i) ***Cultural briefing:*** Explaining the traditions, customs, living conditions, clothing and housing requirements, health stipulations, etc.

(ii) ***Assignment briefing:*** Throwing light on length of assignment, vacations, compensation package, tax implications, repatriation policy etc.

(iii) ***Shipping requirements:*** Shipping, packing, storage, housing facility in the new location etc.

### Post-arrival orientation

Once global employees arrive in the host country, they will require further assistance in '*settling in*'. Someone should receive them and help them in obtaining housing accommodation, establishing bank accounts, getting driving licenses, arranging admissions to school for dependent children etc.

**(iv)** ***Cross cultural training:*** Differences in culture, language and laws may make it difficult for the global employees to be on track quickly. In order to lead a normal life, they need cross cultural as well as language training. The failure to provide such training may create adjustment problems for the expatriate manager and the resultant *culture shock* (the inability to adjust to a different cultural setting) may compel the expatriate to quit the field altogether. Firms can help employees avoid culture shock, of course, by using selection tools to choose the employees with the highest degree of cultural sensitivity. An important part of an expatriate manager's training, further, should be an overview of the legal and ethical issues that are likely to be encountered on the overseas assignment.

B. ***Career development:*** The expatriate's motivation to do well on an international assignment is primarily dependent on the following things:

- Whether the present assignment would help the expatriate to learn new things, expand his knowledge, create a unique position for himself in the organisation ladder, and grow vertically within the firm - once the job is successfully completed.
- Whether the expatriate is enjoying continued support from the headquarters or not.

One of the important deterrents to accepting foreign assignments is the expatriates' concern that they will be '*out of sight, out of mind*'. If they do not have direct and regular contact with their bosses and colleagues at headquarters, they feel isolated and thrown out of the system. To reduce their anxiety levels therefore, global companies must project foreign assignments as stimulating growth opportunities leading to continued career progression. A monitoring system would certainly solve such issues. In this system an expatriate is guided by a senior executive in the headquarters. This executive talks with the expatriate regularly, ensures that the expatriate's name is submitted during promotion and development discussions at headquarters and resolves any headquarters-related problems faced by the expatriate. Another approach has the expatriate coming back to the home office occasionally to foster a sense of belonging to the organisation. Alternatively, mini-sabbaticals could be offered to the expatriate and his family so that he or she can be in touch with current happenings in the headquarters.

## Compensation Practices across cultures

Due to differences in tax and cost of living as well as often difficult living conditions, pay and benefits for employees living abroad must be decided carefully paying attention to three thingsLRayman; Dwyer; Henderson)

- The expatriate's income should at least be equivalent to what he or she is getting at home.
- Additional incentives must be offered for accepting the international assignment (eg sign-on bonus, percentage increase in base salary, lump-sum payment on successful completion of assignment etc).
- It is better to avoid having expatriates fill the same jobs held by locals or lower-ranking jobs. In such cases talented local employees may resent the higher pay and allowances given to expatriates, complain about inequity in pay and may even quit in protest.

According to Henderson, recruiting new employees with the requisite knowledge and skills or influencing current employees to move to a foreign site requires a wide array of compensation related incentives. The site of course must offer significant challenging opportunities for the executive to fully utilize his potential. The transfer incentives must be tempting—covering life style enhancement services, service allowances, premiums in addition to positional rewards that the executive was getting previously.

Most MNCs use what is popularly known as the balance sheet approach which tries to equalise purchasing power across countries. The employer using this approach estimates expenses for income taxes, housing accommodation, goods and services, and reserve and pays supplements to the expatriate in such a way as to maintain the same standard of living he or she would have had at home.

## Performance Appraisal of International Managers

It is not easy to appraise an expatriate's performance. A number of complicating factors come in the way of a fair and equitable appraisal (Harvey; Mendenhall and Addon) *First* there is the question of who actually carries out the appraisal. Cultural differences may distort appraisals done by local management. Additionally, local management does not have enough perspective on the entire organisation to know how well the expatriate is truly contributing to the firm as a whole. *Second*, evaluations from home country managers may always be questioned on grounds of geographical separation. The home-office managers often, may be so out of touch that they can't offer valid appraisals, since they are not fully aware of the harsh realities faced by the expatriate locally. *Third* the criteria used to measure performance such as profits, market share may be good yardsticks theoretically speaking, but when these are affected by local issues such as political instability, changes in government policy, ensuring fairness is not going to be easy. To balance the pros and cons of home country and host country evaluations, performance appraisals should combine the two sources of evaluation. The performance criteria must be linked to be degree of difficulty level in each assignment. Local factors must also be factored into the whole exercise. It is always better to weigh the evaluation more toward the on-site manager's appraisal than toward the home-office manager's distant perceptions of the expatriate manager's performance. *Finally*, it is also important to give an opportunity for expatriates to offer feedback as to how they received support from the home office, the obstacles they had to encounter and the suggestions they have in store for their colleagues who are likely to handle similar jobs in future.

## International Labour Relations

Labour relations structures, laws and practices vary considerably among countries. MNCs, therefore, adopt different labour relations strategies in relation to the environmental factors peculiar to each firm. Some of the important aspects worth considering here may be listed thus (Ramber; Mills)

***The role of unions:*** The role of unions varies from country to country due to many factors such as level of employment, homogeneity of labour, (racial, religious, social class), level of per capita labour income, relations between labour and management, labour laws within a country empowering unions to represent labour effectively etc. In some countries, unions either do not exist at all or are relatively weak. Such is the case in China and a number of African countries. In countries like India with high unemployment, low pay levels, no union funds for welfare and living at the mercy of employer for gaining recognition, the union is forced to seek help from political parties or government. The situation, however, is entirely different in Unites States where the majority union bargains with the employer, not with other institutions.

***Collective bargaining:*** Collective bargaining practices can vary widely from country to country depending on the role played by the respective local governments. In the United Kingdom and France, for example, government actively intervenes in all aspects of collective bargaining. In developing countries, it is quite common for the government to have representatives present during bargaining sessions to ensure fairness and protection to unions, represented by relatively uneducated leaders. Collective bargaining agreements in India focus mostly on wages, benefits and employment conditions (just like the labour agreements in USA). In the United States, local unions bargain with individual employers to settle wages and working conditions. European agreements tend to be brief and to specify minimum wages and employment conditions, with employers free to come out with generous terms. In Australia, unions argue their cases before arbitration tribunals. In France and Germany, industry-wide or region-wide agreements are common. In Japan, local unions carry out the bargaining but combine at some point to determine national wage patterns.

***Labour participation:*** The law takes care of employee representation in many European countries. The employer is legally required to provide for employee representation on safety committees, worker councils or on boards of directors. The worker councils in France are empowered to oversee grievances, problems of individual employees, internal regulations and employee welfare-related issues. A higher form of employee participation in management – known as codetermination – is legally guaranteed in Germany. German law gives three different degrees of participation, depending on the issue in question. German worker councils merely have to be informed and consulted for most economic decisions. But they are permitted to participate in decisions such as dismissals, work procedures and even the design of the work place. At an even greater level of involvement, worker councils have approved rights over decisions such as working hours, training programmes and safety matters.

***Health and safety:*** Employee Health and safety laws and regulations vary from country to country, ranging from virtually non-existent to more stringent than in India. With more and more expatriates working internationally in some of the less-developed nations, safety-related issues have assumed importance in recent times. In countries like Brazil, Nigeria, Philippines, Russia and New Guinea street crimes are quite common and kidnapping has become a way of life. In countries like Turkmenistan, Tajikistan, Bangladesh, Afghanistan medical facilities are primitive, treatment is not as available and medicines are less easily obtained. Before sending executives abroad, therefore, the home-office should understand the local environment, local conditions and the level of difficulty in each global assignment. Proper training and coaching must precede executive travel to such countries where perceptions towards foreign nationals are somewhat negative (like asking expatriates not to wear caps or T-shirts with a foreign tag, equipping expatriate's car with security systems, taking different routes to and from work routinely, keeping expatriates well informed about host country crimes, advising expatriates to look confident always etc.). Many international firms provide bodyguards to escort their key executives working in places where kidnappings, murders, home invasions and robberies occur frequently. Some firms have even gone to the extent of removing sign boards identifying offices and facilities bearing a foreign name with a view to reduce visibility of the firm. In addition to these many firms have started using metal detectors to scan the entry of all people, erected physical barriers such as iron fences, concrete barricades, bullet proof glass, electronic surveillance devices etc. to ensure protection to all employees.

## Repatriation

The final issue in managing international assignments is repatriation (i.e., helping employees make the transition back home) of arriving employees. Since the home office has spent enormous amounts on expatriate's trip abroad including training, compensation, development etc., it is essential to utilise the expertise of the expatriate profitably. It is essential to establish a strategy that allows the home office to take the valuable experience abroad and integrate it with what is happening at home and allow co-workers to learn of the expatriate's experience to improve their own performance. Repatriates must be given a suitable job matching their global experience and knowledge, preferably a high-ranking autonomous position. When such a rewarding position is missing, the expatriate may choose to move to another expatriate assignment with the same employer or with a different employer rather than return to headquarters.

On a personal level, two major issues need special attention. The first is logistics. Personal savings will need to be transferred, personal belongings inventoried and shipped, automobiles and homes possibly purchased and sold, school transfers arranged and spousal employment assistance arranged. The second issue deals with the readjustment and integration into the community for the employee and his or her family. Expatriates often must be acclimatised to home country's life styles, transportation services and other cultural practices, especially if they have been living in less developed countries.

Many progressive international companies try to take care of many of the problems cited above by taking certain sensible steps: (i) giving a written assurance to the international assignee that he or she will be given an appropriate job after completion of the assignment (ii) appointing a sponsor who would keep the expatriate well informed about developments in the home office, including career opportunities (iii) providing the expatriate and his or her family with a reorientation programme to help their integration back into the home culture. Employees on international assignments, it must be remembered, represent valuable assets who need to be managed more systematically and strategically than they traditionally have been, to ensure greater probability of success in global markets.

## REVIEW QUESTIONS

1. Why do some firms gain competitive advantages in international markets? Explain.
2. What are the risks involved in expanding internationally and managing multinational companies?
3. Outline the important characteristics of the ethnocentric, polycentric and geocentric approaches to international staffing.
4. What is the relationship between language and culture? How is it that people from different countries who speak the same language may still miscommunicate?
5. Give some examples of cultural differences in the interpretation of body language. What is the role of such non verbal communication in business relationships?
6. How do perception, stereotyping and ethnocentrism affect communicating with employees across cultures?
7. What accounts for some of the motivational differences between employees across cultures?
8. Identify the important factors that influence the leadership process across cultures
9. While negotiating with people from a different cultural background, what are the key points that must be taken into account by a manager working in a global company?

10. Discuss the concept of work centrality and its implications for motivation.
11. What are some of the challenges faced in training expatriate managers?
12. What makes international staffing so complicated?
13. What are the major costs associated with using expatriate managers overseas?
14. What kind of characteristics are important in selecting an individual for an overseas assignment?
15. What is culture shock? When does it occur? What can be done to reduce its negative effects?
16. Should foreign language proficiency be required for executives assigned overseas? Why or why not?
17. How does appraising an expatriate's programme differ from appraising that of a home-office manager? How would you avoid some of the unique problems of appraising the expatriate's performance?
18. What aspects would be included in a pre-repatriation programme? What factors contribute to re-entry shock?
19. What are some of the challenges faced in training expatriate managers?

## DISCUSSION QUESTIONS

1. If a company new to the international arena was negotiating an agreement with a potential partner in an overseas country, what basic steps should it be prepared to implement? Identify and describe them. Discussion Questions
2. Explain the organisational and individual purposes of expatriation. Why do these need to be incorporated as part of a strategic approach to managing international assignments?
3. .is effective leadership behaviour universal? Or does it vary from culture to culture? Explain.
4. What objections might you expect to hear from employees about overseas assignments?
5. Discuss the effects that different components of the cultural environment can have on HRM in an international firm.
6. If learning (individual and organisational) is an important outcome of an overseas assignment, how can this be worked into a performance appraisal system? How would a manager assess individual and organisational learning?
7. Discuss the following statement: "Global compensation packages should keep expatriates even with what they would receive at home, but not allow them to get rich."
8. Identify four characteristics of multinationals that give labour unions cause for concern (e.g., formidable financial resources, alternative sources of supply, the ability to move production facilities to other countries, a remote locus of authority, operating in many product categories, superior knowledge and expertise in labour relations; the capacity to stage an investment strike etc.)

## CASE STUDY THE CASE OF CULTURAL DIFFERENCES

*By R Chandrasekhar*

It was the best of times; it was the worst of times.

It was the former because Allen Bank's acquisition of a part of the Bradbury Bank-what the latter termed NEM (Newly Emerging Market) operations-seemed an acquisition scripted in heaven. Both were venerable institutions of British origin. Allen was the largest international bank in developing markets. Its core businesses? Retail and corporate banking, treasury ops, and trade financing. The bank employed over 33,000 people across 740 offices in 55 countries. Bradbury bank was smaller, but only marginally so. It employed 28,000 people and was present in 42 countries. Its core businesses were retail and corporate banking and trade financing. However, its NEM business was focussed exclusively on high-networth individuals and large corporates. So, when Bradbury wished to sell its NEM operations-it wanted to exit NEM because most economies there boasted a low credit rating and it wished to lessen its overall credit risk; besides, it wished to focus its efforts on the first world-it was only natural that Allen, which wished to expand its presence in developing countries, buy them.

It was the worst of times because the cultures of the two banks were as different as blues-grass and *Bhangra*-pop. Allen was a systems-driven bank which boasted strong internal controls and placed an emphasis on training and performance. Bradbury was a old-world type, inward-looking firm with weak control systems and condoned pedestrian performance. Worse, it did little to spread its customer base and aggressively acquire new business.

It was also the worst of times because the two companies had different organisational structures. Allen favoured the matrix, with the head of each division or function reporting directly to the regional head of that division or function, and only informally to the country head. Bradbury preferred a linear reporting relationship, with everyone reporting to the country head. Expectedly, Bradbury employees who became part of the rechristened Allen Bradbury Bank (ABB-no relation to the energy giant, although the bank could have learned a thing or two from that company's integration of Asea and Brown Boveri) felt lost. ''There is no symbol of authority I can relate to in my workplace,'' was a commonly-heard refrain.

None of these, though, worried Surinder Sawhney the 53-year-old CEO of ABB, as much as the issue of people. Like most CEOs discover during the process of integration, Sawhney was discovering that ABB seemed to have two people for every position. Worse, Allen-employees considered their counterparts from Bradbury who had been taken on as baggage. ''They're here because that was part of the deal with Bradbury,'' confided one young manager from ABB (he was from the Allen-side). ''By themselves, these people would have never been hired by us.'' Not surprisingly, the acquisition had also thrown a spanner into Allen's well thought out career-progression plans. Sawhney and his HR head were discovering that they would have to re-define these for a larger group of employees. At the same time, they had to convince old Allen employees that they weren't being short-changed in the process. One senior HR manager had suggested that they get senior executives to make short presentations on why they were essential to ABB. Sawhney had thought the idea brilliant; his executives hadn't. Nor had the media. Within days horror stories, mostly apocryphal, about people having to re-interview for their jobs were doing the rounds. And all the while, ABB was steadily losing people. Head-hunters and rival banks were making a beeline for some of ABB's renowned human capital. And insecure employees were signing up with lesser companies rather than negotiate an uncertain future at the bank.

In desperation, Sawhney turned to an old friend Vinay Sen, a HR professional who'd made a career for himself as an independent consultant. That hadn't helped much. True, Sen had shared some interesting thoughts on the issue of synergy. ''Apart from valuation, the most hyped phrase in an M&A deal is synergy,'' he had said. ''People talk of dove-tailing strengths and capabilities, bringing complementary skills, and exploiting cross-marketing opportunities. To me, synergy simply means one plus one, is not two, but six, or may be, eight. When a merger merely maintains the existing equilibrium, it does not make for synergy. It is only when there is a geometric leap in the advantages accruing to a merged entity that synergy makes sense.'' All sound stuff; only, it did little to help Sawhney tackle the problem at hand.

And this, the beleaguered CEO realised, was only the beginning. Convincing the best talent to stay put within the bank was the immediate objective. But there were other long-term ones. Like realising the benefits of the synergy Sen spoke about, and ensuring that ABB ended up with a larger share of the market than any of its constituent entities. Sawhney had read all the right books on getting M&As to work for you, but this was real. And it was painful. ''Heck,'' he thought, ''we don't even share a common e-mail system.''

## Questions

1. 'Integration is critical to the success of a merger'. Examine the statement keeping the Allen and Bradbury case in mind.
2. What should Sawhney do to strengthen both banks and develop a concrete business plan?
3. What are the areas of compatibility and conflict between Bradbury Bank and Allen Bank?
4. What kind of organisational structure should be put in place with a view to ensure smooth translation of rhetoric into action plans?
5. As a consultant what steps do you recommend to implement the integration?

*Source*: Business Today, February 6, 2001